The Beethoven Syndrome

The Beethoven Syndrome

Hearing Music as Autobiography

MARK EVAN BONDS

OXFORD
UNIVERSITY PRESS

OXFORD
UNIVERSITY PRESS

Oxford University Press is a department of the University of Oxford. It furthers
the University's objective of excellence in research, scholarship, and education
by publishing worldwide. Oxford is a registered trade mark of Oxford University
Press in the UK and certain other countries.

Published in the United States of America by Oxford University Press
198 Madison Avenue, New York, NY 10016, United States of America.

Library of Congress Cataloging-in-Publication Data
Names: Bonds, Mark Evan, author.
Title: The Beethoven syndrome : hearing music as autobiography / Mark Evan Bonds.
Description: New York, NY : Oxford University Press, [2020] |
Includes bibliographical references.
Identifiers: LCCN 2019020718 | ISBN 9780190068479 (hardback) |
ISBN 9780190068509 (online) | ISBN 9780190068486 (updf) | ISBN 9780190068493 (epub)
Subjects: LCSH: Music—Philosophy and aesthetics—History. |
Expression (Philosophy)—History. | Beethoven, Ludwig van, 1770–1827—Appreciation—History.
Classification: LCC ML3800 B75 2019 | DDC 781.1/7—dc23
LC record available at https://lccn.loc.gov/2019020718

3 5 7 9 8 6 4 2

Printed by Sheridan Books, Inc., United States of America

Oxford University Press gratefully acknowledges the Joseph Kerman Endowment of the
American Musicological Society, funded in part by the National Endowment for the
Humanities and the Andrew W. Mellon Foundation, for support in
the publication of this book.

To Sam Hammond

Table of Contents

Figures

Acknowledgments

I am grateful to the National Endowment for the Humanities, the Institute for Advanced Study, and the Austrian National Science Foundation (FWF), whose support during the period 2015–17 allowed me to complete the bulk of this study. It is particularly fitting that my time in Princeton at the Institute for Advanced Study was made possible by a fellowship endowed by the late Edward T. Cone, whose writings on the compositional persona provided an important starting point for my research.

I have also benefitted from ongoing conversations with departmental colleagues at the University of North Carolina at Chapel Hill, particularly Andrea Bohlman, Tim Carter, Annegret Fauser, and Stefan Litwin. The staff of the Music Library there—Philip Vandermeer, Diane Steinhaus, and Carrie Monette—provided its consistently unfailing support.

Colleagues at other institutions with whom I wish I could have had more conversations include Francesca Brittan (Case Western Reserve), Todd Cronan and Kevin Karnes (Emory), Ryan Ebright (Bowling Green State University), James Hepokoski (Yale), William Kinderman (University of Illinois), Tomas McAuley and David Trippett (Cambridge), Christopher Reynolds (University of California, Davis), William Robin (University of Maryland), Gilbert Sewall (Phillips Academy), Elaine Sisman (Columbia), Christian Thorau (Universität Potsdam), and Jeremy Yudkin (Boston University). My year in Vienna on a stipend from the Lise-Meitner-Programm was especially valuable, and I will always have fond memories of discussions with my sponsor there, Birgit Lodes (Universität Wien), and with her colleagues John D. Wilson and Elisabeth Reisinger. Evenings with the "three M's" from the Universität für Musik und darstellende Kunst Wien—Marie-Agnes Dittrich, Martin Eybl, and Melanie Unseld—were as delightful as they were thought-provoking. And I owe special thanks to Michael Morse (Trent University), who somehow managed to make sense of a very early draft of this book and pointed out the many ways in which it could be improved.

At Oxford University Press, Suzanne Ryan, was once again the ideal editor and Barbara Norton the ideal copy editor.

As always, my family helped in far more ways than they could possibly realize. While often indirect, those ways were no less important to bringing this project to fruition. To Dorothea, Peter, and Andrew: Thank you.

* * *

Portions of chapters 3 and 5 draw on my essay "Irony and Incomprehensibility: Beethoven's 'Serioso' String Quartet in F Minor, Op. 95, and the Path to the Late Style," *JAMS* 70 (2017): 285–356. Brief passages in chapter 7 appeared in a slightly different form in chapter 13 of my *Absolute Music: The History of an Idea* (New York: Oxford University Press, 2014).

Abbreviations

19CM	*19th-Century Music*
AfMw	*Archiv für Musikwissenschaft*
AmZ	*Allgemeine musikalische Zeitung*
BAmZ	*Berliner Allgemeine musikalische Zeitung*
BGA	Ludwig van Beethoven, *Briefwechsel: Gesamtausgabe*, 7 vols., ed. Sieghard Brandenburg (Munich: G. Henle, 1996–98).
JAMS	*Journal of the American Musicological Society*
KdU	Immanuel Kant, *Kritik der Urteilskraft*, ed. Heiner F. Klemme (Hamburg: Felix Meiner, 2001).
KFSA	Friedrich Schlegel, *Kritische Friedrich-Schlegel-Ausgabe*, ed. Ernst Behler et al. (Munich: Ferdinand Schöningh, 1958–).
MQ	*Musical Quarterly*
NZfM	*Neue Zeitschrift für Musik*

Unless otherwise noted, emphases in quotations appear in the original, and all translations are my own.

The Beethoven Syndrome

Introduction

The Instrumental Self

Beethoven struggled with many things during his life, but neglect was not one of them. By the time he died in 1827, his contemporaries had written so much about his music that the most recent anthology of their collected criticisms runs to almost seven hundred pages.[1] Yet aside from a few reviews from the composer's final years that speculate on the effects of his increasing deafness, these commentaries make almost no attempt to relate his works to his life or vice versa. The overwhelming majority of critics at the time in fact knew little or nothing about him beyond the barest outlines of his career, and the few who did, based mostly in Vienna, did not consider his personal self particularly relevant to the music he was creating. Writing from faraway Thuringia in his 1812 biographical dictionary of musicians, Ernst Ludwig Gerber acknowledged the "serious and gloomy" nature of many of Beethoven's works but explained this by pointing to the wartime conditions being endured by so many composers in German-speaking lands during a period of seemingly endless conflict.[2] In short, no one during Beethoven's lifetime perceived his music as an expression of his inner self.

Yet by the middle of the nineteenth century listeners were routinely hearing Beethoven's music as a revelation of his soul, and they regarded his soul, in turn, as the key to understanding his music. Critics eagerly mapped his life onto his works and his works onto his life. This new way of listening, moreover, extended well beyond Beethoven: audiences were now predisposed to hear the music of *all* composers—particularly their instrumental works—as a personal outpouring of the self, a form of sonic autobiography.

What changed? Why did listeners begin to hear music in such a fundamentally new way in such a short span of time? And why, in turn, has this mode of listening become increasingly suspect over the past hundred years? The inclination of listeners to hear composers *in* their music—the "Beethoven syndrome"—is so deeply ingrained that it is easy to forget just how novel and powerful it was for almost a century. "Syndrome" is not too strong a term.

As in medicine, it is used here to indicate a pattern of symptoms, in this case behaviors that point to an underlying condition. The predisposition to hear music as a form of autobiography began in responses to Beethoven but soon extended to the output of composers in general and dominated musical criticism for almost a hundred years. Listeners routinely turned to biography to explain the general tendencies of what they were hearing in any given artists' output, as well as any unusual exceptions to those tendencies. The rapid decline of such habits of listening in the 1920s reflects a general recognition that this predisposition, while not wholly without foundation, had gone too far. This mode of listening nevertheless remain with us today, even if in diminished form.

The Beethoven Syndrome: Hearing Music as Autobiography explores the changing perceptions of music as a subjective outpouring of the compositional self. Beethoven is the central figure in this account, and his instrumental music was an important catalyst for the new mode of listening that took hold in the second quarter of the nineteenth century. But this change cannot be ascribed to his works alone. It arose out of the convergence of aesthetic, philosophical, cultural, economic, and technological forces. New conceptions about the nature of all the arts, changing constructions of the self, the rising philosophical prestige of the emotions, and the growth of a mass-market music culture all contributed to a new way of hearing music— and above all instrumental music—as a medium of self-revelation.

The discourse on the perception of compositional subjectivity centers on changing conceptions of musical expression and falls into three broad phases:

(1) 1770–1830. Not until the closing decades of the eighteenth century did critics begin to address the relationship between a composer's output and innermost self. Commentators had long kept the two quite separate, for they conceived of expression not as a subjective outpouring of the self, but as an objective construct, which is to say, as the projection of a text (in the case of vocal music) or the representation of an emotion (in the case of instrumental music), consciously crafted in either case to evoke a calculated response in listeners.

(2) 1830–1920. The growing prestige of instrumental music in the late eighteenth and early nineteenth centuries raised fundamental questions about the source and nature of the expression heard in those works. Critics

continued to perceive vocal music primarily as the projection of a text, but they now began to hear instrumental music as a manifestation of its creator's unique individuality. The tendency to hear composers' selves in their instrumental works took hold with remarkable speed in the years just after Beethoven's death. Composers encouraged this perception by advocating an aesthetics of subjectivity in their own writings on music and through their strategies of self-promotion within an increasingly public and competitive marketplace.

(3) Since 1920. In the wake of World War I, the assumption that all expression came from the inner self lost its dominant position almost as quickly as it had attained it: many leading composers and critics returned to an outlook that openly acknowledged expression—and art in general—as an artifice. This renewed conception of expression as an objective construct became a key element of modernist aesthetics, beginning with the New Objectivity of the interwar years and running through the high modernism of mid-century. The inclination to hear a musical work as an audible manifestation of its composer's essential being has nevertheless proven remarkably resilient. The notion of works as life continues to flourish in the public mind, particularly in the realm of popular music, and it continues to play a role in the ways we hear the works of composers from both the past and present.

The three parts of this book correspond to these changing conceptions of musical expression. Part One, "The Paradigm of Objective Expression," surveys the period between approximately 1770 and 1830, when music functioned as an essentially rhetorical art, in which it fell to composers (and, working on their behalf, performers) to move listeners in a particular direction, to persuade them emotionally. Rhetoric is a theory of poetics: it provided a framework of composition in both the oratorical and musical senses of the term, and within this framework, expression was understood as a vital means to the end of moving an audience. Practitioners of the rhetorical arts, whether verbal or musical, anticipated the responses of their audiences and applied their craft accordingly. Listeners of the time, in turn, regarded composers as highly skilled artisans who could be identified through their distinctively individual styles, but not as individuals who had somehow imbued their creations with their own personal identities. Part Two, "The Paradigm of Subjective Expression," examines the period from roughly 1830 to 1920, in which the burden of understanding shifted to listeners, who for the first time in the history of music were now expected to *work*, to make sense of what they were hearing. This was especially challenging if the music at hand had no words. Hermeneutics, in contrast to rhetoric, provides a framework of reception, not production. Within the new paradigm of subjectivity, listeners understood expression as a personal utterance, and they were prepared to hear music—especially instrumental music—as a revelation of the compositional self. Part Three, "Dual Paradigms: Since 1920," examines the ways in which contrasting perceptions of expression have coexisted and mingled, often uneasily, at different times and for different repertoires.

The key issue throughout all three periods—and throughout this book—is not the extent to which composers have sought to express their inner selves, nor the extent to which any given work might reveal something about a composer's inner self, but rather the extent to which the listening public has *perceived* a composer's works as the subjective expression of that inner self.

Subjectivity, it must be said, is a much bigger word nowadays than it used to be, especially when it comes to music. Over the past thirty years or so, many commentators have invoked it to describe a contingent frame of reference implied by a given work;[3] others have posited subjectivity in the music itself;[4] and still others have treated it as a function of agency, an equally capacious concept.[5] Valuable as these approaches may be, they do not for the most part reflect the sensibilities of earlier times, whose listeners understood subjectivity first and foremost as a projection of the compositional self. As a history of listening, then, the present study employs the term *subjectivity* as it was primarily understood in discourse about music throughout the nineteenth century and most of the twentieth: as the projection of a composer's interiority.

The perception of music as an expression of its creator's self seems intuitively familiar to us today, yet it is striking how long it took to appear in music as opposed to the verbal arts. Poets and literary critics had begun to articulate an aesthetics of subjectivity as early as the 1770s in the so-called Sturm und Drang. Lyric poetry in particular, with its first-person perspective, enjoyed unprecedented prestige around this time, and Goethe, the leading poet of his generation, was particularly outspoken in his view of the written word as a vehicle of self-expression. From early on in his life, he maintained, he had routinely transformed personal experiences, both pleasant and unpleasant, into "an image, a poem," and in this manner was able to come to terms with his own subjectivity. He deemed his writings as a whole "fragments of a great confession." The "artist must act from within," he declared, for "dissemble as he might, he can always bring forth only his own individuality."[6] Goethe considered "poetic content" equivalent to the "content of one's own life." He urged young poets to ask themselves of each poem "if it incorporates something experienced and if this experience has developed you." Poetry, as he put it, "compels its possessor to reveal himself. Poetic utterances are *involuntary confessions* in which our interior opens itself up."[7]

The idea of literary creativity as coming "from within" reflects a gradual drift away from the long-standing premise of divine inspiration, which by the late Enlightenment no longer seemed adequate to explain the products of genius. Immanuel Kant's *Kritik der reinen Vernunft* (*Critique of Pure Reason*, 1781) had compelled his contemporaries to rethink their most basic assumptions about human perception and understanding, and his *Kritik der Urteilskraft* (*Critique of the Power of Judgment*, 1790) extended this new epistemological foundation to the realm of aesthetics. After Kant, art could no longer be considered merely a source of pleasure: it could now be regarded as a source of knowledge, generated by an active engagement of the beholder with the work of art. The subjectivity of self now occupied center stage in both the production and reception of art.[8]

In England, William Wordsworth made subjectivity the basis of an ongoing campaign to shape the way in which the public read his verse, and for that matter all verse. Responding to the initially unfavorable reception of his *Lyrical Ballads*, he asserted in the preface to the collection's second edition (1800) that "all good poetry is the spontaneous overflow of powerful feelings." Those feelings would be "recollected in tranquility" but in such a way that "by a species of reaction the tranquility disappears, and an emotion, similar to that which was before the subject of contemplation, is gradually produced, and does itself actually exist in the mind."[9] Wordsworth thus posited the poet's personal emotions grounded in actual, lived experiences as the driving force of the creative process.

Changing conceptions of the self encouraged this new attitude toward subjectivity. Once again Goethe played a key role. He maintained—and demonstrated—that the self could be cultivated through effort and sheer force of will, and that this process was central to the human experience. His ideal of self-development (*Bildung*), articulated most notably in his novel *Wilhelm Meisters Lehrjahre* (*Wilhelm Meister's Years of Apprenticeship*, 1795–96) gave the subjective basis of selfhood newfound prestige. *Bildung* allowed—indeed, compelled—the individual to explore those aspects of selfhood lying beneath the level of consciousness and social conventions—in short, the realm of spontaneous, unreflective emotions.

In the post-Enlightenment world, emotions were no longer something to be contained, repressed, or monitored. What Peter Gay called the nineteenth century's "pilgrimage to the interior," its "preoccupation with the self, to the point of neurosis," had its antecedents, to be sure. But the generation that came of age around mid-century, as Gay observed, was the first to make this sense of self-consciousness "available, almost inescapable, to a wide public," and it did so most forcefully through the arts, which were coming to be seen more and more as outpourings of the innermost self. In retrospect, Isaiah Berlin considered this "the exfoliation of the self" a quintessentially Romantic tendency.[10]

Instrumental music lent itself particularly well to "exfoliations of the self," for it operated outside the strictures of language and for that reason was widely held to spring from a deeper, more primordial, and thus more "authentic" site of the self. And it was in fact instrumental music that provoked a conceptual realignment of the perceived relationship between composers' lives and their works. Vocal music continued to be heard as the projection of a text, and critics recognized that the act of setting words to music would necessarily compel a composer to carefully consider a text's content and character, along with such technical features as its meter, structure, and rhyme scheme. With only rare exceptions, moreover, verbal texts came from an artist other than the composer, whose task it was to enhance and amplify thoughts and emotions set down in advance by someone else.[11] More recent scholarship has made a compelling case for hearing composers in their vocal works, often through the ways in which their music goes against the grain of the given text.[12] But such an approach reflects modern-day sensibilities, not those of the past. Even E. T. A. Hoffmann, in his enthusiastic 1810 review of Beethoven's Fifth Symphony, speculated that the composer's vocal music was "less successful" because "it does not permit a mood of vague yearning but can only depict from the realm of the infinite those feelings capable of being described in words." He reinforced this dichotomy between instrumental and vocal music a few years later in his review of Beethoven's overture, songs, and entr'actes to Goethe's *Egmont*:

> In Beethoven's instrumental music one is accustomed to finding a rich haul of genial contrapuntal turns, daring modulations, etc. But the extent to which the master knows how to rein in his riches and understands how to

use them at the right time is demonstrated by the composition under discussion here, which follows altogether the mind of the poet and clings to its drift without seeking in the slightest to stand out on its own. The reviewer has therefore taken pains to put into an appropriate light and acknowledge the successful aesthetic treatment of the composer's given material.[13]

Hoffmann in effect lauds Beethoven for knowing when to restrain his personal inclinations in the service of a text that has come from the pen of another artist in another medium. Nor was Hoffmann alone in this regard. Two years before, an anonymous reviewer of the *Sechs Gesänge*, Op. 75, had already spelled out the potential for instrumental music to reveal Beethoven's "distinctive interiority" in ways that vocal music could not:

Herr van Beethoven writes nothing that does not betray more or less the stamp of an original spirit, of deep feeling, of a particular disposition, even in its specific manner of elaboration. But in order to demonstrate these assets to their fullest degree, he requires many means and a broad, free field of play. When he is inhibited in this regard—be it through the genre, the words of a text, or his accommodation of the lesser capacities of performers, etc.—then he is rarely able to display his distinctive interiority and is often capable of doing this to only a limited degree and sometimes not at all.[14]

The relationship of the compositional self to purely instrumental music—"absolute music," as it would later come to be called—was thus a different question altogether for eighteenth- and nineteenth-century critics. How to explain the creative starting point of sonatas, string quartets, symphonies, and the like? Composers might occasionally provide clues in the form of programs or descriptive titles, such as the evocative movement headings Beethoven supplied for his *Pastoral* Symphony (1808) or the detailed prose program Berlioz wrote for his *Symphonie fantastique* (1830), but more often than not, they confined themselves to titles that are literally generic and differentiated by little more than keys and opus numbers: Piano Sonata in E Minor, Op. 90; String Quartet in A Major, Op. 41, No. 3; Symphony No. 2 in D Major, Op. 73. Without any distinctive point of reference to the world outside of music, such works provided listeners no immediate way in beyond the broad parameters of genre and the notes of the score.

By the same token, the relatively self-contained nature of instrumental music provided composers greater opportunity to put their own creative powers on display. As the anonymous reviewer of a collection of Mozart symphonies observed in 1799, a composer could demonstrate a higher degree of genius in instrumental genres like the string quartet and symphony than in vocal music, for in the former he must invent "all his material entirely by himself" and is limited beyond this "exclusively and entirely to the language of tones. His thoughts have their specificity in and of themselves, without the support of poetry."[15]

Because of its inherently abstract nature, then, instrumental music lent itself particularly well to the idea of artists creating entirely from within. The representational nature of painting and sculpture—at least prior to the advent of wholly abstract art in the early twentieth century—tended to short-circuit questions about the relationship between the creative subject and the represented object because that object, however stylized, always provided a point of interpretative departure for artists and the public alike. Even in the case of landscapes, which lent themselves particularly well to abstraction, that degree of abstraction was invariably judged in relation to a tangible object.[16]

In this respect, critics working before the era of abstraction treated the visual arts in ways that were analogous to those in which they regarded vocal music: they considered it the task of the artist to project and enhance something that existed before and outside the work of art. Viewers perceived the finished product, however mannered, as the representation of an object, just as listeners heard vocal music as the representation of a text. Artists themselves liked to emphasize their agency in this process, understandably enough, and the notion that every painting is to some extent a depiction of its creator dates back to antiquity: it reemerged in the late fifteenth century and became a cliché over the course of the ninteenth.[17] But this line of thought invariably collided at some point with the materiality of the depicted object, even in the case of self-portraits. Instrumental music, by contrast, offered stylized representations of emotions and inner thoughts, themselves invisible. This allowed listeners to close their eyes, open their ears, and enter into a world without nouns. It was precisely the absence of external referents that gave instrumental music its particular appeal or deprived it of its significance, depending on a given listener's time, place, and aesthetic convictions. Only when visual artists like Wassily Kandinsky, Kazimir Malevich, and Francis Picabia made the conceptual leap to total abstraction around 1910 did they compel critics to see the artist's self as both the source and the object of the work. It is not by accident that this later movement in art history would eventually come to be known as abstract expressionism, the "expression" in question understood as that of the artist. Representation of or through anything remotely identifiable in the external world was no longer an issue. Until then, however, only instrumental music could be perceived and discussed of in such terms, and even this mode of thought, as we shall see, had not entered the mainstream of commentary about music before the 1830s.

The nineteenth century's discourse on subjective expression in instrumental music took place largely in German-speaking lands, for it was then and there that critics and philosophers wrestled most intensively with the philosophical and aesthetic issues surrounding "pure" music. French and English writers weighed in on the matter from time to time, as we shall see, but the mysteries of instrumental music held a special fascination for their counterparts east of the Rhine, many of whom regarded this repertoire as the special province of German composers.[18] As public concerts became increasingly common, critics struggled to explain the significance and creative sources of this expanding body of wordless music. Many of them, including Kant and Hegel, considered it inferior to vocal music on the grounds that it lacked conceptual content, but no one, not even Kant or Hegel, denied its emotional power. To the contrary: writers of the time routinely described instrumental music as the "language of the heart" because of its ability to convey and arouse emotions in ways that words could not.

The idea of hearing such works as emanating from the *composer's* heart, however, did not begin to surface until the mid-1820s, and it offered a radically new way of understanding purely instrumental works as projections of their creators' inner selves. It was around this time that a small handful of critics began to explain the unusual nature of Beethoven's late piano sonatas and string quartets by appealing to the circumstances of his life, specifically his growing deafness. But it was the publication of what would become known as the Heiligenstadt Testament in October 1827, some seven months after Beethoven had died, that effectively legitimized with a single stroke critical interpretations of *all* his music as an expression of his inner self. In this remarkable document, written in 1802 but not discovered until after his death, the composer acknowledged—if only to himself— his struggle against deafness and his resulting estrangement from society. "Had things gotten only a little worse," he declared, he would have committed suicide. "It was only art that held me back. Ah, it seemed to me impossible to leave the world before having produced everything that I felt called upon to bring forth."[19]

The Heiligenstadt Testament changed the way in which audiences heard Beethoven's music. His deafness soon became the centerpiece of the enduring trope of struggle and triumph that listeners perceived in so many of his most celebrated works. Only a year after the composer's death, the critic Joseph Fröhlich could hear the Ninth Symphony as "Beethoven's autobiography, written in music."[20] From the 1830s onward, listeners were for the most part no longer hearing *an* emotion in Beethoven's music but rather *his* emotion. The "Awakening of Happy Feelings on Arrival in the Countryside" in the first movement of the Sixth Symphony (*Pastoral*) was now perceived not simply as an expression of joy in general, but specifically of Beethoven's joy. The "Heiliger Dankgesang eines Genesenen an die Gottheit" in the String Quartet Op. 132, in turn, was no longer heard as a "holy song of thanksgiving by a convalescent," but as Beethoven's personal expression of thanks on his recovery after a documented illness that, as critics were beginning to surmise (correctly), had occurred around the time of the work's composition.[21]

It was the rare critic in the decades after 1830 who did not at some point attempt to relate the composer's music to his inner self, the events of his life, or both. These provided, in effect, a gateway into his works, the works themselves a portal to still higher truths. "With Beethoven's symphonies," the noted journalist and literary critic Julian Schmidt observed in 1853, "we have the feeling that we are dealing with something very different from the usual alternations of joy and sorrow in which wordless music ordinarily moves. We intuit the mysterious abyss of a spiritual world, and we torment ourselves in an effort to understand it. . . . We want to know what drove the tone poet to bottomless despair and to unalloyed joy; we want to gain an understanding from the mysteriously beautiful features of this sphinx."[22]

This retrospective construction of a direct and meaningful connection between Beethoven's life and works opened the floodgates of speculation about musical subjectivity in general. When composers and commentators finally embraced the premise of instrumental music as a first-person art in the 1830s, they made up for their late start with a vengeance. Hector Berlioz's thinly veiled *symphonie à clef*, his *Symphonie fantastique* (1830), encouraged the perception of a vital link between a composer's life and works through an elaborate prose program inspired by his passionate but unrequited love for the Irish actress Harriet Smithson. Critics glommed on to the deeply personal nature of this symphony about an "artist" and his "beloved" almost at once, and they heard the work as a revelation of Berlioz's soul. Robert Schumann in turn incorporated ciphers into his *Carnaval* (1835) that could be decoded easily enough to reveal allusions to Schumann himself, to his then-fiancée (Ernestine von Fricken), and to his pupil and future wife (Clara Wieck), among others. Critics were once again quick to interpret this as an essentially autobiographical work. Chopin's mazurkas and polonaises of the 1830s and '40s were similarly heard as outpourings of their composer's deeply felt patriotism for his native Poland, and Franz Liszt devoted a revealingly disproportionate amount of space to them in his 1852 biography of the composer. By the last quarter of the century, a composer like Bedřich Smetana could openly give his String Quartet No. 1 (1876) the subtitle *From My Life* (*Z mého života*) and point to the opening of its finale as a recreation of the high-pitched ringing that signaled the onset of his deafness. Critics assumed that personal motivations could explain the nature of almost any given work, particularly if it went against convention: they lost no time in linking the gloomy, slow finale of Tchaikovsky's *Pathétique* Symphony (1893), for example, to its composer's subsequent alleged suicide. And while Richard Strauss denied that he was the object of his symphonic poem *Ein Heldenleben* (*A Hero's Life*, 1898), the presence of more than two dozen quotations from his own earlier works reinforced its critical reception as a form of musical autobiography.

Having accustomed themselves to reading biographical elements into what they heard, critics began to perceive self-expression in at least some of the music written by Beethoven's predecessors as well. This approach proved especially attractive in explaining stylistically anomalous works or passages, and it has continued down to the present. More than one commentator heard Mozart's somber Violin Sonata in E Minor, K. 304, for example, as a response to his mother's death in 1778. The noted Mozart scholar Alfred Einstein observed in 1945 that K. 304 "springs from the most profound depths of emotion." Two decades later Erich Schenk heard it, along with the Piano Sonata in A Minor, K. 310, as "painfully resigned acknowledgments" to the loss of his mother. And as recently as 1990 Marius Flothuis attributed the dark nature of K. 304 to the composer's "loneliness, indeed his feelings of despair in the great city [Paris], where he was largely neglected and where his mother fell ill and died."[23] In 1909 the French scholar Théodore de Wyzewa heard Haydn's turbulent minor-mode symphonies of the early 1770s as evidence of the composer's ill-fated love affair with an otherwise unknown woman: only a personal crisis similar to Beethoven's Immortal Beloved could have precipitated a sudden outpouring of such pathos-laden works.[24] The fact that not a shred of documentation supports the woman's existence did not prevent

Wyzewa from conjuring her presence in the composer's life: the music itself provided sufficient and compelling evidence. Biography had long since become the primary tool of musical hermeneutics.

There were dissenting voices, to be sure. The most notable was that of the Viennese critic Eduard Hanslick, who in his *Vom Musikalisch-Schönen* (*On the Musically Beautiful*, 1854) decried the idea of music as an art of subjective expression and advocated in its place an aesthetics of beauty based on purely formal elements. Hanslick accepted the premise that composers' lives could shape the music they wrote, but he insisted that such connections were irrelevant in evaluating any given work. On the whole, however, the public was far more ready to accept the testimony of composers such as Liszt, who declared that "the artist does not deal with form for the sake of form, but rather simply to find in it the voice that can project the impressions of his inner being." It is the composer's fundamental obligation, Liszt declared, to "elevate and ennoble his interiority, to articulate and enrich it."[25]

The aesthetics of personal self-revelation proved a winning formula for composers and public alike, for it reinforced the individuality and elite status of creative artists even while providing listeners with a ready means of access to otherwise challenging works. Church and court patronage declined precipitously in the early nineteenth century, and by 1830 most composers were compelled to fend for themselves in the open market. They quickly learned that their public personae, their individual "brands," could help them promote their music. Berlioz, Liszt, Schumann, and Wagner, all born within the decade 1803–13, belonged to the first generation of composers who consciously fashioned their own distinctive public images through prose criticism. They were the first major composers to write extensively about music in a nontechnical way in venues that reached a broad public. Audiences, in turn, were grateful for a point of entry into an increasingly heterogeneous repertoire. If the bizarre harmonies and timbres of Berlioz's *Symphonie fantastique* could be understood as reflections of his personal life, this made the work that much more comprehensible. If various movements of Liszt's *Années de pèlerinage* could be heard against not only the geographic titles of individual movements but also its composer's actual and documented experience of those places, then these demanding works took on additional and readily understandble layers of meaning. Simplistic as such connections might seem today, they were novel at the time and exerted a powerful effect on the music-consuming public, which for the first time was gradually accepting the idea that it was the responsibility of listeners to come to terms with what they were hearing.

Sincerity played a central role in this new mode of listening. Concertgoers assumed that the autobiographical utterances they were hearing were genuine and heartfelt. This paralleled their habits of reading: a corresponding devotion to sincerity is implicit and at times overt in most nineteenth-century commentaries on literature, reinforced by repeated pronouncements from authors themselves: Wordsworth, Matthew Arnold, and Leo Tolstoy, among others, placed enormous value on the authenticity of artistic emotions, and readers were only too happy to apprehend their works accordingly. "Professing sincerity," as the literary historian Susan Rosenbaum recently observed, was not only a "moral practice but . . . also good business." By putting their "private" emotions on public display, "poets marketed the self, cultivated celebrity, and advanced their professional careers."[26] The same held true for music. By the middle of the nineteenth century, it was not simply the published score alone that was for sale, but also, within its wrappers, the soul of the composer. As a wordless confession from the innermost recesses of the genius-artist, instrumental music offered something more emotionally direct than anything that could be conveyed through the strictures of conventional language.

The ideal of instrumental music as a sincere projection of the inner self reached its zenith around the turn of the twentieth century, at the very moment when listeners were struggling to understand a harmonic idiom rapidly approaching the realm of atonality. "Art," as Arnold Schoenberg declared in a letter to the painter Wassily Kandinsky in 1911, "belongs to the *unconscious*! One must express *oneself*! Express oneself *directly*! Not one's taste, or one's upbringing, or one's intelligence, knowledge or skill. Not all these *acquired* characteristics, but that which is *inborn, instinctive*." Schoenberg would sum up his feelings that same year in the dictum that "art is born of 'I must,' not of 'I can.'"[27]

In the years immediately after World War I, however, leading composers and critics began to turn their backs on the aesthetics of self-expression. Neoclassicism and the New Objectivity rejected subjectivity as the principal basis of expression not only in music but in all the arts, ushering in a return to an earlier conception of expression as a dispassionate construct. The leading musical proponent of this new—or rather, very old—aesthetic was Igor Stravinsky, who in 1923 declared his Octet, for example, to be "not an 'emotive' work" but rather a "musical object . . . based on objective elements which are sufficient in themselves." Stravinsky, like Hanslick before him, did not deny the expressive powers of music, but he saw them as by-products of

the conscious manipulation of musical materials. "Music is, by its very nature, essentially powerless to express anything at all, whether a feeling, an
attitude of mind, a psychological mood, a phenomenon of nature, etc.," he
noted in his autobiography in 1936:

> *Expression* has never been an inherent property of music. That is by no
> means the purpose of its existence. If, as is nearly always the case, music
> appears to express something, this is only an illusion and not a reality. It
> is simply an additional attribute which, by tacit and inveterate agreement,
> we have lent it, thrust upon it, as a label, a convention—in short, an aspect
> which, unconsciously or by force of habit, we have often come to confuse
> with its essential being.[28]

Expressive objectivity would become the aesthetic cornerstone of the high
modernism that dominated art music in the decades after World War II. In
his now-classic work *The Composer's Voice* (1974), the composer and theorist
Edward T. Cone argued that a musical work's creator is present in it only in
the guise of a "persona." "Every composition," he maintained, "is an utterance depending on an act of impersonation."[29] This notion of an assumed,
inherently mutable compositional identity is strikingly consistent with
Enlightenment viewpoints on the nature of musical expression. The turn
toward objectivity in the 1920s, then, was not only a reaction against subjectivity, but also a reassertion of the much older concept of expressive objectivity. The conflation of expression and self-expression in the years between
1830 and 1920 thus constitutes a relatively brief, albeit highly influential, epi-
sode in the broader history of music.

The perception of instrumental music as a manifestation of a composer's
innermost self has nevertheless proven remarkably resilient. Composers
themselves have adopted widely differing viewpoints on the relationship of
their life and works, and their pronouncements have inevitably shaped the
way in which listeners have heard what they have written. Some, like Milton
Babbitt or Pierre Boulez, insisted on the priority of formal structures while
minimizing or denying autobiographical elements in their output. Others
continued to encode life experiences into their compositions even while
keeping the biographical origins of certain musical features hidden from the
general public, as in Alban Berg's *Lyrische Suite* (1926) or Schoenberg's String
Trio, Op. 45 (1946).[30] Still others, like Dmitri Shostakovich and John Cage,
openly acknowledged the autobiographical nature of at least some of their

music, even if the precise nature of those connections is not always clear and often open to contradictory interpretations. More recent composers have found a place for themselves somewhere in this mixed tradition of uneasy coexistence. Neoromanticism and postmodernism, both of which emerged during the third quarter of the twentieth century, accommodate the premise of self-expression without making it foundational to their aesthetics. The notion of works as life flourishes with particular vigor in the realm of popular music, particularly in the case of singer-songwriters, who both create and perform their own works.

We must of course treat artists' professions or denials of subjectivity with caution. At the same time, we cannot ignore them, for such assertions have played an important role in shaping the ways in which listeners hear their works. From Berlioz onward, any number of composers have encouraged the perception of their music as an outward manifestation of their inner selves, and listeners have responded accordingly. It is for this reason that the "Beethoven syndrome" should not be confused with what is sometimes called the "biographical fallacy," the tendency to interpret artists' works through their lives. To call perceptions of compositional subjectivity a fallacy would itself be mistaken.

* * *

The history of hearing music as autobiography is not nearly as linear or straightforward as this brief outline might suggest. The paradigms of expression and the frameworks of listening put forward here were neither monolithic nor mutually exclusive: composers and their audiences could (and did) at times switch between different modes of conveying and hearing expression.[31] Eighteenth-century listeners, for example, had good reason to hear at least certain works as outward manifestations of their composers' personal emotions, such as J. S. Bach's *Capriccio sopra la lontananza del suo fratello dilettissimo*, BWV 992, lamenting the departure of one of his brothers, or Carl Philipp Emanuel Bach's *Abschied von meinem Silbermannischen Claviere in einem Rondo*, H. 272, his farewell to a beloved clavichord he had just sold. Works like these may have been exceptional in their day—"occasional" in every sense of the word—yet they remind us that listening can come in many forms at any given time. In the same way, many of the nineteenth-century listeners who heard expression as emanating from the depths of composers' souls continued to recognize the constructive nature of musical expression to at least some degree, and only the most extreme objectivists of the twentieth century denied the emotional elements of the art. Indeed, one might view the history of discourse on the nature of musical expression as a long-term aesthetic tug-of-war between technical construction on one side and projections of the self on the other. And even though critics have for the most part granted a role to both elements, they have as a whole given precedence to one or the other at different times. These tendencies have been decisive enough to allow the paradigms of objective and subjective expression to serve as useful conceptual coordinates by which to trace profound changes in listening over the last two centuries.

This book, then, is a history of perceptions. The central issue at every turn is the extent to which listeners heard musical expression as an objective construct, as an outpouring of the compositional soul, or as some mixture of the two.

It helps to recognize from the outset that all these modes of listening rest on the characteristically Western construct of the composer as an individual entity, separate and distinct from anyone who might perform music. It is certainly no mere coincidence that perceptions of the compositional self first arose in the decades soon after the crystallization, around 1800, of what Lydia Goehr has called the "work-concept." This regulative concept regarded musical works first and foremost as texts, as opposed to their sounding manifestations in performance. By this line of thinking, performers act upon a text that is regarded (at least ideally) as a fixed object, which in turn has encouraged listeners to perceive performers as recreative artists whose goal is to project the original work of the composer. The work-concept is thus strongly centered on the person of the composer.[32] Performers bring their own subjectivity to bear in bringing these works to life, of course, but a history of perceptions of subjectivity in performance lies beyond the scope of the present study.[33]

It is also important to recognize the danger of taking the concepts of subjective and objective expression to their logical extremes. Cone's notion of the compositional persona has offered a useful means by which to avoid simplistic equations between composers' lives and works. At the same time, the idea of a categorical separation of persona and self is no less problematic: even Cone was ultimately unwilling to sever the two entirely (see p. 185). Carl Dahlhaus and Lewis Lockwood, among others, have rightly insisted that a composer's works and inner self are inevitably related at some level, even if the nature of that connection is difficult to pin down.[34] Artistic creations, as Lockwood reminds us, "do not materialize out of nothing. . . . We can acknowledge that deeply rooted elements in the creative individual's personality, angle of vision, speech habits, interactions with people, and ways of dealing with the world find resonance in many of the artist's works. Such elements combine to shape . . . the inner being that leaves an indelible personal imprint on works that in some way seems unmistakable, even if we cannot define it in detail."[35]

Beethoven's music has proven particularly inviting for speculation on the relationship between a composer's life and works, in part because we know so much about his life, thanks to an abundance of correspondence, conversation books, sketches, and reminiscences by those who knew him. His compositions, moreover, fit an image that has only grown over time. In his acclaimed *Beethoven Hero* (1995), Scott Burnham makes a convincing case for the purely musical foundations of this perception of works as life, arguing that the trajectory of struggle to triumph so typical of the composer's "heroic" works models Western self-consciousness in general. Listeners have thus heard these works as sonic manifestations of the human soul writ large, which in turn has led to a belief that Beethoven himself is the paradigmatic individual in question. "The hero with whom we identify," as Burnham puts it, has thus become "subsumed within the figure of a demigod."[36] Burnham readily acknowledges the importance of factors lying outside the music that have reinforced such perceptions—knowledge of Beethoven's own struggles with deafness, his unhappy love affairs, the tortured nature of the sketches, and so on—but explicitly and purposefully excludes them from his account, focusing instead on those specifically musical qualities that have caused so many listeners to hear Beethoven's music in the ways they do. Burnham is also careful to note that this image rests on a relatively small number of the composer's works, most of them from the so-called heroic era, particularly the Third and Fifth Symphonies. *The Beethoven Syndrome* in no way contradicts Burnham's thesis and indeed reinforces it at many points, even while integrating responses to a much wider range of music—and not just Beethoven's—within a broader range of historical developments. These developments encouraged listeners to hear composers' selves in their instrumental works, beginning around the second third of the nineteenth century and then later, in the early decades of the twentieth, to begin questioning this mode of listening.

There is, in short, a historical dimension to the perception of life as works and works as life, and that history continues to shape the ways in which we listen today. Maynard Solomon asks: "Listening to the *Eroica*, can we expel from our consciousness our knowledge of Beethoven's hero and rescue fantasies, his suicidal thoughts, his family romance, and his nobility pretense?"[37] The question is rhetorical, the answer obvious. But this is not the way in which listeners have always heard the *Eroica*, Beethoven's music, or music in general. With few exceptions, Beethoven's earliest critics listened to what he wrote and talked about it within the framework of rhetoric, and it was not until after his death that listeners began to hear his works—and the works of composers in general—as outward projections of an inner self. *The Beethoven Syndrome: Hearing Music as Autobiography* traces the rise and changing fortunes of this mode of listening.

PART ONE

THE PARADIGM OF OBJECTIVE EXPRESSION: 1770–1830

That every work of art bears some trace of its creator's self is a truism if not a triviality. Music is no exception. The only real question is one of degree. Composers are not automatons, and their lives inevitably shape what and how they write. And just as inevitably, our knowledge of their lives shapes the ways in which we hear what they have written. With relatively few exceptions, however, composers and listeners of earlier times—up until roughly 1830—created and consumed music under premises very different from those of today. In general terms, neither party conceived of musical works as projections of an inner self, but rather as objective constructs. For composers, this meant creating works that would move listeners in desired ways. For listeners, this meant evaluating works on the basis of their effect, not on what a given composer might be trying to "say." With the important exception of the fantasia—recognized already in the mid-eighteenth century as a unique and highly circumscribed genre (see chapter 3)—listeners did not begin to hear expression as a revelation of the compositional self in any significant way until the second quarter of the nineteenth century.

1

The Framework of Rhetoric

Composers and critics of the late Enlightenment agreed that music was the "language of the heart," powerless by itself to convey rational ideas but for that reason all the more capable of moving listeners' passions. They understood the language of music as functioning within the framework of rhetoric, which is to say, the art of persuasion. They identified elaborate parallels between music and language, appropriating concepts and terms from grammar and rhetoric to describe some of music's most basic features, including theme, subject, phrase, sentence, paragraph, cadence, exposition, development, and recapitulation.[1] Some theorists, particularly German ones, went beyond the syntax of music to align it with semantics as well. They proposed long lists of musical figures whose melodic profiles or rhythms could arouse specific emotions in listeners or reinforce the sense of a particular text being set to music. Through repeated use, certain figures acquired specific extra-musical "meanings." A descending chromatic fourth, for example, came to be associated with pain and suffering (as in the "Crucifxus" of J. S. Bach's Mass in B Minor), while ascending leaps could be heard as conveying a sense of joy (as in "Rejoice greatly," from Handel's *Messiah*).[2] These efforts to create a semantics of music were part of a larger, ongoing attempt by such philosophers as Descartes, Hobbes, Spinoza, Locke, and Hume to categorize and inventory the human passions and determine the most effective means of conveying each: drama through gesture and delivery, painting and sculpture through the depiction of facial expressions and physical gestures, and music through various sounding figures that over time came to represent certain emotions.

Enlightenment critics and composers thus understood expression not as a "pressing out" of the compositional self, but rather as the representation of specific emotions intended to elicit corresponding responses in the minds of listeners. In this sense, composers' personal feelings were irrelevant to the job to be done. Here, too, rhetoric provided a model, for the best orators had long been regarded as those capable of advocating either side of any given dispute, regardless of their private opinions on the subject at hand. As the art of persuasion, rhetoric is morally and ethically neutral. This neutrality has long been perceived as both a strength and weakness, for rhetoric can be used to promote evil as well as good.[3] For composers, however, the ethical dimension was largely irrelevant. Listeners judged them on their ability to arouse a wide range of emotions and, in the case of vocal music, to project movingly different kinds of texts.

Expression as a Means of Persuasion

The framework of rhetoric helps explain why eighteenth-century writers so consistently described musical expression as an objective construct, unconnected to a composer's personal emotions. Charles Avison, in his *Essay on Musical Expression* (1752), the first monograph in any language on the topic, defined it in terms of its results, not its origins. He called expression in vocal music the "concurrence of air and harmony, as affects us most strongly with the passions or affections which the poet intends to raise." Avison considered "musical expression in the composer," in turn, as "succeeding in the attempt to express some particular passion" and believed that this success could be measured by the extent to which a given work could evoke that passion in listeners.[4]

The composer is thus an agent of expression, not its source. Even Jean-Jacques Rousseau, composer and confessionalist *extraordinaire*, had nothing to say in his widely read 1768 dictionary of music about the possibility of composers giving voice to their inner feelings. His account of musical expression is thoroughly typical of its time, focused as it is on the technical means of moving listeners. Rousseau describes how composers, having once determined the particular emotion they wish to convey, should go about using the resources of music—principally melody and rhythm, but also harmony and timbre—to awaken that feeling in listeners.[5] He does not bother to ask whether the feelings coincide with those of the creative artist's innermost self, because to his mind and to the minds of his contemporaries, musical expression was an objective construct.

In an era that conceived of music as a rhetorical art, composers repeatedly described the creative process as a means of moving listeners, not as an externalization of their own inner emotions. In an often-quoted letter of 1778 to his father from Paris, Mozart described the premiere of his Symphony in D Major, K. 297, in just these terms:

The symphony began ... and there was a passage right in the middle of the first Allegro that I knew would have to please; all the listeners were carried away by it, and there was great applause. But because I knew, when I wrote it, what kind of effect it would make, I brought it back again at the last moment one more time, and then there were calls for the whole movement to be repeated from the beginning. The Andante also pleased, but especially the last Allegro, for I had heard that all final Allegros, like the first ones, begin with all the instruments together and usually in unison, and so I began mine with two violins alone, piano, for only eight measures and then suddenly a forte, and with it, the listeners (as I had expected) made a "shhh" sound at the piano, and when the forte suddenly came, hearing it and the clapping of hands were one and the same. Right after the symphony, out of joy, I went to the Palais Royal, enjoyed a good ice, prayed the rosary as I had promised, and went home.[6]

Having learned his art within the poetics of rhetoric, Mozart knew that it was his responsibility to anticipate the response of his audiences and fashion his works accordingly. His equally well-known account of composing an aria for *Die Entführung aus dem Serail* (1781) applies this same approach to vocal music. As he reported to his father:

The passage "Drum beim Barte des Propheten" is indeed in the same tempo, but with fast notes, and as Osmin's rage increases, the Allegro assai, in a different meter and in a different key, creates the best effect, for it comes at a point when one would think the aria is already over. For a person in such an intense rage oversteps all order, moderation, and purpose and is no longer aware of himself. So must the music, too, lose awareness of itself. But because the passions, whether intense or not, should never be expressed to the point of arousing disgust, and because music, even in the most gruesome situation, should never offend the ear but instead delight it—so I have chosen not a key foreign to F (the key of the aria) but rather one related to it, albeit not the closest, D minor, but rather one at a further remove, A minor.[7]

Once again, music's technical elements—the working-out of the material through modulations, along with changes in meter and tempo—provide the means to a higher end: to move listeners. The purpose of music is to please, not perplex.

Opinions on Mozart's success in pleasing his contemporaries differed. It is telling that when the Habsburg Emperor Joseph II asked the composer Carl von Dittersdorf his opinion of Mozart's works, Dittersdorf couched his response in terms not of the music itself, but of the ability of others to assimilate it. To evaluate a work was to judge its effect on listeners. In his posthumously published memoirs, Dittersdorf recounted the exchange thus:

Emperor: What do you have to say about Mozart's compositions?

I: He is indisputably one of the greatest original geniuses, and I have as yet never known a composer in possession of such an astonishing wealth of ideas. I wish he were not so profligate with them. He does not let listeners catch their breath, for the moment one wants to contemplate a beautiful thought, another even more magnificent idea is already there in its place, pushing out the former, and this continues in such a way that in the end one cannot hold any of these beauties in one's memory.[8]

Haydn, when asked by his biographer Georg August Griesinger to describe his routine for composing, similarly framed his response with a view to his imagined listeners:

I sat down [at the keyboard] and began to fantasize, according to whether my animus was sad or happy, serious or playful. Once I had seized upon an idea, my entire effort went toward elaborating and sustaining it according to the rules of art. I tried to help myself in this way. And this is what is lacking among so many of our young composers; they string together one little bit after another, and they break off before they have begun, but nothing remains in the heart when one has heard it.[9]

Although neither Griesinger nor Haydn acknowledges it explicitly, the process Haydn describes here is that of writing a work or movement of purely instrumental music. A vocal work, with its preestablished text, would have compelled the composer to begin by carefully examining both the emotional import and technical structure of the words to be set. The composition of an instrumental work entailed no such strictures: its source of inspiration came from within, unbidden. Ultimately, however, for an eighteenth-century composer such as Haydn, it was *only* a starting point. He describes the finished composition not from his own perspective (as a portrayal of the mood that led him to his musical idea), but as a vehicle by which to move his listeners. Moreover, he considers this effect to be a product of technique, the hard work of "elaborating and sustaining" a musical idea "according to the rules of art." Without this artifice, expression falls short, and the listener remains unmoved. Again, the composer is the agent of expression, not its source.

The Composer as Actor

The idea of music as a rhetorical art meant that composers and performers, like orators, had to be good actors—that is, they had to be able to assume and convey on demand a variety of emotional states in a manner that would move listeners. The requisite emotions could be found in the script (for actors), the notated score (for performing musicians), or the text to be set (for composers of vocal music). In each instance, emotional pliability was paramount: actors had to be able to play a variety of roles, just as performers had to be able to play works in a wide range of genres and idioms. Composers of vocal music, in turn, were routinely called upon to project a broad spectrum of emotions, often in a single work, as in the case of opera. Accordingly, theories of the creative process in music from the eighteenth and early nineteenth centuries consistently stressed the need for composers to maintain a high degree of emotional elasticity. The Horatian maxim "Ut ridentibus arrident, ita flentibus adsunt humani voltus: si vis me flere, dolendum est primum ipsi tibi" (As men's faces smile on those who smile, so they respond to those who weep. If you would have me weep, you must first feel grief yourself)[10] would be quoted or paraphrased endlessly in manuals on both rhetoric and music.

This is not to say that composers lacked recognizably individual styles. Critics readily acknowledged characteristic ways of writing, but they did not perceive these as reflections of their creators' inner selves. It was within this tradition that the composer, theorist, and critic Johann Nikolaus Forkel (1749–1818) acknowledged the limits of every composer's distinctive, even unique manner. "Every thought bears a certain imprint of the character of the person who thinks it," he noted in his lectures at the University of Göttingen in the early 1780s, "an imprint that can belong to only one person alone and not to any other individual." Yet, if a musical work is to achieve its goal, "the artist must know how to bend and form his musical ideas so that in the end and in their entirety they correspond to the goals he had established in advance."[11] Composers, in other words, must at times achieve their desired ends in spite of themselves. The Viennese physician, composer, and violinist Amand Wilhelm Smith (1754–1838) similarly acknowledged that the works of the best creative artists bear the imprint of their authors: because their temperaments are so different, "[Emanuel] Bach will never be Dittersdorf, and Dittersdorf will never be Bach." While composers should therefore "observe and take note of their own tendencies and follow them," the successful ones must possess "a sensitive soul that allows itself to be readily transformed into different, even mutually opposing passions."[12]

Critics, then, recognized distinctive traits of individual composers in what they called "artistic character," related to but distinguishable from a composer's personal character. Commentators routinely acknowledged Haydn's disposition toward wit and playfulness, for example, but this was a quality heard at one remove from his personal self. "That certain genres of composition fit him particularly well," the Erfurt organist Ignaz Theodor Ferdinand Arnold observed in 1810, "lies in the individuality of his personal character and its influence on his artistic character, as with all other artists. Cheerfulness comes to him in general more readily than pain or vexation."[13] Still, Arnold couches such artistic tendencies—and not only in the case of Haydn—in terms of relative strengths and weaknesses, not in terms of what individual artists categorically could and could not do.

Critics thus routinely insisted that composers be capable of willing themselves into as broad a range of emotions as possible. And here commentators invariably agreed that personal experience of those emotions was essential. The composer and theorist Johann Mattheson (1681–1764), writing in 1739, advised composers to draw on their own personal experiences in order to project a particular emotion, especially when attempting to represent the various shades of love: "no one," he declared, "will be capable of arousing a passion in the animus of others if he does not know precisely this same passion, as if he had experienced it himself, or is still experiencing it."[14] The key phrase here is "as if" (*als ob*), for, as Mattheson would go on to note, "it is not necessary for a composer to begin setting a lament, a tragedy, or the like, by wailing and weeping. But it is absolutely necessary for him to make room, so to speak, in his mind and heart for the affect at hand. Otherwise things can only go badly for him."[15]

The essence of Mattheson's advice—that composers must be familiar with a wide range of emotions and be capable of drawing on the memory of them as needed—would be repeated over and over throughout the eighteenth century. Avison, for example, noted that if anyone writing a work of sacred music "feels not this divine energy in his own breast, it will prove but a fruitless attempt to raise it in that of others."[16] Writing in the mid-1780s, the composer Christian Friedrich Daniel Schubart emphasized the need for "true" composers to study the human heart diligently in order to "play" on the "heart-nerves" of listeners "in the way one would play a favorite instrument."[17] Here genius remains closely allied to the principles of rhetoric. The Scottish cleric William Duff (1732–1815) argued along the same lines that "every masterly Composer of Music must feel, in the most intense and exquisite degree, the various emotions, which, by his compositions, he attempts to excite in the minds of others." The composer must therefore

> work himself up to that transport of passion, which he desires to express and to communicate in his piece. In effectuating this purpose, Imagination operates very powerfully, by awakening in his own mind those particular affections, that are correspondent to the airs he is meditating; and by raising each of these to that tone of sensibility, and that fervor of passion, which is most favourable to composition.

At this point Duff freely translates "the maxim of Horace," "Si vis me flere, dolendum est primum ipsi tibi," as:

> Would you have me participate [in] your pain?
> First teach yourself to feel the woes you feign.

This, he observes, "is a rule as necessary to be observed by a Composer of Music . . . as by a Tragic Poet."[18] The operative word here is *feign*: a given emotion need not be genuine or spontaneous, but its manifestation must seem so.

The idea of orators "making room" for an emotion, "feigning" it, or actively "transporting" themselves into it derives not only from Horace but from the entire range of classical commentators on the art of rhetoric, all of whom insisted that orators must themselves feel the passions they seek to arouse in their listeners, at least momentarily. As Quintilian observed in his *Institutio oratoria*:

> The prime essential for stirring the emotions of others is, in my opinion, first to feel those emotions oneself. . . . If we wish to give our words the appearance of sincerity, we must assimilate ourselves to the emotions of those

who are genuinely so affected, and our eloquence must spring from the same feeling that we desire to produce. . . . Will he grieve who can find no trace of grief in the words with which I seek to move him to grief? Will he shed tears if the pleader's eyes are dry?[19]

Eighteenth-century compositional treatises consistently encouraged composers to approach their art in this way. Jean-Philippe Rameau, in his 1722 treatise on harmony, urged musicians to "deliver" themselves into the characters they wished to portray musically and "like a nimble actor" place themselves "in the place of those who speak."[20] Heinrich Christoph Koch, author of one the century's most comprehensive compositional manuals, recommended that composers work themselves into the requisite emotional state by reading passages from the works of leading authors who depict that state, or by playing selections by "good composers" who project it, being careful not to incorporate unconsciously too much of other composers' work into their own.[21]

The imperative to transport oneself into a variety of specific emotional states when composing takes center stage in the Swiss aesthetician Johann Georg Sulzer's entry "Expression in Music" (*Ausdruck in der Musik*) in his 1771–74 encyclopedia of the fine arts, the *Allgemeine Theorie der schönen Künste*. Working in collaboration with one of his musical advisors, the composer and theorist Johann Philipp Kirnberger, Sulzer declares expression to be "the soul of music. Without it, music is merely a pleasant mechanism. With it, music becomes the most emphatic kind of speech, which works irresistibly upon the heart."[22] But how does a composer attain "the magical power by which to rule so prodigiously over our hearts?" The emotions to be conveyed in any given work of music, he points out, do not necessarily originate within the soul of the artist. He concedes that no one should attempt to write something "that goes against his character" but insists that a composer must nevertheless cultivate "through diligence and repetition" the ability to "place himself" into emotional states that might be foreign to him, much like the epic poet who must be able to imagine himself into the minds of all his tale's various characters. It would be "foolish," Sulzer observes, to set about composing without first determining the "character" of the piece to be written. He recommends that the composer "imagine some sequence of events, some circumstance, some condition" that would put him in the proper state of mind. Once he has "fired up" his imaginative forces, the composer can then proceed to his task, taking care not to introduce "any musical figures or phrases that lie outside the character of the work."[23] Sulzer grants that a work of music may on occasion arise from a spontaneous, unprompted emotion, but at no point does he suggest this state as a prerequisite for creating a new composition.[24]

When it comes to artistic creativity, the line between real and feigned emotions is often blurred, in both literature and music. Sulzer's hierarchy of verbal utterances in his entry "Poem" (*Gedicht*) is especially revealing in this regard. Everyday speech (*die gemeine Rede*) is a straightforward narration of what we think: it avoids complexity and seeks to make itself clear and readily understandable. Eloquence (*Beredsamkeit*) is "more calculated and artful." Its goal extends beyond mere comprehensibility; it always keeps before it the "aesthetic power" that the tone and cadence of words will have upon the listener to whom it is directed. Poetry (*Dichtkunst*) constitutes a still higher category. Its goal is

> more the animated expression of the object of its representation than the effect it should elicit in others. The poet is himself touched by his object and moved in an animated way to passion, or at the very least to a certain mood. He cannot resist the desire to make known his sensibility; he is carried away. His principal goal is to present in an animated fashion the object that moves him and at the same to express the impression it has made on him. Even if no one should hear him, he speaks, because his sensibility does not allow him to remain silent. He gives himself over to the impressions that his material makes upon him to such an extent that one notices from his tone and from his minimally thought-out expression that he has become completely absorbed in his object. This gives his manner of speech something extraordinary and fantastic, similar to that of individuals who, in experiencing strong emotions, forget themselves and speak and act as if they were alone, even when they are in society.[25]

At this point Sulzer's account looks very much like an endorsement of self-expression: the poet is in effect speaking to himself, without regard for any effect on his audience, real or imagined. But now comes the turn. Having argued that a poem arises in the heat of passion and with minimal reflection, or none at all, Sulzer reveals that this is in fact *not* the case—that the poet's actions are in truth "cold-blooded." He appeals to the morphology of poetry itself.

> Of course no poem could arise without a marked passion and its overpowering force. . . . Only now, because poetry has become a common art, the

imitation of this natural state accomplishes that which in the condition of bare nature could be done only by strong emotional feeling. Thus we see that poets often behave as if they were being driven against their will to pour out their hearts. In this regard it is like dance, which in its origins was nothing other than passionate, enthusiastic movement. Wild peoples, who have as yet transformed nothing into art, dance only when they are transported into passion. But wherever dance has become an art form, one can also dance in cold blood. One nevertheless always acts as if some sort of powerful circumstance had brought forth this fantastic animus. That poetry as well as dance rests on this sort of attitude becomes clear through the fact that both require the support of music, which occupies the senses and spurs on the aroused power of imagination still further. . . . This development of poetry from its origins allows us to identify the true character of the poem.[26]

Without passion there would be no poetry, and among "primitive" peoples—here Sulzer betrays the influence of Rousseau—the resultant form of expression is wholly spontaneous and raw. But the projection of the passions in poetry nowadays, as Sulzer observes, is a calculated, technical business that must feign true passion. His entry "Expression in Music" elaborates even more pointedly on the highly reflective—that is, objective—nature of the ways in which passions can be represented. In the end, his accounts of the creative process in both literature and music are quite standard for his time: an initial moment of enthusiasm is followed by a more extended process of circumspection and refinement.

Sulzer's contortions remind us just how challenging it can be to describe the creative process, and he was not alone in the struggle to reconcile its two very different sides: passionate and dispassionate, spontaneous and reflective, personal and impersonal, subjective and objective. In an unsigned essay entitled "On Artists," published in the *Allgemeine musikalische Zeitung* of Leipzig in 1815, a correspondent identifying himself as "B" laid out the paradoxical nature of this duality with particular clarity. All artists, no matter what their medium, must necessarily alternate between "moments of excitement and enthusiasm" and moments of "mechanical work," in which they hold their creations at a "cold distance" from themselves. The challenge is especially difficult for composers, who must be careful to "fill the gaps of enthusiasm" with "mere artistic craft" only sparingly. Like other artists, the composer must "step out of his individuality altogether" in order to be able to "appropriate to himself musically all the forms of his being." He must nevertheless "pour" into the work "the source of his innermost animus [*Gemüt*]," for "every tone is in a sense the product of his entire life," and it is only through the "highest deception" that he can present to us "the highest truth."[27]

"B" was clearly troubled by the oxymoron "feigned truth." In this, he was extending to music a debate that had begun several decades before in the realm of the theater. The eighteenth century had witnessed a revolution in acting, away from stylized declamation and conventional gestures toward what was thought to be a more natural form of delivery, based on a sympathetic imagination of the whole character to be portrayed on stage.[28] These developments led in turn to a debate about the distinction between an actor's genuine emotions and those projected on the stage. The most famous tract to take up this issue was Denis Diderot's *Paradoxe sur le comédien*, written in 1773–78 and circulated widely in manuscript before its posthumous publication in 1830.[29] The "paradox" is that the best—that is, the most moving—actors do not themselves feel the emotions they express on stage. "Extremes of feeling," Diderot had one of his interlocutors declare, "make for indifferent actors; an average amount of feeling gives you the great mass of bad actors; a complete absence of feeling is what is needed for a great actor."[30] Similar arguments had been made in France and England as early as the 1740s, if not in quite so pointed a fashion.[31]

Performing musicians, counterparts to actors on the stage, were part of this discourse as well. Johann Joachim Quantz, writing in 1752, encouraged musicians to "transport themselves" into the works they were playing. Paraphrasing the dictum of Horace, he argued that these self-induced emotions needed to be genuine in their own way.[32] And as C. P. E. Bach insisted, "One must play from the soul, not like a trained bird."[33] His oft-quoted comment on the necessity of performers to feel the emotion they wish to project to others falls within this tradition of a self-consciously willed state of mind. In yet another variation on Horace's dictum, Bach observed that in performance,

> because a musician cannot move others unless he himself is moved, he must necessarily be able to transport himself into all those affects he would arouse in listeners. He makes his feelings known to them and alters those feelings in such a way as to evoke the greatest empathy. In languid and sorrowful passages he becomes languid and sad. One sees it and hears it through him.[34]

The key verb here is *sich setzen*, to transport or transpose oneself. Bach is speaking in the context of performance, but the principle derives once again from the tradition of oratory and applies to composers as well. The ability to move from affect to affect quickly is essential. "Having barely quieted one affect," Bach observes, "he will then arouse another and subsequently vary the passions constantly."[35]

The theorist Friedrich Wilhelm Marpurg addressed the emotional pliability of performers at some length in 1757:

> The performer should feel what the composer has felt. The latter has prescribed to him his sentiments. The listener must be transported into the same sentiments. . . . Must not the performer comport himself like an actor and know how to transpose himself into this or that affect for a time and in such a way as to follow the intentions of the composer and transpose them to his listeners? He must not follow whatever motions of his soul might be present at the moment. He must take on the composer's prescribed sentiments. . . . The performer must transpose himself into the place of the composer. What has taken place in the latter must also take place in the former.[36]

Similar pronouncements abound throughout the eighteenth century and into the nineteenth.[37] Sulzer urged performers to "play as if from the soul of the composer." Christian Friedrich Daniel Schubart declared that "if I want to perform a sonata by [C. P. E.] Bach, then I must immerse myself entirely into the spirit of this great man so that my own individuality [*Ichheit*] disappears and becomes Bach's idiom."[38] The French violinists Pierre Baillot, Pierre Rode, and Rodolphe Kreutzer called it the duty of the performer "to transmit to the soul of the listener the feeling that the composer had in his soul."[39] And according to E. T. A. Hoffmann, "The true artist lives solely in the work, which he has grasped in the sense of the master and now performs. He rejects asserting his own personality in any way."[40] In 1831 François Fayolle praised the playing of Baillot on the grounds that "he possesses the genius of performance, because he strips away his *I* to become, by turn, Haydn, Boccherini, Mozart, and Beethoven."[41]

Yet there is an underlying paradox in all such pronouncements: performers are encouraged to transpose themselves into the soul of composers, even as composers are encouraged to transpose themselves into emotional states that are not their own. The composer's heart is the lodestar to which players orient their performance, but on closer examination, that lodestar turns out to be mutable.

The simplest way out of this dilemma is to think of composers themselves as actors, at least in the period before about 1830. Historians have been deeply reluctant to recognize, much less accept, this parallel, in spite of its prevalence throughout this period and even (as we shall see in chapter 7) after its reappearance in the twentieth century. This reluctance reflects our current distance from earlier assumptions about the nature of expression as an objective construct. Yet the injunction of so many past authors for composers to portray varied emotional states by relying on imagination and the willed memory of personal experience closely resembles what has since come to be known as the "Stanislavski method," or, more broadly, "method acting," in which actors use personal memory to imagine themselves into the emotional states of the characters and situations they seek to portray on the stage. This approach amounts to what the celebrated teacher of acting Sanford Meisner would later call "living truthfully under imaginary circumstances."[42] Or as the film producer Samuel Goldwyn (among many others) is said to have put it: "Acting is all about sincerity. If you can fake that, you've got it made." The emotions portrayed on stage or on screen are genuine in their own way, even if they are not spontaneous. As far as music is concerned, however, the nineteenth century's legacy of subjective expression and its corollary of emotional sincerity (see chapter 4) have largely occluded this earlier embrace of art as artifice.

Mimesis

Critics of the late Enlightenment recognized the need to reconcile inspiration and craft, the two sides of the creative process. The ancient and protean doctrine of mimesis, which regarded art as a stylized reflection of nature, provided a conceptual template for this. Often translated as "imitation," mimesis is better thought of as "representation," for artists were expected to do more than simply hold a mirror up to the world: they were compelled to re-present it, using the force of imagination to stylize it in such a way as to reveal something not directly evident in nature itself.[43] Critics regarded the exact imitation of any object as neither feasible nor desirable. Johann Elias Schlegel was typical of his generation in emphasizing that the very nature of mimesis entails selectivity, elaboration, and refinement, and that the products of such imitation might at times appear quite dissimilar from their original objects.[44]

By far the most influential eighteenth-century treatise on the subject was Charles Batteux's *Les beaux arts réduits à un même principe* (*The Fine Arts Reduced to a Single Principle*, 1746), which identified mimesis as the quality that unites and elevates the fine arts above the level of mere craftsmanship. Batteux's account reinforces the Enlightenment's conception of artistic expression as an objective construct: the emotions we read about in a poem, see in a painting, or hear in a work of music, he maintained, are representations of those emotions in daily life. Batteux urged composers and painters alike to "forget their state of mind, move outside of themselves, and put themselves into the milieu of the things they wish to represent" in their works.[45] He called music an "artificial portrait of the human passions," for it re-presented human passions not through words or images, but through nonverbal elements of sound, including melody, harmony, rhythm, and timbre.[46]

The title-page vignette of Batteux's treatise captures the mechanism of mimesis in a particularly striking fashion: a putto holds up a mirror for his companion, who reaches toward it but seems overcome, at least in one eye, by the smoke rising out of a nearby lamp (Figure 1.1). The image the putto sees in the mirror, which would otherwise offer a straightforward reflection of nature, is thus distorted, clouded—stylized—by the imagination that emanates from the artist, symbolized by the lamp. These two symbols—the mirror and the lamp—are the icons of the dual sources of artistic creation, and to achieve their maximum effect they must work in tandem. The mirror by itself is incapable of showing anything that is not already evident in nature; the lamp by itself, without regard to the parameters of the natural world and human experience, produces smoke, confusion, opacity. Without the anchoring device of the mirror, unbridled imagination would produce chaos; without the inspiration of the lamp, the mirror alone would produce a sterile, second-hand image of nature. What the observing putto perceives, then, is a synthesis of reflected nature and stylizing imagination. The doctrine of mimesis considers art a product of the mirror and the lamp working together, not in opposition. Batteux's vignette, moreover, presents mimesis not from the perspective of the artist, but from the perspective of the beholder: the observing putto is the audience who responds to the intersection of the known (nature) and the novel (artistic imagination).

This orientation toward the viewer (painting, sculpture), reader (literature), and listener (music) is central to the idea of mimesis. Within a generation, however, that orientation was shifting rapidly, beginning with literature and particularly, as we shall see (p. 54), lyric poetry. Thomas Twining, writing

LES
BEAUX ARTS
REDUITS
A
UN MÊME PRINCIPE·

Ex noto fiɛtum ſequar.
Hor. Art. Poët.

A PARIS,

Chez DURAND, Libraire, ruë S. Jacques,
à S. Landry & au Griffon.

M. DCC. XLVII.
Avec Approbation & Privilége du Roi.

Figure 1.1 Title page of Charles Batteux, *Les beaux arts réduits à un même principe*, 2nd ed. (Paris, 1747)

Batteux's epigraph is an abbreviated version of a passage from Horace's *Ars poetica*: "Ex noto fictum sequar" (From that which is known I shall create). The original passage reads "Ex noto fictum carmen sequar," but Batteux deleted the word *carmen* ("song," in the sense of a poem set to music) so as to extend the reach of Horace's dictum beyond poetry to all the fine arts, which must find their origins to at least some degree in the known quantity of nature. The perception of those arts thus rests on the complementary resources of the mirror (a reflection of nature) and the lamp (the imagination of the artist).

in 1789, took Batteux to task for extending the meaning of "imitation" beyond reasonable limits, for when a lyric poet "is merely expressing his own
sentiments, in his own *person,* we consider him not as imitating."[47] Twining's
perspective is that of the poet; Batteux's is that of the beholder.

There is an important cautionary element to Batteux's vignette as well: the
putto who beholds the image in the mirror seems on the verge of being
overwhelmed by the smoke emanating from the lamp. This image reminds
us that mimesis entails a careful balance between imagination and reflection,
and that the purpose of the fine arts is to elicit a response. Expression is not a
source of psychological release for the artist but rather a construct crafted for
the benefit of the beholder, and it is the combination of clarity and obscurity
that enables a work of fine art to achieve its goals.

The principle of mimesis thus allowed many commentators of the mid-
eighteenth century to accommodate purely instrumental music within the
category of the fine arts even while adhering to the paradigm of objective
expression. As the playwright and librettist Louis de Cahusac declared in
his 1756 entry "Expression in Opera" for Diderot's *Encyclopédie,* "One never
imitates without expressing, or rather: *expression* and imitation are the same
thing." Music itself, he adds, "is an imitation, and that imitation is not and
cannot be anything other than the true *expression* of the feeling one wishes to
portray."[48]

It is largely on the basis of such attitudes toward expression in all the arts
that the earliest biographies of composers made virtually no attempt to relate composers' lives to their works. John Mainwaring's 1760 biography of
Handel, generally regarded as the first major work of its kind for any composer, relates numerous anecdotes that convey a sense of Handel's personality, but at no point does Mainwaring suggest, even obliquely, that this
personality might somehow have manifested itself in music.[49] Nor do subsequent biographical accounts of other composers from the eighteenth and
early nineteenth centuries make any effort in this direction. These include
Franz Xaver Niemetschek's 1798 life of Mozart, compiled "according to
original sources," and Johann Nikolaus Forkel's 1802 biography of Johann
Sebastian Bach, a work of unprecedented scope for its time. Pierre-Louis
Ginguené explicitly conceded at the very outset of his memorial biography of
Niccolò Piccinni, published in 1800, that although the works of great authors
might reveal something of their lives, the same could not be said of artists
working outside the medium of words.[50] And Piccinni was first and foremost
a composer of operas.

Later interpretations of mimesis, as we shall see in chapter 2, would set the mirror and lamp in opposition and value the latter at the expense of the former. Composers who came of age in the wake of the French Revolution tended to forget, misrepresent, or willfully ignore the previously assumed interdependence of these two icons of artistic creativity. The mirror by itself proved an easy target. Imagination, that mysterious force from deep within the soul of the artist, helped artists promote themselves in an increasingly precarious commercial environment that depended more and more on the growing public market for music.

2

Toward the Perception of
Subjective Expression

Beethoven lived in an era when musical expression was understood as an objective construct. Yet it was during this same period that poets, in particular, began to promote the ideal of expressive subjectivity, and Beethoven himself (as we shall see in chapter 3) wrote music that at times baffled critics precisely because of what they heard as subjective qualities in his works. His musical contemporaries were quick to hear subjectivity in his music because they were operating under the prevailing paradigm of objective expression, and they judged his music accordingly, consistently praising its novelty while at the same time lamenting its relative impenetrability. Only after his death did the new understanding of musical expression as a subjective construct encourage listeners to hear—and value—his works as outpourings of his inner self. The qualities we most prize in Beethoven's music today, in other words, were the precise ones that created the greatest difficulties for his contemporaries, not because they were narrow-minded or deficient in their tastes, but because they were hearing his works, along with those of all other composers, within the traditional framework of music as a rhetorical art.

In the meantime, lyric poetry provided a conceptual model for the eventual acceptance of subjective expression in music. The rise of literary self-expression in the 1770s is a story that has been told many times, most notably in M. H. Abrams's classic *The Mirror and the Lamp* (1953), a study that traces the move from what Abrams called a "pragmatic" to an "expressive" theory of art. The "pragmatic" theory had been based on the idea that art's purpose is "to get something done," namely, to move the thoughts and emotions of those beholding the work of art. For authors and readers alike, this places art within the framework of rhetoric. The "expressive" theory, by contrast, shifted the focus to the artist, who now "becomes the major element generating both the artistic product and the criteria by which it is to be judged."[1] Abrams might have been better served by calling this latter phenomenon "self-expressive," for earlier commentators, as we have seen, had written at length about expression as representation, which is to say, as an objective construct.

The Mirror and the Lamp nevertheless remains valuable for the ways in which it traces the dramatic changes that unfolded in perceptions of the literary arts over the course of the late eighteenth and early nineteenth centuries. Abrams identified four "orientations" by which to consider any given work: the mimetic orientation considers the relationship of the work to nature; the pragmatic centers on the relationship of the work to its audience; the expressive (that is, self-expressive) on the relationship of the work to the artist; and the objective orientation emphasizes the relationship of the work to itself. Abrams acknowledged the possibility of considerable overlap among these perspectives, yet they help plot the pronounced shift toward the (self-)expressive theory of art during this time. The goal of *The Mirror and the Lamp*, as Abrams himself identified it, is "to chronicle the evolution and (in the early nineteenth century) the triumph, in its diverse forms, of this radical shift to the artist in the alignment of aesthetic thinking."[2]

This was a gradual process, one that developed slowly in different regions at different times. Poets and critics of the late eighteenth century actively encouraged the perception of expressive subjectivity by variously transforming, undermining, or rejecting the doctrine of mimesis. The term itself remained (*Nachahmung* in German, *imitation* in French), but critics used it more and more in the narrow sense of "imitation," as opposed to its earlier, broader sense of representation, itself part of a broader synthesis of reflection and imagination, with the mirror and the lamp working in tandem. By severing the tie between the two, Romantic poets and critics created a ready target, for "imitation"—the mirror—carries with it the odor of the secondhand, the derivative, the faux. Writers whose careers began in the last third of the eighteenth century would in fact use mimesis as an aesthetic whipping boy, a way of dismissing the aesthetics of earlier generations and asserting their own novelty. They cultivated a narrative of liberation that applied not only to themselves as individuals but to art—and for that matter, life—in general.

The self-deceptive nature of this narrative has long since been recognized: mimesis was simply too broad and malleable a concept to be overthrown all at once, and even the Romantics, who emphasized the creative powers of the mind, acknowledged the mind itself as a phenomenon of nature. Nature thus remained a touchstone of art, even if the aspect of it being reflected was sometimes difficult to make out. The Romantics' repeated appeals to the poem as a heterocosm, an autonomous universe of its own, ultimately rested on the premise of art as a representation not of the products of nature (*natura naturata*) but rather of its creative powers (*natura naturans*), which included the creative powers of the mind. All of this remained well within the conceptual parameters of mimesis.[3] Thus it was not difficult for Karl Philipp Moritz and others of his generation to shift the object of the mimetic mirror inward. In his *Über die bildende Nachahmung des Schönen* (*On the Formative Imitation of Beauty*, 1788), Moritz insisted that what artists imitate is not visible nature but the invisible forces of nature, the process of creation, including the process of creation within artists themselves. Moritz held that the act of imitation resides within artists themselves, not the objects they depict.[4] In the minds of the early Romantics, external objects were less important than the creative energy behind them. "What am I to do with all these branches and leaves? With this exact copy of grasses and flowers?" asks the artist-hero of Ludwig Tieck's novel *Franz Sternbalds Wanderungen* (*Franz Sternbald's Peregrinations*, 1798). "It is not these plants or these mountains that I want to depict in prose but my animus, my mood, which governs me at precisely this moment; I want to hold these fast and communicate them to others who can understand them."[5]

From the 1770s onward, then, authors vigorously promoted this new aesthetics of self-expression. For them, the artist was no longer merely an agent of expression but its very source. In his 1801–2 Berlin lectures on the fine arts, August Wilhelm Schlegel associated the term *expression* with the spontaneous, immediate, and unreflected cries and gestures we make in response to a given situation; these, he maintained, are revelations of "what goes on inside us," and they are "unintended and often involuntary. The word 'expression' [*Ausdruck*] is quite aptly chosen for this: the interior [*das Innere*] is pressed out, as it were, through an extrinsic force; or the expression is the external imprint from within."[6]

Such assertions reflect a conception of art far removed from the framework of rhetoric. Art is now the outward manifestation of an inner feeling and no longer the evocation of a feeling in the mind and mood of an audience.

Art as a Window on the Self

Subjective expression is a projection of the inner self, and conceptions of that self changed dramatically over the course of Beethoven's lifetime.[7] The neologism of "the I" (German: *das ich*; French: *le moi*) that first appeared in the 1770s reflects its reconceptualization as distinct entity.[8] Kant's "Copernican revolution" in philosophy, beginning in the 1780s, reconfigured the mind's relationship not only to the world around it but to itself, and the nature of "the I" became the most pressing philosophical issue for the first generation of post-Kantian philosphers, which included such figures as Fichte, Schelling, and Hegel. The central question was whether or not—and if so, how—the mind could observe itself. The challenge was compounded by the presence of the unconscious, a level of mind that by its very nature was inaccessible to direct observation but for that very reason all the more foundational. From Plato onward, philosophers had wrestled with the concept of the unconscious, and while they differed on its workings, all agreed on its prestige as the site of the primal self, unsullied by the strictures of reason, language, or social convention.

The debate about the nature of the unconscious took on new urgency toward the end of the eighteenth century.[9] In a momentous shift in the history of aesthetics, philosophers began to recognize that while the unconscious might defy observation, its *products* could provide indirect evidence of its workings. They began to regard works of art as arising out of a synthesis of conscious thought with the unconscious and, as such, as capable of offering at least an occluded window onto the nature of the unconscious, which is to say, the primordial self. The philosophical stakes of art thus increased with the growing conviction that it could serve as a means of self-knowledge and, by extension, knowledge in general.[10]

Hume and Kant are the primary figures here, and imagination is the key concept. The Cartesian system had conceived of imagination as a faculty of mediation between the senses and reason, and an imperfect one at that.[11] But imagination, as Hume maintained in his *Treatise of Human Nature* (1738–40), was fundamental to human understanding, in that it does not merely mediate perceptions and reason but integrates them, allowing us to comprehend the sensory impressions we take in from the external world. Without imagination, Hume argued, we could not meaningfully connect the causes and effects of what we observe. Yet this same faculty posed a threat, for "nothing is more dangerous to reason than the flights of the imagination, and nothing has been the occasion of more mistakes among philosophers." Where, then, to draw the line? Reason by itself was inadequate, yet imagination, although vital, could not be trusted; "we have, therefore, no choice left but betwixt a false reason and none at all." Hume's despair was palpable: "For my part I know not what ought to be done in the present case."[12]

Kant famously credited Hume with having interrupted his "dogmatic slumber" by pointing out this seemingly intractable problem.[13] Kant's solution—the basis of his self-proclaimed "Copernican revolution" in philosophy—was to conceive of the imagination as both a cognitive *and* a creative faculty. This "transcendental synthesis" of the senses and reason gave imagination (*Einbildungskraft*) newfound prestige. It was something no longer to be tempered, moderated, or mistrusted, but instead embraced as the faculty that grounded all knowledge. Whereas Hume had been reluctant to grant imagination any productive capacity, Kant's conceived of it as basic to all thought. He called it "a productive cognitive faculty . . . very powerful in creating, as it were, another nature out of the material which the real one gives it."[14] For Kant and the subsequent generations that engaged with his philosophy, the "transcendental imagination" was more than a reproductive conduit by which to process sensory impressions: it was the productive faculty that unified the self.[15] It was around the turn of the nineteenth century that an awareness of the self—*Selbstgefühl*—became foundational to thought and expression in both philosophy and the arts, with the arts increasingly viewed as an extension of philosophy.[16] Subjectivity was no longer something to be tolerated or even eliminated; it was to be embraced and amplified.

This new way of thinking about the self changed conceptions of art in fundamental ways. Kant argued that the value of art lies not in the objects themselves, but in their ability to stimulate the "free play of imagination" in those who behold them. This in itself represents an unprecedented rejection of rhetoric, which Kant had elsewhere assailed not because it could be abused—that was a charge that had dogged rhetoric since antiquity—but rather on the grounds that it robbed listeners of their moral freedom. Kant's dismissal of rhetoric, as David Wellbery points out, "is not contingent, but categorical, a perniciousness in principle, and in this sense his argument marks an historical caesura."[17] If the "purposeless purposiveness" of art was to incite the "free play of the imagination," then art could eventually come to be seen—as it indeed would be in the later doctrine of *l'art pour l'art*—as existing for its own sake, free from all moral or pragmatic agendas. The idea that the purpose of an artwork was to move an audience in a particular direction could not survive in a philosophical framework that considered art's chief value to lie in its ability to stimulate the "free play of imagination."[18]

This new prestige of imagination enabled art to function as a means of self-integration, which is to say, as a means of knowledge. Fichte, Schiller, Schelling, and Hegel all made the case for this in different ways. They saw the aesthetic experience as an activity that more than any other could bridge the gap between imagination and reason, subject and object. The imagination, by uniting the conscious and the unconscious in the act of aesthetic contemplation, could reconcile "the 'I'" with the "not-'I'" (Fichte), duty with desire (Schiller).[19] For Schelling, art served as the "general organon and capstone of the entire vault of philosophy." Art can "always and continuously proclaim anew what philosophy cannot represent externally, namely, the unconscious element of action and production and its original identity with consciousness. For this very reason, art occupies the highest place for the philosopher, for it opens, as it were, the holiest of holies, where One Flame burns, so to speak, in eternal and primordial union that which nature and history have separated."[20] Only through the contemplation of art, a tangible product of imagination, Schelling argued, can we sense the nature of the unconscious. This in turn allows us to gain at least some idea of the self as the site of integration of subject and object. For Hegel, the fine arts offered a mode of "revealing to consciousness and bringing to utterance the Divine Nature, the deepest interests of humanity, and the most comprehensive truths of the spirit."[21] Language was inadequate to the task. As Schiller so trenchantly put it:

> Warum kann der lebendige Geist dem Geist nicht erscheinen!
> *Spricht* die Seele so spricht ach! schon die *Seele* nicht mehr.

> Why can the living spirit not manifest itself to the spirit?
> When the soul *speaks*, then alas! it is already no longer the *soul* which speaks.[22]

Genius was a vital catalyst for this newly discovered epistemological power of the arts. Genius had fascinated since ancient times, but the discourse on it, as in the case of imagination, took a new turn in the second half of the eighteenth century. Philosophers and critics continued to regard it as an inborn quality that could not be taught or learned and that eluded rational explanation. But from the 1750s onward "genius" came to be associated more and more with those individuals in possession of this quality, as opposed to the quality itself. This new usage reflected the growing conviction that genius, unusual and rare as it might be, was an integral part of the self. The conception of genius as a form of divine possession, the "madness" of the *furor poeticus* so often invoked by the ancients—what Goethe called the

daemonic—never disappeared entirely, but it gradually gave way to the conviction that the source of genius was to be found not in some spirit that had
taken possession of the artist temporarily, but within the artist's enduring
and central self.[23] In an increasingly secularized world, and particularly in
the wake of the French Revolution, the words "self" and "mind" gradually
supplanted "soul."[24]

Originality was the hallmark of genius. In his influential *Conjectures on
Original Composition* (1759), Edward Young had advocated a move away
from the conventions of neoclassical poetry and helped inspire a generation of poets who proclaimed both their originality and individuality. "Too
great Awe" for the writers of antiquity, he observed, "lays Genius under re-
straint, and denies it that free scope, that full elbow-room, which is requisite for striking its most masterly strokes."[25] Young advised those who would
cultivate their genius to "Dive deep into thy bosom. . . . *Reverence thyself.* . . .
Let not great Examples, or Authorities, browbeat thy Reason into too great a
diffidence of thyself. . . . The man who thus reverences himself, will soon find
the world's reverence to follow his own."[26] Young was right. In the decades
that followed, the concept of genius was evoked so often to explain the unconventional features of poetry and literature of the time that the late 1760s
and 1770s came to be known as the *Geniezeit*, the "Age of Genius," its chief
representatives Herder, Goethe, and Schiller.[27]

Kant's position on genius was particularly influential on thinking about
the fine arts. In his *Kritik der Urteilskraft* (1790), he identified originality as
its primary characteristic and made a basic distinction between superior
mental powers of deduction and creative ("original") genius. He maintained,
for example, that Newton's discoveries in science, though profound, could be
demonstrated in a series of logical steps, whereas works of fine art—works
of beauty—could not be deduced in any comparable way through rules or
precepts. Not even their creators could describe how they came into being.[28]
Kant thus saw the fine arts as products of original genius, which he defined as
a union of imagination and understanding, thereby broadening the concept
to encompass the creative process as a whole, from its origins in an internal
inspiration through the external representation of that inspiration in a work
of art.[29] "Genius," he famously declared, "is the talent (natural gift) that gives
the rule to art." Because this talent is an "inborn productive faculty of the
artist," it "belongs to nature," and on this basis Kant proposed that such a relationship "could also be expressed thus: *Genius* is the inborn predisposition of
the mind (*ingenium*) *through which* nature gives the rule to art."[30]

But what did Kant mean by "rule" in art, and why did this term figure so prominently in his definition of genius? If originality was the chief attribution of genius (as all agreed), why would he have grounded its definition in an interplay of originality and rules, the latter of which are by definition *not* original? For an artwork to stimulate anyone's imagination, Kant maintained, it first had to be intelligible at some level, for "there can also be original nonsense."[31] It was therefore not enough for artists simply to have original ideas: they must be able to convey those ideas in ways that could be grasped by others. Kant's "rules" are thus best understood not as codified prescriptions, such as the Aristotelian unities of drama (action, time, and place) or the rules of French neoclassical theater (five acts, no mixture of tragedy and comedy, dramatic verisimilitude, etc.), but rather as broader conventions or norms that serve to promote intelligibility. "Every art," he asserted, "presupposes rules which first lay the foundation by means of which a product that is to be called artistic is first represented as possible."[32] Indeed, "there is no fine art in which something mechanical, which can be grasped and followed according to rules, and thus something *academically correct*, does not constitute the essential condition of the art." Genius itself can do no more than "furnish rich *material* for products of art; its elaboration and *form* require a talent that has been academically trained, in order to make a use of it that can stand up to the power of judgment." A "lawless freedom of imagination," whatever its richness, produces "nothing but nonsense."[33]

There is a striking resonance here with Haydn's later account of his own creative process in music (see p. 24). Through fantasizing at the keyboard, he declared, musical ideas came to him unbidden: this corresponds to the "rich material" of genius. In order to make this idea apprehensible to others, however, Haydn focused his efforts on "elaborating and sustaining it according to the rules of art" (sie den Regeln der Kunst gemäß auszuführen und zu souteniren). And if Griesinger's transcription of Haydn's follow-up to this statement is accurate—"Thus I sought to help myself" (So suchte ich mir zu helfen)—then the composer chose to describe the creative process in terms of helping not his music, but rather *himself* by tempering his powers of invention, which had manifested themselves in the "rich materials" that had sprung up out of his unconscious. Kant's "mechanical" or "academically correct" component of the artistic creation corresponds to what Haydn called the "rules of art," which allowed the products of his own imagination to become intelligible to listeners. Haydn saw the two phases of composition as mutually dependent—neither sufficient, both necessary.

These "rules of art" were in any case mutable, as Kant himself acknowledged, and as Haydn would iterate on multiple occasions. When told by Griesinger that Johann Georg Albrechtsberger "wanted to banish all fourths" from strict composition, Haydn responded: "What does that mean? Art is free and should not be bound by any restraints of craft. The ear—assuming it is an educated one—must decide, and I consider myself as competent as anyone else to prescribe laws about such things. Such artificialities have no value; I wish instead that someone would try to write a truly new kind of minuet."[34] Griesinger's report very nearly puts Kant's characterization of genius in Haydn's mouth: the composer deems himself "competent . . . to prescribe laws"—another word for rules—about his art. And indeed, Griesinger recognized it as such:

> Haydn's aesthetic character was the product of a happy natural gift and unceasing study. Whoever heard him talking about his art would not have sensed in him a great artist; and in Haydn could be found a complete confirmation of Kant's observation that "where an author owes a product to his genius, he does not himself know how the ideas for it have entered into his head, nor is it in his power to invent the like at pleasure, or methodically, and communicate the same to others in such precepts as would enable them to produce similar products.[35]

The *Kritik der Urteilskraft* is a treatise on taste, not poetics, yet Kant (like others before him) consistently emphasized the centrality of taste to the creative process as well. "Taste, like the power of judgment in general," he declared,

> is the discipline (or corrective) of genius, clipping its wings and making it well behaved or polished; but at the same time it gives genius guidance as to where and how far it should extend itself if it is to remain purposive; and by introducing clarity and order into the abundance of thoughts it makes the ideas tenable, capable of an enduring and universal approval, of enjoying a posterity among others and in an ever progressing culture. Thus if anything must be sacrificed in the conflict of the two properties in one product, it must rather be on the side of genius: and the power of judgment, which in matters of beautiful art makes its pronouncements on the basis of its own principles, will sooner permit damage to the freedom and richness of the imagination than to the understanding.[36]

Later generations would tip the aesthetic scales in the opposite direction, toward genius, thereby compelling beholders to make increasingly greater efforts to comprehend what they were reading, seeing, or hearing. Even if the proferred artwork might initially seem confused and confusing, those contemplating it were now willing to give the benefit of the doubt to artists, at least in the first instance. Kant and his contemporaries could for the most part have scarcely imagined such a scenario as the norm, as "exemplary." For them, the artist's task was to stimulate the imagination, not confront it. And to achieve this end, to realize this Kantian "purposiveness," artists had to make their ideas intelligible. This helps explain the emphasis Haydn placed on his imagined listener in describing his creative process to Griesinger. It is also entirely consistent with his oft-quoted praise of Mozart, as reported by Mozart's father, Leopold: "Herr Haydn said to me: I say to you before God and as an honest man: Your son is the greatest composer known to me, either personally or by reputation. He has taste and beyond that the greatest knowledge of composition."[37] The "taste" to which Haydn refers here is not that which Mozart directs toward the music of others but rather toward his own in the process of composing it. In Kantian terms, Haydn was praising Mozart's ability to clip the wings of his own genius. It is striking that Haydn did not (at least by Leopold's account) praise Mozart's originality or powers of invention but rather his sense of when and how to rein in his imagination. Indeed, Haydn's comments may be understood as an implicit rebuttal to those contemporary critics who criticized Mozart's music as overly rich in musical ideas.[38]

Haydn's pronouncement, then, is part of a much broader tradition of thought which recognized that artists had to walk a fine line between convention and originality. Too great an emphasis on the former would lead to boredom in the minds of listeners; too great an emphasis on the latter would lead to unintelligibility. Even Christian Fürchtegott Gellert (1715–69), one of the fiercest opponents of rule-bound poetry and drama, recognized that genius served no purpose if its ideas could not be transmitted to others:

> Yet what can the best genius achieve without instruction, without art, without training? What splendidness will the greatest spirit bring forth if it has not yet been educated in fields of knowledge, if it has not yet been equipped with a supply of beautiful and useful thoughts, adorned with a multitude of lively images, and with the treasures of language and expression?[39]

Gellert's own storehouse of rhetorical devices is on full display here: imagination without the means of expression is sterile.

Beyond the homegrown figures of the *Geniezeit* in German-speaking lands—Hamann, Herder, Goethe, Schiller, Karl Philipp Moritz, C. F. D. Schubart, Gottfried August Bürger, and Max Klinger, among others—it was Shakespeare who came to be regarded around this time as the paradigmatic genius of literature.[40] As in the case of any artist recognized as a genius, critics accorded him a considerable degree of deference. This meant that audiences were willing not merely to pardon his offenses against convention but to make an effort to comprehend their meaning and import. The arts have always been predicated upon a certain degree of engagement by readers, viewers, and listeners—even so-called passive reception requires a modicum of attentiveness—but the effusions of an acclaimed genius like Shakespeare demanded more.

Goethe, Herder, and Christoph Martin Wieland led these efforts to make sense of what so many readers of their time found baffling and strange in Shakespeare. Biography offered one way in. In the sketch of the Bard's life appended to his 1760s German-language translation of the dramas, Wieland went so far as to assert that it was Shakespeare's ignorance of the ancients that allowed him to be so original. Early exposure to Greek and Roman classics would certainly have developed his mind and given his works "an orderliness, a propriety and perfection he now lacks. But with all those advantages, he would no longer have been Shakespeare, no longer the primordial genius, the son of Fantasy . . . whose wild tones, like the forest song of the free nightingale, move the responsive strings of our hearts faster and deeper than the tutored, artificial song of the caged canary."[41]

Goethe also emphasized Shakespeare's independence from convention. In his speech opening the Shakespeare festival he organized in Frankfurt in 1771 (the first of its kind in German-speaking lands), he praised the poet for having demonstrated that the prescribed Aristotelian unity of place was "as oppressive as a prison," the unities of plot and time "burdensome shackles on our imagination."[42] Herder's "Shakespeare" essay of 1773 similarly extolled the playwright's works as counterweights to French neoclassicism and lauded them as examples of *Volkspoesie*, the poetry of a community innocent of convention.

The centrality of original genius in aesthetic discourse eventually filtered down to music criticism as well. What Mary Sue Morrow has called "rule mongering" gave way by the 1780s to genius as *the* criterion of compositional quality.[43] Critics nevertheless continued to operate within the conceptual framework of rhetoric, for they persisted in judging the products of genius on the basis of their effect.

Changing conceptions of genius and the self inevitably fostered a growing sense of individualism. The very word (along with its cognates) was itself an invention of the early nineteenth century.[44] Its novelty lay not in the belief that each individual is unique, but rather that this uniqueness could be cultivated. The German ideal of *Bildung*—self-cultivation—is the most obvious of many late-Enlightenment manifestations of this new-found conviction.[45] "Originality," as the philosopher Charles Taylor puts it, became a "vocation," and "expressive individuation" became "one of the cornerstones of modern culture." This notion is so basic today, as Taylor points out, that "we barely notice it, and we find it hard to accept that it is such a recent idea in human history and would have been incomprehensible in earlier times."[46]

Somewhat paradoxically, the cult of individuality encouraged a concurrent premise of universality, by which the experience of any one individual could now (at least in theory) hold the key to unlocking the mystery of the human condition in general. The universal self, in other words, could be found in the individual self.[47] This concept of universal individuality had enormous consequences for the arts: the artist was no longer simply the creator of a distinctive style or manner but now a potentially unique source of knowledge, with implications for all. As August Wilhelm Schlegel put it in 1808:

> Where, then should the artist seek his sublime mistress, creative nature, in order to consult with her, as it were, given that she is not preserved in any external phenomenon? He can find it in his own interiority, in the center of his being through spiritual intuition: there alone and nowhere else. Astrologers called man a microcosm, a small universe, which can be justified philosophically quite well. . . . What determines the degree of the artist's genius and puts him in a position to portray a universe within the universe is the clarity, the force, the fullness, the all-encompassing nature with which the universe is reflected in a human spirit, and with which this reflection is in turn mirrored within him.
>
> One could therefore define art as nature, transfigured and condensed for our contemplation through the processive medium of a consummate spirit.[48]

On the cusp of the nineteenth century, then, philosophers and critics alike were increasingly inclined to view the creative artist's innermost self as at once the source, the vehicle, and the object by which an artwork could make its greatest effect. More than a personal mannerism or style, subjectivity was now regarded as the essence of art and beyond that of knowledge itself. Novalis declared the most engaging artworks to be those that are "a genuine effluence of *personality*," and Fichte opened one of his several discourses on epistemology with this imperative to would-be philosophers:

> Take notice of yourself: above all, turn your gaze away from that which surrounds you and toward your interior. This is the first demand that philosophy makes of its apprentices. It is not about that which is external to you, but rather entirely about you yourself.[49]

This turn inward was thus at the same time a turn outward. Only by discovering the self could philosophers and artists identify and project universal truths.

The Prestige of the Passions

Passions, sentiments, feelings, affects, emotions: by whatever name, these subjective qualities assumed unprecedented importance in conceptions of the self during the second half of the eighteenth century.[50] Passions were nothing if not natural. "A passion," as Hume observed in 1740,

> is an original existence, or, if you will, modification of existence, and contains not any representative quality, which renders it a copy of any other existence or modification.... The consequences are evident. Since a passion can never, in any sense, be call'd unreasonable ... 'tis impossible, that reason and passion can ever oppose each other.[51]

Hume would go on to work out the implications of this provocative assertion, but his conclusions are less important for the moment than his move to put reason and the passions on more or less equal footing. In so doing he paved the way for Rousseau, who would locate the central self in feelings (projected through cries of passion) rather than in thought (projected through language) on the grounds that the former preceded the latter, both in the development of the individual and in the history of humankind. Rousseau would carry out his quest for the nature of the inner self most famously in his *Confessions*, completed in 1769 but published only in 1782, four years after his death. He opened with a bold pronouncement:

> I have resolved on an enterprise which has no precedent, and which, once complete, will have no imitator. My purpose is to display to my kind a portrait in every way true to nature, and the man I shall portray will be myself.
>
> Simply myself. I know my own heart and understand my fellow man. But I am made unlike any one I have ever met; I will even venture to say that I am like no one in the whole world. I may be no better, but at least I am different.[52]

Nature thus remained the touchstone of truth. Rousseau's hyperbolic claims of novelty and verisimilitude epitomize his era's belief in the possibilities of self-development and the universality of the individual.[53] Rousseau may not have been the founder of confessional culture, but he was certainly its first great popularizer, and his work would inspire a slew of subsequent autobiographies, by Benjamin Franklin (1791), Goethe (1811–14), and De Quincey (1821), among others. Ultimately, these all amount to what the historian Peter Gay would later call "exercises in self-definition."[54]

Music offered an intriguing avenue to unlocking the inner self. Figures such as Condillac, Rousseau, Sulzer, and the Scottish cleric John Brown argued that as a nonverbal expression of emotion, music preceded rational language for the expression of ideas.[55] According to this line of thought, music could provide an unparalleled window on the unconscious, that otherwise inaccessible realm of profoundly personal existence. Sulzer, as noted earlier, pointed to "the first poets, singers, and dancers" as having expressed sentiments from deep within themselves and without reflection; unlike their later counterparts, they did not imitate or represent emotions but instead gave voice to what they truly felt, without the slightest degree of artfulness.[56] Folk music, once considered a lower form of the art cultivated solely by the uncultivated, skyrocketed in aesthetic prestige toward the end of the eighteenth century precisely because of its origins in a "natural" society, uncorrupted by literacy and technology.[57]

The idea of music as coming from deep within the human soul is an ancient one. It was only through music—not words—that Orpheus could overpower the guardians of Hades and transcend the otherwise unbridgeable gulf between the realms of life and death. For Plato, "rhythm and harmony permeate the inner part of the soul more than anything else," including language and gesture.[58] Eighteenth-century commentators who called music "the language of the heart" were co-opting a phrase already in widespread use to describe a type of verbal language that was direct, heartfelt, and spontaneous, and as such readily distinguishable from the more carefully worked out "language of understanding." As Sulzer pointed out, "Words which by themselves would make only a weak effect could become the language of the heart if sung."[59] To Herder's way of thinking, "The sentiments of our heart would lie buried in our breast if the melodic stream did not convey them in gentle waves to the hearts of others. And it is for this reason that the Creator made the music of tones the organ of our formation; it is a language of sentiment, a language for fathers, mothers, children, and friends."[60] In contrast to the painter, according to Novalis, "the musician draws his art entirely from within, without the slightest hint of imitation."[61] Hegel followed in this vein by calling melody the "pure resonance of the inmost self. . . . the innate soul of music."[62] As late as 1849 Wagner was still identifying musical sound—*Ton*—as "the organ of the heart, music its artistically conscious language."[63]

In theory, then, critics acknowledged music, independent of any sung text, as the ideal medium for conveying primordial emotions. Yet very little of this aesthetic would find its way into discourse about the repertoires being performed in concert halls, salons, or theaters of the eighteenth century. Even Rousseau, it will be remembered, described musical expression in terms of the technical means by which composers could achieve the desired goal of moving listeners.

Literary critics of the time, on the other hand, were becoming increasingly quick to look for evidence of authorial sincerity. Passions are by their very nature sincere, and sincerity—the "congruence between avowal and feeling," as the literary critic Lionel Trilling succinctly defined it in his now-classic study of the idea in literary criticism—assumed unprecedented importance in the second half of the eighteenth century. The word, as Trilling observed, has since "lost most of its former high dignity. When we hear it, we are conscious of the anachronism which touches it with quaintness. If we speak it, we are likely to do so with either discomfort or irony."[64] The growing weight accorded to authorial sincerity nevertheless indelibly altered the perceived relationship between writers and their texts.

Sincerity was in one sense wholly compatible with rhetoric; indeed, the ideal orator was expected to give every appearance of genuine sincerity. Yet sincerity itself was understood as having no need for rhetoric, the artful presentation of an argument. Sharply divided opinions about the sincerity of Samuel Richardson's novel *Pamela* when it first appeared in 1740 provided an early indicator that this quality had in any case taken on new importance in the judgment of literature.[65] The enormous commercial success of Rousseau's *Julie, ou La nouvelle Héloïse* (1761) was due in part to its being perceived as an essentially autobiographical novel, long before Rousseau allowed as much in his *Confessions*. In a bit of self-promotion that would become known only after his death, he acknowledged that the origins of *Julie* could indeed be traced to his own unhappy love affairs. "Everybody was convinced," he recalled, "that it was impossible to express feelings so vividly unless one had felt them. . . . In that they were right, and it is true I wrote the novel in a state of burning ecstacy."[66] In the "Conversation about Novels" that served as a "second preface" to *Julie*, Rousseau (in the guise of "R.") pointed out that in contrast to the isolated countryside,

> it is only in the world that one learns to speak forcefully. First of all, because one must say everything differently and better than others would, and second, because being obliged at every moment to make assertions one doesn't believe, to express sentiments one does not feel, one attempts to give what one says a persuasive turn to make up for the lack of inner persuasion. Do you believe that really impassioned people have those intense, strong, colorful ways of speaking that you admire in your Dramas and Novels? No; passion wrapped up in itself expresses itself with more profusion than power; it doesn't even try to persuade; it doesn't even suspect that anyone could mistrust it. When it says what it feels, it does so less to explain it to others than to unburden itself.[67]

Goethe's own epistolary novel, *Die Leiden des jungen Werthers* (*The Sorrows of Young Werther*, 1774), created an equal public sensation a decade later and encouraged similar speculations about the relationship between a work's author and fictional characters. Like Rousseau, Goethe encouraged this perception, acknowledging much later in life that in the act of writing this novel he had "fed it with blood from my own heart, like a pelican." Having produced the work in a mere four weeks, "almost unconsciously, like a somnambulist," he "felt, as if after a general confession, once more happy and free, and entitled to a new life."[68]

Lyric Poetry

Poetry, and above all lyric poetry, was the artistic genre most closely associated with self-expression in the second half of the eighteenth century. As an expression of mood rather than a narration of events, the lyric forms—broadly understood to include elegies, songs, sonnets, and odes—had long been associated with an author's state of mind. Aristotle had defined lyric poetry as the genre in which the poet speaks directly, unconnected to characters or a plot, but it was not until the late Enlightenment that it established itself as what M. H. Abrams would later call "the poetic norm."[69]

Sulzer, always a useful barometer of mainstream thought in his time, observed that "the lyrical poem, even when it is directed toward another individual, takes after the monologue quite closely. . . . Where other poets speak upon reflection, the lyric poet speaks entirely from sentiment."[70] In his explication of "The Original Work of Art" (*Originalwerk*), Sulzer deems "original" any poem that gives voice to its creator's genuine—sincere, unpremeditated—feelings:

> It is easy to see how many advantages works that are original necessarily enjoy over those that are not. The former are true utterances of genius, whereas the latter are representations of sentiments that are feigned and not actually present. The former always show us nature, the latter only art. A poet who is moved to lyrical enthusiasm by an object and then begins to sing because he desires to express what he feels and cannot resist that desire creates an original ode that is a true likeness of his animus. At other times, however, an ode may be called for by circumstances outside of art; or the poet may imagine himself to be in a circumstance, in a condition in which he is actually not, and he searches for sentiments that are natural to those circumstances but that he himself does not really have, and it is in this assumed attitude that he poeticizes. A different work will then materialize, however, one that displays more art than nature. Such a work is rather deceptive, in that the poet attempts to deceive us merely in order to demonstrate art.[71]

In any case, and in contrast to later critical theories, Sulzer never suggests that knowledge of poets' lives will promote a better understanding of their works. "Original" feelings can help poets create better poetry, but it does not follow that readers must assume or imagine those feelings to be those of poets themselves as individuals.

Goethe, too, promoted the cause of lyric poetry, particularly in his early years, when he cultivated the image of the artist as projecting entirely from within. He was, in effect, living out a declaration he had put into the mouth of his fictional Werther: "I return into myself and find a world!"[72] In later life Goethe was more inclined to stress the author's sense of imagination and distance from his personal experience. "As long as a poet expresses his few subjective emotions," he declared to Eckermann in 1826, "he cannot be called a poet. But he is poet when he knows how to appropriate the world to himself and how to express it."[73] He told Madame de Staël, in turn, that "the poet must retain his *sang-froid* in order to excite more forcefully the imagination of his readers." His French visitor went on to note, quite astutely, that he may not have held this opinion earlier in his life.[74] So great was the influence of the early Goethe, however, that the history of German literary criticism after him, as Katrin Kohl has observed, would become "the story of heroic individuals, and the study of texts the study of the 'inner' life they express."[75] In this respect, the legacies of Goethe and Beethoven run parallel.

In his Berlin lectures of 1801–4 on drama and literature, August Wilhelm Schlegel called lyric poetry "the musical expression of emotions through language. The essence of the musical spirit consists of this: that we seek to retain, even perpetuate inwardly, a given emotion with pleasure, be it delightful or painful." He identified *Poesie* as "the most intimate expression of our entire being."[76] In similar fashion, Hegel called lyric poetry's content "the subjective, the inner world, the observing, sentient animus . . . that can therefore take as its sole form and final aim the self-expression of the subject."[77]

More than any other English poet, William Wordsworth made subjectivity his calling card. He repeatedly called attention to the intensely personal nature of his own creations. Many of his poems are written in the first person, often in a seemingly colloquial tone; a number of them even incorporate the time and place when they were written, further emphasizing (or at least alleging) their origins in the poet's own life, such as *Lines Composed a Few Miles above Tintern Abbey, on Revisiting the Banks of the Wye during a Tour. July 13, 1798*, or *Composed in One of the Valleys of Westmoreland, on Easter Sunday*.[78] Writing to a friend in 1816 about *The White Doe*, Wordsworth concluded that "the poetry, if there be any in the work, proceeds whence it ought to do, from the soul of Man, communicating its creative energies to the images of the external world." As M. H. Abrams noted, this assertion captures the fundamental change that took place in poetry around the beginning of the nineteenth century: Aristotle's efficient cause—the poet—had now become poetry's final cause.[79] Wordsworth never denied the craft of poetry altogether, but he consistently downplayed it, insisting that a poet is a "a man speaking to men."[80] He "took frequent occasion," as the literary critic David Perkins wryly observed, "to tell his readers that they were enjoying unpremeditated effusions." Spontaneity was the new hallmark of expression, even if this did not accurately reflect the way in which poets (including Wordsworth himself) actually produced their works.[81]

Wordsworth was not the only one to encourage such readings. Many of his most notable contemporaries—including Coleridge, Hazlitt, Byron, Shelley, and Keats—went out of their way to convey an aura of spontaneity. As Byron wrote in 1821 to a fellow poet, "I can never get people to understand that poetry is the expression of *excited passion*." For Shelley, poetry, in contrast to logic, "is not subject to the control of the active powers of the mind," and "its birth and recurrence have no necessary connexion with the consciousness or will." Keats claimed that he "never wrote one single Line of Poetry with the least Shadow of public thought."[82]

French poets of the time espoused similar ideals of self-expression. François-René de Chateaubriand (1768–1848) declared that "the great writers have produced their lives in their works. One really paints only one's own heart."[83] André Chénier (1762–94) called the heart "the sole poet," for the heart "dictates," while the poet merely "writes." The poet has no choice but to "obey this divine master and take its hand."[84]

Critics extended this presumption of self-expression to earlier poets as well. It is scarcely coincidental that autobiographical readings of Shakespeare's sonnets began to appear in the closing decades of the eighteenth century. The English critic Edmond Malone, writing in 1780, was the first to read the life as a key to the works.[85] Apparently unaware of Malone's work, August Wilhelm Schlegel bemoaned in his 1809–11 lectures on drama that it had never occurred to anyone to connect the sonnets with the poet's life. "They quite obviously portray actual situations and moods of the poet, they acquaint us with the passions of the man and indeed include as well remarkable admissions about his youthful mistakes."[86] For Wordsworth, the sonnets were the "key" with which "Shakespeare unlock'd his heart." It was in these poems, he maintained, that the poet "expresses his own feelings in his own person." Subsequent critics, including Heinrich Heine and Ralph Waldo Emerson, would continue to read the sonnets as autobiographical.[87]

Such readings became possible only after the premise of self-expression had established itself. This new way of interpreting poetry, moreover,

correlates with the declining force of rhetoric as a poetics.[88] By its very nature, lyric poetry stands in opposition to rhetoric, or at least seeks to convey
the impression that it does, in that it gives the appearance of being the expression of a soul unconcerned with its effect on an audience. Whereas rhetoric calculates the appropriateness and force of verbal devices and weighs
their use and placement accordingly, lyric poetry does no such thing—
or again, more precisely, strives to create the impression of doing no such
thing—centered as it is on the poet, not on readers or listeners. This goes
hand in hand with the rise of sincerity, from which self-expression cannot
be separated. Self-expression is by definition sincere, which makes any real
or imagined audience secondary if not altogether irrelevant in the crafting
of the poem. Shelley likened the poet to "a nightingale, who sits in darkness
and sings to cheer its own solitude with sweet sounds; his auditors are as men
entranced by the melody of an unseen musician, who feel that they are moved
and softened, yet know not whence or why."[89] Thomas Macaulay encouraged
the lyric poet "to abandon himself, without reserve, to his own emotions."
"Analysis," he concluded, "is not the business of the poet."[90] Along similar
lines, John Stuart Mill insisted that "all poetry is of the nature of soliloquy"
and distinguished between "poets of culture" and "poets of feeling," with the
latter moving beyond rhetoric and the "affectation" of emotion. "Eloquence,"
Mill explained "is *heard*, poetry is *over*heard. Eloquence supposes an audience; the peculiarity of poetry appears to us to lie in the poet's utter uncon-
sciousness of a listener. Poetry is feeling confessing itself to itself, in moments
of solitude."[91]

Such pronouncements are of course themselves calculated: the claim that
poets are *not* concerned with their audience is itself a rhetorical strategy. It
also plays into the declining prestige of rhetoric around the beginning of
the nineteenth century.[92] By 1800 subjectivity and its attendant qualities—
sincerity, spontaneity, and imagination—were becoming essential hallmarks
of value in the verbal arts. Commentators valued these qualities in music as
well, though to a far more limited extent; a comparable acceptance of subjectivity within the abstract art of instrumental music would have to wait for at
least another generation.

3

Hearing Composers in Their Works

Throughout the early decades of the nineteenth century, readers who were willing to perceive poetry and novels as self-expressive remained largely reluctant to hear music in the same way. Audiences continued to listen to vocal works as the projection of a text, and they tended to judge instrumental music on the basis of its effect, giving little if any regard to the creative self behind such works. At a time when objective expression remained the presumed norm in music, Beethoven was the one composer critics consistently heard as drawing attention to his presence. He elicited this response by cultivating two seemingly opposite but ultimately complementary qualities in his music, nearness and distance: the former through fantasy, the latter through humor and irony.

Fantasy

The deepest roots of musical self-expression lie in the genre of the fantasia, both as an extemporaneous free improvisation (typically by a soloist on a keyboard instrument) and as a notated approximation of the same. All music originates in and bears at least some evidence of the imagination—the fantasy or "fancy" of the composer—but listeners perceived this quality more immediately and prominently in the fantasia than in any other genre.[1] Its inherently (or at least seemingly) spontaneous nature predisposed listeners to hear fantasias as a window on the performer-composer's inner self.

Musically, the fantasia distinguishes itself from all other genres in a ways that typically involve some combination of (1) a free trajectory of ideas that unfold in a manner bearing little or no resemblance to the prevailing conventions of large-scale form; (2) musical ideas that seem fragmentary, unrelated to one another, or both; (3) a freedom of rhythm and tempo that at times eliminates the concept of meter altogether; and (4) unconventional harmonies and harmonic progressions, including sudden, unprepared modulations to distant keys. To make matters even more unpredictable, fantasias could and sometimes did incorporate conventional forms, well-rounded themes, developed ideas, a clear sense of meter, and conventional harmonies and harmonic progressions. In short, there was simply no way of knowing in advance, even in the most general terms, what to expect when one heard a fantasia, whether it was performed extempore or from a notated score. The generic designation constituted, in effect, a warning label to listeners: Expect the unexpected.

The perception of the fantasia primarily as the product of imagination, with correspondingly little or no room for circumspection, made it a decidedly anomalous genre. Eighteenth-century commentaries consistently refer to its exemplars as having "no theme," in the sense that they lack a *central* theme, a musical idea to be developed—"elaborated and sustained," as Haydn put it—over the course of the whole. Instead, fantasias were heard as revealing the changing moods of performer-composers in the process of inventing their own material. Rousseau, for one, called the fantasia "a piece of instrumental music one performs while composing it."[2]

The fantasia's perceived enactment of its own creation was aided in no small measure by its inherently intimate nature. Often performed on the clavichord, an instrument suited for small spaces because of its limited dynamic range, it opened what Annette Richards has called a realm of "intensely private emotion, of *Empfindsamkeit* and *Einsamkeit*, sentiment and solitude."[3] This combination of intimacy and spontaneity encouraged listeners to hear these sentiments as emanating from the depths of the composer's innermost self. Johann Friedrich Reichardt said that when C. P. E. Bach fantasized, his "entire soul" was "present in the process."[4] Bach himself endorsed fantasias that "do not consist of memorized, learned passages or stolen thoughts, but that instead must arise out of a good musical soul," conveying a speechlike quality capable of moving "from one affect to the other" in a manner that was "hurtling" and "surprising."[5]

Indeed, there is good evidence to support the notion that certain of Bach's fantasias are to at least some degree autobiographical. He gave one of them the title *C. P. E. Bachs Empfindungen*—"C. P. E. Bach's Sentiments"—thereby suggesting not the representation of an objective emotion, but the outward projection of an inward feeling identified by the composer as his own.[6] He confided to the composer and critic Carl Friedrich Cramer that he had written his Fantasia in A Major, H. 278, in a single day, "*in tormentis*," during a painful fit of gout, and on the basis of this account Matthew Head has made a persuasive case that multiple features of the score reflect the kinds of bodily pain associated with that disease.[7] Charles Burney's oft-quoted 1773 report of Bach's fantasizing at the keyboard further highlights the physical intensity of the genre as a whole:

> After dinner . . . I prevailed upon him to sit down again to a clavichord, and he played, with little intermission, till near eleven o'clock at night. During this time, he grew so animated and *possessed*, that he not only played, but looked like one inspired. His eyes were fixed, his under lip fell, and drops of effervescence distilled from his countenance. He said, if he were to be set to work frequently, in this manner, he should grow young again.[8]

Burney's description reminds us of the centrality of the performer-composer in the freely improvised fantasia. With no central theme or formal conventions to follow, listeners were compelled to attend not only to the sound but also to the very body of the individual from whom the music emanated.

Less often cited but in its own way even more revealing is the 1768 account of Bach's fantasizing made by the poet Matthias Claudius. In a letter to his colleague Heinrich von Gerstenberg, Claudius compares Bach's performance of Adagio movements to the delivery of an orator "who has not memorized his speech but is instead filled with its content," who does not rush his delivery but instead "quite calmly allows one wave after another to stream out of the fullness of his soul, without any artificiality in the way it all flowed out."[9] The suggestion here is that Bach is able to convey a sense of improvisation by enacting spontaneity, even though he is "full of the content" before he begins. Claudius's account highlights the crucial but ultimately unanswerable question about the relationship of the planned to the unplanned, the calculated to the spontaneous.

Gerstenberg, the recipient of Claudius's commentary, would go on to provide two different text underlays to Bach's widely admired Fantasia in C Minor, one from Socrates' final speech in Plato's *Apology*, the other from Hamlet's famous soliloquy ("To be or not to be").[10] But these are two different kinds of monologues: Socrates' has an audience, while Hamlet's, a true soliloquy, does not. The resolute Socrates, determined on his course of action, addresses his followers to convince them that his decision to drink the poison is correct; the irresolute Hamlet addresses no one save himself and is interrupted before he can come to any conclusion. Rhetoric is still in play here, if on a different level, in that there *is* in fact an audience for Hamlet's monologue, but those who witness this moment of thinking out loud are in effect eavesdroppers. Theater-goers recognized this sort of monologue as different in kind from standard interactions because it is a moment when the character on stage, alone with his thoughts, is speaking his true mind, unsure of which direction his own argument is taking him.

It is this quality of eavesdropping that set the free fantasia apart from all other genres in the minds of eighteenth- and early nineteenth-century listeners. It is, as Laurenz Lütteken has observed, a "monological" genre, and the music listeners were hearing was not in the first instance intended for them. What they were hearing—or rather, overhearing—was the soul of the performer-composer communing with itself in the medium of music.

The potential of the fantasia to reveal an artist's innermost being comes to the fore in Friedrich Rochlitz's 1804 account of his encounters with "Karl," a taciturn and socially withdrawn inmate of an insane asylum who, without musical training of any kind, could fantasize for hours at the keyboard. These nonverbal outpourings, Rochlitz maintained, mirrored the genuine and often rapidly changing conditions of Karl's true state of mind, offering a window on that which lies beneath or beyond the level of verbal articulation: the soul, the true self.[11]

Freely improvised fantasias were in all likelihood seldom entirely spontaneous, however much performers wished to cultivate that impression and however much listeners wished to believe it.[12] It is no doubt for this very reason that Rochlitz emphasized Karl's utter lack of musical training, thereby enhancing the value of the fantasia as a diagnostic tool of the primordial self. Under more normal circumstances, musicians would typically rely on certain techniques, patterns, and conventions when improvising, and it is altogether possible for a performer to "think out" an improvisation to at least some extent in advance. But the degree of such calculations cannot be determined in any meaningful way, and it is listeners' assumptions about the spontaneous nature of the fantasia that have carved out for it a singular place among musical genres.

To what extent notated fantasias capture any previously improvised performance(s) is also impossible to say, though eyewitness accounts tend to vouch for some reasonably close degree of correspondence even while acknowledging the inherent differences between the two.[13] In 1787, for example, Carl Friedrich Cramer observed that on the basis of some recently published fantasias, music lovers who had never heard C. P. E. Bach fantasize in person could get "some sense" of the experience, even if that sense would "always be incomplete." For one thing, Cramer observed, if a notated fantasia transcribed what Bach had actually played, it could be performed properly by few others, if by anyone at all.

> The connoisseur will nevertheless be able to see in the [published] fantasias before us the manner of the composer, the unusual ways in which he moves from one key to another, sometimes slowly, sometimes with a *salto mortale*, how he prepares daring modulations and alters tempos according to the way in which his genius considers good in the free fantasia.[14]

Heinrich Christoph Koch, in his musical dictionary of 1802, took similar note of the inevitable gap between improvised and notated fantasias even while acknowledging their common musical features. Carl Czerny, in turn, reported that Beethoven's Op. 77, his only written-out fantasia for solo keyboard, presented "a faithful image of the manner in which he extemporized and therefore did not confine himself to the development of any particular theme, but rather surrendered himself to his genius for constantly inventing new subjects."[15]

Whether freely improvised or notated, the fantasia thus enjoyed a unique exemption from the premise of music as a rhetorical art: listeners, hearing what they took to be a private, spontaneous flow of ideas, assumed responsibility for making sense of what they were hearing. They gave performer-composers a dispensation, in effect, from the otherwise standard obligation to present a musical whole that was apprehensible and persuasive in its emotional trajectory.

But too much fantasy in any composition not explicitly labeled as such was consistently regarded as a defect. Critics and composers recognized fantasy as the necessary starting point for the invention of ideas but never failed to note the imperative that fantasy—outside the genre of the fantasia itself—be tempered by circumspection. This in itself was an extension of a longer tradition derived from literature. In the standard German-language manual of literary poetics from the mid-eighteenth century, for example, Johann Christoph Gottsched had admonished writers to be aware that not all products of the imagination are beautiful or appropriate to the task at hand. Artists who let their fantasy take full rein, Gottsched declared, are like the young Phaeton, who must guide a chariot led by wild horses but lacks the understanding and powers to restrain them and therefore has no choice but to allow them to take him wherever they will.[16]

This attitude is implicit in Haydn's account of his own process for composing instrumental music, cited earlier: "I sat down [at the keyboard] and began to fantasize, according to whether my animus was playful or sad" (see p. 24). Haydn touches here on the essence of the fantasia: it reflects the composer's passing mood and is not dictated by external considerations of any kind. But Griesinger's question was not about how Haydn fantasized but rather about how he composed, and here Haydn implicitly criticized those younger artists who in effect conflated fantasizing and composing by "string[ing] together one little bit after another" and "break[ing] off before they have begun," with the result that "nothing remains in the heart when one has heard it."[17] In other words, while Haydn *began* to compose by fantasizing as the keyboard, the resulting work was not itself a fantasia (unless he designated it explicitly as such), for once he had settled on a suitable idea, the process of fantasizing effectively ceased. This is not to say that imagination stopped altogether at this point in the compositional process, but rather that the focus on working out a particular musical idea precluded the (quasi-) spontaneous and unpredictable trajectory of ideas produced by the act of freely fantasizing.[18] The object of the composer's attention, in other words, shifted from interior thoughts to the elaboration of those thoughts for an intended audience. While the invention of a theme might come from within, its working out was governed in no small part by the composer's imagined listeners.

Haydn's answer to Griesinger's question about how he composed was in fact a fairly stock response, part of a long tradition that related fantasizing to composing even while maintaining a clear distinction between the two. The North German organist and composer Michael Johann Friedrich Wiedeburg (1720–1800) had espoused essentially the same procedure more than a quarter of a century before when he called fantasizing "nothing other than composing without much circumspection or artfully long contemplation." Like Haydn, Wiedeburg recommended fantasizing as a way to create a theme that could then "be varied in all kinds of ways," the equivalent of Haydn's process of "elaborating and sustaining" a central musical idea.[19] This same sequence of steps appears in the composer Johann Wilhelm Hertel's 1783 autobiography. Writing in the third person, Hertel (1727–89) describes how, in contemplating the nature of the text to be set to music, he sat down at the keyboard and played "little more than unconnected phrases and harmonies that would have been completely incomprehensible and intolerable to anyone else." Yet these fragments allowed him to "fire up his entire soul in such a way that one could almost see on any given day whether he had an Allegro or an Adagio in his head." Hertel then set it aside for a time, returning to it "with complete cold-bloodedness" when committing it to paper, taking into account the music's effect (*Wirkung*) on others.[20]

This division between an initial, unconscious phase of fantasy-driven inspiration and a subsequent, conscious phase of "cold-blooded" circumspection is also evident in comments by Christian Gottlob Neefe (1748–98), one of Beethoven's teachers in Bonn. Neefe, too, warned against the dangers of an excessive reliance on fantasy: "What kind of musical monstrosities would we have if one simply piled one idea on top of another without any relationship, if one were to allow an unbridled fantasy without at the same time employing heart and mind? No listener would be able to grasp and perceive such music."[21] Like Hertel and Haydn, Neefe conceived of composition as a process that originates within the self but at some point fairly early on shifts decisively toward desired effects on an imagined audience. Fantasy is essential in the initial stages, but all three composers explicitly rejected a continued reliance on it beyond a certain point. In short, an overabundance of fantasy in works created and heard under the premises of music as a rhetorical art creates an excess of the smoke that emanates from the lamp of artistic imagination (see p. 36).

It is for this reason that "fantasy" and its cognates served as code words throughout Beethoven's lifetime for the unusual, the idiosyncratic, the bizarre. Koch, in his musical dictionary of 1802, went so far as to define *Bizarria* as "a type of fantasia in which the performer gives himself over primarily to a peculiarly singular mood.[22] And in the entry for *Fantasie* in the abridged version of the same dictionary from 1807, Koch emphasized that the "chaos of the images and concepts" arising out of fantasy, if it is to serve any purpose in art, requires the simultaneous assistance of "reason, through which these images and concepts are selected, ordered, and placed in sequence."[23]

The aesthetics of the fantasia thus cannot be mapped onto any other genre of music, as has been proposed on more than one occasion.[24] It was a genre unlike any other and was heard as such.

Beethoven, Neefe's pupil, grew up in the tradition that viewed fantasy as a necessary but insufficient quality in the creative process. He mastered the practice of free improvisation and cultivated it throughout his career as a performer. In the margins of a sketchbook from 1807–8 he noted that "One truly fantasizes only when one pays no attention at all to what one is playing; thus in public one would fantasize in the best and truest sense by yielding without constraint to precisely whatever one pleases."[25] This approach to improvisation is supported by multiple descriptions of Beethoven's fantasizing at the keyboard, all couched in more or less the same terms. Louis Baron de Trémont, a French officer who visited the composer in Vienna in 1809 and witnessed him fantasizing at the keyboard, described the experience:

> If he was well disposed on the day agreed upon for his improvisation, he was sublime. There was inspiration, drive, beautiful melodies, and free harmony, for—governed by musical feeling—he did not think about achieving specific effects, as he did when he held a pen in his hand. These things appeared of their own, without rambling.[26]

The distinction between fantasizing and composing comes through with special clarity here. It is the act of *not* taking listeners into account—of giving no thought to the effect of the music—that Trémont identifies the fundamental difference between the two.

Not surprisingly, then, the one work by Beethoven hailed during his lifetime as explicitly autobiographical should be a fantasia. The Fantasia in C Minor for Piano, Orchestra, and Chorus, Op. 80 (more commonly known as the Choral Fantasy), which was premiered in 1808, begins with an extended passage for unaccompanied solo piano that moves rapidly through a series of triadic passages to a succession of fragmentary ideas. But a theme eventually emerges, and it is picked up by the orchestra, which then enters into dialogue with the soloist. Toward the end, voices join in as well, intoning a text that praises the power of art.[27] The Erfurt organist and critic Ignaz Ferdinand Cajetan Arnold, reviewing the published work in 1812, took special note of its genre as one that offered access into that most mysterious of all artistic worlds: the realm of creative genius. Typically for his generation, Arnold (1774–1812) regarded musical genius as a quality, not as a synonym for the individual in its possession. Still, he emphasized the way in which the Choral Fantasy could provide a glimpse into Beethoven's "workshop of ideas."

> If the genre of the fantasy constitutes the true apex of genius, which creates from within itself, which depicts the portrait of its own soul, and which makes the form of art the pure reflective mirror of its interiority, whose fullness emerges in clarity: then such a work must be all the more precious to friends of art, the more purely the genius of its creator presents itself, without extraneous aids and without the limitations of any prescribed

form. The fantasy is the monologue of the artist, in which he articulates purely that which is his own and perceived by himself, whereas he can stand in only a dialogical relationship to received genres, such as the oratorio, the opera, etc. That is, he can give only that which the established forms offer him. . . . In the free fantasy, by contrast, all chains are broken and the genius of the artist is re-established in its primordial rights—older than the genres—as creator, as ruler in the realm of sounds. If every artist followed this suggestion—or better, if the genius of most artists accommodated itself less to conventional genres and understood itself to operate in the realm of its own freedom, its own spiritual emancipation—then every fantasy (assuming that the artist is in fact thinking of a fantasy independently and not merely imitating one) would be a true autobiography and provide the clearest insight into his creative inner self, in which one could observe his command and his presence, so to speak, in the workshop of his mind. . . . Here we find set down a rich body of evidence not only for the study of art but also for the psychological features of Beethoven's artistic character.[28]

Arnold's comments bring together a number of threads that run through discourse about the fantasia in the late eighteenth and early nineteenth centuries: the unusual nature of the genre itself; its independence from conventions of form; its essence as a compositional monologue; its capacity to realize artistic "freedom"; and its ability, more than any other genre, to reveal the "psychological features" of a composer's "artistic character." The distinction between personal and artistic character is still in evidence here, but the distance between the two has diminished markedly.

Adolph Bernhard Marx's later commentary on the Choral Fantasy reinforces all the major elements of Arnold's response. Reviewing a performance in Berlin in 1825, Marx called the work Beethoven's "musical self-portrayal" (*seine musikalische Karakteristik*). And even though Felix Mendelssohn was at the keyboard, Marx declared that it was Beethoven he heard fantasizing, "weaving his ideas from darkness and light" until the instruments "come to life according to his spirit," the whole culminating with the entrance of the chorus.[29] The following year Marx introduced his lengthy review of the Ninth Symphony by drawing attention to its similarity with the Choral Fantasy, calling these two works the only ones in which Beethoven, "certainly without being aware of it," had "elevated his artistic identity to the content of a work of art." If listeners had paid heed to the title "Fantasia" of the earlier work, he maintained, then a great deal of misunderstanding and misjudgment could have been avoided.[30]

In these and other similar responses we see not only the acceptance but the expectation of compositional subjectivity in a work explicitly labeled a fantasia. It is all the more revealing, then, that the most consistent criticism leveled against Beethoven's instrumental music during his lifetime, even from those who counted themselves among his admirers, was an overabundance of fantasy. As early as 1799, an anonymous reviewer of the Op. 10 piano sonatas praised him as a "man of genius" who "follows his own path." But too often, in this critic's view, Beethoven's "abundance of ideas" caused him to "pile thoughts wildly one on top of the other" and to "group them in a rather bizarre manner," which in turn produced an "obscure artfulness or artful obscurity" that was "more a liability than an asset."

> Fantasy, which Beethoven possesses to an unusual degree . . . is something quite valuable and indeed indispensable for a composer who feels the calling of a great artist and who disdains writing in a manner that is overly popular and superficial but who instead would much rather produce something that has a strong inner vitality and invites the connoisseur to hear it repeatedly. But in all the arts there is an overabundance that derives from a too great and too frequent striving for effect and a display of learnedness in composition. . . . This reviewer, who has now begun to value Herr van Beethoven, having made the attempt to accustom himself gradually to his manner, can therefore not suppress the wish . . . that it might please this composer, rich in fantasy, to allow himself to be guided throughout his works by a certain economy, which is certainly preferable to its opposite. There are indeed few artists to whom one must shout: Save up your treasures and treat them economically! For not many are so overly rich in ideas and so skilled in combining them. This is therefore less a direct reproach of Herr v. B. than a well-intentioned appeal, which if it does reproach on the one hand nevertheless preserves something honorable on the other.[31]

Beethoven faced such criticism repeatedly throughout his career, and not just toward the end of it. When the earliest reviewer of the *Eroica* Symphony called it "a very extended, daring, and wild fantasy," it was not meant as a compliment. Self-identifying as one of Beethoven's "most genuine admirers," this anonymous critic felt compelled to concede that for all the symphony's "beautiful and striking passages," its "strident and bizarre" features made it "extremely difficult to gain an overview of the whole." A sense of coherence seemed to "disappear almost completely."[32] And an unnamed French critic, after hearing a portion of an unidentified symphony by Beethoven in 1811, gave us a memorable image: "Having penetrated the listener's spirit with a sweet melancholy, he shreds it at once with a mass of barbarous chords. It strikes me as if we were seeing doves and crocodiles penned up together."[33]

This perception of an overabundance of fantasy, with its juxtaposition of incongruous and irreconcilable elements, is evident once again in an 1811 review of the String Quartet in E♭ Major, Op. 74. The anonymous critic begins by praising the "high simplicity" (*hohe Einfachheit*) of the composer's Op. 18 quartets as worthy of Haydn and Mozart. But the more recent quartets of Op. 59 "breathe an entirely different air," for in them the composer had indulged the "most remarkable and strangest notions" of his "original fantasy," thereby uniting "the most disparate things in a fantastic manner," all in a "deep and difficult art."[34] As for the first movement of Op. 74, "The paltry melodic coherence and the back-and-forth humoristic digressions from one idea to another give more the appearance of a free fantasy than of an ordered whole."

> Beethoven's genius has no need of our praise, and it will scarcely take note of our desires. Yet when an artist in creating beauty—be he a poet or a composer—believes that he can give himself over *exclusively* to the play of his subjective fantasy, without regard to the unity and purity of the effect, then the art-loving recipient may be allowed to hold fast exclusively to the unity and beauty of the end product and indicate what it is that has impeded a sense of pure, full pleasure. The present author declares all this with a frankness that is second nature to him in art as in life, and with the conviction that friends of gracious art think as he does: *that he has no desire to see instrumental music lose its way in this fashion.*[35]

References to "rules," "ordered wholes," and the like should not be read simply as mindless allegiance to convention: critics of the time valued originality and had no particular investment in convention for its own sake. The underlying premise of such concerns, shared by such earlier composers as Hertel, Wiedeburg, Neefe, and Haydn, was the imperative of intelligibility, a sine qua non if a given composition was to achieve its desired effect. Listeners of the time could not be moved by music that left them puzzled and confused. What they sought instead, as the anonymous critic of Op. 74 suggests, was a degree of clarity sufficient to allow them to absorb the ideas at hand. To the extent that listeners were deprived of the signposts inherent in conventional formal structures, their pleasure in a work was correspondingly diminished. "Rules" and "ordered wholes," in other words, should be understood as shorthand terms for those conventions that could help listeners follow the trajectory of a given work. Forkel had made this point explicitly long before in asserting that the purpose of rules is to ensure intelligibility. Rochlitz had similarly noted that while adhering to such rules does not ensure the quality of a work, deviating from them creates the danger of the work's becoming "considerably less effective."[36]

The formulations differ, but the juxtaposition of praise for fantasy and censure for its excess—always in that order—recurs repeatedly in contemporaneous responses to Beethoven's instrumental music. The entry for him in a biographical dictionary of artists published in Vienna in 1812 lauds the richness and novelty of his musical ideas but goes on to observe that "one cannot deny that at times he lets himself be carried away too much on the wings of his fantasy and leads his listeners into realms that are often incomprehensible."[37] Giuseppe Carpani, in his biography of Haydn, identified Beethoven as his one true successor but despaired about the profusion of fantasy in the younger composer's music. To support his view, Carpani relayed a second-hand account of Haydn's opinion of Beethoven, and while the report's veracity may be questionable, its terminology is revealing.

> A friend of mine once asked *Haydn* what he thought of this young composer. The old man responded in all sincerity: "His early works pleased me greatly, but I must confess that I do not understand the latest ones. It always seems to me that he writes *fantasias*.[38]

In a lengthy essay on the composer published serially in the *Allgemeine musikalische Zeitung* in 1815, the Leipzig philosopher and critic Amadeus Wendt praised Beethoven at some length but joined the chorus of those who found fault in the predominance of fantasy and fantasia-like elements in his music. Precisely because it is so self-revelatory and largely free of self-reflection, the fantasia "presses against the boundaries of music and of art in general":[39]

> More than any other genre, the musical fantasia is forgiven its sins against form and rules if a great spirit presides over it; it is a delightful product when the technical assurance of the master is on display

involuntarily yet pervasively. But to transfer the character of the fantasia to other kinds of music and *thereby make musical fantasy dominant in the realm of the world of notes* can only lead to great aberrations. A lavish richness of ideas and an unconquerable originality can reveal themselves in this way, but the clarity, comprehensibility, and order by which the work of art becomes an enduring pleasure, as opposed to the work of a passing mood, will then be lacking. Here it is that I once again speak of Beethoven's *great aberrations*, for it is not my purpose to be his eulogist (to which I feel neither called nor authorized), but rather to consider impartially his influence on the most recent music, as well as his character, according to my ability and insight.

Many works of Beethoven, including various symphonies and sonatas, can be comprehended and appreciated only as *musical fantasias*. Even the attentive listener often loses sight of the main idea in them and finds himself in a magnificent labyrinth, where lush vegetation and marvelously rare flowers draw attention to themselves, yet without the thread that leads back to one's peaceful home. The artist's fantasy flies on ahead unceasingly; moments of rest are rarely permitted, and the impression that was made at first is often eradicated by what comes later. The principal idea has disappeared completely, or it shimmers only the dark distance in the flow of moving harmony.[40]

"The impression that was made at first is often eradicated by what comes later": we hear in this an echo of Haydn's lament that a too-rapid succession of unrelated ideas leaves listeners cold. Wendt in effect accuses Beethoven of musical narcissism, of turning his mind inward, away from his audiences. Fantasy in itself is not a bad thing, Wendt acknowledges; but when it interferes with comprehensibility, it undermines a composer's ability to move listeners. Wendt concludes with the hope that Beethoven might in the future "strive more toward the honor of the art of music *in general* than toward *his* art."[41]

A year later Franz Schubert noted in his diary that the *Bizarrerie* of much modern-day music was traceable "almost exclusively" to "one of our greatest German artists"—there can be little question that Schubert had Beethoven in mind here—"who unites, confounds, and makes no distinction between the tragic and the comic, the agreeable and the repulsive, the heroic and the howling, the most holy and the Harlequin."[42] In private correspondence not long afterward, the renowned lexicographer Ernst Ludwig Gerber voiced despair at the excess of fantasy in all genres of modern instrumental music, and he singled out Beethoven as the principal culprit:

> It seems to me now as if fantasy, like a despot, has appropriated to itself absolute power over music in general. Granted one cannot imagine music at all without fantasy, yet it must be regulated through taste and reason. But now any limits or boundaries to fantasy are unimaginable. Everything goes everywhere and nowhere; the crazier, the better! The more wild and bizarre, the more fashionable and effect-laden. There is a never-ending pursuit of distant keys and modulations, of unharmonic progressions, of ear-splitting dissonances, and of chromatic passages, without rest and without cessation for the listener. Yet in this manner we hear and play nothing but pure fantasias. Our sonatas are fantasias, our overtures are fantasias, and even our symphonies, at least those by Beethoven and his kind, are fantasias. If one now factors into this the mischief and the struggle that instruments pursue among and against one another, it remains impossible for the layman to take satisfaction from such a *charivari*.[43]

We are inclined today to read such responses as revealing more about the limited imaginations of Beethoven's contemporaries than about his music. It is certainly tempting to dismiss Gerber's despondency as the attitude of a seventy-year-old whose tastes had been formed half a century before. But the musings of Wendt—thirteen years younger than Beethoven—and the nineteen-year-old Schubert (who had already made a name for himself with his song *Erlkönig*, Op. 1) should give us pause. To regard such readings as myopic ignores the broader premises in which all these commentators functioned. Audiences nowadays expect and even demand a high quotient of individuality and originality in new music. We want composers to project a distinctive voice, and when we hear a new work in the concert hall, we are prepared to accommodate what is presented to us. We may or may not approve of what we hear, but we accept the responsibility of coming to terms with it. Within the framework of music as a rhetorical art, however—the framework that dominated throughout Beethoven's lifetime—audiences assumed no such thing: the burden of comprehensibility lay with composers, not listeners. The notion that listeners might be expected to extend themselves in order to grasp the trajectory of the composer's thought—again, with the notable but clearly circumscribed exception of the fantasia—did not take hold to any meaningful extent until after Beethoven's death. It was not merely perceptions of his music that changed but assumptions about how to listen to music in general, particularly instrumental music.

And so it was for many listeners trying to make sense of Beethoven's music during his lifetime: they were hearing *too much* of him in his works, too much of what they perceived to be his own internal, inwardly directed fantasizing, a process that seemed to minimize or preclude any consideration on the part of the composer toward his anticipated listeners' responses to his music. This is of course precisely what later generations would come to value in Beethoven's compositions—the quality that makes his music sound so distinctively like his and no one else's.

Beethoven spent his entire professional career working in a musical culture that functioned within a framework of rhetoric. To varying degrees at different times and within different genres, and often within a single work or even movement, he both accepted and resisted that framework. It was not until the early 1830s, however, that critics in general came to accept the essentially subjective nature of expression as the new norm for both composing and listening. This shift is readily apparent in Wendt's later writings: by 1831, the same critic who sixteen years before had chided the composer for an overabundance of fantasy was now far more accepting of Beethoven's tendencies in this direction, for

> his fiery, inventive fantasy develops a wealth of ideas. . . . The symphony is for him [in contrast to Haydn and Mozart] an extended *orchestral fantasy* in the true sense of the word. He is an opponent of repetitions and always great in his constantly forward motion. And if this motion appears to go against established law, it lays down, like the path of a comet, a new law. The course of this multifaceted spirit is the course of a hero.[44]

Wendt's change of heart bears witness to an epochal shift in the history of music. Critics of the time lacked the terminology to describe this shift, and it would became clear only in retrospect. Beethoven's contemporaries recognized the qualities that made his music different but had to rely on the older vocabulary of fantasy and the fantasia, a genre whose principles of subjectivity would eventually permeate all forms of instrumental music. Listeners eventually adjusted—at times enthusiastically, at times reluctantly—to this new premise, which meant that they now had to invest effort in listening. This was an effort to which they were not accustomed. Once the aesthetics of the fantasia entered the compositional mainstream, around 1830, listeners could no longer rely on the standards of earlier formal conventions to comprehend the music they were hearing. They looked instead, as we shall see in Part Two, to the composer's life and soul.

Humor and Irony

Humor and irony offered composers two further means by which to draw attention to their presence in their works. Both of these devices entered the core repertoire of instrumental music—that is, genres beyond the fantasia—in the second half of the eighteenth century, and Haydn and Beethoven were their most prominent practitioners. Their contemporaries recognized the broader implications of this development and commented on it some length, usually disapprovingly.

Critics working at the turn of the nineteenth century typically used the term "humor" not in the modern sense of the comic, but rather in the sense of humorism, the ancient theory which holds that an individual's emotional state is determined by the relative proportion of the four bodily fluids, also known as humors: blood, phlegm, yellow bile, and black bile. The predominance of any one of these, it was believed, manifested itself in a person's disposition, mood, or, to use the German term for it, *Laune*. A preponderance of blood made one sanguine, while a preponderance of phlegm made one phlegmatic, of yellow bile, choleric, and of black bile, melancholic. To compose according to one's *Laune* meant to write in a way that betrayed one's inner physical disposition, which is to say, a disposition beyond one's own control.

"Betray" (*verraten*) is precisely the verb the philosopher and critic Christian Friedrich Michaelis uses in a brief but illuminating essay of 1807 on humor in music. It is an essay worth considering in some detail, for it signals an important shift not only in how composers wrote music, but also the ways in which listeners heard it. More and more artists, Michaelis maintains, most notably Haydn, were creating works that reflected their particular humor (*Humor*) or disposition (*Laune*) to a greater extent than ever before, and as a result listeners were becoming increasingly aware of the presence of composers in those works.

Michaelis begins his essay by noting the prominence of humor in recent works of literature; that he names no specific authors suggests that he could assume his readers' familiarity with the prose of such novelists as Laurence

Sterne (widely translated into German) and Jean Paul.[45] He also seems to have felt no need to justify the idea that techniques of the literary arts might be extended to music as well. "Music is humoristic," he declares, "if it betrays the disposition [*Laune*] of the artist more than the rigorous application of a systematic artistic practice."[46] Humoristic music, in other words, reveals the inner nature of the composer *nolens volens*, and in a way that other kinds of music do not and cannot. We apprehend humoristic works as sonic manifestations of the self.

The musical ideas in a humoristic composition, Michaelis explains, are "distinctive and unusual, following one another not in the way one would expect according to convention." They instead "surprise us through their entirely unexpected turns and transitions, and through entirely new and unusually juxtaposed figures."[47] Without violating the rules of harmony and often employing the art of counterpoint "in the most refined manner," the humoristic composer "sets himself apart from that which is conventional" through the twists and turns of his ideas, sudden modulations to distant keys, and the equally unexpected return to the tonic and the principal idea. He "gives his thoughts free rein with unreserved daring" and avoids "the common formulas of composition" in such a way that the whole resembles the "spontaneous inspirations of a fanciful or humoristic narrator, who unites the most seemingly opposite things and who, in his unusual mood, gives a new perspective on even the most well-known things." Humoristic music is "at times comic and naïve, at times serious and sublime."[48] It can seem muddled at first, but only because it runs counter to expectations established by convention.

While the musical features Michaelis identifies are essentially the same as those associated with the fantasia, their emotional sources are different in ways that are revealing. Michaelis makes a categorical distinction between works that manifest *Humor* as opposed to *Laune*, even while noting that listeners rarely encounter either quality in its pure state. Music dominated by humor tends to be "witty and of a happy, pleasant character," whereas music dominated by *Laune* "carries the traces of an obstinate mood in which sentiments crisscross in an extraordinary way and in which [the composer's] fantasy cannot play in an entirely free manner."[49] He equates the music of *Humor* with scherzo and scherzando movements, the music of *Laune* with the capriccio, which he acknowledges to be synonymous with "the fantasia, and particularly the free fantasia."[50] The implication, then, is that a composer's *Laune* can be so powerful, so "obstinate," as to overwhelm even the free play of imagination. Fantasy yields, in effect, to an essentially pathological condition over which the composer would seem to have little or no control, or over which the composer chooses to exert no control, at least for the moment. This points all the more strongly to the notion of music as a "betrayal" of the composer's inner self: the self-editing mechanisms of reflection and contemplation are absent.

Another distinction between the products of *Humor* and *Laune* lies in their respective orientations toward listeners. Scherzo-like humoristic music "betrays its intention to exhilarate and amuse listeners," and the composer is able to "express his subjective individuality" in spite of this higher, outwardly directed goal. In this category, "the composer moves more freely" than in music dominated by *Laune*, because he does so through the deliberate elaboration of "a certain object of his own choosing, of a certain attractive or droll theme, which he at times varies in his own manner and at times contrasts with other themes." Humoristic music, then, involves a greater degree of conscious manipulation than the free fantasia: it does not wander from idea to idea but instead revolves around a central theme, which achieves its effect through the manner in which the composer treats it, all with the broader intention to "exhilarate and amuse."[51]

Music dominated by *Laune*, on the other hand, is not oriented toward listeners and as a result is less flowing and less readily comprehensible. It is more apt to move from one idea to another without warning, for in such works the composer "seems to depend" on the "obstinacy of a mood, on the peculiarities of his momentary disposition" to an extent that he cannot set for himself a specific goal of "entertaining listeners and acquiring their sympathy through consciously perceptible regularity." Instead, the composer "appears to be driven exclusively by an inner compulsion to show himself as he now is" and to "exhibit the extraordinary progression and changes of his sentiments and conceits."[52] *Laune* exerts a power that comes from deep within: self-expression trumps intelligibility. The premises and resources of rhetoric no longer apply.

Michaelis concludes by noting the growing importance of humor in contemporary music:

> Humoristic music was very rare among earlier composers, as they gladly adhered to strict regularity, and as their imagination did not so easily take the daring flight that brought them above and beyond the conventional. Handel's genius, rich in ideas, might belong perhaps to the most outstanding ones that dared to strike out on a freer path and at times gave

music the interesting expression of the fanciful. Our most recent music, by contrast, is for the most part humoristic, especially since Joseph Haydn, the greatest master of this genre, set the tone for it in his original symphonies and quartets. Johann Sebastian Bach often tended in the direction of this manner, though he kept himself within limits by means of his artful harmony. Carl Philipp Emanuel Bach also composed in this style not infrequently. But Haydn was the first to do so with general effect, and he prompted a great many famous musicians of recent times to write in this character. The humoristic was also not foreign to Mozart's rich genius, but he seemed more attuned to the serious and sublime than to the comic and naïve, and as much as he knew how to write in a joking mood, he never tarried there very long, or he readily transitioned to the great and imposing or to the heartfelt and affecting. Duos, quartets, and quintets for various instruments would seem to lend themselves extremely well to the fanciful style, and not only Haydn, but also Pleyel, Viotti, Rode, Kreu[t]zer, Clementi, and Beethoven have allowed a rich source of that humor to flow that in their music. In some cases it tends more toward toward playful jocularity, in others toward effusive earnestness.[53]

What Michaelis describes here is the infiltration of humor into genres beyond the fantasia, including sonatas, quartets, and symphonies. He lays out a spectrum of compositional possibilities: "conventional" works in which composers aim for comprehensibility; humoristic works, in which the agency of the composer becomes evident even as the work reflects the composer's concern for its effect on listeners; and works dominated by *Laune*, in which the inner mood of the composer inhibits the presentation of ideas in a readily comprehensible manner.

Michaelis was not the first to notice these developments. As early as 1776 Carl Ludwig Junker had challenged his readers "to name a single work by Haydn in which *Laune* is not a marked quality," assuring them that they would, in fact, find no such composition.[54] This was not, in Junker's opinion, to Haydn's credit. Michaelis, writing a generation later, was far more sympathetic to this quality in music. His account owes a deep but unacknowledged debt to Jean Paul's *Vorschule der Ästhetik* (1804), which makes humor, broadly conceived, a foundational element of literary aesthetics. Jean Paul repeatedly emphasizes the ways in which humor reveals the innermost self of the author, declaring at one point that "the self plays the leading role with every humorist," and that it is in humor that "the 'I' steps forth parodically."[55]

The technique of authors calling attention to themselves in the course of a narrative is something Jean Paul values in the works of Cervantes, Swift, and Sterne, and he even goes so far as to call attention to the similarities between the music of Haydn and the prose of Sterne, who

> repeatedly speaks at length and weightily about certain phenomena before finally concluding that not a single word of it all, in any case, has been true. One can sense something similar to the audacity of annihilating humor, and at the same time an expression of disdain for the world, in certain music—for example, Haydn's, which annihilates entire passages through one that is foreign, and which storms along between pianissimo and fortissimo, Presto and Andante.[56]

Humor, in short, provided a means by which authors could draw attention to their agency and in so doing reveal a glimpse of their inner selves. The playwright Ludwig Tieck identified humor as way of indicating the "specific and idiosyncratic manner of a person, his most distincitve essence." Humor, he observed, "occasionally correlates with *Laune* and is in any case a quality in which playfulness and seriousness are coupled, as for example in the case of Sterne."[57] Tieck might well have said the same of Beethoven, a personal acquaintance of his whose even more jarring juxtapositions of the serious and comic earned him the repeated epithet, even during his own lifetime, as a "musical Jean Paul."[58]

The self-revelatory nature of humor runs contrary to one of the underlying precepts of rhetoric, that orators not call attention to their craft or to their agency as orators. Gotthold Ephraim Lessing recognized the applicability of this principle to all the arts. In his *Laokoon* (1766), he pointed out that art strives to make present in the mind of the beholder something that is in fact not physically there. This illusion is essential if an artwork is to be successful in its goal of moving the emotions of the beholder. And this end is possible only when that individual ceases to be aware of the vehicle by which a work makes its impression. The artist himself, the creator, must not enter into the mind of the beholder; if he does, the work will lack sufficient illusion to achieve its effect.[59] Lessing put forward this basic idea even more pointedly a year later in his *Hamburgische Dramaturgie*:

> And how weak must be the impression made by the work, if in that very moment [of beholding it] one's greatest desire is to juxtapose it against

the figure of the master who made it? The true masterpiece, it seems to me, fills us with itself so entirely that we forget about its creator and perceive it not as the product of a particular individual, but rather of nature as a whole. . . . If one is so curious about the artist, then the illusion must be very weak, one must sense little that is natural and yet be all the more aware of the artifice.[60]

Anyone listening to an oration or musical composition can be surprised or even moved by an unexpected turn of events within the presentation, but one's awareness of the orator, performer, or composer, by Lessing's lights, should be indirect at best, and if at all, then preferably only in retrospect, upon reflection. A revealing exception in music, he concedes, would be a bravura showpiece written primarily as a vehicle for soloists to display their virtuosity. But he points out that this is just the kind of composition that many critics disparage as empty, precisely on the grounds that it seeks merely to dazzle rather than to move the listener's passions: the performer's inescapable presence, and listeners' attention to it, preclude a sufficient degree of aesthetic illusion. As Johann Maass noted of instrumental music in general: "The composer's best art is this: to compose in such a way that one notices no art at all."[61]

Yet this was precisely the principle that Haydn, Beethoven, and other contemporary composers identified by Michaelis had begun to violate on a consistent basis. Humor compelled critics to hear new music on composers' terms. The encounter was not always a happy one, as Amadeus Wendt's 1818 review of Beethoven's Eighth Symphony makes abundantly clear.

The long-renowned humor of this genial composer, evident in extraordinary leaps, achieves such audacious heights here that the listener smiles more than is moved. The question cannot be repressed: Where is music heading, now that a composer's every willful idea violates the law of melody and that he cuts off the thread of melody wherever it pleases him? In short, where is music heading if the art serves as an arbitrary game for the often labored *Laune* of an individual, even if that *Laune* is endowed with all the luster of talent and experience? . . . One can, it must be acknowledged, grow accustomed to that which is peculiar the more often one hears it. . . . I also gladly concede that one can only gradually penetrate a deep artwork completely. But the first, unprejudiced contemplation and hearing usually gives us the correct overall impression, which on repeated listening I find only

confirmed. . . . The first movement and above all the finale have all the defi-
ciencies of Beethoven's music—and of the *present* time.[62]

Irony, closely related to humor, shares many of the same musical
features: sudden shifts of tone, unmediated leaps from one affect to another,
and blatant violations of musical conventions, which is to say, of listeners'
expectations. But whereas listeners heard humor as an almost unavoidable,
quasi-pathological manifestation of the compositional self, they heard irony
as a calculated device in which composers deliberately called attention to the
artifice of art. In this sense, irony was perceived less as a revelation of self
than as an active assertion of self.

Musical irony comes in many forms. Its locus classicus is the end of the finale of Haydn's String Quartet in E♭ Major, Op. 33 No. 2 ("The Joke"), where
the music repeatedly and blatantly violates the conventions of musical closure: the unsuspecting listener has every reason to believe that the piece is
over when in fact it is not, and when it actually does end, it seems to be still
in progress, for Haydn has repurposed the movement's opening phrase into
its final cadence. This is, in effect, a musical pun: the movement's beginning
is identical to its ending. And just as when we hear a verbal pun, we become
conscious of the punster's wit and the arbitrary nature of language. By violating the conventions of closure so flagrantly, Haydn calls attention to them
and in so doing exposes the craft of his art. We become aware, in effect, of the
ordinarily invisible puppeteer who has been pulling the strings of his cred-
ulous listeners. All of this serves to establish a certain sense of distance between the composer and his work, thereby calling attention to his agency.
The ending of this quartet lays bare the gap between art as a technique and art
as an aesthetic experience.

Haydn's irony, here and throughout his oeuvre, is of the moment: once the
work is over, we understand in retrospect the way in which he has played
with our expectations.[63] Whether or not we appreciate these manipulations
of convention is a matter of personal taste. A fair number of Haydn's
contemporaries clearly did not. They objected to the unmediated mixtures of
serious and comic, high and low in his music.[64] It would seem that they preferred not to be reminded of the illusory nature of what they were hearing.

Beethoven also played repeatedly with listeners' expectations, but even
more intensively and on an even broader scale, and he, too, met resistance
on this front. His use of irony extends at times across an entire movement or
work, leaving listeners mystified as to the motivation or logic behind what

they have just heard. The String Quartet in F Minor, Op. 95 (1810), offers
an illustrative example of this. Beethoven labeled it *Quartetto serioso* on the
autograph score, a description that aptly characterizes the work's three first
movements and most of its finale. But just as the minor-mode finale seems
to drawing to a close, the tone shifts abruptly from one of somber gravity
to one of almost weightless levity. The contrast is all the more striking because of the absence of any readily audible thematic connections between the
finale's coda and any other material we have heard up to this point. This is not
like the later String Quartet in A Minor, Op. 132, in which the finale's main
theme, heard hitherto only in the minor mode, makes its final appearance in
major. Instead, we are faced with a fleeting coda that seems wholly unconnected to what has gone before.[65]

This coda, as Lewis Lockwood observes, has "baffled many a dedicated
Beethovenian."[66] Critics were slow to take up the challenge. It was not until
1863 that A. B. Marx, a dedicated Beethovenian if ever there was one, mus-
tered the courage to address it at all. He himself had avoided discussing
the quartet altogether in the 1859 first edition of his life-and-works study
of the composer, only to confess in the second edition that he could gain
no "clear idea of the whole, or even merely a sense of unified psychological
development." He deemed the final forty-three measures an entirely separate, fifth movement and refused to call it a coda on the grounds that it
lacked any recognizable connection to the preceding Allegretto agitato.[67]
Almost fifty years later Vincent d'Indy was less forgiving. For him, the
finale's coda was "without interest or utility of any sort," the movement as
a whole perhaps at best an example of how *not* to compose. Walter Willson
Cobbett, writing in 1930, was equally dismissive: "One might imagine it
some light Rossinian operatic finale which had strayed into this atmos-
phere of sustained beauty, and we think that no interpretation could pal-
liate this error of a genius."[68]

More recent commentators have found the ending of Op. 95 no less puzzling. Basil Lam calls it a "comic-opera coda, absurdly and deliberately unrelated" to the work as a whole, "the Shakespearian touch that provides the
final confirmation of the truth of the rest." David Wyn Jones observes that
the last movement "almost defies comprehension," particularly "the final
move in the coda to an exhilarating F major. . . . The self-avowed difficulty of
the quartet as a whole invites comparison with the late quartets, but the later
works find a cohesion that is more satisfying than that evident in Op. 95." For
William Kinderman, the coda is "problematic" because it "blithely ignores

the dramatic tensions of the work up to that point," and those tensions, rather than being resolved, "are forgotten and seemingly transcended." Daniel Chua has similarly argued that this ending is full of "clichés so incongruous to everything else in the quartet that the situation is one of *aporia* rather than humour." The coda as a whole manifests "a creative refusal to respond to the struggle" that had gone on up to this point in the finale.[69]

Why would Beethoven end such a consistently somber, serious work in this way? The move correlates with a fascinating report about the way in which he improvised at the keyboard, as recalled by his pupil Carl Czerny in 1852:

> His improvisation was most brilliant and striking: in whatever company he might chance to be, he knew how to produce such an effect upon every hearer that frequently not an eye remained dry, while many would break out into loud sobs; for there was something wonderful in his expression in addition to the beauty and originality of his ideas and his spirited style of rendering them. After ending an improvisation of this kind he would burst into loud laughter, and banter his hearers on the emotion he had caused in them. "You are fools!" he would say. Sometimes he would feel himself insulted by these indications of sympathy. "Who can live among such spoiled children," he would cry.[70]

It would be easy to dismiss this as yet one more entertaining but probably apocryphal anecdote were it not supported by certain moments in music that Beethoven committed to paper, most notably in the coda of Op. 95. But this raises the question of *why* Beethoven would want to insult his listeners, either through improvisation or through notated works. The answer reflects the beginnings of a gradual shift from the principles of rhetoric to the principles of hermeneutics. By abandoning the framework of rhetoric in a pointed fashion at this moment, Beethoven presented his listeners with what amounts to a puzzle to be solved, or at least contemplated, for in its most sophisticated forms, irony promotes the plausibility of utterly contradictory meanings.[71]

All of this is in keeping with contemporaneous developments in literature and philosophy. Beethoven, as we know, was a profound devotee of Shakespeare, and irony was a hallmark of Shakespearean drama, not merely on the level of individual characters or scenes but frequently across entire plays, as August Wilhelm Schlegel argued. Most poets, he observed, are "partisan" in that they "demand blind belief" from their readers. But "the more passionate the rhetoric, the more easily it falls short of its goal," for perceptive readers can become all too aware of being manipulated, and when we see through the artifice, we question our submission to the will of the artist. However:

> If on the other hand by a dexterous maneuver the poet occasionally turns the coin over onto its less shiny side, he thereby places himself in a secret understanding with a select circle of his readers, those who are most perceptive. He shows them that he has anticipated their objections and that he is not a captive of the objects being presented, but rather hovers freely above them, and that he if wanted to do things differently he could utterly annihilate that which he himself had magically conjured up.[72]

This twofold capacity of the artist—to move an audience and yet at the same time demonstrate a certain emotional remove from the material at hand—is characteristic of early nineteenth-century attitudes toward irony as an artistic device that could be understood at once as both engaged and distant. But it was in any case antirhetorical, in that it rejected the task of moving listeners toward a particular emotional state and instead challenged them to interpret what they were hearing. It forced listeners to think about compositional motivations, which is to say: about composers themselves.

Beethoven's Subjectivity in an Age of Objectivity

When the Erfurt musician and critic Ignaz Theodor Ferdinand Arnold published his "Gallery of the Most Famous Musicians of the Eighteenth and Nineteenth Centuries" in 1810, he ignored Beethoven but had this to say about the music of Haydn, who had died the year before:

> There is no musical idea, be it ever so simple or ornate, that would not become interesting through inversion, fragmentation, transposition, and similar such devices. The sureness and facility in the arts of counterpoint, supported by an inexhaustible imagination, lead the ear unexpectedly into wildernesses and depths, into which it gladly follows such sure guidance and for which it is richly rewarded. Haydn does this like a clever orator, who, when he wants to convince us of something, proceeds from the basis of a sentence that is universally recognized to be true, one with which everyone agrees, one that everyone must be able to understand; but he knows

so cunningly just how to use this idea, that he can soon convince us of anything he wishes to, even if it is the very opposite of the idea originally proposed.

Haydn's music enters our ears quite smoothly, for we have a sense that we are hearing something that is easily grasped and already familiar to us. But we soon find that it is not that which we had thought it was or should become. We hear something new, and we marvel at the man who knows so cleverly how to offer us, under the guise of the well known, something never heard before. Precisely this endearing popularity gives his compositions— for all their harmonic extravagance and instrumentation—an inexhaustible clarity, general intelligibility, and comprehensibility so that we grasp the most difficult things with ease.[73]

No one had ever talked about Beethoven's music in this way. A Viennese reviewer, writing in 1806, expressed disappointment that "because of an obvious desire to be completely novel, Beethoven is not infrequently incomprehensible, disconnected, and obscure." Another critic, reviewing the piano sonatas of Op. 10, grumbled about the music's "obscure artistry or artistic obscurity."[74] Beethoven himself was well aware that his music was difficult to follow. As early as 1796 he had declared to the pianist and composer Johann Andreas Streicher that "even if only a few understand me, I am satisified."[75] As a young composer facing critical headwinds, Beethoven can be forgiven for such a defensive statement. Still, the assertion is remarkable for its time, given the prevailing conception of music as a rhetorical art, in which it was assumed that composers bore responsibility for writing works that were intelligible and therefore capable of "persuading"—moving—listeners. This did not mean that listeners expected to hear only simple, easily digestible music. As Arnold's glowing account of Haydn's music suggests, complexity and novelty were not in themselves barriers to intelligibility, provided they were applied in the right way. Artfulness was acceptable as long as it appeared artless. And indeed, another critic a decade earlier had praised Haydn's music in just these terms, lauding its synthesis of "artistic popularity" and "popular artistry."[76]

"My language is understood throughout the world," Haydn is said to have claimed late in his life.[77] The veracity of the report is for the moment less important than its formulation, which reflects the high value placed on intelligibility in his time. Mozart, too, had accepted as self-evident his responsibility to connect with a wide range of listeners. In an often-quoted passage from a letter of 1782 to his father, he described how his new piano concertos, K. 413–15, were

> a mean between too difficult and too easy. They are very brilliant, pleasant to the ears, without falling into emptiness, of course. Here and there, *connoisseurs alone will derive satisfaction*, but in such a way that the *non-connoisseurs will be pleased* without knowing why.[78]

Not every critic found Mozart's music so broadly appealing. The most common reproach was that he aimed at too sophisticated an audience. Joseph II's reported claim that *Die Entführung aus dem Serail* contained "far too many notes" and Cramer's remark that the six string quartets dedicated to Haydn were "too highly seasoned" are the best-known such judgments.[79] Still, even if his tendency was to write music that was more demanding than most, Mozart would likely never have claimed to be satisfied if his music were "understood by only a few."

Beethoven's music posed challenges of an altogether different order. Audiences were willing to listen attentively but were unprepared and unwilling to accept works that left them simply puzzled. They did not expect to be confronted with the incomprehensible. Yet that is precisely the word that would surface in commentaries on his music repeatedly throughout his lifetime. He composed in an age dominated by the framework of rhetoric, yet by challenging listeners to understand what he had written, his works anticipated—often to a considerable degree—the framework of hermeneutics that would later supplant rhetoric. Beethoven never rejected the parameters of rhetoric and could never escape them entirely: they were too deeply engrained in his early training, and his finances depended in large measure on sales of his music to the public. Even toward the end of his life he declared that his "primary goal" in writing the *Missa solemnis* had been to "arouse religious feelings and make them lasting in singers and listeners alike."[80] On the whole, however, over the course of his career we can see him moving farther and farther away from the basic principles of music as a rhetorical art.

A small number of commentators began to acknowledge this tendency in positive terms, if somewhat tentatively, around 1810. After hearing string quartets by Haydn, Mozart, and Beethoven in a single performance in 1809, the composer Johann Friedrich Reichardt ruminated on the different ways in which these "three genuine humorists" had cultivated the same genre, "each according to his own individual nature." He compared the means by which each had projected himself through his music:

> Haydn created the quartet out of the pure, bright source of his lovable, orig-inal nature. As regards naïveté and *Laune*, he thus remains unique. Mozart's more powerful nature and richer fantasy was more pervasive, and in many a movement he articulated the highest and deepest of his inner being; he was himself more of a performing virtuoso and thus demanded much more in the way of artful elaboration. In this manner he built his palace on Haydn's lovingly fantastic garden house. Beethoven had made himself at home from early on in this palace; all that was left to him was the building of a daring, defiant tower in which to express his own nature in his own forms, a tower [*Thurmbau*] onto which no one will readily add something without breaking his neck.[81]

Reichardt's imagery is architectural: Haydn's garden house is close to nature, full of fantasy yet still "lovable"; Mozart's imposing palace, an expansion of that garden house, reveals even more in the way of fantasy, which is to say, more of the composer's own self; and Beethoven's tower atop that palace is so extreme that any further extension of it would be dangerous if not altogether impossible. Reichardt's choice of the word *Thurmbau* is delightfully ambig-uous: it can mean either the building of a tower or the tower itself, and a very specific one at that: the Tower of Babel. Without saying so directly, Reichardt suggests that Beethoven's tower, "daring" and "defiant," runs the risk of taking musical language beyond the point of intelligibility, a language *not* under-stood throughout the world.

In his review of the Fifth Symphony the following year, E. T. A. Hoffmann would trace a similar progression from Haydn to Mozart to Beethoven, moving from a foundation of natural innocence and naïveté (Haydn) to a higher degree of self-consciousness (Mozart) and culminating in the outer reaches of the otherworldly (Beethoven). And again like Reichardt, Hoffmann recognized the peril of unintelligibility and framed his critique, revealingly, in praise not of Beethoven's creative imagination—which even his detractors acknowledged—but rather his capacity for reflection, cir-cumspection, and rational deliberation—in short, his objectivity, the very quality his critics so often found lacking. Hoffmann was quite explicit on this point. Beethoven, he observed, "separates his 'I' from the inner realm of tones and rules over that realm as an unfettered master."[82] At a time when subjectivity was the central issue of German philosophy (most prominently in the writings of Fichte, Schelling, and Hegel), this evocation of the philosophical flashpoint of what Fichte called "I" and the "Not-'I'" (the *Ich* and *Nicht-Ich*) carries pointed implications. Only through an acute awareness of that which lay beyond himself could Beethoven achieve his desired effect, and Hoffmann's analysis of the Fifth Symphony ultimately revolves around that effect: at no point does he characterize the work as a volcanic eruption of the composer's self. In this respect, Hoffmann's review treats expression very much in terms of Enlightenment objectivity.[83]

Nor would this conceptual foundation of expressive objectivity fade anytime soon. As late as 1826, an anonymous critic opened his comparison of Beethoven and the novelist Jean Paul with the observation that "undoubtedly the most genial composer of our time rules over his genius as if it were a slave."[84] The Viennese critic Friedrich August Kanne, in a review of several of the composer's later works, including the *Missa solemnis* and the Ninth Symphony, similarly noted that Beethoven's fantasy was tempered by his "sublime circumspection."[85] The best way to counter the charge of an excess of fantasy, Beethoven's advocates seemed to agree, was to play up his capacity to distance himself from his own work and create from a detached, critical perspective.

An excess of compositional subjectivity nevertheless remained a sticking point in contemporary assessments of Beethoven's music. When Hoffmann reworked large portions of his 1810 review into an essay penned by his fictional *Kapellmeister*, Johannes Kreisler, he could take a more aggressive stance. Freed from the strictures of journalism, he openly attacked those who professed incomprehension in the face of what Beethoven had written:

> Beethoven's mighty genius intimidates the musical rabble; they try in vain
> to resist it. . . . But what if it is only *your* inadequate understanding which
> fails to grasp the inner coherence of every Beethoven composition? What if
> it is entirely *your* fault that the composer's language is clear to the initiated
> but not to you, and that the entrance to his innermost mysteries remains
> closed to you?[86]

Even from the pen of a fictional character, an indictment of the listening public's competency was remarkable for its time, given the fundamental premise of a rhetorical framework for the production of music, a framework that placed the burden of intelligibility on composers, not listeners.

In time, other critics gradually began to accept subjectivity as a desirable quality. The Berlin-based critic, librettist, actor, and composer Karl (Carl) Blum (1786–1844) publicly thanked Beethoven in 1814 for having "poeticized" the "minuet" of the Fifth Symphony—its untitled third movement—from the "depths of your rich animus."[87] Later that same year he expanded on the idea of hearing the composer in his work:

> But what other living composer is capable, as he is, of doing exactly the op-
> posite, of allowing his innermost sensibility to resonate through harmony?
> His soul is like the ocean: if it is calm, then it reflects heaven and all its stars
> in its waters. But if the all-powerful breath of nature blows upon it, then it
> surges and crashes, foaming and breaking on the shore. Thus it is with *him*.
> If his soul is calm and still, then amiable and luminous rays break forth in
> endless quantity and in every direction, and a world of wonders is opened
> up to us by their magic shimmer. But if the innermost core of his being is
> moved by hostile forces, then sure enough, waves of harmony tumble forth
> thunderously and break next to each other and on top of each other. Yet
> even in this hurricane a quiet, heavenly tone often enters in, one that points
> to a calming of the storm.[88]

Blum was the first critic to use the term *irony* specifically in connection with Beethoven's music. His comments are particularly rich in that they touch on two of the most important qualities consistently associated with irony in the early nineteenth century. First, it is subtle: it "hovers" over the artwork as a whole and only occasionally imposes itself with force. Second, irony is perceptible only to some—whether August Wilhelm Schlegel's "select circle of readers" or Beethoven's "few" who understood his music:

> In the works of the greatest poets there is often an irony that hovers gently
> above the whole but that breaks through incisively at times; it is easily
> perceived by thoughtful observers. I would adduce here, among many,
> Shakespeare, Cervantes, and Goethe. Beethoven's compositions have not
> been considered nearly enough from this perspective; yet only in this
> way will that which is *seemingly* unpleasant and alien be recognized as
> exquisite and necessary. Genuine poetic irony hovers over many of his
> most outstanding works, at times gently, but also at times incisively and
> frightfully.[89]

Here Blum identifies the three authors whom critics of Beethoven's time associated with irony more often than any others. If Shakespeare and Cervantes would seem to be predictable choices, Goethe might come as a surprise. Yet Goethe's contemporaries repeatedly noted the presence of irony in his writings. The most famous instance was Friedrich Schlegel's widely discussed essay of 1798 on *Wilhelm Meisters Lehrjahre*, in which Schlegel praised the "irony hovering above the entire work," even while noting that not every reader would perceive it.[90] *Schweben*—to hover, to be in suspension between two points—is the word Blum would later use, and it is a word often invoked in connection with irony. Schlegel lauded the novel's "aura of dignity and momentousness," which could nevertheless "smile at itself."[91] Goethe's air of detachment, he maintained, gave the novel an air that was at once both serious and humorous, weighty and light: "One should not let oneself be fooled when the poet treats persons and events in an easy and lofty mood, when he almost never mentions his hero without irony, and when he seems to smile down from the heights of his spirit upon his masterwork, as if this were not for him the most solemn seriousness."[92] For the critic Adam Müller, Goethe had no equal in "the art of contradiction, the reflective exchange of algebraic signs, the form in which any possible contradiction can manifest itself, thus in rooted motion, in true irony, in universality."[93] Jean Paul similarly viewed Goethe as one of the great "humorists," together with Cervantes, Sterne, Voltaire, Rabelais, and Shakespeare—in short, with those authors widely perceived at the time as ironists.[94]

The tendency to hear Beethoven in his music—either as a reflection of his deepest innermost self or as detached observer—would become increasingly evident over the last decade of his life. An anonymous reviewer writing for the *Allgemeine musikalische Zeitung* in 1817 felt reason to hope that the more melodious nature of the Violin Sonata in G Major, Op. 96, along with other recently published works, was a sign that the composer's outlook on life was now "satisfied, friendly, and cheerful." For "artists of *his* kind . . . give voice to themselves in their works."[95] Thus it was only among extraordinary artists, according to this critic, that the ideal of self-expression manifested itself. Another contributor to the same journal later that year took a young composer's new overture to task for its attempt to imitate Beethoven too closely. The problem, to this reviewer's mind, was that what makes Beethoven's music so captivating and inimitable is that it is distinctively his own, and it is his own because (as in the case of Jean Paul's prose) he has created it "from his innermost, powerful, and intrinsically original nature."[96]

Such observations would nevertheless remain relatively isolated before the mid-1820s. The scales tipped in favor of subjectivity only later, toward the end of Beethoven's life and then with great intensity in the years immediately after his death.

For the time being, the process was slow. Two of Beethoven's compositions that today are considered to be of a particularly personal nature—the Piano Sonata Op. 81a ("Les Adieux") and the *Missa solemnis*, Op. 123—illustrate just how much later perspectives have colored earlier ones. The assumption that these express deep personal emotions revolves around the composer's relationship with their dedicatee, his patron and pupil, Archduke Rudolph, the younger brother of the Habsburg Emperor Franz I. The piano sonata in particular has long been regarded as the most transparently autobiographical of all Beethoven's compositions. The titles of its three movements ("Das Lebewohl," "Abwesenheit," and "Das Wiedersehen" [The Farewell, Absence, and Reunion]), its dedication to Archduke Rudolph, and the inscriptions on an autograph manuscript of the first movement ("Wien am 4ten May 1809/bei der Abreise S Kaserl. Hoheit/des Verehrten Erzherzogs/Rudolph" [Vienna, 4 May 1809, on the departure of His Imperial Majesty, the Honored Archduke Rudolph]) would seem to support this interpretation. The archduke was in fact forced to flee Vienna in the face of the invading French army in early May 1809, and he did not return until late January 1810.

Based on the chronology of the sources, however, it now seems fairly certain that these movement titles were applied to the work after the fact. Poundie Burstein in particular has questioned the traditional perception of this sonata as a token of the composer's supposedly deep personal affection toward the archduke.[97] Drawing on the earlier work of Susan Kagan, Burstein summons considerable evidence to show that the composer's relationship with Rudolph, while cordial, was "not so close that being apart from each other for a few months would cause either one of them intense sadness, contrary to what is suggested by the standard programmatic explanations of op. 81a."[98] Indeed, the evidence suggests quite the opposite: that Beethoven viewed his lessons with the archduke as a drain on his time and energies. As he wrote to Ferdinand Ries (a former pupil by this time), "My unfortunate connection to this archduke has brought me close to beggardom; I can't see starving, I have to give. So you can imagine how I suffer in this situation!"[99] Beethoven nevertheless recognized his debt to Rudolph and dedicated numerous important works to him from 1809 onward, including the Piano Concertos Opp. 58 and 73 ("Emperor"), the Violin Sonata Op. 96, the Piano

Trio Op. 97 ("Archduke"), the Piano Sonatas Opp. 106 ("Hammerklavier") and 111, the *Missa solemnis*, Op. 123, and the *Grosse Fuge*, Op. 133.

Burstein makes a convincing case that Beethoven's reasons for dedicating Op. 81a to the archduke had more to do with finances than friendship. This teacher-student relationship was an unusual one, to say the least: Rudolph was by far Beethoven's most generous and loyal patron at the time, one of three members of the nobility who had recently pooled their resources to provide the composer with an annuity that would keep him in Vienna. The archduke was also in a position to help Beethoven realize his lifelong dream of a permanent appointment of some kind, ideally at the Habsburg court. The image of Beethoven as a *Kapellmeister* runs counter to the popular image of his independent spirit, but his desire to secure a court appointment and with it a reliable source of income is well documented throughout his entire career.[100] Given the financial and professional implications of his relationship to the archduke, he had little choice but to comport himself with deference. When Rudolph declined his right of succession to become archbishop of Olmütz (Olomouc), where Beethoven had hoped to be given a stable and highly desirable post, Beethoven was by his own admission beside himself and could not pretend otherwise, for Rudolph's decision effectively marked the end of the composer's hopes for an improvement in his financial situation. In a remarkable letter to Breitkopf & Härtel from February 1812, he acknowledged his momentary inability to do something artists in particular must be able to do easily: namely, to convey a mood different from the one in which they genuinely find themselves.

> For now I can write only what is absolutely necessary. You say that good humor sparkles in my last letter; artists have to be able to throw themselves often into anything and everything, and so this, too, might have been affected, for I am precisely not in good humor at the moment. The incident with the Archduke has fatal consequences for me. If heaven will only give me patience until I go abroad, then I shall be in a condition once again to find myself within myself.[101]

Eight years later Rudolph accepted a second opportunity to assume the archbishopric of Olmütz, and Beethoven composed his *Missa solemnis*, Op. 123, to mark the occasion. He was hopelessly late in delivering the work, however, for he did not finish the score until 1822 and even then continued to make revisions for some time afterward. Finally, in March 1823, he sent

Rudolph a manuscript copy of the Kyrie with the inscription: "Von Herzen—Möge es wieder—zu Herzen gehn!" ("From the heart—May it return—to the heart!"). This, too, has been widely invoked as evidence for the deeply personal nature of the work and his affection toward the archduke.[102] As Birgit Lodes has persuasively demonstrated, these words were intended for Rudolph alone: they appear only in the presentation manuscript and not in the published score issued by Schott (Mainz) in March or April of 1827.[103] The inscription to the archduke seems to have become public knowledge only in 1860, when Wilhelm von Lenz conveyed a mangled version of it he had received at second hand from the violinist Karl Holz: "von Herzen ist's gekommen, zum Herzen soll's dringen" (It has come from the heart, it should penetrate the heart).[104] But from that point on, the inscription served as a touchstone for Beethoven's desire to communicate his personal feelings to others through music, even in a work—or more to the point, especially in a work—whose text had been set to music countless times before.

What has gone largely overlooked in all this is the thoroughly stock nature of Beethoven's inscription. It was widely used during the composer's lifetime in two contexts that converge in the *Missa solemnis*: music and religion. Throughout the eighteenth century and well into the nineteenth, German-language writers routinely referred to music as "the language of the heart" (*die Sprache des Herzens*), a "language" that operated outside the conventions of verbal semantics and syntax and for that very reason was considered all the more effective in expressing emotions in ways and to a degree that words could not. Spiritual faith, too, was something that words alone could not fully convey: it was in the end a matter of the heart, surpassing all understanding.

In 1819 alone—the year in which Beethoven began work on the *Missa solemnis*—the phrase appeared no fewer than three times in the *Allgemeine musikalische Zeitung* of Leipzig, a journal the composer is known to have followed fairly closely:

- Anonymous, "Nachrichten. Wien. Uebersicht des Monats November," *Allgemeine musikalische Zeitung* 21 (1819), 8: "Unschuld und Grazie war Dem. Wranitzky als Pamina; ihr gefühlvoller Gesang kam vom Herzen und drang zu aller Herzen" (Mademoiselle Wranitzky, as Pamina, was innocence and grace; her emotional singing came from the heart and penetrated all hearts).
- Anonymous, "Nachrichten. Dresden," *Allgemeine musikalische Zeitung* 21 (1819), 387: "Der Gesang soll aus dem Herzen kommen und zum

Herzen gehen" (Singing should come from the heart and go to the heart").

- J. C. H., "Einige Worte über die musikalische Bildung der jetzigen Zeit," *Allgemeine musikalische Zeitung* 21 (1819), 574: "wie selten da der fromme Blick, der nur zu fragen scheint, ob, was vom Herzen kommt, denn auch wieder zu Herzen gehe?" (how seldom do we see there [on the stage] the pious gaze that seems only to ask if what comes from the heart might then also go the heart?).

The fact that Beethoven's inscription was a stock phrase does not in itself undermine its sincerity: those who use clichés often employ them in a heartfelt manner, and it would be petty to take Beethoven to task for a lack of verbal originality. His application of this particular phrase to a work of sacred music, moreover, was as appropriate as it was conventional. By the same token, it cannot be read unequivocally (as it so often has been) as an original statement from the depths of his creative soul.

We must be similarly circumspect about the isolated reports committed to writing long after the fact that allege Beethoven to have commented explicitly on the subjective nature of his music. The instrument maker Johann Andreas Stumpff (1769–1846) visited Beethoven in the fall of 1824, but not until sometime after 1840 did he record his recollection of the encounter. The composer, according to Stumpff, voiced frustration at expressing his emotions in music: "When I try, now and then, to give musical form to my turbulent feelings—ah, I find myself horribly disappointed."[105] This report may be accurate, in spite of having been set down by an individual in his early seventies at least sixteen years after the event. It resonates in any case with the kinds of discourse about music that had become commonplace only in the 1830s.

A similar account, also recorded many years after the event, comes from the pen of Karl Holz (1798–1858), the violinist who had played in Iganz Schuppanzigh's string quartet and had served for a time in the 1820s as Beethoven's secretary. Holz, writing a year before his death to Wilhelm von Lenz, recalled that for Beethoven,

the crowning achievement of all his movements for string quartet, and his favorite, was the E♭ *Cavatina* in 3/4 from the Quartet in B♭ [Op. 130]. He truly composed it in tears of melancholy and admitted to me that his own music had never before made such an impression on him, and that even thinking back on this piece always cost him renewed tears.[106]

We cannot dismiss such reports out of hand. Still, it is striking that accounts like these are so few in number and did not begin to surface until decades after the composer's death. This is not altogether surprising, for it was only then that discourse about the relationship of composers to their creations had begun to change so fundamentally. Conversely, it was only by this point that works like *Wellingtons Sieg* were coming to be regarded as vestiges of moral failure.[107] Critics could reach such conclusions only by assuming that composers revealed their inner selves in their music.

Beethoven himself did come came tantalizingly close to articulating an awareness of self-expression on at least one occasion. In 1824 the publishing firm of B. Schotts Söhne in Mainz—a firm with which he had done business before on many occasions—solicited from him a presumably small-scale work to be included in an issue of its newly launched music journal, *Cäcilia*. Beethoven thanked the publishers for their invitation but noted that "as far as my humble self is concerned, I would gladly serve you if I did not feel an innate higher calling to reveal myself to the world through my works."[108] The composer's lifelong distinction between "greater" and "lesser" works is well documented, and to his mind, self-revelation would seem to have been a feature of the latter.[109] Yet even if Beethoven considered his "greater" works a revelation of his inner self, it would be some time before the wider musical public would begin perceiving them in that way.

PART TWO

THE PARADIGM OF SUBJECTIVE EXPRESSION: 1830–1920

For the generation that came of age in the decade after Beethoven's death, the idea of subjective expression in music became the new norm. Listeners continued to hear instrumental music as the "language of the heart," but from around 1830 onward the heart they heard was now that of the composer. The framework of rhetoric gave way to the framework of hermeneutics: audiences began to think about what they were hearing from the perspective of the composer, seeking to understand what each was trying to "say" in every new work. With persuasion no longer perceived as an end, it fell to listeners to interpret. The idea of learning how to listen caught on quickly, and periodicals aimed at music lovers began to proliferate. The *Allgemeine musikalische Zeitung* of Leipzig, established in 1799, was the first to achieve success as a long-running venture; this testifies not only to the quality of the journal itself but also to a sufficiently broad readership that recognized its growing responsibility to come to terms with what they were hearing.

Composers, for their part, both contributed to and profited from the new premise of expressive subjectivity. They embraced the role of oracle. Liberated, as it were, from the obligations of comprehensibility, they were now in a position to cultivate increasingly idiosyncratic styles, which in turn were heard to reflect their distinctive individualities. By the middle of the nineteenth century listeners assumed that any composer with pretensions to seriousness of purpose would possess a unique "voice" that projected a deeper, inner self. The paradigm of subjective expression also encouraged the growth of an essentially new category of openly or semi-openly autobiographical instrumental music, which helped further strengthen the general perception that all instrumental music was at some level autobiographical.

4

The Framework of Hermeneutics

Rhetoric has always been a theory of poetics, of how to construct an argument, whether for civic or aesthetic purposes. Strictly speaking, then, the idea of "rhetorical listening" is oxymoronic, for while rhetoric anticipates habits of listening, it does not prescribe them, even if repeated applications of its principles have shaped those habits to a considerable degree.[1] At its most successful, rhetoric compels listeners to respond in a particular manner, and in music it fell to composers and performers, working in tandem, to move audiences. Listeners had to attend to the music, certainly, but the idea that an audience might have to make an effort to "understand" a work was simply foreign to eighteenth-century thought. Indeed, the very phrase "to understand music" (*Musik verstehen*) did not appear in German-language discourse aimed at the general public until around 1800.[2] By 1850 it was assumed that listeners would indeed make such an effort.

In their attempts to understand the abstract art of instrumental music, listeners operated on the basis of two fundamental premises: *sincerity* and *oracularity*:

1) **Sincerity**: Once listeners began to hear a work's musical ideas as emanating from deep within the soul of the composer, they heard these ideas as fundamentally sincere. This presumed sincerity of musical expression precluded any sense of distance between a work and its creator and at the same time reinforced the assumption of a meaningful connection between a composer's life and works.

2) **Oracularity**: The presumption of sincerity fostered a growing perception of composers not as orators who sought to persuade, but as oracles who used the intrinsically abstract, opaque medium of instrumental music to utter truths to be deciphered by listeners. This in turn created a hermeneutical imperative: for the first time, listeners were willing to assume responsibility for making sense of what they were hearing.

These new assumptions were applied retrospectively to earlier repertoires as well, most intensively to the music of Beethoven, who by the second quarter of the nineteenth century had become *the* paradigmatic composer of instrumental music. Listeners heard his works as outward manifestations of his inner self and made this a new benchmark of aesthetic judgment for all composers, living or dead. Critics relegated instrumental music that did not express the inner self to a lesser category of works they considered entertaining but not enlightening, enjoyable but not profound. Textual authenticity also assumed growing importance over the course of the nineteenth century: making sense of an oracle's utterances was of little value if those utterances had not been transmitted correctly.

The Perception of Sincerity

The growing perception of music as coming from deep within the soul of the composer carried with it the presumption of emotional authenticity, which is to say, sincerity. E. T. A. Hoffmann was among the first to articulate the idea of instrumental music as a first-person art. Aspiring composers who studied the works of masters "truly and deeply," Hoffmann maintained in an essay first published in 1814, could "enter into a mysterious rapport" with the "spirit" (*Geist*) of their predecessors, which in turn would kindle a dormant power that could lead to a kind of "ecstasy." In so doing, younger composers could "awaken to a new life" and "perceive the miraculous sound" of their own "inner music." "Only *that* composition"—and here Hoffmann uses the word *Tongedicht*, literally a "poem in tones"—"that emanates truly and powerfully from the interiority [of the composer] penetrates to the interior of the listener. The spirit understands only the language of the spirit." This, Hoffmann declared, is the "true effect of a composition that emanates from within."[3]

For an aspiring composer to study the work of an acknowledged practitioner had long been standard pedagogical advice. What is new here is Hoffmann's emphasis on learning more than just technique. The careful study of a score, he maintains, will bring novice composers into a spiritual communion with the master artist who created it. The artist's self, in short, is there in the score for those who can comprehend its notation, and if students are to achieve mastery themselves, they must understand the soul of that master artist.

By the 1820s a small but growing number of music critics were emphasizing the self as both the source and the object of musical expression. Even
the Leipzig philosopher and critic Amadeus Wendt, who could scarcely be
counted among the more radical thinkers of his time (see p. 71), was beginning to accept the premise of subjectivity. Wendt remained committed to
the idea of expression as representation, but by 1826 he was arguing that the
proper object of representation was an image within the animus (*Gemüt*) of
the artist:

> Expression occurs any time we speak of the externalization of something
> *internal*. Expression thus presumes something *internal*, and in art, this is
> the property of the object to be represented, insofar as it has been contem-
> plated and perceived in the artist's own individual way. Along with the ob-
> ject, the artist thus presents to us his own inner state. . . . Expression in art
> thus depends initially on the [artist's] perception of the material. . . . If this
> representation adheres more to the particular quality of the object, which
> is presented accurately and vividly, we tend to call this expression charac-
> teristic. . . . On the other hand, expression is often more subjective, that is, it
> presents in unmediated fashion the psychic state of the artist. True expres-
> sion encompasses both.[4]

Along similar lines, the poet, composer, and critic Carl Borromäus von
Miltitz, writing in 1834, maintained that composers in every instance do
their best work when they allow themselves to be taken over by the inspiration of the moment, which Miltitz compares to a state of clairvoyance. This,
he advises, will allow them to make the "state of their soul" (*Seelenzustand*)
intelligible to the outside world.[5] Miltitz does not dismiss circumspection
and technique altogether, but his tone is typical of writers from the 1830s
onward, who speak far more enthusiastically about the lamp than the mirror.
   Instrumental music's growing philosophical prestige in the early decades of
the nineteenth century owed much to the conviction that it offered a window
onto the human soul. If the true self lies below the level of consciousness,
and if art provides indirect access to that subconscious level (see pp. 41–43),
then instrumental music, because of its nonverbal nature, holds at least the
potential to provide access to the otherwise inaccessible realm of the human
interior. Schelling had laid the groundwork for this in the conclusion to his
System des transzendentalen Idealismus (1800), and Arthur Schopenhauer
would take it further still in his *Die Welt als Wille und Vorstellung* (1819),

even if his thought would have to wait another forty years or more to enter the philosophical mainstream. In the meantime, even a minor philosopher such as Franz Anton Nüsslein could assert in 1819 that "music is rooted in the depths of the human animus" and therefore constitutes a "resonance of the internal self."[6] Hegel, in his lectures on aesthetics, called "subjective interiority" the "true object" of music and maintained that this art could allow "interiority" to become "intelligible to itself." In this respect, music's essence lay in the purity of its subjectivity; and here, as noted earlier, Hegel pointed to melody as the "pure resonance of the inmost self . . . the most distinctive soul of music."[7] In Hegel's system, however, this did not ultimately work to music's advantage, for music lacked the objective, conceptual elements that could provide the necessary dialectical insights available to poetry and above all to philosophy.[8] The essentially inward, subjective nature of music was by this point nevertheless beyond all question.

Among poets and literary critics, meanwhile, the creed of subjective expression was growing ever more extreme. The "recollected in tranquility" qualifier to Wordsworth's idea of poetry as the "overflow of powerful feelings" (see p. 5) was minimized and at times suppressed altogether. Byron called poetry "the lava of the imagination whose eruption prevents an earth-quake," emphasizing the cathartic effect of the artwork on its creator, and by the early 1830s Victor Hugo was insisting that literary works should "gush forth in a single stream" without subsequent revision.[9] Alphonse de Lamartine, in turn, could declare in all apparent seriousness that his poems were "written as they were felt."

> Here are four books of poetry written just as they were felt, unconnected, without order, without apparent transitions . . . real poems, not feigned ones, ones that give more feeling of the man himself than the poet, an intimate and involuntary revelation of his impressions of each day, pages from his inner life inspired at times by sadness, at times by joy, by solitude or society, by despair or hope, in his moments of ennui or enthusiasm, prayer or passion.[10]

Such claims were part of a much larger and longer assault on the principle of mimesis, that convenient scapegoat for Romantic artists, a synecdoche for the failure of earlier generations to incorporate genuine—sincere—emotions into their art. As the poet John Keble put it in 1838, "Aristotle, as is well known, considered the essence of poetry to be *Imitation.* . . . *Expression* we say, rather than *imitation*; for the latter word clearly conveys a cold and in-adequate notion of the writer's meaning."[11] Once again we see the confusion caused by the use of a single word—*expression*—to convey two (deceptively) related but different phenomena.

Literary critics deemed sincerity the key to quality, even if they did not al-ways agree on how to recognize it. Thomas Carlyle, for example, writing in 1828, considered it central to the poetry of Robert Burns:

> The excellence of Burns is . . . his *Sincerity*, his indisputable air of Truth. . . .
> The passion that is traced before us has glowed in a living heart; the opinion
> he utters has risen in his own understanding, and been a light to his own
> steps. He does not write from hearsay, but from sight and experience; it is
> the scenes he has lived and labored amidst, that he describes; those scenes,
> rude and humble as they are, have kindled beautiful emotions in his soul,
> noble thoughts, and definite resolves; and he speaks forth what is in him,
> not from any outward call of vanity or interest, but because his heart is too
> full to be silent. . . . Let a man but speak forth with genuine earnestness the
> thought, the emotion, the actual condition of his own heart; and other men,
> so strangely are we all knit together by the tie of sympathy, must and will
> give heed to him.[12]

Matthew Arnold, a generation later, found a distinct *absence* of sincerity in the same poet:

> But for supreme poetical success more is required than the powerful appli-
> cation of ideas to life; it must be an application under the conditions fixed
> by the laws of poetic truth and poetic beauty. Those laws fix as an essential
> condition, in the poet's treatment of such matters as are here in question,
> high seriousness;—the high seriousness which comes from absolute sin-
> cerity. The accent of high seriousness, born of absolute sincerity, is what
> gives to such verse as
>
> "In la sua volontade è nostra pace . . ."
>
> to such criticism of life as Dante's, its power. Is this accent felt in the passages
> which I have been quoting from Burns? Surely not; surely, if our sense is
> quick, we must perceive that we have not in those passages a voice from the
> very inmost soul of the genuine Burns; he is not speaking to us from these
> depths, he is more or less preaching.[13]

Just how two such highly respected critics could differ so fundamentally in evaluating the work of the same author illustrates the elusive nature of sincerity. Yet this seems never to have threatened the perceived significance of this quality in nineteenth- and early twentieth-century aesthetics. Leo Tolstoy provided its supreme manifesto when he defined art as

> a human activity consisting in this, that one man consciously, by means of certain external signs, hands on to others feelings he has lived through, and that other people are infected by these feelings and also experience them.
>
> *The stronger the infection, the better is the art as art*, speaking now apart from its subject matter, that is, not considering the quality of the feelings it transmits. And the degree of the infectiousness of art depends on three conditions:
>
> (1) on the greater or lesser individuality of the feeling transmitted;
>
> (2) on the greater or lesser clearness with which the feeling is transmitted;
>
> (3) on the sincerity of the artist, i.e., on the greater or lesser force with which the artist himself feels the emotion he transmits.
>
> But most of all is the degree of infectiousness of art increased by the degree of sincerity in the artist.
>
> I have mentioned three conditions of contagiousness in art, but they may be all summed up into one, the last, sincerity, i.e., that the artist should be impelled by an inner need to express his feeling. That condition includes the first; for if the artist is sincere he will express the feeling as he experienced it. And as each man is different from everyone else, his feeling will be individual for everyone else; and the more individual it is — the more the artist has drawn it from the depths of his nature, — the more sympathetic and sincere will it be. And this same sincerity will impel the artist to find a clear expression of the feeling which he wishes to transmit.
>
> Therefore this third condition—sincerity—is the most important of the three.[14]

The weight Tolstoy gives to sincerity anticipates the aesthetics of early twentieth-century expressionism. The painter Wassily Kandinsky was one of many artists who took up Tolstoy's creed. "With an open eye," he declared, the artist "must watch his inner life, and his ear should always be attuned to the voice of inner necessity. Then he may draw on all permissible means and, just as readily, all proscribed means. This is the only way to express the mystically necessary. All means are sacred if they are internally necessary. All means are sinful which are not drawn from the spring of inner necessity."[15]

Kandinsky's "inner necessity" is in fact a term that had been used repeatedly by composers, including both Wagner and Schoenberg. And it no mere coincidence that all these artists forged styles the public found difficult to grasp: Wagner because of his extreme chromaticism and avoidance of conventional operatic forms, Schoenberg because of his atonality (or "pantonality," as he preferred to call it), and Kandinsky because of the increasingly abstract nature of his paintings. The strangeness of their respective idioms, it would seem, made it all the more important for these artists to insist publicly and repeatedly that their art was the product of inner necessity, the driving force of sincerity.

Sincerity carried economic implications as well. With the precipitous decline of court patronage at the turn of the nineteenth century, composers scrambled to find alternative sources of income.[16] Many, like Beethoven and Czerny, cobbled together a living from published music, commissioned works, private teaching, and performances. Others, like Anton Reicha and Luigi Cherubini, occupied teaching positions at institutions such as the Paris Conservatoire. The economics of freelance production encouraged the public to perceive composers as autonomous artists who wrote how they wanted when they wanted and in genres of their own choosing. In reality, composers had to keep an eye on the marketplace, promoting their works and the process their personal uniqueness as artists. The premise of self-expression supplied a fulcrum by which to establish a distinctively individual "brand." In this respect, composers were now engaging in a practice that poets had been cultivating for at least two generations. This was, after all, the period in which we can now recognize the origins of celebrity culture.[17]

Audiences welcomed this development because a knowledge of composers as individuals offered a way into their music, no matter how stylistically challenging the idiom. Armed with an understanding of the artist who had created a work of nonrepresentational instrumental music, listeners who lacked formal training in the nuts and bolts of harmony, voice leading, and the construction of small- and large-scale forms—which is to say, the vast majority of listeners—could now find a way into what they were hearing. Composers benefited from this dynamic as well. At least part of Berlioz's strategy in advertising the close relationship between his life and his *Symphonie fantastique* (1830) was to convince potentially skeptical listeners of the sincerity of his music in the face of its unconventional formal design, radical harmonic idiom, and novel timbres. The listening public was, after all, more likely to accept or at least tolerate difficult music if at a very minimum it perceived that music to be sincere. No one likes to be hoodwinked, and sincerity would go on to play a major role in French musical aesthetics throughout the remainder of the century.[18]

Few poets were bold enough to cast public doubt on the sincerity of sincerity, but Edgar Allan Poe was remarkably blunt about the matter:

> Most writers—poets in especial—prefer having it understood that they compose by a species of fine frenzy—an ecstatic intuition—and would positively shudder at letting the public take a peep behind the scenes, at the elaborate and vacillating crudities of thought—at the true purposes seized only at the last moment—at the innumerable glimpses of idea that arrived not at the maturity of full view—at the fully matured fancies discarded in despair as unmanageable—at the cautious selections and rejections—at the painful erasures and interpolations . . . which, in ninety-nine cases out of the hundred, constitute the properties of the literary *histrio*.[19]

Such frank acknowledgments were rare, however; sincerity remained a supreme ideal. The poet and critic Edmund Gosse called it "indeed . . . the first gift in literature and perhaps the most uncommon." Tolstoy saw it in "peasant art," which explained its powerful effect, but found it to be "almost entirely absent from our upper-class art, which is continually produced by artists actuated by personal aims of covetousness or vanity." Sincerity, in any case, held the moral high ground, for it was by definition perceived as authentic and as such "true."[20]

It is largely for this reason that irony in instrumental music went into a steep decline after the death of Beethoven. Vocal music remained capable of incorporating it to great effect, as in such songs as Robert Schumann's "Ich grolle nicht" from *Dichterliebe*, a setting of poems by Heinrich Heine, himself a master of verbal irony.[21] The text says one thing, the music quite another. Schumann—a fervent admirer of the fiction of both Hoffmann and Jean Paul—was in fact the only composer of stature after Beethoven whose instrumental music bears the obvious hallmarks of irony in the form of contrasting "voices," as in his *Carnaval* (1835) and *Kreisleriana* (1838). But even those works give their listeners fair warning of a potential contrast between appearance and substance, the former through its reference to a season of masked identities, the latter through its subtitle (*Fantasien*) and its title's evocation of E. T. A. Hoffmann's fictional virtuoso of literary irony, Johannes Kreisler. With the exception of transparently parodic works (such as Gabriel Fauré and André Messager's *Souvenirs de Bayreuth* or Emmanuel Chabrier's *Souvenirs de Munich*, both send-ups of Wagner) it was not until the closing years of the nineteenth century that listeners began to hear occasional instances of compositional self-distancing, most notably in the music of Gustav Mahler, whose works are full of seemingly incongruous juxtapositions and contrasting moods that arrive and depart without warning. Particularly clear examples appear in the slow movement of the First Symphony (1888), which opens with a distorted, minor-mode version of the folk song variously known as "Bruder Martin" or "Frère Jacques" and then alternates between hauntingly lyrical songlike melodies and passages that evoke the sound of a klezmer band. The slow movement of the Fourth Symphony, in turn, begins with a solemn homage to the "Contemplative Quartet" from act I of Beethoven's *Fidelio* but eventually dissolves in disarray before gathering itself again just before the end.[22] Such moments of irony created no little consternation for Mahler's critics, who presumed a degree of compositional sincerity that he refused to deliver consistently. His standing as a composer suffered during his lifetime in no small measure because of critical resistance to its perceived lack of earnestness. More subtle forms of distancing through allusion—such as, for example, the references to Beethoven's Ninth in Berlioz's *Harold en Italie*, Brahms's First Symphony, and Antonín Dvořák's Ninth Symphony, "From the New World"—were not heard as such by contemporary audiences.[23]

In a parallel development, the prestige of philosophical and literary irony was already on the wane by the end of the 1820s. After a brilliant outburst early in the century in the writings of Friedrich Schlegel, Novalis, Jean Paul, Hoffmann, and Tieck, among others, it quickly fell out of fashion. Hegel disparaged it, and even Schlegel distanced himself from his earlier enthusiasm for it.[24]

The nineteenth century's blanket presumption of aesthetic sincerity also helps explain why critics of the time had difficulties with works like Beethoven's "Serioso" String Quartet, Op. 95 (see p. 81). Even A. B. Marx, that most sympathetic of the composer's critics, confessed his inability to offer any reasonable explanation for the seemingly bizarre change of tone in the brief coda of its final movement. Marx seems to have been unable to free himself from the assumption that the music *had* to be sincere. It would be another century and a half before anyone entertained the idea that Beethoven might be toying with his listeners or calling attention to the overwrought seriousness of the quartet as a whole. The best that commentators could do in the meantime was to explain the music through the events of its composer's life: the lighthearted coda was evidence of Beethoven's having moved on from a rejected proposal of marriage, and the unusual nature of the late works as a whole could be explained away as a consequence of his growing deafness, his increasing isolation from society, his declining health and sense of impending death, his disillusionment with the political scene, the legal and personal turmoils associated with guardianship of his nephew, and so on. Even in the twentieth century, Theodor Adorno's notion of the late works as incorporating the composer's self-critique of his earlier music rests on the underlying premise of compositional sincerity.[25]

The Perception of Oracularity

The perception of artists as mediators of higher truths was scarcely novel in the years around 1830: the concept of *furor poeticus* as a form of divinely inspired madness is as old as antiquity. Once the basic tenets of philosophical idealism had begun to penetrate discourse about music in the years around 1800, they were applied with special vigor to purely instrumental works, which, because of their indeterminate content, lent themselves particularly well to the expression of that which was beyond the capacity of language.[26] The inherent opacity of instrumental music made it a particularly powerful medium through which oracular composers could "speak." Critical discourse throughout the first third of the nineteenth century reflects a growing belief that a work of instrumental music could indeed convey something beyond its audible surface, even if the work's title divulged nothing more than the technical elements of its literally generic identity ("Symphony No. 5 in C Minor, Op. 67"). Increasingly, listeners came to perceive composers not simply as mediators of truths, but as sources of those truths. And it was now the responsibility of listeners to interpret the utterances of those oracles.

Beethoven was the paradigmatic oracle. In the eyes of the composer and critic Jacques-Auguste Delaire, writing in 1830, he had drawn his inspiration from within:

Living in isolation, he turned inward toward himself; he descended into the source of his being to study the movements of his interior life, tranquil or agitated. And all his works are a translation of his sentiments, of his emotions; he has put into them all his hates, all his sorrows, all his outbursts of anger, all his feelings of vengeance, all his dreams of happiness. There, all his impressions are painted as if in a magic mirror, and he himself is the wizard who reveals these mysteries to us. . . . It is a volcano that erupts, it is a lava that flows and burns along its way!![27]

Audiences thus gradually began to listen from a new, imagined perspective: that of the composer. This empathetic approach is so deeply ingrained in concert-hall listening practices today that it can be challenging to grasp just how radical an idea it was in the second quarter of the nineteenth century. Up until that point, audiences had listened largely from their own perspectives. Even the rhapsodic accounts of Wilhelm Heinrich Wackenroder, Tieck, and other early Romantics from around 1800 had consistently centered on the effects of the music they heard on themselves; they paid little if any regard to the identity or nature of the creative minds behind what they were hearing or the motivations that drove composers to write in the particular ways they did. It would be another three decades before listeners, driven by the new paradigm of expressive subjectivity, would hear music from the perspective of the composer. This new way of listening correlates with what have since become standard elements of concert-hall ritual: an ideally silent and motionless audience, along with program notes to guide listeners through each work, explaining its origins and (often) its composer's putative intentions.[28]

Changes in habits of listening shaped not only the reception of music but its production as well. Composers could now take—and to some extent were expected to take—more and more liberties in what they wrote, knowing that critics would be more willing to give the benefit of the doubt to any work that was technically competent. Perhaps nowhere is this new aesthetic articulated more concisely and forcefully than in the often-cited review of an early performance of Beethoven's String Quartet in B♭ Major, Op. 130, that appeared in the *Allgemeine musikalische Zeitung* in May 1826. Although well disposed toward the quartet as a whole, the anonymous critic could make no sense of the work's finale (later published separately as the *Große Fuge*, Op. 133), calling it

incomprehensible, like Chinese. When the instruments have to struggle with enormous difficulties in the regions of the South and North Poles, when each of them presents a different figuration and crosses the others *per transitum irregularem* amid countless dissonances, when the players, suspicious of each other, do not attack entirely cleanly: then the Babylonian confusion is truly complete.[29]

Yet this same critic, having accused Beethoven of writing in what amounts to a foreign language, goes on to concede that "we nevertheless do not want to dismiss things too hastily. Perhaps the time will come when that which on first sight seemed to us opaque and muddled will be recognized as clear and pleasing forms."[30] This final comment resonates with the words of Paul in 1 Corinthians 13:12 ("For now we see through a glass, darkly; but then face to face"), the critic's implication being that what we now perceive imperfectly may in the future become evident. In any case, this review of Op. 130's original finale treats its text with the kind of respect normally accorded Holy Writ. The consequences of repeated hearings of Beethoven's late works were more than merely hypothetical for another anonymous critic reviewing the String Quartet in E♭ Major, Op. 127. Anyone acquainted with the musical life of larger or smaller German cities, this reviewer observed, will know that Beethoven's music is not easy to understand. And for that reason, listeners must hear his works multiple times, because only then will certain features become clear, and in the process, at least some of those who were formerly harsh critics might well become "passionate devotees."[31]

A deferential attitude in the face of such challenging works would have been all but unthinkable a mere ten or fifteen years before. The anonymous reviewers of Opp. 130 and 127 were in effect accepting the rebuke to Beethoven's critics that had been issued more than a decade before by Hoffmann's fictional Kreisler: that the inability to comprehend Beethoven's music lay not with the composer but with listeners who lacked understanding (see p. 87).

Hoffmann/Kreisler's perspective eventually carried the day, as listeners accepted the responsibility of interpreting the language in which composer-oracles were now framing their pronouncements. Opacity was no longer regarded as a defect but as a provocation to interpretation, an indicator of depth.[32] Beethoven's Ninth, as Richard Taruskin has observed, unleashed a tradition of symphonies that loaded themselves up with "symbols and sphinxes." By the end of the century Mahler could say of his Third Symphony with a certain degree of pride that "people will take a while to crack open the nuts I've shaken out of the tree for them."[33]

It was during the second quarter of the nineteenth century that listening came to be regarded as a hermeneutic act. This new approach to the art fueled the profusion of journals and books aimed a rapidly expanding public of concertgoers. In the process of persuading their readers *how* to listen, critics like Hoffmann and—a generation later—Schumann, in his extended review of Berlioz's *Symphonie fantastique*, were reinforcing the unspoken premise that listening required more than mere attentiveness: it demanded an unprecedented degree of engagement with the work at hand, which is to say, with the creative mind behind the music.

The perception of composers as oracles made listeners far more willing to extend themselves. "The *incomprehensible*," as one Mannheim critic observed in an 1828 essay on Beethoven's music, "is rooted in the *infinity* of poetic genius."[34] And after a performance of the Ninth Symphony in Vienna in February that same year, another reviewer observed that

> we are gradually beginning to learn how to disentangle the thread of this artful musical fabric; its miraculous outlines step forth ever more clearly, and scarcely a couple of short years will have passed before this gigantic work will be as generally known and understood as its predecessors [i.e., Beethoven's earlier symphonies], which at the time of their appearance were also decried as the equivalent of Egyptian hieroglyphs.[35]

Not everyone accepted the idea of listening to music in this way. An anonymous critic for the *Allgemeine Musikzeitung* of Frankfurt, a journal dedicated to "promoting theoretical and practical music for musicians and friends of music in general" and edited by "an association of musicians and academics," quoted the passage above soon after its publication, gave it the heading "Another Word on Beethoven," and glossed it:

> "We are gradually beginning to learn how to *disentangle* the thread (!) of this artful musical fabric; its miraculous outlines step forth ever more clearly, and scarcely *a couple of short years* (!!) will have passed before this gigantic work will be as generally (?) known and understood as its predecessors (??), which at the time of their appearance were also decried as the equivalent of *Egyptian hieroglyphs* (and rightly so!)."

What can one say in the face of such a verdict? One must fall silent when one sees that there are those whose blind idolatry goes so far as to defend a rhapsody which no one as yet has understood and which they themselves hope to comprehend *in a few years*. Is it then the purpose of music to decipher *Egyptian hieroglyphs*? Instead of affording pleasure, is to become a painful toil of the mind? Should the ear and heart be left out in the cold? And how many persons are there—if it is otherwise possible—who are capable of solving such a problem? Is true music only for those few who have been initiated into the depths of mysticism, or is it for all cultivated persons? Well, it's not worth the effort to say any more about the foolishness of those who deny all *feeling* in order to revere a pseudo-art that, like algebra, occupies the head alone and allows the heart to atrophy.[36]

At issue here is not Beethoven's Ninth, or even Beethoven's music in general, but the very act of listening. For the first time in the history of music, audiences were expected to work, to employ their own imaginations in order to engage with composers on a higher level of thought.[37] This new relationship between listeners and composers bears striking parallels to the realignment between readers and authors that had been encouraged around the turn of the nineteenth century by such philosophers as Herder, Schiller, Novalis, and Friedrich Schlegel, the last of whom differentiated between two types of authors, one "analytic," the other "synthetic":

> The analytic author observes the reader as he is and makes his assessment accordingly, applying his machinery to produce the requisite effect. The synthetic author constructs and creates for himself a reader as he should be; he imagines him not as static and dead, but as alive and reciprocating. He allows that which he has created to appear step by step before the reader's eyes, or he entices him to create it himself. He has no wish to create a specific effect on him, but rather joins with him in the holy relationship of the innermost *Symphilosophie* or *Sympoesie*.[38]

For Schlegel, the "analytic" author operates within a framework of rhetoric, taking into account the capacities of an anticipated audience, one of the long-standing parameters of rhetorical decorum. The "synthetic" author, by contrast, operates in an oracular fashion, creating a work with which readers must actively engage in order not merely to grasp it but to extend it, to build on it in a dialectical process. Author and reader together thereby enter into what Schlegel calls a "holy relationship" based on a process of reciprocal philosophizing or poeticizing. From the reader's perspective, this goes beyond what we would today call hermeneutics, for *Symphilosophie* creates an even more fluid dynamic, a continuous dialogue of spirits in which criticism becomes a creative enterprise in its own right, one that includes readers as well as authors, and by extension listeners as well as composers.[39] "The true reader," Novalis asserted, "must be the extended author." Or, as Schlegel put it, "True criticism is an author raised to the second power."[40]

To paraphrase Schlegel, then, we might well say that Beethoven was seeking to create for himself listeners as they should be, to set in motion an experience in which the listener is "alive and reciprocating," not merely passive and receptive, or "static and dead," to use Schlegel's even more graphic formulation. Beethoven was moving in step with those literary figures of his generation who perceived it as their duty to engage with and elevate readers who might be open to such an approach. They accomplished this at least in part by presenting texts that placed immediate and considerable demands on their readers. Irony and incomprehensibility were important means of creating such demands.[41] The literary critic Gary Handwerk has pointed to numerous works of the period that "utilize an interruptive structure similar to parabasis in their abrupt shifts from one narrative level to another, from fairy tale or fantasy or dream to realism and back again," citing as examples Friedrich Schlegel's novel *Lucinde*, Novalis's *Heinrich von Ofterdingen*, Brentano's fairy tales, and Hoffmann's novellas and short stories.[42]

Within the parameters of the rhetorical tradition, incomprehensibility (*obscuritas*) had long been regarded as a defect. But over time a growing number of critics, including Lessing, Herder, and Friedrich Schlegel, had come to regard artful incomprehensibility as a hermeneutical provocation, a challenge to interpretation, an incitement to readers to engage purposefully with texts that are themselves purposefully difficult.[43] By these lights, clarity was no longer a quality to be embraced without reservation, and incomprehensibility no longer one to be avoided at all costs.

Friedrich Schlegel's widely discussed (and widely misunderstood) 1800 essay "Über die Unverständlichkeit" (On Incomprehensibility) was a manifesto for this new outlook. It was in effect the coda to a literary finale, the last salvo in what the Schlegel brothers had determined would be the final issue of *Athenäum*, the journal they had founded, coedited, and to a great extent coauthored over the previous three years. The essay defies easy description or characterization: it embodies Schlegel's ideal of the synthetic author, for it challenges readers to make sense of its difficult prose and sometimes dizzying line of argumentation. It enacts its own subject, claiming at times to be ironic when seemingly straightforward and at other times not to be ironic when seemingly full of irony. "Comprehensibility" and "incomprehensibility," as Schlegel both argues and demonstrates, are relative terms, and our understanding of the universe rests on the incomprehensibility of its chaos. *Unverständlichkeit* is not a product of *Unverstand*—a lack of understanding—but rather an index of deeper insight into the shallowness of what is too often perceived as clarity. The prose takes surprising twists and turns and ends with a poem of Schlegel's own—a gloss on Goethe's poem "Beherzigung"—that he hopes "one of our outstanding composers will find worthy of providing with a musical accompaniment." For "there is nothing more beautiful on earth," he concludes in an apparent non sequitur (for music had up to this point not been mentioned at all) than "poetry and music working together in beloved union to ennoble mankind."[44]

Schlegel was not alone in recognizing the chimeric nature of clarity and the depths that would be revealed by the incomprehensible. His brother August Wilhelm had identified nature itself as the paradigm of unfathomability (*Unergründlichkeit*) and artistic genius as an "image in miniature" of nature itself in the process of creating (*natura naturans*):[45] "It is precisely from obscurity that the magic of life derives, in which the root of our being becomes lost," and this obscurity produces an "inexhaustible secret. This is the soul of all poetry."[46] Schiller, in turn, famously called Goethe's *Wilhelm Meisters Lehrjahre* "calm and deep, clear and yet incomprehensible, like nature itself."[47] And Novalis's unfinished *Die Lehrlinge zu Sais*, brought to press posthumously by Tieck and Schlegel in 1802, opens with an extended meditation on acceptance of the incomprehensible as the means by which to gain a deeper understanding of the universe. Adam Müller's 1806 essay on Aristophanes likewise endorsed incomprehensibility as an engine of insight. All these writers distinguished between incomprehensibility as a product of mere authorial incompetence and incomprehensibility as a product of authorial imagination and agility. The riddle, in Brian Tucker's memorable phrase, had moved "from an irritant to an ideal."[48]

It is thus not surprising that literary hermeneutics should enjoy its first modern flowering around the turn of the nineteenth century. While by no means a new discipline at the time, it acquired increasing prestige and extended its scope to include even works of music on occasion. Hermeneutics presumes a quality of depth in the object of contemplation, an assumption that there is more to any given work than what appears on its surface, and the application of these assumptions to instrumental music in the first half of the nineteenth century, above all in German-speaking lands, reflects the growing status of the art.[49] As Ian Bent has demonstrated, hermeneutic methodologies inform E. T. A. Hoffmann's lengthy 1810 review of Beethoven's Fifth Symphony.[50] Hoffmann seeks to explain the relationship of the work's parts to its whole and in so doing elucidate the seemingly incomprehensible. The hermeneutic impulse is even more clearly evident three years later in Hoffmann's reworking of this review into an essay penned by his fictional *Kapellmeister*, Johannes Kreisler. One passage quoted earlier is worth repeating here and reading from the perspective of hermeneutics:

> Beethoven's mighty genius intimidates the musical rabble; they try in vain to resist it. . . . But what if it is only *your* inadequate understanding which fails to grasp the inner coherence of every Beethoven composition? What if it is entirely *your* fault that the composer's language is clear to the initiated but not to you, and that the entrance to his innermost mysteries remains closed to you?[51]

Hoffmann's 1810 review and "Kreisler's" 1813 essay together exemplify the kind of dialectical engagement between author and reader that Friedrich Schlegel, Novalis, and others had been advocating in literary circles for a decade or more. Here we see criticism becoming its own art form, an extension of the artwork in question. And it was above all Beethoven's instrumental music that posed the most immediate challenge to his contemporaries, for music without a text raised the specter of incomprehensibility. Incomprehensibility, as the literary critic Robert S. Leventhal has argued, proved to be the "hinge of hermeneutics" in the early nineteenth century.[52] Two distinctly different critical traditions arose around this time in response to the threat of texts that defied comprehension. Friedrich Schleiermacher's approach—continued by Wilhelm Dilthey, Hans-Georg Gadamer, and others—assumed the integrity of a text as an integrated whole and sought to eliminate incomprehensibility to the fullest extent possible.[53] Friedrich Schlegel's destabilizing, disintegrative hermeneutics, by contrast, viewed incomprehensibility as a spur to interpretation but itself ultimately inescapable, insurmountable, and immune to any totalizing "answer" or "solution." This tradition went largely underground in the nineteenth century (with the exception of Nietzsche) and for a good part of the twentieth but would reemerge in the work of such diverse critics as Walter Benjamin, Theodor Adorno, Jacques Derrida, and Paul de Man.

The two primary approaches to musical hermeneutics in the nineteenth century were technical and biographical. What we now think of as formal analysis—the examination of structure, harmony, voice leading, and so on—was available only to those few who possessed the requisite knowledge of music's technical elements. Biographical analysis, by contrast, was open to all, even to those who could not read musical notation. A knowledge of composers' lives thus became the most widespread means of understanding their music.

This understanding entailed more than mere knowledge, however: it meant understanding an author's intentions "better than the author himself," as the most common formulation of the day would have it: variants of this phrase appear in the writings of Kant, Fichte, Schleiermacher, Schelling, and Schlegel.[54] If authorial creation was a synthesis of conscious and unconscious acts, then one of the goals of hermeneutics was to articulate that unconscious element to the extent possible. As the historian of philosophy Ernst Behler put it, an "author's creation" is to be approached as an "unconscious act to be made conscious by the reflective interpreter."[55]

In his emphasis on knowledge of a text's author, Herder was a key figure in the modern history of hermeneutics. As early as the 1770s he maintained that "the life of an author is the best commentary on his writings if he is true and at one with himself":

> One should be able to regard every book as the imprint of a living human soul. . . . Every poem, particularly an entire, extensive poem—a work of the soul and of life—is a dangerous betrayer of its creator, and often at those moments when the author least thinks he has betrayed himself. Whenever it is worth the effort, this lively approach to reading, this divination of the soul of a creator, is the only way of reading and the most profound means of self-cultivation. . . . Such reading is a competition, a heuristic: we climb upward with the author to creative heights, or we discover error and aberration at the site of their birth. The more vividly one knows the author and has lived with him, the more vivid one's dealings with him.[56]

Herder's hypothetical author would seem to be an amalgam of a real and imagined individual, the latter grounded in one's knowledge of a given writer's works as a whole. Still, the vogue of literary biography seems not very far beyond the horizon, as would indeed prove to be the case. Authors' lives would become a key, and in the minds of many *the* key, to understanding a given work.

A generation later, it was Schleiermacher's influential *Hermeneutik und Kritik*, published posthumously in 1838 but based on lectures delivered and discussed widely between 1805 and 1833, that set out the new hermeneutical agenda. Building on the work of his predecessors, particularly Herder and Friedrich Schlegel, Schleiermacher (1768–1834) was instrumental in establishing hermeneutics in its modern form. He insisted that all texts—not just difficult ones—are susceptible to misunderstanding and thus in need of interpretation, and in his interpretation of biblical texts he established a methodology by which to interpret writings of all kinds. Every utterance, he maintained, stands at the intersection of the "grammatical," that is, the capacities of the language in question, and the "psychological," the historical position and internal makeup of the author. This demanded a simultaneous understanding of the language of a text (through such parameters as semantics, syntax, and grammar) and the psychology of the individual who created the text, including its author's historical position, knowledge, and motivations at the moment of creation. Schleiermacher insisted that interpretation depended at least in part on reading a text from its author's perspective, and that the more we can put ourselves in the author's position, the better equipped we are to explicate the text at hand. This entailed a knowledge of the author's life, "for every utterance is to be understood always and only in relation to the entire life to which it belongs," on the grounds that "every utterance is discernible only as a moment in the life of the person uttering it."[57] This moment in turn is conditioned by the individual's life as a whole, including questions of era and nationality. Any interpreter must therefore determine the circumstances that moved an individual to make a particular utterance.[58]

Schleiermacher's theory of hermeneutics thus regards all authorial statements as subjective at some level, not in the narrow sense of assuming that all statements are necessarily sincere (that is, genuinely felt by the author) but in the sense that the author's historical context, psychological makeup, and personal motivations all play major roles in the creation of any given text. A reader's knowledge of the author will therefore facilitate understanding of that text. Given that we "have no direct knowledge" of what may have been in the author's mind, however, "we must try to raise to the level of consciousness many things that may have remained unconscious in his mind." Schleiermacher summarized the goal of what he called the "divinatory method" as the "initial understanding of an utterance just as well as and then subsequently better than its author."[59]

The biographical aspect of interpretation advocated by Schleiermacher was already well under way by the time his lectures were published in 1838, but their appearance in print gave philosophical legitimacy to his method. This seemingly simple idea of interpreting a work of literature through the life of its author, far from self-evident in the first quarter of the nineteenth century, grew exponentially in the decades that followed. Thomas Carlyle was a leading figure in this regard, both as a critic and as a historian. He followed Kant's dictum on genius as that which gave the rule to art, and he urged others to treat it as such. "Genius," Carlyle declared, "has privileges of its own; it selects an orbit for itself; and be this never so eccentric, it is indeed a celestial orbit, we mere stargazers must at last compose ourselves; must cease to cavil at it, and begin to observe it, and calculate its laws."[60] Carlyle went so far as argue that a principal value of a work of literature was the insight it could potentially provide into the person of its author. As M. H. Abrams would wryly put it, Carlyle was "king among those who read an author not for what he made, but for what he was."[61] Of Jean Paul, for example, Carlyle said: "That his manner of writing is singular,—nay, in fact, a wild complicated Arabesque, no one can deny. But the true question is,—how nearly does this manner of writing represent his real manner of thinking and existing?"[62] No one would have asked such a question a generation before. That Carlyle should have posed it in the year of Beethoven's death exemplifies the shifting framework of criticism from rhetoric to hermeneutics, a perspective that was slowly beginning to infiltrate discourse on music as well.

"History," as Carlyle pointedly observed three years later, "is the essence of innumerable Biographies." And later still: "The History of the world is but the Biography of great men."[63] This "great man" approach would soon be applied to music. In 1834 Raphael Georg Kiesewetter issued the first historical survey of the art organized fundamentally around composers, associating each historical epoch with one or more names. For example:

> The Epoch of Hucbald (10th century)
> The Epoch of Guido (11th century)
> The Epoch without Names (12th century)
> The Epoch of Franco (13th century)
>
> . . .
>
> The Epoch of Palestrina (1560–1600)
> The Epoch of Monteverdi (1600–40)

The Epoch of Carissimi (1640–80)

. . .

The Epoch of Haydn and Mozart (1780–1800)
The Epoch of Beethoven and Rossini (1800–32)[64]

Such quasi-Hegelian readings of history would become standard for all the arts over the course of the nineteenth century. As John Ruskin put it in 1869,

> Great art is the expression of the mind of a great man, and mean art, that of the want of mind of a weak man. A foolish person builds foolishly, and a wise one sensibly; a virtuous one beautifully, and a vicious one basely. If stone work is well put together, it means that a thoughtful man planned it, and a careful man cut it, and an honest man cemented it. If it has too much ornament, it means that its carver was too greedy of pleasure; if too little, that he was rude, or insensitive, or stupid, and the like. So that when once you have learned how to spell these most precious of all legends—pictures and buildings,—you may read the characters of men, and of nations, in their art as in a mirror;—nay, as in a microscope, and magnified a hundredfold; for the character becomes passionate in the art, and intensifies itself in all its noblest or meanest delights. Nay, not only as in a microscope, but as under a scalpel, and in dissection; for a man may hide himself from you, or misrepresent himself to you, every other way; but he cannot in his work: there, be sure, you have him to the inmost. All that he likes, all that he sees,—all that he can do,—his imagination, his affections, his perseverance, his impatience, his clumsiness, cleverness, everything is there. If the work is a cobweb, you know it was made by a spider; if a honeycomb, by a bee; a worm-cast is thrown up by a worm, and a nest wreathed by a bird; and a house built by a man, worthily, if he is worthy, and ignobly if he is ignoble.[65]

Ruskin's claim amplifies Goethe's earlier claim that "dissemble as he might, he [the artist] can bring forth only his individuality."[66] And it was now up to readers, viewers, and listeners to grasp that individuality in the work of art.

Responses to Beethoven's compositions in the 1820s—to be discussed in detail in chapter 5—were among the earliest manifestations of this new approach in music. But these responses did not play out in isolation, for the heated dispute that erupted in the 1820s over the authenticity of Mozart's Requiem (1791) centered on precisely the same issue: the connection between a composer's inner life and his works. In the case of the Requiem,

unfinished at the time of the composer's death, the key question was one of
authenticity: how much of it was by Mozart, and how much of it had been
completed by others? With more and more critics gradually beginning to
hear music as self-expression, it made all the difference whose "self" they
were hearing. This work, after all, amounted to Mozart's dying words, and
for that very reason critics were inclined to hear in it a deeper sense of the
composer's self than in other vocal works. Hoffmann declared that it had
arisen from Mozart's "innermost," and that of all his sacred compositions,
this was the only one in which he had "opened up his interiority."[67] And
Georg von Nissen, who married Mozart's widow, Constanze, declared in his
1828 biography that the composer could not have written the Requiem in the
way he had unless he were himself already half dead, a *Halbverklärter*, "half-
transfigured."[68] Here, for once, listeners could hear Mozart *in* his music.

When after a careful study of the sources the composer and theorist
Gottfried Weber concluded in 1825 that the Requiem "could scarcely be
called a work by Mozart at all," the stakes went far beyond matters of mere philology. The Abbé Maximilian Stadler—one of several who had played a role
in completing the work—responded with a spirited defense of the Requiem's
fundamental authenticity. Still others weighed in on the matter, and a back-
and-forth debate over authorship continued into the early 1840s.[69] The viru-
lence of the dispute reflects how deeply critics and their readers cared about
the accurate transmission of oracular utterances. This provides yet further
evidence in support of what Lydia Goehr has called the "work-concept" and
its attendant emphasis on the person of the composer and the growing importance of congruence between the text (and performance) of a composition and its composer's intentions.[70] More and more, consumers of music
wanted to know with certainty that a published work by Mozart—or Haydn,
or Beethoven—was indeed what it claimed to be.

The 1820s nevertheless remained a period of transition, for not everyone
accepted the emerging aesthetics of subjectivity. The composer-critic Franz
Stoepel, for one, posed this question in 1827:

> What, then, can be heard in a symphony by Beethoven, Mozart, or even
> *Haydn*? This is music and nothing but music, tone and nothing but tone.
> There are no love stories with various fine intrigues or a dashing *Don Juan*
> or a cunning *Figaro*; in short, it is boring. It is true that many otherwise
> quite reasonable people say that they can think of an endless number of
> things while listening, that they can best hear the rich life of the soul of

those great men, that the purest and richest poetry prevails in these works, etc. But we believe that the most beautiful work of art is one that requires us to think very little or preferably not at all, one in which the roasted pigeon, so to speak, flies directly into our mouths.[71]

Within a decade Stoepel's view would be widely regarded as quaint and old-fashioned. Music, and above all the wholly abstract art of instrumental music, now demanded effort not just from composers and performers, but from listeners as well.

5

First-Person Beethoven

With the growing perception of composers as oracles, Beethoven the individual became the key to understanding his music. Public awareness of his deafness was the immediate stimulus for such an approach, and it proved to be the earliest and most important catalyst for hearing his voice in his music. Critics could "explain" the unusual nature of his late works by pointing to his inability to hear. Deafness, in turn, exacerbated what many perceived to be his misanthropic tendencies, which led to still greater social isolation, all of which were heard to manifest themselves in a personal style that even his most enthusiastic supporters conceded could be difficult to grasp.

The reminiscences, biographies, and letters that came to light in the years immediately after the composer's death helped bolster the perception of his works as an outpouring of his inner self. Critics took palpable pleasure in regarding Beethoven's life as a nonfictional *Bildungsroman*, a record of personal growth and development audible in his compositions. Private documents that surfaced only after his death—the 1801 letter to Wegeler acknowledging for the first time his growing deafness, the letters to the "Immortal Beloved," and above all the Heiligenstadt Testament—provided compelling evidence of the composer's desire to unburden himself. In the end, his instrumental works came to be regarded as wordless counterparts to these verbal confession.

From Rhetoric to Hermeneutics

The commentaries on Beethoven's music that appeared during the initial years of the *Berliner Allgemeine musikalische Zeitung* between 1824 and 1827—the last three years of the composer's life, as it turned out—reveal in concentrated form the pivot from a rhetorical to a hermeneutic framework in discourse about music. The journal's publisher had introduced readers to its first editor, Adolph Bernhard Marx, as a "brilliant young man deeply immersed in the style of criticism and artistic views of E. T. A. Hoffmann."[1] Like Hoffmann, Marx cultivated a style of reviewing that went beyond the standard surface-level characterization of the work at hand. Without declaring it openly, he encouraged readers to listen from the perspective of the composer, to go beyond the effect of works and think more about their source and import, and to become, as Novalis had put, "the extended author."

Marx's 1825 review of a performance of the Choral Fantasy, Op. 80, opens with a paragraph that incorporates virtually all the tropes that would become central to the reception of Beethoven's music over subsequent decades. It is couched squarely within the framework of hermeneutics:

> To some listeners, Beethoven's magnificent Fantasy [Op. 80] . . . will certainly not yet have revealed the great spirit [*Geist*] that dwells within it. And indeed, how is it possible that a mixed audience could grasp—in passing, as it were—a work that took weeks, perhaps months to ripen within a great artist, a work that springs out of a new idea, that seeks out new aspects of our interiority in order to move us with new sounds, new intimations and perspectives? One has to be accustomed to and experienced in following the flight of the artist's spirit in its every manifestation, or one has to have so much reverence for artworks and so much self-recognition that one returns again and again to any work that gives even a vague sense of the new and the good. In the meantime, one must also be prepared to relinquish all previous opinions and principles, in order to allow that which is new to have its effect on us and to allow it to unfold itself to us in its fullest. Anyone who disdains to do this is a poorly informed judge of all progressive works and deprives himself of pleasure in them and of the further development of art. The works that are generally accepted and beloved at once are precisely the most worthless, for this kind of success demonstrates that they consist only of that which is conventional, that which has been long known generally.[2]

Marx hears the presence of the composer in the work, holds listeners responsible for the work's effect, and insists that listeners approach it with an open mind and be prepared to hear it multiple times.

Critics would eventually extend these premises, implicit to some degree already in the genre of the fantasia (see p. 59), to instrumental compositions of all kinds. And it was the works of Beethoven's last decade that elicited a series of unusually lengthy and penetrating commentaries from Marx and his associates at the *Berliner Allgemeine musikalische Zeitung*. Together these reviews laid out the agenda of the hermeneutic perspective that would soon become the norm in responses not only to Beethoven's music, but to instrumental music in general. Marx's like-minded contributors in this project were Ludwig Rellstab (1799–1860), better known at the time as a critic than as a poet, and Christian Gottlob Rebs (1773–1843), an educator and music director in the Saxon town of Zeitz. Four reviews in particular, published between March 1824 and June 1826, merit closer consideration: they address the last two piano sonatas, Opp. 110 and 111 (Marx), the String Quartet Op. 127 (Rellstab), and the Ninth Symphony (Rebs).

1) Piano Sonata in A♭ Major, Op. 110
(A. B. Marx, 10 March 1824)[3]

Marx opens by presenting the most extended public revelation to date of Beethoven's deafness and social isolation. The clear implication is that an understanding of the composer's personal circumstances at the time of the work's composition will enhance an understanding of the music. The theme of struggle and triumph take center stage here:

> It is an uplifting spectacle to see human energy *fighting against and triumphing over* a powerful adversity. Beethoven's genius survives such a battle. Deafness has robbed him of every livelier means of communication. Among the hundreds of thousands in the Imperial city he lives isolated and lonely. The jubilant call of joy, the expression of love and veneration have fallen silent around him. His hand moves across the strings and he does not perceive the chords that delight everyone. What a heavy blow for the tone-poet to lose his hearing, to be cut off from the sense that was the most highly developed in him, the sense that gave him the richest nourishment![4]

The hardship of deafness has nevertheless ultimately worked to Beethoven's advantage, for it has liberated him from the conventional obligation of pleasing his contemporaries and at the same time forced him to turn inward, bringing him into ever-closer contact with the inner source of his creative powers:

Beethoven had the power to withstand this struggle and has emerged from the fight more invigorated and uplifted than before. The more the external world cut itself off from him, the deeper he turned back into his interiority. . . . He fulfills his mission with ever-greater purity, and his gifts become that much richer for those who understand him—and all the more inaccessible for those who have never understood how to grasp his own distinctive essence.[5]

It is only human, Marx observes, that in such an isolated state the composer would at times cast a nostalgic eye toward happier times. "The present sonata," he says, appears to be "an overflow from the innermost heart. Let us cease once and for all treating a work of art as if it were a lifeless product. One can believe to have understood it only when one has discovered and demonstrated its import in the soul of its creator." The opening Allegro, he declares, is "the lament of the isolated man"; it is full of "the gentlest expression of melancholy, endearing in its grace and majesty."[6] Furthermore, "Once the melody dies out, as if in the throes of sighing," the second-movement Allegro molto in F minor interweaves, quite unexpectedly, "a well-known folk song, which just as unexpectedly closes with a gentle echo:

> The artist seems to say to us: "All these things—the trivial joys that defraud individuals of their time and of that which is elevating, the desolate passion in whose rapture many a life is squandered—have never held power over me. Like an empty wind, they have whirled past me (Trio in D♭ Major). Thus it should have been and had to be (Coda)."[7]

In the subsequent recitative and arioso, "Beethoven wants to open his innermost heart—and how painfully—in the melody of the Arioso, . . . in the lament of a deeply wounded, abandoned heart in the weeping second voice toward the end." For anyone who does not hear this, Beethoven will remain "forever mute, and will also never understand me"—by which Marx means himself.[8]

This is an extraordinary review, one in which Marx at the end seems as resigned to fate as the composer—and the work—he is describing. By putting words in Beethoven's mouth, he almost literally hears the composer in his music.

2) Piano Sonata in C Minor, Op. 111
(A. B. Marx, 17 March 1824)[9]

Having published a signed review of Op. 110 in the previous week's issue of his journal, Marx realized that he could not offer a similarly ecstatic notice of another sonata so soon afterward, and so he chose the form of an unsigned letter to the editor—in reality a letter from himself to himself—that expresses deep skepticism about Op. 111. This, however, soon proves to function as a foil for the views of the wholly enthusiastic "Edward," a talented young musician who had recently visited the author of the letter and played through the sonata at sight. The fictive Edward provides a mouthpiece by which Marx could voice statements far more extreme than would otherwise have been appropriate within a straightforward review:

> I shall spare you, Sir, the dithyramb into which Edward threw himself after a long silence, the way in which he sighed that Beethoven, having died, had appeared to humanity in the form of a gigantic spirit, which announced: You never recognized me. Observe: this was my mighty life, these pains have purified me, these rays of hope from Elysium, these sounds from the blessed years of youth have strengthened me and nourished my timid heart. And now I die. "Yes, he has died," cried Edward, and in vain I asked if this report was reliable enough to be printed in your journal.[10]

Edward declares the first movement of Op. 111 to be an allegory of Beethoven's life, the second movement the death of the great man. "Indeed," he asks, "what artist would give something other than that which he has experienced within himself?"[11] He rejects the conventional notion of art as a source of consolation:

> Consolation is for the weak. Holy art teaches us by showing us and allowing to feel what we must endure. It strengthens us, in that it makes known to us the awakening powers in our own breast. It elevates us in that it shows us, like nature itself, within decline an ascent, a new life, and at the end of the finite the infinite.[12]

Edward—Marx's mouthpiece—knew full well that Beethoven was still alive. But his belief in the autobiographical essence of this music is so strong that he insists on hearing the second movement as an allegory of a death occasioned by the widespread misunderstanding of Beethoven's spirit. The artist has sacrificed himself on the altar of an uncomprehending public, and Edward's commentary is filled with thinly veiled Christological imagery. For him, Op. 111 is a spiritual self-portrait. Marx could not have made such bold assertions in his own name, but, like Hoffmann's Kreisler a decade before, a fictive mouthpiece allowed him to move beyond the conventions of standard criticism.

3) String Quartet in E♭ Major, Op. 127
(Ludwig Rellstab, 25 May 1825)[13]

Rellstab, having heard one or more performances of the as-yet-unpublished String Quartet Op. 127 in Vienna in March 1825, reflects on the work in an extraordinary essay that lays out a virtual blueprint of biographical hermeneutics.[14] A composition, he maintains, can be as much a relic as the sword or clothing of a great man. Op. 127 is itself altogether

the expression of the most noble soul, of the purest zeal for art itself. Nowhere is there a trace of anything that is there for the purpose of any other [soul] than itself. Genius wanted simply to manifest itself and only itself: everything else was of no consequence, nothing. And so too should we accept it as such. Such works cannot and must not be otherwise. What appears to be foreign, dark, and confused in them has its clarity and necessity in the soul of their creator, and it is there that we must seek guidance. Anyone who is able to imagine himself into the soul of a man who for the last fourteen painful years has lived alone in the world of life and joy, anyone who is able to think without *the* sense that is the source of the noblest and purest pleasure of the spirit; anyone who grasps that even the most powerful genius is constrained by and subjected to finite limitations: that individual will also wish that the memory of hearing might grow weaker, even in the case of a Beethoven, that the lively colors of musical tones might fade more and more. For that individual's heavenly fantasy would then be different from those whose worldly ears perceive with difficulty. And in all humility and without presumption, we might say that a genius who has suffered a significant change and disruption in his being must necessarily produce and create differently from the person who goes through life powerfully and intact. For this reason, we do not want to attack hastily that which strikes us as foreign and incomprehensible; instead, we want to acknowledge that there can be no correct evaluation where there is no standard of measurement.

Let no one, however presume, from this that Beethoven's newest work is somehow incommensurable with our ability to apprehend. No, thank heaven, there is still sufficient connection between him and us that we have a common language for our emotions, even if that language is not understandable in every last respect and detail—and where after all would that be case, *strictly speaking*, between even as few as any two individuals?

And it is in this language that Beethoven has spoken to us in such a miraculous way, in a way that has touched us to our core. It is a serious statement that he makes to us, the considered utterance of combat-riven pain from a soul that has been deeply wounded and yet is just as deeply full of hope. It is the manly pain of a Laocoön that enmeshes itself with secret threads throughout the entire work, which seems to mock itself in a deep Scherzo and yet in so doing seizes us all the more deeply and harrowingly in our breast.

Thou mighty genius who so divinely bestows gifts full of blessing on us: Should you alone be the one who suffers? No, from such a spring gushes strength and uplift, and you will fortify and console and uplift yourself, even if the luminous rays of sweet musical sounds, which you so miraculously create, should nevermore penetrate the mute night of your mortal life.[15]

The framework of rhetoric has all but vanished here: the work is the manifestation of a great soul, and nothing in it serves any purpose other than for that soul to make itself known. It is up to us to comprehend that manifestation. Rellstab applies many of Schleiermacher's basic hermeneutic principles and calls into question the facile assumption that full and mutual understanding can be taken for granted, even between two individuals who share a common language. To comprehend the utterance of another individual as fully and completely as possible, Rellstab maintains, we must enter into the mind—and indeed the soul—of that individual and take into account all the circumstances that have led to that utterance. We must therefore listen to it from the perspective of its creator, imagining ourselves into the pain he has suffered from his deafness and social isolation. Rellstab in effect turns Beethoven's disability into an asset and in one particularly provocative assertion claims that the world might well wish his deafness to become even more profound.

4) Symphony No. 9 in D Minor, Op. 125
(Christian Gottlob Rebs, 28 June and 5 July 1826)[16]

Rebs begins by taking note of the "artistic egoism" of the age, in which artists place their self-interests above those of art, projecting their own disposition (*Laune*) arbitrarily. Such egoism

> can be small and repellent if the composer lacks the powers of fantasy and feeling and posits empty affectation in place of art. But there is also an egoism that makes its appearance with Promethean daring and piles Pelion on Ossa in order to reach the gods in their abode. Beethoven—I must acknowledge my opinion openly—strikes me as such a giant in this most recent symphony. . . . Through his power, he repels in a hostile fashion as often as he draws us in and delights us. He creates tension, he deafens, he fatigues us . . . and he does all this, it would seem, because he wants to do this. I want to emphasize here, however, that I am speaking only of the general impression this work made upon me by two performances executed with uncommon diligence by our orchestra. I do not want to make any pretense toward a verdict in the case of such a master. I stipulate only that whoever has gotten to know this work compare the impression it has made upon him with the one expressed here, without taking the master's personal circumstances into account.[17]

For Rebs, the idea of regarding a work as a manifestation of the compositional self is so self-evident that he feels compelled to ask others to disregard it in reaching their own conclusions about this new symphony. Yet there can be no question that this is a work by Beethoven, who is now more readily discernible in his music than ever before:

> The features of his uniqueness are raised here [in the first movement] to an unprecedented height. . . . Some of it is less the result of an inner objective necessity than the arbitrariness of a cheeky disposition, so that in its character the whole approaches that of the fantasia and capriccio.[18]

"Inner objective necessity" smacks of rhetoric, of that which is needed for a work to make its effect on audiences. The evocation of the fantasia and capriccio, in turn, implies that what we are hearing is in fact something more akin to inner *subjective* necessity. While Rebs would go on to praise the second and third movements, he had little positive to say about the work's finale, even going so far as to recommend that it be omitted from future performances. Even in this decidedly mixed review, the critic was clearly hearing Beethoven in his music.

* * *

Critics did not pivot in unison toward a framework of hermeneutics: plenty of them continued to listen within the framework of rhetoric and respond accordingly, which in the case of Beethoven's late works usually meant responding negatively. Still others seem to have combined elements of the two. One anonymous reviewer, reporting on a March 1827 performance of the Ninth Symphony in Stettin, noted that "there could be no doubt" that Beethoven had composed its finale "in an animated mood of joy, or at the very least after transposing himself into that state." Having allowed for the possibility that the composer's state of mind may have been self-induced, this same critic goes on to ask, "Which smooth and polished artist reveals his 'I' in such a natural way as Beethoven did in this finale?"[19]

The Heiligenstadt Testament

The publication in October 1827 of what would come to be known as the Heiligenstadt Testament convinced the musical public beyond all doubt that a knowledge of Beethoven the individual would help them understand his music.[20] This was a message, in effect, from beyond the grave, a profoundly self-confessional document written in Heiligenstadt in October 1802 but discovered only after the composer's death. In it Beethoven acknowledges that his advancing deafness has driven him from society and made him seem "antagonistic, obstinate, or misanthropic." He laments his loss of the one sense so vital to a musician, a sense he felt he possessed to a degree that "few others in my profession have or have had."[21] He resolves to circulate in society only when circumstances compel him.

Addressed to his two brothers but directed to humanity in general, the document opens with the words "O ihr Menschen"—roughly, "To all humanity." This is, in effect, Beethoven's *apologia pro vita sua*:

> If I approach any gathering of people I am overcome with a deep anxiety for fear of the danger that my condition will be noticed. . . . What a humiliation

when someone standing next to me heard a flute from afar and *I heard nothing*; or when someone heard a shepherd singing and I heard nothing. Such incidents brought me to the edge of despair, only a little more of this and I should have taken my own life. It was only art that held me back. Ah, it seemed to me impossible to leave the world before having produced everything that I felt called upon to bring forth. And so I endured this miserable life, truly miserable. . . . Patience, it is said . . . is what I must now choose as my guide. . . . Already in my twenty-eighth year I am compelled to become a philosopher. This is not easy for an artist, more difficult than for just anyone. Lord, you look down on my innermost self; you know and recognize that a love of humanity and a proclivity to good deeds lie there within. O ye who at some point read this, consider that you have done me wrong, and may the Unhappy One console himself by finding one of his kind who in spite of all the impediments of nature nevertheless did everything in his capacity to be accepted into the circle of worthy artists and humans.[22]

Rochlitz's brief introduction to the text helped emphasize the document's singularity. He gave it lead billing in the 17 October 1827 issue of his weekly *Allgemeine musikalische Zeitung* and assured readers that his transcription of the original was exact, including its occasional "awkward phrasing" and "incorrect punctuation." To understand the document, he claimed, one must know that it was written at a time of "life-threatening illness." Beyond this, Rochlitz provides no further commentary and lets the document speak for itself.

Rochlitz's quasi-diplomatic nature of his transcription reinforced this aura of portentousness. Abandoning for a moment the standard two-column format of his journal, he reproduced as best he could the actual layout of the document's postscript. Here, in a portion of the text dated 10 October 1802, a few days after the original, the composer had written at a ninety-degree angle, "For my brothers Karl and ***, to be read and carried out after my death," and Rochlitz faithfully set these words in type in the same way.[23] The visual effect is striking, unlike anything else readers had seen in his journal before (Figure 5.1).

Scholars have since scrutinized this document repeatedly for what it has to tell us about Beethoven's creative output.[24] Yet its powerful and immediate impact on the way listeners heard his music has never been adequately considered. This was, after all, the first public evidence from Beethoven's own hand to link his suffering to his music, and the revelation that art alone had held him back from suicide was electrifying. The document's publication

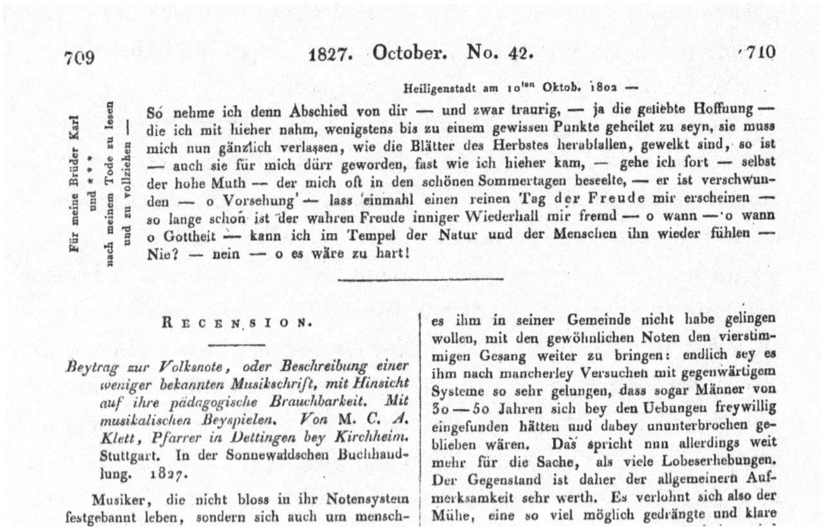

709 1827. October. No. 42. 710

Heiligenstadt am 10ten Oktob. 1802 —

Für meine Brüder Karl und *** nach meinem Tode zu lesen und zu vollziehen —

Só nehme ich denn Abschied von dir — und zwar traurig, — ja die geliebte Hoffnung — die ich mit hieher nahm, wenigstens bis zu einem gewissen Punkte geheilet zu seyn, sie muss mich nun gänzlich verlassen, wie die Blätter des Herbstes herabfallen, gewelkt sind, so ist — auch sie für mich dürr geworden, fast wie ich hieher kam, — gehe ich fort — selbst der hohe Muth — der mich oft in den schönen Sommertagen beseelte, — er ist verschwunden — o Vorsehung — lass einmahl einen reinen Tag der Freude mir erscheinen — so lange schon ist der wahren Freude inniger Wiederhall mir fremd — o wann — o wann o Gottheit — kann ich im Tempel der Natur und der Menschen ihn wieder fühlen — Nie? — nein — o es wäre zu hart!

RECENSION.

Beytrag zur Volksnote, oder Beschreibung einer weniger bekannten Musikschrift, mit Hinsicht auf ihre pädagogische Brauchbarkeit. Mit musikalischen Beyspielen. Von M. C. *A. Klett, Pfarrer in Dettingen bey Kirchheim.* Stuttgart. In der Sonnewaldschen Buchhandlung. 1827.

Musiker, die nicht bloss in ihr Notensystem festgebannt leben, sondern sich auch um mensch- es ihm in seiner Gemeinde nicht habe gelingen wollen, mit den gewöhnlichen Noten den vierstimmigen Gesang weiter zu bringen: endlich sey es ihm nach mancherley Versuchen mit gegenwärtigem Systeme so sehr gelungen, dass sogar Männer von 30—50 Jahren sich bey den Uebungen freywillig eingefunden hätten und dabey ununterbrochen geblieben wären. Das spricht nun allerdings weit mehr für die Sache, als viele Lobeserhebungen. Der Gegenstand ist daher der allgemeinern Aufmerksamkeit sehr werth. Es verlohnt sich also der Mühe, eine so viel möglich gedrängte und klare

Figure 5.1 Detail from Rochlitz's publication of Beethoven's Heiligenstadt Testament in the *Allgemeine musikalische Zeitung* 29 (17 October 1827): 709–10

When Friedrich Rochlitz published the Heiligenstadt Testament for the first time, he broke away from his journal's standard two-column format (visible in the beginning of the unrelated book review underneath) to run the text across the width of the full page, with a smaller font set vertically, reflecting the layout of Beethoven's original handwritten document. This striking departure from standard practice served to emphasize the extraordinary importance of this text.

ratified in a single stroke the kinds of readings that Marx and his associates had been making earlier in the decade in the *Berliner Allgemeine musikalische Zeitung*. With the publication of the Heiligenstadt Testament, biographical interpretations of the music became the norm. Critics now had an authorial voice to validate the tropes of suffering and overcoming that had begun to circulate even before the document's discovery. They could now read his works either as an artistic enactment of struggle-to-triumph (as in the case of the Fifth Symphony) or as a form of cathartic sublimation (as in the case of the Second Symphony, believed at the time to have been written coterminously with the Heiligenstadt Testament itself).

After its initial appearance in October 1827, the text was disseminated with remarkable speed. It was republished in Vienna some three weeks later and then appeared in English in two different London journals, once before the end of 1827 and then again in 1828. The *Philadelphia Monthly Magazine* published a summary with selected quotations in 1828, and a Dutch translation was issued that same year.[25] Ignaz Ritter von Seyfried reproduced the text in its original German in the biographical notes he appended to his 1832 collection of Beethoven's studies in figured bass, counterpoint, and composition, but when François-Joseph Fétis translated Seyfried's book into French in 1833, he moved those biographical notes to the very front of the volume, implicitly pointing to the life as the basis for an understanding of the works. Indeed, the very idea of publishing any composer's technical studies reflects the extraordinary interest in Beethoven's personal development as a composer just five years after his death.[26] Several Parisian journals, including the *Revue musicale* and *Le Voleur*, republished the French text of the testament later that same year, and Castil-Blaze incorporated it into his lengthy encyclopedia entry on Beethoven, also published in 1833.[27]

It is against this background that Joseph Fröhlich, in his 1828 essay on the Ninth Symphony, could dilate at such length on the trope of the composer's suffering as a source of strength. Such trials, Fröhlich maintained, enabled Beethoven to create "a complete portrait of his soul," for the Ninth was "Beethoven's autobiography, written in music."[28] A. B. Marx, in turn, reviewing the String Quartet in F Major, Op. 135, in 1829, could conclude that

> the content of the last works would seem to be connected most intimately to Beethoven's subjectivity and his particular circumstances. One grasps that the sequence of ideas [in these works] might strike the coolly resolved listener who remains outside the work as confusion and error; whereas the deepest, innermost soul of the composer in all its richness of sentiment pours memories and sorrows into the breast of the engaged, empathetic friend.[29]

Interiority and subjectivity soon became standard themes in discussions of both the man and his music. The composer and critic Alfred Julius Becher was one of many who identified Beethoven as having changed the very nature of composition itself. "Mighty Beethoven," he declared in 1834, "the summit of the current era of music and the greatest composer of all times, emptied in a flow the entire fullness of his feelings, the complete abundance of his ideas in his symphonies." Conventional in his earliest works, Beethoven had eventually presented "real ideas and self-conscious states of mind" in his music, "in contrast to the mere representation of situations."[30] Writing for the *Gazette musicale de Paris* that same year, A. B. Marx applied this new way of thinking to the Piano Sonata in C♯ Minor, Op. 27 No. 2 ("Moonlight"):

> A page from his personal life is provided to us by his sonata (quasi una fantasia, in C♯ Minor, Op. 27 no. 2), which he wrote at a time when he found himself disappointed by a tender sentiment he felt obliged to renounce. Those whose hearts feel this sympathy for Beethoven . . . will readily recognize in the Sonata Op. [1]3 and in other works by him that manifest these particular sentiments the state of the composer's soul at the time he wrote them, even if in those moments he had no concern to make those states known to the public by the kinds of explicit headings found in Op. 81[a], Op. 26, and his next-to-last string quartet, among other works.[31]

By 1835 the stage was set for new revelations that would confirm what was quickly becoming an article of faith: that Beethoven's compositions were relics of personal catharsis. Enter Bettina Brentano von Arnim (1785–1859). She knew both Goethe and Beethoven personally, and one letter to her from the composer is indisputably authentic, giving all the more credence to the many others that are almost certainly fictitious, including her own letters that she claimed to have written to both artists. In one, supposedly sent to Goethe in 1810 but not published until a quarter of a century later, after the poet's death, she recounted her first meeting with the composer. "Beethoven considers himself the founder of a new sensuous basis of spiritual life," she declared, quoting him as saying, "I must spurn a world that has no inkling that music is a higher revelation than all wisdom and philosophy."[32] Four years later she published three letters Beethoven had supposedly written to her. In the last of these, dated August 1812, "Beethoven" describes his meeting with Goethe in Teplitz, including the moment when the imperial family had met the two of them on foot: Goethe had removed his hat and bowed, but Beethoven had simply marched on. Schumann's *Neue Zeitschrift für Musik* spoke enthusiastically about the letter in 1839, and Anton Schindler would republish it in his biography of the composer the following year.[33]

For the moment, the authenticity of these letters is less important than their effect at the time they were published, when they were believed to be genuine. They reinforced the image of Beethoven as willful and indifferent to social—and thus, by extension, musical—conventions, and they encouraged the growing tendency to hear his works as quasi-Goethean "fragments of a great confession."

The many openly fictional accounts of Beethoven's life published in the decades after his death transmitted these dual themes of interiority and self-expression to an even wider public. Ernst Ortlepp's *Beethoven: Eine phantastische Charakteristik* (1836), to take but a single example, includes a remarkable conversation between Beethoven and Haydn's ghost, who tells the composer that he will die soon after finishing the Ninth Symphony, his "swan song":

> "You will finish it!" replied Haydn, "and it will resound for another thousand years! From heaven I bring to you the blessing and power to achieve this: that your last creation contains everything that as yet lay unuttered in the deepest depths of your soul, that it shall become an image of your holy self, at first not understood and rejected, then intuited and regarded with astonishment, and later grasped and beloved, and finally venerated and praised for all eternity!"[34]

Haydn takes his leave, and Beethoven resolves to make Schiller's "An die Freude" the centerpiece of the symphony's finale:

> "Yes," he cried, "before I die, they must finally hear everything that has weighed upon my soul. I want to paint with powerful strokes the great battle between world-weariness and world-joy . . . and so they should certainly see that I elevate myself victoriously over worldly suffering, like a colossus that towers toward heaven!"[35]

Fiction and criticism became blurred at times. Chrétien Urhan made sense of the seemingly disparate movements Beethoven's Ninth by comparing it to Berlioz's *Symphonie fantastique*, hearing in it "a summary of *the entire life* of Beethoven . . . there he has set down the secret of his entire interior life and the diverse transformations of his soul. It is his moral biography!"[36] Joseph d'Ortigue, an associate of both Berlioz and Urhan, experienced in Beethoven's string quartets a "tête-à-tête" in which the composer unburdened "at length" and in "a mysterious language" the "secrets of his heart," his "sufferings, his joys, his passions," which had "penetrated to the marrow of his bones and stirred the very last fibers of his being."[37]

Biographies

Posthumous attempts to explain the works through the life got off to a fast start with Johann Aloys Schlosser's *Ludwig van Beethoven*, published in Prague in September 1827, six months after the composer's death and a month before the publication of the Heiligenstadt Testament.[38] It is a curious work, full of more than its share of howling inaccuracies. A native of Prague, Schlosser does not disclose his sources: he claims to have finished the preface in Vienna in June of that year, which suggests that he could have interviewed any number of individuals who had known Beethoven, or even met the composer himself, but at no point does he claim to have done either. In any case, Schlosser is at times quite specific about the close relationship between life and works. He reports that Beethoven suffered "pains caused by a delusion of his heart" around 1809, and that "these sufferings expressed themselves quite clearly in all the works of that time." He alludes to these circumstances again obliquely later in his account, aligning them with the works of Opp. 40–60 and speculating that the curious mixture of the serious and comic in many of these compositions reflects a "state of mind occasioned by something extraordinary, to which I have referred previously."[39] He further singles out, as a representation of the composer's "inner history," the Fifth Symphony for "its combination of reminiscent and prophetic sounds." The first movement's "fiery Allegro sets the fundamental tone of a portentous, powerful life," while the "melancholy grief" of the second is "elevated by a hope-filled glimpse of eternity," presumably the C major sections with trumpets and timpani. In the third movement we hear "the descending storm of fate," but with the opening of the finale "every earthly oppression falls away and the victorious spirit soars into the sun-drenched ether of eternal freedom."[40] To Schlosser's mind, Beethoven's Fifth is about Beethoven, a musical autobiography that looks both backward and forward.

More than a decade would pass before music lovers would have access to a narrative of the composer's life from the perspective of close associates. Franz Wegeler (1765–1848), a childhood friend from Bonn, and Ferdinand Ries (1784–1838), Beethoven's erstwhile pupil in Vienna, published their "Biographical Notes" to wide acclaim in 1838.[41] Their account reinforced the inclination of listeners to hear his works in the way they read Goethe: as fragments of a great confession. Their biography made public for the first time the composer's letter to Wegeler of 1801 in which he confessed his growing deafness. Subsequent critics would never tire of quoting one passage in particular: "I will grab fate by the throat, it shall certainly not break me completely."[42] That the context of this vow is medical rather than musical made no difference to those predisposed to hear the life in the works. The portion of the letter in which this oft-quoted line appears consists largely of Beethoven's complaints about his condition and his current doctor, along with queries about Wegeler's opinion of other physicians and possible treatments, including Galvanism. There is not the slightest suggestion that the act of "grabbing fate by the throat" might manifest itself musically. Wegeler also included in this new biography Beethoven's previously unpublished letter to him of 29 June 1800, in which the composer says that he "lives in my musical notes alone," but which again would typically be quoted without its fuller context, in which he adds that he "often works on three or four pieces at the same time."[43] Yet another of the book's revelations was Ries's firsthand account of Beethoven's fury at the news that Napoleon had crowned himself emperor, which led the composer to tear up the title page of the symphony that was to have been dedicated to him, the *Eroica*.[44] From this point on, no one could hear the work in the same way.

Anton Schindler's highly anticipated 1840 biography provided readers with still more evidence encouraging readers to connect the composer's works and inner self. Although now regarded as an unreliable source— Schindler is known to have forged entries in the conversation books and to have exaggerated both the duration and intensity of his contact with the composer—his position as an off-and-on unpaid personal assistant in the last decade of Beethoven's life helped give his biography an unprecedented aura of authority, particularly for the later years.[45] He declared early on that his biography would be " concerned primarily with the *circumstances and living conditions under which Beethoven created such great and immortal works*, that is, with matters of fact that one would have had to have experienced then and there and moreover at the side of the great man, in order to measure their greater or lesser effect on his entire being."[46] Beethoven, according to Schindler, possessed the "true soul of an artist," and this soul revealed itself to varying degrees in "every one of his works."[47] His biography traces the origins of the "Moonlight" Sonata, for example, to the composer's passion for Giulietta Guicciardi and asks: "What genius could have written the Fantasia in C♯ Minor without such a love? And let it be said here, if only in passing: it was his love for Giulietta, the dedicatee of this work, that inspired him to create it."[48] By this point, Hector Berlioz's *Symphonie fantastique*, portraying its creator's obsession with the actress Harriet Smithson, had firmly established itself in the concert repertoire; the "Moonlight" Sonata could now take its place as Beethoven's contribution to the genre of fantasy-like works inspired by passionate and unrequited love. That *fantasia* and *fantastique* should figure into both titles is no mere coincidence: the fantasia, as noted earlier (see p. 59–74), had long been heard as a confessional genre.

Schindler's biography also presented, for the first time, the text of the letter to the "Immortal Beloved," an unnamed woman to whom Beethoven had expressed a deep passion.[49] Along with the Heiligenstadt Testament (also reproduced in his book), these letters had come into Schindler's possession in late March of 1827 when he was clearing out the flat in Vienna where the composer had recently died. The publication of these letters created such a sensation that Schindler would go on to issue a partial facsimile of them in the third (1860) edition of his biography. They offered for the first time a glimpse into a very different side of the composer as a man of passionate intensity; this intensity, in turn, provided the key for many subsequent commentators to interpret a variety of works as either the outpouring or sublimation of the composer's love interests.

Equally sensational was Schindler's account of Beethoven's explanation of the "meaning" of the opening of the Fifth Symphony: "Thus fate pounds at the portal!"[50] This nugget appears fairly late in the book, after repeated evocations of "fate" (such as "Fate implanted itself firmly into his ears and prevented him from hearing speech and tone") and only one page after Schindler's observation that the fugal passage in the *Eroica*'s Marcia funebre "bears witness at precisely that point to a struggle with fate."[51] No one at the time had any particular reason to doubt Schindler's apparently firsthand report, making the perception of Beethoven's music as essentially autobiographical all the more viable, particularly when combined with the composer's oft-quoted earlier pronouncement to Wegeler that he would "grab fate by the throat."

By mid-century autobiographical readings had become standard fare. The composer, poet, and critic Peter Cornelius, for example, declared in 1854 that

> everyone who listens to Beethoven's creations—from the layperson . . . to the most refined connoisseur . . . is conscious that something more and different speaks out of these works than those by Haydn and Mozart. People strive to account for this in the most diverse ways. Some call it depth, humor, subjectivity; some compare Beethoven to Shakespeare, Jean Paul, Byron. We for our part seek an explanation for the unusual in Beethoven by imagining his entire, full, and solemn life as if it were the labor pains of

birth, labor pains of specific thoughts expressed through the language of tones.[52]

A year later the critic Wilhelm von Lenz observed that the "postscript" to the last of the "Immortal Beloved" letters could be found in the "languishing" and "swelling" dissonant seconds of the horns in the trio of the *Eroica*'s Scherzo, which "speak of an unnamed love." Giulietta Guicciardi—the woman in question, in Lenz's opinion—"lives here" in this "embodiment of the noblest passion." Lenz heard the Op. 59 string quartets, in turn, as Beethoven's self-portrait.[53] Alexandre Oulibicheff perceived Beethoven as both the author and hero of the Fifth Symphony.[54] Readers who, like Oulibicheff himself, are looking for "Beethoven himself, his most intimate self" would find an "embarrassment of riches" in the string quartets of Op. 18, riches Oulibicheff proceeded to identify, saving his prime example for last: in the finale of Op. 18 No. 6, labeled "La Maliconia," in whose harmonically tortuous passages we hear Beethoven's own melancholy.[55]

A. B. Marx, in his wide-ranging 1859 biography of the composer, noted that the "Pastoral" Symphony "opens up to us, as does every one of his poems, Beethoven's soul and makes us aware of that which a return to the bosom of nature has given him."[56] Beethoven's symphony is thus no longer a symphony about nature, but about Beethoven's response to nature. Marx called the Andante of the "Archduke" Piano Trio, Op. 97, a "night prayer" and apostrophized it with these words: "Beethoven's soul rested in you."[57] Such commentary is consistent with Marx's broader belief that compositional pedagogy should not be restricted to the technical elements of music but instead encompass the development of the individual as a whole.[58]

The critic August Wilhelm Ambros heard the first-person voice in virtually everything Beethoven wrote: "He wants to express in music and through music everything that lives in him—the highest and the lowest."[59] So deeply is Beethoven's self embedded in his works and so varied are the moods of each that

we would like to pose the question to him as to what moved him. . . . We are no longer interested in the musical poetry [*Tondichtung*] alone: we are also interested in the musical poet [*Tondichter*]. Accordingly, we assume almost the same perspective toward Beethoven as toward Goethe: we consider his works as a commentary on his life. In the case of both great men, one could also turn the statement around and say just as correctly that we view their lives as commentaries on their works.[60]

Like so many critics of his generation, Ambros believed that Beethoven had fundamentally changed the course of music. Instrumental works from the generation of Bach and Handel had been a mere "play of forms" (*Formenspiel*), and while Haydn and Mozart had created a greater sense of equilibrium between form and content (which is to say, emotional content), it remained to Beethoven to give priority to that content. Only through repeated hearings can we realize just how much the form has "grown" to meet the content, and that the works are in fact "musical organisms full of eternal life."[61]

Ludwig Nohl, yet another mid-century biographer, declared the "Appassionata" Sonata, Op. 57, "one of the most passionate outpourings" of Beethoven's "painfully agitated, almost resentful inner self."[62] He traced the origins of the "Moonlight" Sonata and the "Tempest" Sonata in D Minor, Op. 31 No. 2, to "the time of suffering and renunciation" in the composer's life. In the case of the "Tempest" Sonata specifically, it is the Heiligenstadt Testament that provides "the best commentary on both its crushing doubt and gentlest melancholy." And when Nohl called the Heiligenstadt Testament a "commentary" on the work, he meant this quite literally, for, having transmitted the beginning of the document earlier in his book, he at this point proceeded to quote the remainder of it in its entirety.[63] The Heiligenstadt Testament had become, in effect, an extended program note from Beethoven's own pen.

The centennial of Beethoven's birth in 1870 elicited renewed assessments of the relationship between the composer's life and works. So revealing was the power of his instrumental music, according to the noted American critic John Sullivan Dwight, that "through one symphony you get a clearer insight into a being like Beethoven than through any life of him that could be written."[64] Richard Wagner's "Beethoven" essay similarly insisted that the person of the composer had to be the "focus" of any attempt to say something about "the rays of light of the miraculous world that emanates from him." Any attempt to describe the "true essence" of his music "without falling into tones of rapture" was otherwise doomed to failure. Wagner accordingly interpreted the String Quartet in C♯ Minor, Op. 131, autobiographically, as the "image of a day in the life of our saint."[65]

The 1871 publication of Beethoven's "diary" (the so-called *Tagebuch*) from 1812–18 provided yet further coordinates by which to map the composer's inner self onto his works.[66] This unsystematic and occasional collection of jottings and observations, some of them commonplace, others quite intimate, opens with an entry that includes these lines:

> You must not be a *human being, not for yourself, but only for others*: for you
> there is no longer any happiness except within yourself in your art. O God!
> Give me strength to conquer myself, nothing at all must fetter me to life.[67]

As if to underscore the compositional process as a synthesis of the spiritual
and technical, the entry that immediately follows turns to the finer points
of voice leading: "The precise coinciding of several musical voices generally
hinders the progression from one to the other."[68]

The growing attention to Beethoven's compositional sketches over the
course of the nineteenth century captures the era's unceasing efforts to grasp
the mysteries of artistic creation. As early as 1821 an anonymous reviewer for
the *Allgemeine musikalische Zeitung* had noted the value of such sources, comparing them to preliminary drafts made by visual artists.[69] Seyfried provided
the first reproductions of Beethoven's sketches in his 1832 survey of Beethoven's
studies in figured bass and counterpoint, and systematic study of these materials
began in earnest a generation later with the work of Gustav Nottebohm. But
even Nottebohm conceded that the sketchbooks do not reveal the "moment
of creativity" we seek in Beethoven's music. Nor is that moment to be found in
the finished work: we must look instead to "Beethoven the artist himself, in the
unity of his entire being and spirit, in the harmony of the powers of his soul."[70]

The sketches in any case reinforced the image of Beethoven as a *Kraftgenie*,
that is, a genius who created through sheer force of will, as opposed to a
Naturgenie, exemplified by Mozart, whose works were perceived as having
been produced without strenuous effort.[71] In this respect, the sketches
helped humanize Beethoven, even while making all the more pronounced
the contrast between him and the seemingly of-another-world Mozart.[72]
Beethoven's sketches ultimately came to be seen, as Douglas Johnson has put
it, as "artifacts of the struggle," artifacts that could be—and were—correlated
with the documented struggles of the composer's life.[73]

This mapping of the compositional self onto the works spanned the entire
spectrum of literature about Beethoven, from the most popular biographies,
aimed at a wide readership, to the most scholarly, aimed at specialists. Paul
Bekker, a highly respected critic who appealed to both audiences, declared in
1911 that "the vehemence of his feelings nullifies all restraining rules of decorum" in his works:

> A soul reveals its deepest secrets. A personality buffeted by elemental storms
> drops all veils and exclaims its own experiences with ruthless openness to

an amazed humanity. No stimulus from outside can give Beethoven deeper impulses than that which he receives from within himself. He thus elevates this self to an object of artistic representation and chooses as his medium of communication the language in whose magical forms he says everything that humans are capable of thinking and feeling: wordless instrumental music.[74]

And it was not just Beethoven's life that critics projected onto his works: they saw in his very appearance—above all the famous scowl—an unwillingness to engage with the world on anything other than his own terms. While the scowl may be traced to the life mask produced by Franz Klein in 1812, it became increasingly prominent over time, and posthumous images of the composer almost invariably portray him as turned inward, self-absorbed, and without any interest in presenting himself in an even mildly agreeable manner.[75] There is no feigned happiness here, only the outward signs of an inward struggle. The fascination with Beethoven's physiognomy is itself yet another index of the conviction that the inner self is a key to the works. As early as 1835 Anton Schindler was reporting at length on the composer's physical characteristics; the point of such a detailed account would scarcely have been imaginable a generation before.[76] Evidence to the contrary, moreover, was simply ignored. Ludwig Rellstab, who had visited the composer several times in the spring of 1825, reported years later that he had found nothing in Beethoven's countenance that matched the "asperity, that stormy wildness . . . that has been given his physiognomy in order to bring it into conformity with his works."[77] Rellstab recognized the posthumous attempts to link outward and inward appearances, but by the middle of the nineteenth century the trope of Beethoven's interiority was too firmly established to be dislodged.

The tendency to hear Beethoven in his works reached its zenith around the turn of the twentieth century. Even as sober a critic as George Grove could hear the composer's passion for the Immortal Beloved—whom he thought to be Therese von Brunsvick—in the Fifth Symphony: "Considering the extraordinarily imaginative and disturbed character of the Symphony, it is impossible not to believe that the work—the first movement at any rate—is based on his relations to the Countess, and is more or less a picture of their personality and connection. . . . In fact, the first movement seems to contain actual portraits of the two chief actors in the drama."[78]

Perhaps more than any number of similar verbal accounts from this time, a single likeness captures the almost mystical qualities so many turn-of-the-century critics associated with Beethoven and thus by extension his music. In a fantastical image created in 1903 by the artist Hugo Höppener ("Fidus," 1868–1948), a grotesquely oversized bust of the composer glares out beyond us, sphinxlike, the corners of the mouth turned down (as always), while a nude female strains on tiptoes to touch his lips and chin (Figure 5.2). Beethoven is at once enormous and impenetrable. His collars look like small mountain ranges. The secret of this sphinx—which is to say the secret of his music—lies deep within. The persona, moreover, is hyperbolically masculine: taciturn and externally forbidding.[79] The best we can do when we

Figure 5.2 Hugo Höppener ("Fidus"), "Beethoven," *Die Jugend* 11 (1903): 171.

Whatever its shortcomings, kitsch has the capacity to expose popular attitudes in ways that are remarkably revealing. This 1903 image captures not only the perception of Beethoven as a larger-than-life sphinx but also his status as the most "masculine" of all composers.

approach him is to extend ourselves to reach his level. The starry vaults of the Ninth Symphony have taken on human form.

* * *

When Hans Heinrich Eggebrecht surveyed the history of Beethoven reception in the composer's bicentennial year of 1970, he organized his findings around a dozen or so themes so persistent as to warrant the label "constants." Foremost among these were "The Music of That Which Has Been Experienced" and "The Biographical Content of the Music (Unity of Life and Work)."[80] The more listeners learned about Beethoven, the more they heard him in his music. Yet Eggebrecht's survey, for all its value, ignores all criticism published during the composer's lifetime and as such fails to expose the pronounced contrast between contemporaneous and posthumous responses to his music. They were quite different. Listeners—and listening itself—had changed.

6

After Beethoven

Beethoven's shadow was more than just musical. His style, composers and critics agreed, could not be imitated. But his subjectivity—or more precisely, his *perceived attitude* of subjectivity—could be emulated quite readily, and it became the new norm soon after his death. Critics, moreover, heard compositional subjectivity not only in new music but also in selected works of the past.

The increasingly public nature of the Western musical world—in the form of ever larger concert halls, cheaper technologies of print and print distribution, and the more economical manufacture of instruments, especially the piano—created a growing demand for guides that could help listeners comprehend an instrumental repertoire that was becoming stylistically ever more diverse and technically difficult. The number of new music journals grew exponentially in the second quarter of the nineteenth century, as did the publication of music itself, including for the first time miniature scores produced specifically for the purpose of study rather than performance.[1] Composer biographies, a rarity before 1800, had become commonplace by mid-century.

These are all symptoms of a fundamental change in the most basic premises of concert-hall listening. Audiences now assumed that the instrumental music they were hearing came from deep within the soul of the composer. This phenomenon itself has long been recognized; what has gone largely unnoticed is the speed with which this new mode of listening took hold in only a decade or two.

Written Lives

Prior to 1830, the concertgoing public had relatively little knowledge of composers, particularly living ones.[2] Sources of information tended to restrict themselves to basic biographical data, such as the facts of professional employment and some indication of works produced. This approach is evident in such publications as W. C. Printz's *Historische Beschreibung der edelen Sing- und Kling-Kunst* (1690), Johann Gottfried Walther's *Musicalisches Lexikon* (1732), Johann Mattheson's *Grundlage einer Ehren-Pforte* (1740), J.-B. de La Borde's *Essai sur la musique ancienne et moderne* (1780), and Ernst Ludwig Gerber's *Historisch-biographisches Lexikon der Tonkünstler* (1790–92), issued in a revised and expanded form as the *Neues historisch-biographisches Lexikon der Tonkünstler* (1812–14). The travelogues of Charles Burney (published 1771–73) and Johann Friedrich Reichardt (published 1774–1810), provided firsthand but brief accounts of composers at various locales throughout Europe. Composer autobiographies were few in number and tended to be limited in scope.[3] André-Ernest-Modeste Grétry's *Mémoires, ou Essais sur la musique* (1789) and Christian Friedrich Daniel Schubart's *Leben und Gesinnungen* (1791) were as much collections of essays on various musical topics as they were personal memoirs.

In this respect, composers differed from visual artists, who from the Renaissance onward—thanks in large part to Giorgio Vasari's *Vite de' più eccellenti pittori, scultori, e architettori* (1550; 2nd ed., 1568)—had attracted far more interest during their lifetimes as individuals and who in turn had been far more active in promoting themselves. This included taking whatever steps they could to ensure an enduring posthumous reputation. In a telling moment, Vasari chided Correggio for not having painted a self-portrait, thereby depriving subsequent generations of a likeness of himself.[4] Visual artists enjoyed one decided advantage over composers in this regard: a painting, sculpture, or building would under normal circumstances survive beyond—and often well beyond—the life of its creator. Composers harbored no such illusions: until the closing decades of the eighteenth century, with only rare exceptions (most notably Lully and Handel), music was rarely performed after a composer's death. Outside of the church, most of the compositions listeners heard had been written within their own lifetimes.[5]

The first separately published composer biography of any substance, John Mainwaring's 1760 account of Handel, was likely commissioned by the composer himself as a counterpart to the stone likeness of his person in Westminster Abbey, for which he had made explicit provisions in his will. No comparable biography of any composer would appear again until Franz Xaver Niemetschek's life of Mozart (1798) and Johann Nikolaus Forkel's life of Johann Sebastian Bach (1802), followed by the several biographies of Haydn that appeared in 1810, the year after his death.

The custom of publishing biographies only after the death of their subjects certainly did not help the listening public learn about composers while they were still alive and present in the concert hall. At the same time, there seems to have been little demand for such information: as long as concertgoers heard music as a form of objective expression they had no compelling reason to think about the inner psyche or for that matter the very identity of a given work's creator. Listeners might well marvel at a composer's technical ability, and certain names on a concert program or a title page promised a higher quality of music—hence, for example, the many works falsely marketed under Haydn's name during his lifetime—but they did not attend a concert or buy a new work of published music anticipating a revelation of the announced composer's inner self. Only when they began to perceive expression as the subjective outpouring of a creative soul did the identity and psyche of the composer become centrally important to the experience of listening. Approaching a new work from the perspective of the composer who had written it also happened to be the easiest and least technically demanding way of coming to terms with it.

The use of biography as a hermeneutic tool was already firmly established in literary criticism by the 1820s. Goethe, as noted earlier, saw value in biographies for the interpretation of poetry and fiction, and not just his own. In the foreword to his own memoirs (1811), he declared that any given biography would ideally "portray the individual in relation to his times and . . . show to what extent the whole works against or in favor of him, how he creates out of this a view of the world and of humanity, and—if he is an artist, poet, or author—how he projects this outwardly." He conceded that this goal was scarcely achievable, for no individual truly knows himself or his times, nor can anyone really evaluate all the many forces in play in the creation of any given artwork. The effort, he felt, was nevertheless worthwhile.[6]

The public appetite for biographies of composers grew rapidly in the second quarter of the nineteenth century. Journals expanded the number and scope of biographical profiles of composers still alive, and in a departure from earlier custom, publishers began to issue monographs on living composers, such as Stendhal's *Vie de Rossini* (1824), G. Imbert de Laphalèque's *Notice sur le célèbre violoniste Nicolo Paganini* (1830), and J. W. Christern's *Franz Liszt, nach seinem Leben und Werke, aus authentischen Berichten dargestellt* (1841). Two major reference works of the time made available an unprecedented quantity of biographical information that included living composers: Fétis's *Biographie universelle des musiciens* (8 vols., 1835–44) and Gustav Schilling's

Encyclopädie der gesammten musikalischen Wissenschaften oder Universal Lexikon der Tonkunst (6 vols., 1835).

Composers themselves were eager to make themselves known. In 1826 the Gesellschaft der Musikfreunde in Vienna sent out a call to Austrian composers to submit particulars of their lives and eventually received more than two hundred such accounts.[7] This enthusiastic response can be explained in part by composers' growing realization that financial success depended on their appeal to an expanding public. Court patronage, which declined precipitously after 1815, was no longer the source of employment and income it had once been, and composers were learning to use the public press as a vehicle of self-promotion. The first composers to write extensively about music for the general public—Berlioz, Schumann, Liszt, and Wagner—were all born within a span of ten years, between 1803 and 1813. Beyond providing income, writing prose helped each of these composer-critics raise their profile with readers who were also potential listeners. As Fétis caustically noted in his review of the *Symphonie fantastique* in 1835, Berlioz was writing in four different journals of divergent political tendencies in an attempt to "insinuate faith in his name."[8] In the meantime, composers themselves, including Berlioz, had begun to create their own autobiographies in sound.

Audible Lives

The assumption that composers' selves would be audible in their works had become so self-evident by the 1830s that a critic for the *Allgemeine musikalische Zeitung* of Leipzig, reviewing a new nocturne by the Irish composer John Field, could express surprise at its *lack* of any apparent connection with its composer's life. Having opened the review by noting Field's recent ill health, the writer marveled that "it is as if the master's soul had remained so utterly child-like as it once had been, as if life with its experiences had passed over him without casting even a single shadow."[9]

Composers who doubled as critics did their part to encourage such perceptions. Foremost among these was Berlioz, who in both his music and his prose blazed the trail of self-projection. His *Épisode de la vie d'un artiste: Symphonie fantastique* (1830; the title and subtitle would be reversed only later) is the manifesto of compositional subjectivity. It inspired generations of subsequent composers to write themselves into their music. The identity of the "artist" in this work was never much of a secret: Berlioz and his associates fed the Parisian press with the story of his obsessive passion—his idée fixe—for the Irish actress Harriet Smithson. While still at work on this new symphony, he described it to a friend as "my novel, or rather my story, whose hero you will easily be able to recognize." In another letter, he called the *Symphonie fantastique* a work "in which the development of my infernal passion is to be portrayed."[10]

Berlioz's outward expression of his inward turn was part of a broader movement in all the arts.[11] He was inspired in no small measure by his literary idols, who included Byron, Lamartine, Chateuabriand, and Hugo, the last of whom had declared in 1824 that "it is not in fact from the springs of Hippocrene, from the Castalian fountains, nor indeed from the stream of Permessus that the poet draws his inspiration, but quite simply from his soul and his heart."[12] Berlioz cultivated this attitude with apparent effortlessness. "What dominated him more than reasonably," his friend the composer Ferdinand Hiller recalled in 1879,

> was the constant contemplation of himself, of his own passionate feelings, his entire conduct and drive. He was one of those people who feel the need to appear interesting to themselves, to give an elevated meaning to the slightest thing that they do, feel, or suffer, the good as well as the bad, whatever comes their way. And yet he did not give the impression of being vain, which is all the more remarkable, given that he talked about himself often and almost exclusively. Not that he didn't bring God and the world, music and poetry, peoples and countries into his the realm of his outpourings, but he always remained—if I may express myself in genuinely German terms—subjective in the highest degree.[13]

The openly autobiographical nature of the *Symphonie fantastique* became an idée fixe of its own for contemporary critics. Almost without exception, they prefaced their responses to the work, whether positive or negative, with extended remarks on the composer. Berlioz himself set this tradition in motion in a biographical profile published in 1832 under the name of his friend Joseph d'Ortigue but in fact largely written by the composer.[14] After a lengthy account of his life up to 1830, Berlioz-Ortigue has this to say about the *Symphonie fantastique*:

> All these biographical details. . . are indispensable for understanding this extraordinary composition. It is impossible nowadays to judge a

serious work in isolation, that is, without following the trace, thread by thread, back to the man himself, and without accounting for the author's circumstances . . . One must ask what the artist felt.[15]

D'Ortigue dutifully opened his review of a concert performance a few months later with a long meditation on the relationship of artists in general to their specific times—whether they are ahead of or behind them—before introducing Berlioz the individual. He said nothing to about the work itself until almost halfway through his critique.[16] Heinrich Panofka, reporting to the *Neue Zeitschrift für Musik* from Paris, opened his essay on the *Symphonie fantastique* and *Harold en Italie* with an enthusiastic narrative of the composer's "in many respects interesting life" so that readers would have a "better understanding" of these works.[17] Only when he had gone beyond the halfway point of his account did he turn to the specific works at hand, and even then, his focus remained squarely on the composer: the *Symphonie fantastique*, he reported, is "a drama, the passionate effusion of a youth's heart, which Berlioz expresses to us through music; it is a period of his life that he renders to us in tones."[18] Such biographical introductions did not always work to Berlioz's advantage: when François-Joseph Fétis, the doyen of Parisian music critics, opened his 1835 review of the *Symphonie fantastique* with a disparaging portrait of his former student, he recounted his memory of a recalcitrant Conservatoire pupil who had displayed neither interest nor ability in counterpoint.[19] Yet even here, the net effect was to reinforce the premise of the composer's life as the key to understanding the work. This biographical approach was virtually without precedent at the time: the only real antecedents had been notices from the 1820s that had introduced Beethoven's newest works with brief acknowledgments of the composer's increasing deafness as an explanation for their unusual nature.

Robert Schumann's lengthy 1835 review of the *Symphonie fantastique* follows this pattern of biographical exegesis as well, devoting considerable attention to the composer's life before turning to the music. Berlioz, he observes, "belongs more to those Beethovenian characters whose artistic development correlates precisely with their life stories, in which every changing moment of the life causes a moment of rising or falling in their art."[20] After dismissing the work's program—the movement titles and word of mouth would have sufficed, he insists—Schumann makes an extraordinary statement:

Standing before the workshop of genius, humans possess a characteristically beautiful shyness: they want to know nothing, indeed just as Nature
herself evinces a certain delicateness in covering up roots with earth. Let
the artist, then, seal up his labor pains: we would learn dreadful things if
were able to see the occasion for the genesis of all his works.[21]

As we now know, Schumann had by this point himself already begun composing his own autobiographical music, having started work on *Carnaval*
the year before (see p. 10). Following his own advice, he relied on titles—
most of them fairly transparent—and word of mouth to communicate the
connections between his music and his life.

The programmatic titles and accompanying prose program for the
Symphonie fantastique in any case reflect the new orientation toward the self
as muse. Berlioz recognized that by setting out his sources of inspiration explicitly he could at once draw attention to himself and help listeners understand the work's new and challenging idiom. Program music was by no means
a new phenomenon at this time: fully developed instances of it date from as
early as the turn of the seventeenth century. But the perception of music as an
oracular art changed the perception of the verbal clues composers were now
providing for such works. Audiences were beginning to read these as keys to
unlock what might otherwise seem to be opaque utterances. The framework
of hermeneutic listening, in other words, fueled the new prestige of program
music, and vice versa.

As a critic, Berlioz consistently equated the ideal composer with one whose
presence was palpable in the music. Nowhere does this come through more
clearly than in his 1851 account of hearing a performance of Beethoven's
Piano Trio in C Minor, Op. 1, No. 3:

I throw my door wide open. . . . Enter, enter, welcome, proud melody! . . .
Heavens! how noble and beautiful it is! . . . Where, then, did Beethoven
find those thousands of phrases, each of them more poetically character-
ized than the others, and all different, all original, without even the family
resemblance one finds in the melodies of great masters renowned for their
fecundity? And what ingenious developments! What unexpected turns of
thought! . . . How swiftly that indefatigable eagle flies! How he hovers and
balances in his harmonious sky! He dives into it, loses himself in it, soars,
descends again, disappears; then returns to his starting-place, his eye more

brilliant, his wings stronger, intolerant of rest, quivering, athirst for the infinite.[22]

For Berlioz, Beethoven and his music were one.

Robert Schumann also looked to literary figures for inspiration, both as a composer and as a critic. The influence of such writers as Friedrich Schlegel, Jean Paul, and E. T. A. Hoffmann on both his music and his prose is well documented.[23] And again like Berlioz, Schumann gave his contemporaries ample basis on which to hear his own music as autobiographical. He shared the "keys" to his early piano works with friends and critics alike.[24] In his *Carnaval*, Op. 9, for example, he embedded autobiographical elements within a web of musical ciphers (or "Sphinxes," as he called them) that form the basis of each movement's opening idea, permutations of the notes E♭ ("Es" in German, pronounced the same way as the letter "S"), C, H (the German for B♮), and A, which in succession outline the musical letters in the name SCHumAnn but when rearranged could also indicate ASCH, the hometown of his then-fiancée, Ernestine von Fricken. Many of the titles of individual movements of *Carnaval*, in turn, refer to Schumann's own alter egos (Eusebius, Florestan), persons in his immediate circle (Chiarina = Clara Wieck, Estrella = Ernestine von Fricken), other composers (Chopin, Paganini), or figures from the commedia dell'arte (Harlequin, Pierrot, Columbine). In keeping with the spirit of Carnival season, the identity and implications of these individual musical motives are "masked," though not to the extent that they defy recognition. If anything, the very presence of those masks calls attention to the presence of the individuals, objects, or ideas behind them. *Papillons*, Op. 2, and the *Davidsbündlertänze*, Op. 6, incorporate similarly veiled autobiographical elements as well.

In his writings, both private and public, Schumann reinforced the premise of music as an autobiographical art, and not only for himself. He accepted the autobiographical foundation of Berlioz's *Symphonie fantastique* and questioned only the extent to which that foundation should be made known to the public. Liszt's "own life," he observed in turn, "is in his music." [25] And in 1843 he wrote to his friend the composer and critic Carl Koßmaly:

> With some reticence I enclose here a packet of my older compositions.
> You will easily see what is immature and imperfect among them. They are
> mostly reflections of my turbulent earlier life; man and musician always
> sought to express themselves simultaneously in my case; it is still so even

now, even though I have certainly learned to better control myself and also my art. Your empathetic heart will discover how many joys and sorrows lie buried together in this little heap of notes.[26]

Schumann's comment about improved self-control is borne out by the nature of the music he wrote from the early 1840s onward. David Ferris has made a convincing case that the composer in effect withdrew his early, "private" piano works of the 1830s from public performance on the grounds that they were too personal and excessively subjective. Anthony Newcomb, in turn, has pointed to marketplace considerations as another reason for the change in the composer's style after 1840.[27] Whatever the cause, this stylistic shift was recognized during Schumann's lifetime: Franz Brendel, who had succeeded him as editor of the *Neue Zeitschrift für Musik*, observed in 1845 that his predecessor had "descended" from his earlier "lonely heights" to produce piano works that were less subjective.[28]

Critics of the time nevertheless continued to hear Schumann's later music as a revelation of his inner self, in part because this had become the standard mode of hearing all instrumental music with any claims to depth. Ernst Gottschald's wide-ranging essay of 1850 on the Second Symphony offers a case in point.[29] Couched in a series of letters to a friend and written under the pen name "Ernst von Elterlein," this account resonates with the tumultuous political events of the day, alluding repeatedly to the conflict between "liberal" and "conservative" forces. The sinuously interweaving lines of the first movement's slow introduction reflect Schumann's animus as one "still captive" to an "alienating sense of solitude," but the simultaneous rising fifth motif in the trumpets and horns project "*his* innermost soul, which endures steadfastly and unshakably" throughout the "trial by fire" that ensues. The foundational idea [*Grundidee*] of the work is the "*victory-crowned* struggle of a particular individuality"—Schumann's—"after its inwardmost amalgamation with a spiritual universality in which all egotistical boundaries are eliminated, boundaries which separated individual spirits from one another but which now love one another as equals, for they dwell in the realm of liberty, equality, and fraternity."[30] The work thus follows a trajectory similar to that of Beethoven's Fifth Symphony: the composer has " 'willed,' 'suffered,' and 'acted,'" and in the end triumphs. Gottschald thus proclaims Schumann Beethoven's heir in the realm of the symphony.[31]

Convincing or not, Gottschald's analysis rests on the underlying—that is, unstated—premise that it is Schumann's soul we are hearing in this music.

His account, moreover, presents the piece from the composer's perspective, describing it as if we were witnessing its coming into being. To understand the composer's motivations is to understand the finished product.

Schumann had in fact shared at least some of those motivations with his circle of friends and acquaintances, including perhaps Gottschald himself, who was a regular contributor to the *Neue Zeitschrift für Musik*. Schumann wrote to the composer and conductor Georg Dietrich Otten that he had written the symphony in December 1845 while "half ill; it seems to me that one would have to hear this" in the symphony: "Only in the finale did I begin to feel myself again. And in fact upon completing the entire work I felt better once more. But otherwise, as I have said, it reminds me of a dark time."[32] In his posthumous biography of the composer, his friend Joseph von Wasielewski quotes him as having confessed that the work had been sketched out "at a time when I was in great physical pain; indeed, I can well say that it was, so to speak, the resistance of spirit that clearly influenced it, and through which I sought to fight against my condition. The first movement is full of this struggle and is quite moodily restive."[33]

Critics propagated such sentiments with gusto. Ida Marie Lipsius (writing under the pen name "La Mara"), a prolific biographer of eighteenth- and nineteenth-century composers, said of Schumann that he "put a piece of himself into every one of his compositions. His music is therefore inextricable from his life, perhaps more so than the life and work of any other master."[34] Albert Tottmann drew a sharp distinction between Mendelssohn and Schumann on this very basis. Reverting to the earlier vocabulary of rhetoric, Tottmann compared Mendelssohn to "an orator in tones" whose "richly colored, rousing diction wins over the ear and the heart of all listeners at once." Schumann, by contrast, "wrote with his heart's blood. Like Beethoven, he too, with his introspective nature, wrote nothing that he had not already felt and experienced in his innermost soul." For this reason, Tottmann maintained, Schumann's music was less appealing to the broader musical public because it was less readily comprehensible.[35] Yet Mendelssohn's advantage was fleeting: nothing in his life conformed to what was perceived as the Beethovenian model of self-expression. His works largely resisted alignment with his life, and over time his reputation suffered accordingly.

Frédéric Chopin arrived on the musical scene around the same time as Schumann, which is to say, at a moment when listeners were starting to hear any serious instrumental composition as an outpouring of its creator's inner self. That Chopin performed so much of his own music in public helped reinforce this perception. Reviewing the recent publication of the *Tarantella*, Op. 43, an anonymous critic for the *Athenaeum* of London declared in 1842 that

> the man and his music are one. The former, frail as a shadow, pale, gentle, gracious in demeanour, and as unworldly in all his incomings and outgoings, as if he pursued his imaginative career in a wood rather than in that most worldly of cities, Paris,—offers one of the many examples furnished by contemporary annals of music, studied and wrought out poetically. . . . The extreme delicacy of M. Chopin's physical conformation, which makes his appearances in public very rare, and, comparatively speaking, ineffective, has also had its influences in determining the character of his works. It is at once to be perceived, that the latter have been written by one endowed with a man's strength, but a woman's *sensitiveness* of finger: and that, in their execution, force can be better dispensed with than flexibility. . . . But a certain fragility and delicacy, akin to those of form and feature, are discernible in M. Chopin's compositions. He seems incapable of continuous effort.[36]

"The extreme delicacy of M. Chopin's conformation": the formulation suggests an ideal against which Chopin is being compared, and a male ideal at that. Though Beethoven is not cited by name, few readers of the *Athenaeum* would likely have missed the drift of such an observation.

Chopin's pupil Wilhelm von Lenz, in turn, described his teacher's mazurkas as "the diary of his soul's journey through the sociopolitical territories of his Sarmatian dream world."[37] Lenz was but one of many nineteenth-century critics fixated on the composer's homeland. The critic James William Davison, writing in 1843—still during the composer's lifetime—noted that the mazurkas portray "in vivid colours the patriotism and home-feeling of the great Polish composer (we need hardly remind our readers that Poland boasts the honor of having given birth to Chopin), affording vent in passionate eloquence, to the beautiful and secret thoughts of his guileless heart."[38]

Recent scholarship has largely debunked the narrative of Chopin as a politically engaged artist who wrote music that reflected the aspirations of the exiled Polish community in Paris.[39] This narrative nevertheless flourished during his own time and long afterward. Franz Liszt, in his biography of Chopin, published three years after the latter's death, dwelled on the polonaises and mazurkas at the expense of more "cosmopolitan" genres such as the preludes, etudes, waltzes, scherzos, and sonatas. To understand

Chopin's music, Liszt maintained, one must understand Poland and the Polish people. In the end however, Chopin's soul could be heard at the core of all his works, regardless of genre:

> As the devout in prayer, so he poured out his soul in his compositions, expressing in them those passions of the heart, those unexpressed sorrows, to which the pious give vent in their communion with their Maker. What they never say except upon their knees, he said in his palpitating compositions, uttering in the language of tones those mysteries of passion and of grief which man has been permitted to understand without words, because there are no words adequate for their expression.[40]

A number of the Chopin's contemporaries heard his music as emanating from an even deeper source of his self, from the realm of dreams, which is to say, from sleep's fantasy.[41] Such assertions would have been unthinkable only a generation before. Dreams have always demanded interpretation, but only in Chopin's lifetime did compositions come to be regarded as dreams in their own right. The vocabulary of discourse on instrumental music was changing rapidly.

Form versus Content

The perception of Chopin's works as audible manifestations of his inner self was part of a broader effort to rescue instrumental music from the charge of formalism. This was a term that Liszt, Wagner, and their critical allies liked to preface with the word *empty*. Music that relied on form alone was by definition music that did not come from the depths of the compositional soul. Form was at best a means to an end and most certainly not an end in its own right. To Liszt's mind, the artist's true task was to "project the impressions of his inner being, to elevate and ennoble his interiority, to articulate and enrich it."[42] A. B. Marx, in his 1859 biography, declared that Beethoven, as an artist, "had no truck with abstractions devoid of life; his calling, like that of all artists, was to create life, life from his own life."[43]

The frequency and vehemence of such assertions created a backlash from such critics as Ludwig Bischoff (1794–1867) and Eduard Hanslick (1825–1904), who insisted that music was a self-contained art that could arouse emotions but did not in itself express them. No major composer of the time endorsed such views, however. In many respects, the two sides talked past each other: both hammered away at the idea of "expression" but applied the term in very different ways. The "conservatives" implicitly adhered to an earlier conception of expression as an objective construct without explicitly identifying it as such, whereas the "progressives" understood expression as a subjective outpouring of the compositional soul.[44] Hanslick conceded the inescapable influence of composers' inner selves on their works but in his typically legalistic fashion—he had been educated as a jurist—separated the act of artistic creation from that of aesthetic judgment:

> In a strictly aesthetic sense, we can say of any given theme that it *sounds* proud or sad; we cannot, however, say that it is an expression of the proud or sad feelings of the composer.[45]
>
> What the composer who is full of feeling and spirit brings forth, be it graceful or sublime, is first and foremost *music* (an objective construct). By principle, the *subjective* moment always remains subordinate, though it will always be present in various proportions to the objective element according to differences among individual composers. Compare those subjective natures who aim to give voice to their powerful or sentimental interiorities (Beethoven, Spohr) against those whose aims are directed toward the clear and formative (Mozart, Mendelssohn). The works of the former will differentiate themselves from one another by unmistakable peculiarities, and taken together they will reflect the individuality of their creators, yet each work like the other will bring forth purely musical autonomous beauty for its own sake. Only within the boundaries of this artistic construct is a work more or less subjectively endowed. To take this to its logical extreme: it is possible to imagine a music that is *pure music*, but not one that is *pure feeling*.
> . . .
> Thus, in the *composition* of a work of music we find an externalization of the distinctive, private affect only insofar as is possible within the boundaries of a predominantly objective, formative undertaking.[46]

Elsewhere in his treatise, Hanslick turns to the example of Beethoven to illustrate his point:

> An aesthetic evaluation knows nothing and should know nothing about the personal circumstances and the historical environment of a composer, but instead should hear and believe only that which is articulated in the work of

art itself. Such an evaluation will accordingly ascertain in *Beethoven's* symphonies, even without knowing the name and the biography of its creator, a sense of storming, struggle, unsatisfied longing, and a defiance that is conscious of its power. But that the composer had republican sympathies, was unmarried, deaf, and possessed all the other characteristics a historian of the art might consider illuminating: these can never be read out of these works or used to evaluate them.[47]

A generation later Edmund Gurney (1847–88) refuted the connection of composers' lives and works even more forcefully. "The fashion of imagining and overstraining connections between a man's music and his life," he argued, "is due to a tendency, amiable but in Music especially ill-advised, to make heroes of artists." Like Hanslick, Gurney downplayed the subjective element of composition and conceded nothing more than the possibility of a "dim affinity to the external course of emotional life," which he considered in any case peripheral to both the creation and perception of music in general.[48]

It was nevertheless composers who commanded the greatest public attention, particularly those who wrote prose as well as music, and of these, none marketed himself more effectively than Wagner.[49] His essays and treatises gave him a platform by which to assert the central importance of compositional necessity (*Notwendigkeit*): only that which was internally motivated—both in the process of artistic creation and within the product itself—could be of value. The fact that he wrote the words as well as the music to his own stage works allowed him to make the case for the inherently subjective nature of his creations. Of his opera *Der fliegende Holländer*, for example, he avowed that "my course was new; it was bidden me by my inner mood [*Stimmung*], and forced upon me by the pressing need to impart this mood to others."[50] Or, as he wrote to Mathilde Wesendonck in 1860: "Our kind [i.e., artists] look neither right nor left, forward or backward; we are indifferent to time and the world, and one thing alone rules us: the need to need to unburden ourselves of that which is inside of us."[51] "Necessity" is by its very nature sincere, and "the language of music," Wagner declared, is "the most primordial organ of expression for the inner human." Music's calling is to satisfy the "needs of the soul."[52]

One particularly characteristic feature of Wagner's criticisms is their advocacy of approaching any given work of music from its composer's perspective. Our capacity for understanding, he insisted, grows with empathy. In his 1857 essay on Franz Liszt's symphonic poems, for example, he urged listeners to trust composers and promised that this trust would be rewarded, for "if we love a great artist, we are saying we adopt and appropriate to ourselves, in effect, those individual peculiarities that made the artist's creative perspective possible."[53] Such an assertion may well seem quite unremarkable today, but the idea of putting faith in a composer, even one whose works might upon first hearing seem difficult to grasp, reflects a new way of listening to music, one that had established itself only during Wagner's lifetime.

Wagner's turn to Schopenhauer in the mid-1850s would cause him to reconfigure composers as transmitters of the primordial Will. In practice, however, this only enhanced their status as oracles whose pronouncements went beyond the projection of mere individuality by incorporating truths of universal value.[54] Friedrich von Hausegger's influential *Die Musik als Ausdruck*, which first appeared serially in the *Bayreuther Blätter* in 1884 and soon thereafter in book form, was one of many later publications that promulgated Wagner's Schopenhauerian views on the nature of musical expression. "The artist," Hausegger declared, "creates unconsciously, and all the surprising correspondences between his tonal object and those prevailing motions of the apparatuses of expression are not the product of observation, but rather the product of a direct urge toward expression that has awakened and grown within him."[55]

Later Composers

Composers who came of age in the second half of the nineteenth century for the most part considered it self-evident that their inner selves would be on public display in what they wrote. Assertions of subjectivity were commonplace. Speaking of his Fourth Symphony (1878), Pyotr Ilyich Tchaikovsky declared to a colleague that there was "not a single phrase" in it "which is not deeply felt, which is not the echo of some sincere emotion. The only exception is perhaps the middle of the first movement where there are tensions and joins and glueing together; in short, *artificiality*." Tchaikovsky's comments on his *Pathétique* Symphony profess an even greater degree of subjectivity.[56] Mahler repeatedly called attention to the subjective nature of his music, and while he avoided public pronouncements on this point, he had a good idea that others would make his views known to a wider audience.[57] According to Natalie Bauer-Lechner, Mahler declared in 1893 that

> my two symphonies [First and Second] exhaust the content of my entire life; what I have set down in them is experience and suffering, truth and poetry in music. And if one knew how to read well, my life would in fact

manifest itself transparently to that person. Creativity and experience are so intimately linked for me.[58]

The essence of Bauer-Lechner's report is confirmed at many points in Mahler's correspondence. As he wrote to the critic Arthur Seidl in 1897, "Only when I experience do I 'poeticize in tones'; yet only when I poeticize in tones do I experience!"[59] Alma Mahler's various accounts about the autobiographical nature of the Sixth Symphony went unquestioned until only recently, largely because it was assumed for so long that her husband's music was at its core self-disclosive.[60]

Edward Elgar (1857–1934), a near-contemporary of Mahler's, held much the same attitude about his works. His *Variations on an Original Theme* (better known as the *"Enigma" Variations*), like Schumann's *Carnaval*, are cued to acquaintances from his life. And of his Violin Concerto, his Second Symphony, and *The Music Makers*, Elgar confided to Alice Stuart-Wortley: "I have written out my soul in the concerto, Sym. II and the Ode and you know it . . . in these three works I have *shewn* myself."[61]

Arnold Schoenberg never tired of letting others know that his music was self-expressive. In his 1912 lecture on Mahler, he declared that "in reality, there is only one greatest goal towards which the artist strives: *to express himself*. If that succeeds, then the artist has achieved the greatest possible success; next to that, everything else is unimportant, for everything else is included in it."[62] Twenty-five years later Schoenberg was still proclaiming his belief in this idea: "I write what I feel in my heart, and what winds up on paper has first circulated through every fiber of my body."[63] Composition was for him a spontaneous process, one that could not be summoned up at will. The sincerity—the necessity—of creation could not be simulated:

> Expressive content wishes to make itself understood; its upheaval produces a form. A volcano erupts, the devastation makes an ornamental effect; a steam-kettle explodes, and the objects it strews around fall at points one could exactly calculate on the basis of relationships of tension, weights, distances, and resistances. One can, however, also lay the same objects out, so that they imitate an explosion's sense of order, and the temperament implied by the distances and weights. But there is a difference after all. . . . It makes some difference whether an ornament has as its author the explosion of a steam-kettle or the arranging hand of an interior decorator. . . . There is no point in arranging the indices of a volcanic eruption, for the expert will

see at a glance that nothing more than a spirit-burner has been raging. . . .
They [rogue artists] would do us and themselves more of a service if they
told a little truth about the sad state they get into whenever life is too much
for them."[64]

Béla Bartók, for his part, confessed in 1909 to Márta Ziegler (later his wife)
that "I did not believe this until I experienced for myself that one's work actually shows more exactly than a biography the noteworthy events and driving
passions of a life."[65]

Indeed, already by the end of the nineteenth century, the idea of music as
a form of autobiography had become so commonplace that Ludwig Speidel
(1830–1906), one of Vienna's leading music critics, could question Bedřich
Smetana's motivation for giving his String Quartet No. 1 (1876) the subtitle "From My Life": "A composer could actually write 'From My Life' above
each of his pieces of music, because from where should he otherwise take his
music, unless he steals it?" Speidel conceded that Smetana's case was slightly
different in that the finale of his quartet made reference to his deafness, "a fact
of history and autobiography."[66] Another Viennese critic, writing in 1893,
described the same quartet as "a history of the heart translated into notes."[67]

Not every composer encouraged such perceptions of their music.
Johannes Brahms, for one, actively went out of his way to discourage
listeners from hearing anything having to do with his private life in his
works. A protégé of Schumann, he had initially followed the lead of his
early mentor, incorporating biographical ciphers into his music even while
withholding public commentary on them.[68] But after an unhappy early experience with musico-political polemics, he withdrew behind a largely impenetrable façade and offered no clues to the biographical impulses behind
his music. Contemporary critics had to content themselves with generali-
ties or speculation: that Brahms's frequently elegiac tone was a by-product
of his personal inclination toward melancholy, or that he had written his
Deutsches Requiem (1868) in response to the death of his mother. Only after
the composer's death was the public able to learn of more specific possible
intersections between his life and works, above all through Max Kalbeck's
four-volume biography (1904–14).[69] A close friend of the composer, Kalbeck
transmitted numerous anecdotes from private correspondence and personal
reminiscences. The public could now learn that the opening of the Piano
Concerto in D Minor, Op. 15, was inspired (at least according to Kalbeck)
by the news that Schumann had attempted to drown himself in the Rhine,

and that the String Sextet in G Major, Op. 36, reflected his having "cut himself loose" from Agathe von Siebold, his "last love."[70] In this respect, Kalbeck created a more "Beethovenian" Brahms, at least posthumously, one whose works reflected his life and inner self.

Women composers of the nineteenth and early twentieth centuries occupy an exceptional place of their own in the history of perceptions of self-expression. Critics rarely viewed them as individuals, instead essentializing them as exemplars of half the world's population. Until well into the twentieth century, commentators felt obligated to weigh in on the relative "virility" or "femininity" of any new work composed by a woman, particularly if it was a large-scale instrumental genre such as a symphony or concerto. The idea that she might have an identity, experiences, or emotions beyond the category of "the feminine" seems to have been beyond the reach of most observers, even in their commentary on works they admired. Critical responses to new music by such composers as Augusta Holmès (1847–1903), Ethel Smyth (1858–1944), and Cécile Chaminade (1857–1944) are typical in this regard. A number of reviewers who praised Holmès's *Ode triomphale*, written for the Paris Exhibition of 1889 to celebrate the centenary of the French Revolution, extolled the work's "virility," without any apparent awareness of irony.[71] Along similar lines, one American reviewer of Ethel Smyth's *Der Wald* (the first opera by a woman to be performed at the Metropolitan Opera, in 1903) declared that "not as the music of a woman should Miss Smyth's score be judged. She thinks in a masculine style, broad and virile." The same reviewer then proceeded to ignore his own dictum by comparing Smyth's orchestration to that of Holmès and Chaminade; in her generous use of brass instruments in particular, he observed, "the gifted Englishwoman has successfully emancipated herself from her sex."[72]

But too much virility could create problems of its own. In an otherwise glowing 1890 review of Chaminade's *Concertstück*, Op. 40, Louis de Romain declared that

> we are in the presence of a work written with undisputable authority, of a work that is strong and virile, indeed too virile, and that is this fault I would be tempted to address here. For my part, I almost regretted not having found more of those qualities of grace and tenderness that reside in the nature of women, qualities whose secrets they possess so well.[73]

Such responses are products of an era that assumed an audible relationship between a composer's life and works, with the important difference that in the case of women composers critics stopped short of perceiving the kind of individuality accorded their male counterparts. This helped perpetuate a vicious critical circle: if a work composed by a woman was deemed "too masculine," it could not possibly be sincere, for it meant that the composer was not being true to her own self. Music judged as "too feminine," on the other hand, revealed its creator's inability to transcend a decidedly one-dimensional subjectivity. Only in the last fifty years or so has this situation begun to change.[74]

Retrospective Subjectivity

The paradigmatic shift in the perception of musical expression that occurred around 1830 changed the ways in which listeners heard at least some music of the more distant past as well. Beethoven, it was agreed, had been the first composer to write in a consistently self-expressive manner; and many critics had no difficulty applying the aesthetics of self-expression to the music of still earlier generations, especially in the case of passages, movements, or entire works that were somehow puzzling or anomalous within a composer's output. In the case of Haydn, one movement in particular demanded—and received—biographical interpretation: the finale of the "Farewell" Symphony of 1772 (No. 45, in F♯ Minor), which features a gradual departure of the musicians, leaving only two solo violinists at the very end. This highly unusual movement spawned a variety of explanations that differed in their particulars but agreed on one central point: that the pantomime of the shrinking orchestra was intended to send a message of some kind to Haydn's master, Prince Nicolaus Esterházy.[75] The actual events leading up to the "Farewell" Symphony are less important for the present purposes than the disproportionate amount of critical attention given to this one movement out of the more than one hundred symphonies Haydn had penned. Nicolas-Étienne Framery, in a brief biography published the year after Haydn's death, devoted no fewer than seven out of forty-seven pages—some 15 percent of his book—to this one work. By his account, a depressed Prince Nicolaus has quarreled with Haydn, and the finale plays out the consequences of the resignation Haydn had just submitted.[76] Good stories get works talked about.

The nineteenth century's fundamental belief in the inherently autobiographical nature of music manifests itself graphically in connection with another exceptionally unusual moment in Haydn's output shortly after the beginning of his oratorio *Die Schöpfung* (The Creation, 1797–98). Originally entitled "Haydn se rendant en Angleterre" (Haydn Arrives in England, Figure 6.1), this 1872 painting (now apparently lost) by the Belgian historical painter Edouard Jean Conrad Hamman (1819–88) was at some point rechristened "Haydn Composing his 'Creation.'" The image shows the composer on his way to London on in late December of1790, seated resolutely on the open deck of a ship in the middle of a raging storm in the English Channel. The deck pitches at a precarious angle as a deck hand hurries to adjust the rigging; one of the women recoils in horror while another scurries for shelter below. Haydn alone is upright and calm, his mind clearly elsewhere, his gaze fixed on the bolt of lightning striking not so terribly far away. The import of the lithograph's new title would have made sense to anyone familiar with Haydn's oratorio. A storm at sea was the locus classicus of the sublime

HAYDN COMPOSING HIS "CREATION."

Figure 6.1 Edouard Jean Conrad Hamman, *Haydn Composing His "Creation"*
Originally titled *Haydn se rendant en Angleterre*, this 1872 image by the Belgian painter Edouard Jean Conrad Hamman (1819–88), depicts the documented storm the composer experienced at sea on his way to England on 31 December 1790. A later, unknown publisher gave it the title of *Haydn Composing His "Creation,"* a work the composer would in fact not begin writing until seven years later. The new title links the sublimity of a storm at sea—the classic manifestation of the sublime in nature—with the moment of creation ("And there was Light") as depicted in Haydn's oratorio, a moment that would become the quintessential exemplar of the sublime in music. Such an extraordinary achievement, the caption suggests, could have only originated in the composer's personal experience.

in nature—both terrifying and awe-inspiring—and the opening of Haydn's *Schöpfung* had long since become the supreme example of the sublime in music. At the moment when the chorus intones the final word of "Und es ward Licht" (And there was light; Gen. 1:3), the orchestra, its forces reduced up till now, explodes in an instant to its full capacity, trumpets blaring, drums pounding. The sound erupts as suddenly as a lightning bolt. The clear implication of the image and its new title is that this celebrated moment in Haydn's music can be traced back to a specific moment in his life seven years before. Haydn had in fact described this journey and the storm at sea in a letter written shortly after his arrival in England on New Year's Day 1791.[77] Once again biography steps in to explain the anomalous: only someone who had experienced the sublime in nature could represent it so powerfully in art. And by the logic of the image's new title, experience and creativity cannot be separated: Haydn is composing even as he experiences.

Nineteenth- and early twentieth-century critics were inclined to regard Mozart's music largely as impersonal, beautiful in its own way but not revealing of its composer's self. Biographies consistently reinforced the image of Mozart as "otherworldly," his works correspondingly suprahuman. Otto Jahn, for example, in his magisterial biography of the composer, observed that the more perfect the artwork, the more difficult it becomes to trace its origins: in the end, such music could be "understood and enjoyed only as a finished product."[78] Tchaikovsky, in turn, considered Mozart's music a refuge from the turmoils of life, "an expression of life's joys as experienced by a healthy, wholesome nature, *not corrupted by introspection.*"[79] And Ferruccio Busoni could declare that "with Beethoven, the human becomes for the first time the central argument of music," whereas Mozart, by contrast, was "divine" (*göttlich*).[80]

Certain anomalous works, invariably in the minor mode, nevertheless demanded—and received—biographical explanation. The case of the Requiem, widely regarded as having been shaped by the composer's sense of his own imminent death, has already been noted (see p. 118). Friedrich Rochlitz claimed in 1799 that Constanze had told him that the String Quartet in D Minor, K. 421, the only minor-mode work of the six quartets dedicated to Haydn, had been written when she was in labor with the couple's first child, in 1783, and that her husband had shuttled between her and his writing desk, comforting her in her pain but returning at frequent intervals to his work. The birth itself, she testified, had occurred when her husband was occupied with the middle of the minuet movement. The point of the anecdote, it would seem, was to illustrate the composer's intense powers of creative concentration. By the time Mary and Vincent Novello visited the twice-widowed Constanze in Salzburg some thirty years after Rochlitz's report, the entire scenario had become audible in the music: Constanze now maintained that "the agitation he suffered and her cries are to be traced in several passages" in the quartet.[81] The Novellos' account would remain essentially unknown until its publication in the middle of the twentieth century, but the English critic Edward Holmes, one of Vincent Novello's professional associates, conveyed its essence in his 1845 biography of Mozart, asserting that "the various and profound feelings displayed in that magnificent work afford internal evidence of the truth of these domestic circumstances, and show the agitated state of mind in which it was produced."[82] As told in the middle of the nineteenth century, then, the story demonstrated the autobiographical, self-expressive nature of Mozart's music, or at least of this particular work. And like most good anecdotes, it is a story that would prove irresistible to subsequent commentators. Even Wolfgang Hildesheimer, in his decidedly sober 1977 biography of the composer, felt obligated to speculate that "the sudden *forte* of the two octave leaps and the following minor tenth (bars 31–32 of the Andante)" reflected the pains of childbirth, for "these are figures that otherwise do not occur in Mozart."[83]

Ever since the middle of the nineteenth century, Mozart's biographers have tended to treat minor-mode works or movements as somehow more revealing of the composer's true self than those written in the far more common major mode. In need of evidence that the "divine" Mozart could become as "disturbed and agitated as much [as] if not more" than any other mortal, Alexandre Oulibicheff pointed without hesitation to the first, third, and fourth movements of the Symphony in G Minor, K. 550, particularly the finale, and all three in the minor mode.[84] Even Jahn agreed with the conventional wisdom of his day that the compositions in minor were "deeper" and "more meaningful."[85] Ludwig Nohl, in his widely read 1863 biography, insisted that Mozart's works were "generally independent of his state of mind," yet repeatedly treated those in the minor mode as exceptions to this rule. He wondered what might have precipitated the "deep conflict" that found its expression in the Fantasy in C Minor, K. 457, and he declared that the Quintet in G Minor, K. 516, "betrays something of the deep emotions" of Mozart's "heart" at the time of its composition, in spite of its having been written almost simultaneously with the Quintet in C Major, K. 515.[86] Nohl further confessed that he had not been able to understand the unusual nature of the A-Minor Piano Sonata, K. 310 (300d), especially its finale, until he learned that Mozart had composed it toward the end of his time in Paris in 1778. The work's turmoil, its "wrestling with itself," he realized, mirrored the composer's "struggles between duty and inclination," and "nothing can give us more certain evidence to the state of his soul" at the time "than this sonata." The belief that minor-mode works and movements provided isolated glimpses into the composer's true emotions conformed to the Beethovenian dynamic of suffering as a source of inspiration. In this respect, his nineteenth-century biographers were giving Mozart what Karen Painter has aptly called a "Beethovenian Afterlife."[87]

That afterlife has continued down to the present, even if scholars have become considerably more cautious in speculating about the connections between composers' lives and works. Commentators have been able to hedge their bets in various ways. Two of the most common are to cite the assertions of others without confronting them directly, or to leave open the plausibility of direct connections in isolated instances. Julian Rushton combines both tactics in his observations on Mozart's Piano Sonata in A Minor, K. 310, the same work that had so perplexed Nohl. This sonata, Rushton observes,

> has been associated with the pain and turbulence of the period of his mother's illness and death but may have been written earlier, affected by a turmoil of feelings connected with Aloysia [Weber] or his severance from the guiding hand of Leopold. Or he may have written it because he felt like writing that kind of piece. Not every joy and pain perceived in Mozart's music can possibly originate from events; he was an artist, not an autobiographer.[88]

Rushton's "not every joy" suggests that some joys and pains *do* in fact reflect compositional subjectivity.

Johann Sebastian Bach would prove particularly difficult for later critics intent on hearing a personal self in his instrumental music. That his profound sense of faith was on clear display in his sacred vocal music was beyond dispute. But what about the substantial body of instrumental music? Aside from the *Capriccio sopra la lontananza del suo fratello dilettissimo*, BWV 992, critics have struggled to hear personal subjectivity in these works. Professional motivations are clear enough: Bach wrote the majority of his organ music while employed as an organist, orchestral works in an effort to find employment as a court musician, and so on. Beyond this, however, evidence of his self in such works remained elusive, and over the course of the nineteenth century Bach's instrumental music gradually came to be seen as the cornerstone for the tradition of "pure" music—what would later come to be called "absolute" music—which is to say, a play of forms "without content," as Hans-Georg Nägeli put it in 1826, or as "forms set in motion through musical tones," as Eduard Hanslick would later argue in his *Vom Musikalisch-Schönen* (1854).[89]

Two Categories of Music

The framework of hermeneutics that began to take hold in the second third of the nineteenth century helped nurture a new categorical distinction between music that warranted interpretation and music that did not. These categories have persisted down to the present and correspond more or less to what we now think of as "art" (or "classical") music, on the one hand, and "popular" music, on the other. The difference between the two lies partly in issues of style but just as importantly in modes of perception, and specifically the presumed presence or absence of depth in a given work. It was not until the 1810s and '20s that critics began to talk about depth in instrumental music to any significant degree (see p. 113), and for this reason it was only around 1830 that we begin see the first signs of a conceptual divide between what would come to be known in German as "serious music" (*ernste Musik*, also known as "E-Musik") and "entertainment music" (*Unterhaltungsmusik*, "U-Musik").[90]

It was thus that listeners attended to more demanding musical genres within the framework of hermeneutics. In the realm of instrumental music, this meant symphonies, sonatas, and various forms of chamber music, particularly the string quartet. An entire publishing industry grew up in the nineteenth century to assist music lovers in their efforts to understand these repertoires, beginning in the 1820s and '30s with the appearance of a number of major new music journals aimed at the general public, most notably *The Harmonicon* (established 1823), the *Berliner Allgemeine musikalische Zeitung* (1824), *Cäcilia* (1824), the *Revue musicale* (1827), *Le Ménestrel* (1833), the *Gazette musicale de Paris* (1834, merging with the *Revue musicale* in 1835 to form the *Revue et gazette musicale de Paris*), the *Neue Zeitschrift für Musik* (1834), and *The Musical World* (1836). Program notes distributed at concerts became increasingly common; these, too, oriented concertgoers to the works they were about to hear.[91] Audience behavior changed, too: listeners grew silent and still, comporting themselves as if in a sacred service. According to the best available documentation, this began around 1830.[92] Later decades saw a growing number of musical "guide books," analogues of publications aimed at tourists visiting new sites.[93] Hermann Kretzschmar's enormously successful "Guide through the Concert Hall" (1887–90), updated in dozens of new editions well into the twentieth century, spawned numerous imitators. Kretzschmar would in fact appear to have been the first writer to use the term "hermeneutics" specifically in connection with music.[94] Hans von Wolzogen's guides to the leitmotifs of Wagner's music dramas also proved enormously popular and helped listeners focus on the carefully interwoven melodic (and largely instrumental) elements of those works.[95]

At the other end of the spectrum, listeners approached "entertainment" music within the older framework of rhetoric, exerting little if any effort to come to terms with what they were hearing. They relied instead on composers and performers to move them. In earlier times, this mindset had prevailed for all music. Kretzschmar and his followers accordingly ignored waltzes and quadrilles by Josef Lanner and by members of the Strauss family, in spite of their immense popularity. The notion of "understanding" such music was simply foreign, and no author or publisher of the time seems to have sensed anything resembling a commercial market for commentary that addressed this sort of repertoire: to their minds, there was little or nothing to be understood, even if there was much to be enjoyed.

Hierarchical distinctions between "higher" and "lower" genres of music were not altogether new. In his *Allgemeine Theorie der schönen Künste* of 1771–74, for example, Johann Georg Sulzer set the symphony above all other instrumental genres, likening recent ones to Pindaric odes on the grounds of their sublimity. Philipp Gäng's treatise on the fine arts, published in Salzburg in 1785, also acknowledged gradations of gravity, noting that "a witty, humorous poem, a small, trifling piece of music, etc., can please us greatly without our being aware of a particular inclination in the work or an affect on our souls; these are beauties that are merely pleasing." Koch, in his musical dictionary of 1802, similarly noted that as a genre, divertimentos "have for the most part no definite character but are merely paintings in tones that aspire to delight the ear, as opposed to expressing a particular sentiment with its various modifications."[96]

But such comments fall well short of the categorical distinction between two entirely different kinds of music that would emerge a generation later.

This new attitude manifests itself openly in the very first sentence of Gustav Schilling's 1844 biography of Franz Liszt:

> The idea of music as an art of the soul has long enjoyed the widest general belief and no longer encounters the slightest contradiction. As a result, fortunately, every play of tones for the sake of mere pleasure and entertainment has fallen into the concept of everyday music making.[97]

"Everyday music making" points to a category distinguishable from—and inferior to—music as "an art of the soul." The only real question still open to debate, Schilling maintained, is the depth and nature of a given work of music's meaning or significance (*Bedeutung*). Music—or "real music," Schilling might as well have said—was no longer an art of mere pleasure.

PART THREE
DUAL PARADIGMS: SINCE 1920

In the years during and immediately after World War I, a number of leading composers and critics began to reject the aesthetics of self-expression. The New Objectivity (*Neue Sachlichkeit*), as it came to be called, marked a return to the concept of expression as a construct, and objectivity became a cornerstone of the high modernism that dominated musical aesthetics throughout the middle decades of the twentieth century. Composers and listeners alike no longer consistently equated expression with self-expression, especially in works that aspired to depth and seriousness. The idea of music as a revelation of the compositional self was nevertheless too deeply ingrained in musical culture to disappear altogether, and a belief in the aesthetics of subjectivity has continued to manifest itself in a variety of ways down to the present.

To complicate matters further, concert-hall audiences have continued to listen within a hermeneutic framework, regardless of whether they hear expression as a subjective or objective construct. They listen, in other words, from the perspective of the composer, and they accept responsibility for understanding the work at hand. In the realm of popular music, by contrast, the framework of rhetoric persists. We find ourselves today in an era of dual expressive paradigms and dual frameworks of production and reception.

7
The Return of Objectivity

The return to a paradigm of expressive objectivity began in the literary arts, not music. And more than any other group of writers, it was the symbolist poets who helped overturn prevailing assumptions about the nature of expression. Stéphane Mallarmé, Paul Verlaine, Arthur Rimbaud, and other like-minded poets viewed their art primarily not as an unburdening of the self but as a linguistic construct. This return to a paradigm of expressive objectivity did not, however, entail a simultaneous return to the framework of rhetoric. Quite the contrary: the opaque and often mystical nature of symbolist poetry compelled readers to apply themselves more diligently than ever before to come to terms with such enigmatic texts.

Form was the new locus of expression. Reversing Wordsworth's dictum from the beginning of the century, Oscar Wilde declared in 1890 that "all bad poetry springs from genuine feeling." The "real artist," he maintained, is the one who "proceeds, not from feeling to form, but from form to thought and passion":

> He does not first conceive an idea, and then say to himself, "I will put my idea into a complex metre of fourteen lines," but, realising the beauty of the sonnet-scheme, he conceives certain modes of music and methods of rhyme, and the mere form suggests what is to fill it and make it intellectually and emotionally complete. From time to time the world cries out against some charming artistic poet, because, to use its hackneyed and silly phrase, he has "nothing to say." But if he had something to say, he would probably say it, and the result would be tedious. It is just because he has no new message, that he can do beautiful work. He gains his inspiration from form, and from form purely, as an artist should. A real passion would ruin him. Whatever actually occurs is spoiled for art. All bad poetry springs from genuine feeling. To be natural is to be obvious, and to be obvious is to be inartistic.[1]

T. S. Eliot endorsed a similar aesthetic of personal distance. For him, "the progress of an artist is a continual self-sacrifice, a continual extinction of personality. . . . The more perfect the artist, the more completely separate in him will be the man who suffers and the mind which creates." Poetry "is not the expression of personality but an escape from personality."[2] Russian formalists of the 1910s and '20s, along with the Anglo-American school of "New Criticism" of the 1930s, similarly rejected the biographical interpretations of literary texts that had for so long dominated the field.[3]

The Spanish philosopher José Ortega y Gasset (1883–1955), one of the most articulate advocates of aesthetic detachment in the interwar years, used music to illustrate his case for a "new sensibility" in all the arts. "From Beethoven to Wagner," he complained in 1925, music had amounted to an art of "confession," with each composer creating "great structures of sound to accommodate his autobiography." Our aesthetic pleasure from such works, he maintained, was the equivalent of a "contagion," an "unconscious phenomenon" that made art "blind," inhospitable to intellectual engagement on the part of listeners. Ortega y Gassett hailed Debussy as the first composer to "relieve" music of "private sentiments," to "dehumanize" it by producing works that now made it "possible to listen . . . serenely, without swoons and tears."[4]

Composers and musicians themselves had already started making similar appeals around this time. In a 1920 manifesto entitled "Junge Klassizität" (Young Classicism), Busoni (1866–1924) called for a renewal of earlier values through a "renunciation of subjectivity." He called for a musical style that would include a

> casting off of the "*sensuous*" and the *renunciation of subjectivity* (the path to objectivity—the author stepping back from his work—a purifying path, a hard road, a trial by fire and water), the reconquest of cheerfulness (*Serenitas*): not the corners of Beethoven's mouth, and also not the "liberating laughter" of Zarathustra, but the smile of the wise, of the godhead and—*absolute* music. Not profundity and disposition and metaphysics; but rather : music through and through, distilled, never under the mask of figures and concepts borrowed from other realms.[5]

Objectivity became all the rage in the in the interwar years. Edgard Varèse announced in 1925 that music (including his own) can "express nothing but itself."[6] The collaborations of Bertolt Brecht and Kurt Weill—most notably in *Die Dreigroschenoper* (1928) and *Aufstieg und Fall der Stadt Mahagonny* (1930)—produced stage works that openly called attention to their artificiality. In 1928 the composer and critic Heinz Tiessen (1887–1971) proposed a distinction between "I-Music" and "It-Music" (*Ich-Musik* and *Es-Musik*), the former centered on personal expression, the latter on the "unfolding of the musical substance from within itself."[7] The terminology never caught on, but it captured a distinction which by that point had been firmly established. Five years later Aaron Copland praised the Mexican composer Carlos Chávez (1899–1978) for his "gift for the expression of objective beauty of universal significance rather than as a mere means of self-expression." Copland called Chávez's music modernist not on the basis of its style but on the basis of its objectivity, which "exemplifies the complete overthrow of nineteenth-century Germanic ideals which tyrannized . . . music for more than a hundred years."[8]

No composer of the time promoted the idea of objective expression more zealously than Igor Stravinsky. He opened a 1924 essay on his recently completed Octet with a series of clipped, declarative statements:

> My Octuor is a musical object.
>
> This object has a form and that form is influenced by the musical matter with which it is composed.
>
> The differences of matter determine the differences of form. One does not do the same with marble that one does with stone. . . .
>
> My Octuor is not an "emotive" work but a musical composition based on objective elements which are sufficient in themselves. . . .
>
> My Octuor, as I said before, is an object that has its own form. Like all other objects it has weight and occupies a place in space, and like all other objects it will necessarily lose part of its weight and space in time and through time. The loss will be in quantity, but it can not lose in quality as long as its emotive basis has objective properties and as long as this object keeps its "specific weight." One cannot alter the specific weight of an object without destroying the object itself.[9]

The matter-of-fact tone and quasi-scientific terminology ("objective elements," "specific weight") epitomize a self-conscious sense of emotional detachment. The composer and educator Nadia Boulanger (1887–1979), Stravinsky's close associate at the time, had adopted a similar rhetoric in her review of an early performance of the Octet in Paris in 1923. "In this work," she observed, "Stravinsky reveals himself as a constructivist, a geometer. . . . No transpositions, everything is music, purely."[10] Stravinsky would elaborate on these basic ideas in his autobiography of 1935:

> For I consider that music is, by its very nature, essentially powerless to *express* anything at all, whether a feeling, an attitude of mind, a psychological mood, a phenomenon of nature, etc. . . . *Expression* has never been an inherent property of music. That is by no means the purpose of its existence. If, as is nearly always the case, music appears to express something, this is only an illusion and not a reality. It is simply an additional attribute which, by tacit and inveterate agreement, we have lent it, thrust upon it, as a label, a convention—in short, an aspect which, unconsciously or by force of habit, we have often come to confuse with its essential being.[11]

The cause of objectivity would be taken up with even greater intensity in the years after World War II. Paul Hindemith (1894–1963), who had been a driving force of the New Objectivity aesthetic in the 1920s, would remind his fellow composers in 1952 that if they thought they were projecting their personal emotions through their works, they were deluding themselves:

> If the composer himself thinks he is expressing his own feelings, we have to accuse him of a lack of observation. Here is what he really does: he knows by experience that certain patterns of tone-setting correspond with certain emotional reactions on the listener's part. Writing these patterns frequently and finding his observations confirmed, in anticipating the listener's reaction he believes himself to be in the same mental situation. From here it is a very small step to the further conviction that he himself is not only reproducing the feelings of other individuals, but is actually having these same feelings . . . He believes that he feels what he believes the listener feels; he tries to construct musically the ultimate ring of this strange chain of thought—and consequently he does not express his own feelings in his music.[12]

The parallels to Sulzer's notion of "transporting" or "transposing" one's self in the compositional process are striking indeed. Leading composers and critics of the twentieth century no longer equated expression with self-expression, and they looked on the latter as an older, outmoded way of doing business.

The Composer as Chameleon

Composers' repeated avowals of expressive objectivity led listeners and critics to rethink the relationship between composers and their works. By its very nature, objectivity called into question the premise of aesthetic sincerity that had shaped musical listening for almost a century and the arts in general for even longer. It was the rare nineteenth-century poet who openly acknowledged the discrepancies between public perceptions of creativity and its reality: Edgar Allen Poe, as noted earlier (p. 104), was among the few who had insisted on a distinction between spontaneous and assumed emotions. John Keats, who professed sincerity in public, acknowledged in private the necessarily malleable nature of the poetic self, and in one particularly vivid image he compared poets to chameleons:

> As to the poetical Character itself . . . it is not itself—it has no self—it is everything and nothing—It has no character—it enjoys light and shade; it lives in gusto, be it foul or fair, high or low, rich or poor, mean or elevated. It has as much delight in conceiving an Iago as an Imogen. What shocks the virtuous philosopher, delights the camelion Poet. It does no harm from its relish of the dark side of things any more than from its taste for the bright one; because they both end in speculation. A Poet is the most unpoetical of anything in existence because he has no Identity; he is continually in for and filling some other Body.[13]

Keats's portrayal of the artist as chameleon extols the ability of the individual genius-artist to transcend personal inclinations and convey the entire spectrum of human experience. By this line of thought, the lack of a fixed identity gives the artist a decided advantage.[14]

When this image finally entered musical discourse in the 1920s, it was directed primarily at Stravinsky, and rarely in a positive sense. A chameleon, after all, adapts itself to its surroundings and has no "true" color, which is to say, no true identity. The strongly nationalistic Alfred Heuß, editor of the *Zeitschrift für Musik*, writing in 1928, called Stravinsky not simply a chameleon, but an "international chameleon," a composer who lacked not only a personal identity but a national one as well. Olivier Messiaen applied the image rather more neutrally in 1939, calling him a "chameleon-musician, the man of a thousand and one styles," even while emphasizing the element of rhythm as a unifying feature of Stravinsky's output, a trajectory outlined "from his first work to his most recent."[15] The composer's advocates would follow Messiaen's lead and come to his defense by granting the charge up to a point but finding some sort of true identity underneath the surface after all. As the critic Donal J. Henahan noted in 1967, "For decades, scholars have ticked off the multiform styles that our foremost composer has picked up and used, but with noticeable anxiety they have gone on to exonerate him of shallowness and fashion-chasing, pointing out that no matter what color the chameleon wears, the 'real' Igor can be discerned underneath the stylistic skin." Along these same lines, the conductor Alan Gilbert observed more recently in program notes for a concert with the New York Philharmonic that "Stravinsky was a chameleon: he wrote in many different styles, and was absolutely convincing in all of them, but still maintained in all his works the 'Stravinsky voice.'"[16]

Adorno never actually used the term "chameleon" in his comments on Stravinsky, but it seems to lie just below the surface of almost everything he wrote about him. Adorno was particularly critical of the lack of "expressive fluctuation" in his music, with its static harmonies, "impersonal" tone, and lack of "compositional spontaneity." "The subject that in music is prohibited from speaking of itself actually ceases to 'produce' and contents itself with the empty echo of an objective musical language that is no longer its own."[17] For all his modernist credentials, Adorno was very much a traditionalist in matters of musical expression.

What lies behind each of these assertions is the premise that composers possess—or *should* possess, even if only far below the surface—a "true" voice, one that transcends style and is stable, recognizable, and by implication genuine.[18] The *absence* of a "true" voice, after all, suggests dissemblance, deceit. The legacy of sincerity persists in spite of claims to the contrary. It has simply come to manifest itself in ways that are more subtle.

The assumption that every composer possesses a "true" voice in any case runs counter to the older tradition of compositional objectivity. Mozart, by all available evidence, took every bit as detached an approach to his art as Stravinsky. Contemplating an extended visit to Paris in 1778, he dismissed any doubts that he could adapt his music to the prevailing tastes there. "One thing is certain," as he wrote to his father from Mannheim, "I wouldn't be anxious at all, for as you know, I can assimilate and imitate pretty much kind or style of composition."[19] And when a Viennese critic in 1817 called Beethoven "our Proteus," the appellation was given with pride and respect.[20] The Protean artist, able to overcome self-inclinations at will, was considered

superior to those ruled by their innate proclivities. "To be truly free and educated," as Friedrich Schlegel had noted in 1797,

> an individual would have to be able to tune himself at will at any time phil-
> osophically or philologically, critically or poetically, historically or rhetori-
> cally, à-l'antique or à la moderne, in an entirely arbitrary fashion and to any
> degree, in the way one tunes an instrument.[21]

In this sense, creative mutability was long perceived as a manifestation of
personal command over one's own self. This outlook is certainly consistent
with Beethoven's attraction to Eastern philosophy and its emphasis on an
overcoming of the self and its desires. Schlegel's observation also resonates
with the opening recitative of the Ninth Symphony's finale, a text written not
by Schiller and possibly by Beethoven himself: "O Freunde, nicht diese Töne!
Sondern lasst uns angenehmere anstimmen" ("Oh friends, not these tones!
Let us instead tune ourselves more agreeably") The trope of "tuning" oneself
in a desired fashion extended to the very act of artistic creativity. Beethoven
himself put this ability on display on more than one occasion, as for example
in his dual settings of the same text (Metastasio's "L'amante impaziente") in
two radically different ways (Op. 82, Nos. 3 and 4), or by providing a new
finale to the String Quartet in B♭ Major, Op. 130, a movement that stands in
utter contrast to the work's original finale, later published separately as the
Große Fugue, Op. 133.

The prestige of stylistic mutability went largely underground after
Beethoven's death, however, and did not resurface until the last quarter of
the twentieth century in the idea of the compositional "persona," articulated
most influentially, as noted earlier, by Edward T. Cone in The Composer's
Voice (1974). Though he did not evoke the image of the chameleon explicitly,
Cone made a strong case that composers did not express their inner selves
but instead assumed a temporary identity outside their own. This notion
of an artistic "persona" has a long background in literature, and Cone duly
acknowledged his debt to Wayne C. Booth, who in his Rhetoric of Fiction
had documented that tradition in rich detail.[22] Cone extended this notion to music, maintaining, for example, that the "artist" in the Symphonie
fantastique is not Berlioz himself but rather "a persona," a "figure identifiable
as Berlioz but not identical with Berlioz. . . . The persona's experiences are
not the composer's experiences but an imaginative transformation of them;
the reactions, emotions, and states of mind suggested by the music are those

of the persona, not the composer."[23] This is strikingly consistent with the Enlightenment ideals of expressive objectivity.

While Cone's thesis may well have been applicable to (and endorsed by) a large majority of his mid-twentieth-century colleagues, it does not correspond to the ways in which most nineteenth- and early twentieth-century composers portrayed themselves, nor does it reflect the ways in which listeners heard their music. As a composer himself, Cone (1917–2004) was a modernist, and, typically for his time, he struggled with such figures as Berlioz and Richard Strauss who wrote music that was openly or semi-openly confessional. Indeed, Cone implicitly applauded the "greater detachment of the composer from his subject" in Berlioz's move from the "I" of the *Symphonie fantastique* to the "he" of *Harold en Italie* (1832) and beyond that to the wholly third person of *Roméo et Juliette* (1840). Richard Strauss, in turn, came up short in Cone's estimation, for he "seems to have grasped [the] principle" of the persona "imperfectly, if at all," in such works as the *Sinfonia domestica* and *Ein Heldenleben*.[24]

The Composer as Medium

Another way for twentieth-century composers to distance themselves from the idea of self-expression was to claim that they were not themselves the source of higher truths but rather merely the vessel for their transmission. This outlook, implicit already in ancient notions of divine inspiration and in later perceptions of the composer as oracle, gained new prestige in the nineteenth century through the philosophy of Schopenhauer, who considered music not simply as a representation of the Will, the most elemental force of all human life, but a projection of the Will itself, with no meaningful distinction between the individual and universal. For him, "the universal imageless language of the heart" is conveyed by the "holy, mysterious, inner speech of tones."[25] Music is the most immediate manifestation of the universal self, the composer its medium. "The composer reveals the innermost essence of the world and proclaims the deepest truth in a language that his reason does not understand, in the way a magnetic somnambulist informs us about things of which she herself has no idea when she is awake. In the case of the composer, therefore, more than any other artist," he declared, "the man and the artist are entirely separate and distinct."[26].

Popularized by Wagner, such Schopenhauerian pronouncements resonate with multiple assertions by Mahler, who considered himself a mouthpiece of the universe even while emphasizing the deeply personal nature of his symphonies (see p. 157). This dynamic constituted a burden, for he considered his art a sacrifice for the good of all humanity. Speaking of the first movement of his Third Symphony, he told Natalie Bauer-Lechner in 1896:

> Genuine horror grips me when I see where it is leading, which path is earmarked for this music, and that it has fallen to me to be the bearer of this gigantic work. Today it came to me in a flash, in the way one's own experience sometimes illuminates and reveals something one has known for a long time: Christ on the Mount of Olives, compelled to drain the cup of sorrows to the dregs—and who wanted it to be this way. Whoever is destined for this cup cannot and will not refuse it yet at times must be overcome by a deathly fear when he thinks about what still stands in front of him. I have the same feeling in thinking about this movement and in anticipation of what I will have to suffer for it, and of not being able to experience that it will be recognized and acknoweldged.[27]

Nietzsche, for his part, ridiculed the idea of the composer as the "ventriloquist of God." For him, the idea of the composer as a medium of the divine smacked of charlatanism.[28] But the image of the composer as medium persisted into the twentieth century, at least in certain quarters. "I am the vessel through which *Le Sacre* passed," Stravinsky famously declared in 1962, long after the event.[29] While this might seem at first an avowal of modesty, it in fact positions him as the chosen mouthpiece of a higher force, a mediator between the divine and the human. As an alternative to the doctrine of self-expression, this outlook was in its own way no less self-aggrandizing.

The Composer as Engineer

Throughout the second half of the nineteenth century, composers and critics who considered themselves to be at the forefront of change embraced what was loosely known as "The Music of the Future," an ideology that scorned "pure" or "absolute" music as hopelessly isolated and empty. The only genuinely progressive instrumental music, according to this school of thought, was that which engaged with the broader world of ideas through some verbal indication of content, either a prose program (Berlioz's *Symphonie fantastique*) or a programmatic title (Liszt's *Eine Faust-Symphonie*, with movements labeled "Faust," "Gretchen," and "Mephistopheles"). By the 1920s the situation was completely reversed. One by one, composers who considered themselves in the forefront of progress rejected program music and embraced the aesthetics of formalism. Debussy, Schoenberg, and Stravinsky all gradually abandoned or repressed programmatic elements in their instrumental works, and even Richard Strauss turned away from the inherently programmatic genre of the symphonic poem.[30]

The "new" aesthetics of objectivity that blossomed in the wake of World War I encouraged a rapid rise in the technical analysis of music, which implicitly hypothesized the composer as an engineer, an architect of abstract forms, forms whose beauty—or autonomous significance, for those growing number of commentators who rejected the centrality of beauty—was nonreferential, unfettered to the world outside of sound. Even in the case of Beethoven, the compositional self was no longer an object of central interest for such authors as Heinrich Schenker, Hans Mersmann, Fritz Cassirer, and Walter Riezler, whose commentaries pointedly downplayed, ignored, or ridiculed the kinds of biographical issues that had so occupied writers of previous generations.[31]

This more structurally oriented approach to Beethoven's music reflects broader changes in the scholarly study of music altogether. Guido Adler, widely regarded as one of the founding figures in the nascent discipline of musicology, positioned the study of musical styles at the center of the field. He accorded biography its place, but that place was decidedly secondary. His *Der Stil in der Musik* (1911) and *Methode der Musikgeschichte* (1919) mark a decisive turn away from the "great man" approach to music history. Adler proposed a discipline centered less on a succession of works by canonic composers than on the collective transformation of musical styles through the entire corpus of music. He believed that such an approach would help establish musicology on a more "objective" basis, comparable to the field of art history. Technical analysis, dealing exclusively with the structure of the notes in a score, was by its very nature more dispassionate and less speculative than biographical analysis. Style was now the "most important unifying ideal" for thinking about the history of music; biography and expression were no longer issues of central concern.[32] Adler's approach found widespread acceptance among his fellow musicologists. Hermann Abert, the noted biographer of Mozart, observed in 1920 that "we still hear repeatedly the point of view that behind every good piece of music there must be an important event in the composer's life. Nowadays, what we hear is very often quite the opposite, namely, that the life of an artist has absolutely nothing to do with his art."[33]

The high-modernist aesthetic that arose after World War II intensified the pursuit of objectivity. Composers with any aspirations to modernist credentials worked hard to project an aura of objectivity in their music. In the wake of even greater mass carnage, and with the growing threat of nuclear annihilation, the imperative of breaking with the past and finding new modes of composing became all the more pressing. The leading figures of the musical avant-garde—including such diverse figures as Pierre Boulez, Luigi Nono, John Cage, and Karlheinz Stockhausen—disagreed on many points, but they were united in their rejection of subjective expression as a defining element of earlier aesthetics. Objective detachment was the order of the day for those composers who wished to be considered on the cutting edge of their art.

In the West, at least, this meant a radical intensification of objectivity that manifested itself in such techniques as total serialism (Messiaen, Boulez), indeterminacy (Cage, Xenakis), and novel sonorities (Varèse, Stockhausen). The range of new timbres grew exponentially with the emerging technologies of magnetic tape, which eliminated the human element in performance; this, too, enhanced the aura of objectivity. Boulez summed up these tendencies in his 1963 comments on his Third Piano Sonata:

> Form is becoming autonomous, is tending toward an absolute it has never known before; it rejects the intrusion of the purely personal accident. The great works to which I have referred—Mallarmé, Joyce—constitute the bases of an epoch. "anonymous" in them, one might say, "speaking for an author's voice." If it were necessary to find a profound motive for the work I have tried to describe, it would be *"anonymity."*[34]

This is not to say that modernist composers rejected the premise of expression altogether, but rather that they discouraged the notion that it emanated first and foremost from the compositional self. And it has been heard as such: the theorist Joseph Straus, for example, has recently argued that

Stravinsky's late music—much of it serialist—is "not only structurally rich but movingly expressive as well," for it "vividly represents a wide range of human emotions and experiences."[35] The key word here is *represents*. As far as expression is concerned, the trajectory of aesthetic thought had in a sense come full circle with Stravinsky, back to a construction that would have been very familiar to composers and critics of the late Enlightenment.

8

The Endurance of Subjectivity

In spite of modernism's aesthetics of objectivity, both the projection and the perception of subjectivity have endured. Having grown accustomed to hearing composers in their works over the course of multiple generations, beginning in the 1830s, listeners could not and did not suddenly change their assumptions about the nature of musical expression. The belief that music— particularly instrumental music—comes from deep within the human psyche was too firmly rooted in Western thought to be dislodged altogether.

The growing prestige of objectivity in the 1920s nevertheless displaced the perception of compositional subjectivity as the default mode of listening. Composers' claims of self-expression since that time have been considerably more muted and ambiguous than in the century before. Critics, in turn, have become far more cautious about drawing direct connections between an artist's works and inner self, even if the nature of that connection continues to fascinate.

The shifting landscape of expressive paradigms is readily evident in the flood of commentaries on Beethoven that appeared in 1927, the centenary of his death. Arnold Schmitz went to the heart of the matter in *Das romantische Beethovenbild* by calling into question the long-standing perception of his music as a product of personal experience. "The romantic image of Beethoven," he maintained, "does not present the true Beethoven but rather the stock character of the romantic artist. This image is painted with colors that come from the palette of romantic philosophy but do not correspond to historical reality."[1] Schmitz was among the first to attempt to dismantle Beethoven's scowl. Hermann Abert, one of the leading music historians of his generation, agreed that the time was right for a new approach. "An exasperated attitude toward Beethoven is now making itself felt among younger persons," he observed. "They find his pathos oppressive, exaggerated, even intolerable; they consider his pointed subjectivity a downright calamity for the art. All indicators point toward turning a new page in the history of Beethoven's art."[2] The views of Schmitz and Abert are further confirmed by the responses to a 1927 survey of young musicians about their attitudes toward Beethoven: most of them rejected, either implicitly or explicitly, the traditional view of his music as deeply expressive of an inner self.[3]

How, then, to listen to Beethoven's music if not as an expression of his inner self? J. W. N. Sullivan's *Beethoven: His Spiritual Development*, also published in the centennial year of 1927, provided a blueprint for many subsequent commentators by changing the terms of the debate. Sullivan scrupulously avoided the excesses of earlier critics in interpreting specific works through specific events of the composer's life, yet he insisted that "in his greatest music, Beethoven was primarily concerned to express his personal vision of life. This vision was, of course, the product of his character and his experience. Beethoven the man and Beethoven the artist are not two unconnected entities, and the known history of the man may be used to throw light upon the character of his music."[4] Sullivan's more generalized approach to the issue of life-and-works drew deeply (if covertly) on the principles of Freudian psychology. The composer's emotional states were "the fruits of countless experiences as realized and co-ordinated by the artist, and they enter into the very texture of his spiritual being."[5] These accumulated experiences formed the basis of the composer's elemental self, and that self found its expression in his music:

> The quality that survived the experience depicted in the first movement of the ninth symphony and enabled the composer to achieve the state depicted in the third movement was precisely the primitive unconquerable energy depicted in the Scherzo. This quality was the most primitive and most lasting thing in Beethoven. It is almost symbolic that his last recorded action, when lying unconscious on his death-bed, should have been the shaking of his fist towards heaven in response to a shattering peal of thunder.[6]

The logic here is somewhat circular: the music is evidence of the composer's psyche, and the psyche manifests itself in the music. To his credit, Sullivan avoided the excesses of nineteenth-century biography and refrained from making direct associations between the composer's life and his works even while identifying possible subterranean links between them. This tradition has continued down to the present in the highly influential writings of Maynard Solomon, who repeatedly sounds a note of caution about using psychoanalytic techniques to interpret the music even while going to great lengths to elucidate Beethoven's state of mind at various stages of his life. Solomon is careful to suggest rather than assert. His question quoted earlier—"Listening to the *Eroica*, can we expel from our consciousness our knowledge of Beethoven's hero and rescue fantasies, his suicidal thoughts, his family romance, and his nobility pretense?"—suggests without asserting that these same issues had a bearing on the composition of the *Eroica*.[7]

Not all writers have been so circumspect. The temptation to hear subjectivity in Beethoven's music has proven irresistible at times, even when authors explicitly reject such an approach. In his recent *Beethoven: Anguish and Triumph*, for example, Jan Swafford observes that

> if Beethoven was not a Romantic artist setting out mainly to express himself, it is still hard not to connect his emotional storms of 1810 with the String Quartet in F Minor, [Op. 95, "Serioso"]. . . . Whether the fury and the tenuous moments of hope in the *Serioso* represent Beethoven's state of mind that year is another of that year's elusive questions. But there is no question that the *Serioso* sounds like a cry from the soul.[8]

The implication, once again, is that what we hear ("a cry from the soul") is an echo of what the composer put into the work.

This strategy of implication has by no means been limited to Beethoven. Scholars have shown a particular inclination to hear personal subjectivity in the music of Schubert. Even Edward T. Cone, who called for a clear distinction between a composer's self and his or her persona (see p. 14), could not resist hypothesizing about connections between Schubert's innermost being and at least some of his works. He used the *Moment musical* in A♭ Major, Op. 94, No. 6 (1824), to expound on the possibilities of an "isomorphic" relationship between the two. Cone deemed the work's unusual harmonic structure "a model of the effect of vice on a sensitive person" and related this to the incurable syphilis Schubert knew, by this point in his life, that he had contracted.[9] Cone was careful to couch his hypothesis in a series of questions: "What personal experiences might Schubert have considered relevant to the expressive significance of his own composition?" "Did Schubert's realization [of having contracted syphilis] . . . induce, or at least intensify, the sense of desolation, even dread, that penetrates much of his music from then [1824] on?" "Is it too fanciful to hear a similar reaction embodied in the tonal structure of the *Moment musical*?"[10] Like Solomon, Cone prefers questions to answers, allowing the questions themselves to insinuate that hearing a work as an expression of its creator's "true" self—as opposed to one projected through the assumed identity of a persona—penetrates to a deeper level of interpretative import.[11]

A similar premise of personal subjectivity underlies much of the more recent dispute surrounding Schubert's alleged homosexuality.[12] On one level, the debate has centered on an evaluation of the biographical evidence, but the question of how and to what extent—if any—the composer's sexual orientation influenced his works has rarely been far from the surface. Time and again, those seeking to show a relationship between the two have pointed to unusual passages in the music to validate their claims. As in the case of Haydn and Mozart (see p. 161), it is invariably the unconventional that evokes biographical explanations. "The appearance of apparently unintegrated musical features in canonized masterpieces," as James Webster has astutely observed, is treated as a "problem" that induces scholars to "scour the records of [the composer's] life and character for an 'explanation.'" Even a figure as respected as Carl Dahlhaus, Webster notes, sanctioned such an approach.[13]

In the case of composers who came of age after 1920, certain lives have attracted subjective readings more than others. Dmitri Shostakovich (1906–75) has proven almost irresistible in this regard, in part because he himself made so many provocative (and often contradictory) comments about the self-expressive nature of his works. For example, he confided to his daughter, Galina, that his Eighth String Quartet (1960) was autobiographical, an assertion supported by the work's incorporation of his musical monogram at several junctures, along with self-quotations of various earlier works: both procedures hark back to Schumann's *Carnaval*.[14] In a letter to his friend the theater critic and historian Isaak Glikman, Shostakovich called this same work a memorial to himself but went on to note mordantly that he had "shed the same amount of tears" over this "pseudo-tragic quartet" as "I would have to pee after half a dozen beers."[15] Respected specialists differ widely in their readings of this and other works, but all are in agreement that his music is autobiographical at some level, even if that presence is deeply enigmatic.[16] Wendy Lesser's recent study interprets all fifteen of his string quartets through the lens of the composer's life, taking her cue from his widow, Irina's, assertion that they constitute a "diary" which records "the story of his soul." Yet even Lesser resists the notion of a straightforward, "vulgar" biographical interpretation of the Eighth String Quartet, pointing to its deep ironies as a form of self-expression, in that these ironies mask the "true" identity of the projected subject, or more precisely, that they expose the fragmented nature of that identity.[17] For whatever reason—no doubt a mix of personal, political, and professional considerations—Shostakovich preferred to create an enig-matic aura about the connections between his life and his works. In so doing, he nevertheless encouraged the notion that links of some kind did in fact exist, that his works could indeed be heard as an outward manifestation of his inner self, even if that "true" self was ultimately indecipherable.

If Shostakovich's comments on self-expression relied on misdirection, contradiction, and irony, other composers shaped perceptions of their music through insinuation, suggesting but never quite stating that what they were writing was in some way an expression of the inner self. Even Aaron Copland, the self-proclaimed modernist who in 1933 had praised the music of Carlos Chávez for having "completely overthrown" the nineteenth-century Germanic "tyranny" of the art as a "mere means of self-expression" (see above, p. 173), could not resist speculating on the nature of composi-tional subjectivity some twenty years later:

> Still, the serious composer who thinks about his art will sooner or later have occasion to ask himself: why is it so important to my own psyche that I compose music? What makes it seem so absolutely necessary, so that every other daily activity, by comparison, is of lesser significance? And why is the creative impulse never satisfied; why must one always begin anew? To the first question—the need to create—the answer is al-ways the same—self-expression; the basic need to make evident one's deepest feelings about life. But why is the job never done? Why must one always begin again? The reason for the compulsion to renewed cre-ativity, it seems to me, is that each added work brings with it an element of self-discovery. I must create in order to know myself, and since self-knowledge is a never-ending search, each new work is only a part-answer to the question "Who am I?" and brings with it the need to go on to other and different part-answers.[18]

Copland's final question is eerily similar to one posed almost a century be-fore by A. B. Marx, who had maintained that it was only by "looking inward" when writing "a tranquil Adagio" that a composer could "receive an answer to the question: 'Who am I'?"[19] Copland was careful to frame his musings in the abstract, leaving it to readers to connect these thoughts with his own per-sonal approach to composition. But the implication, as he surely knew, would be clear enough. He was also careful not to suggest how listeners might dis-tinguish between self-expression and the by-products of self-discovery.

Copland's strategy of insinuation would be taken up by later composers who were unwilling to dismiss the idea of self-expression entirely yet reluctant to indulge in the self-proclaimed subjective fervor that had been standard fare a hundred years before. George Rochberg (1918–2005) offers a good example of this. In the mid-1960s he was one of the first major composers to break modernist ranks by embracing idioms and traditions of the musical past, including tonality. Colleagues who considered themselves on the cutting edge of musical style accused him of apostasy.[20] But Rochberg appealed to expression as the driving force behind this change, insisting that

> music is much more than a product of sheer rationality and intellect—that side of ourselves on which modernism has placed such a high premium. . . . Music is a direct utterance of the human soul, the release of the human heart in sound in as many of its forms of sensibilities as we are capable of imagining and realizing.[21]

Like Copland, Rochberg couched his thoughts on expression in terms of the universal rather than the personal: "Music is . . . ," not "My music is. . . ." At the same time, he seems to have encouraged a parallel narrative that linked his turn away from serialism and atonality with the long illness and eventual death of his twenty-year-old son, Paul, in 1964. Rochberg never actually made this claim himself, at least not in public: it does not appear in his published essays and program notes, nor even in his extensive and often deeply personal correspondence with the Hungarian-Canadian composer István Anhalt. Its is particularly conspicuous by its absence in a 1976 interview with Guy Freedman, who gave Rochberg ample opportunity to expand on the reasons behind what Freedman called the composer's "metamorphosis."[22] The narrative of a personal tragedy as the catalyst for a new way of composing has nevertheless become a standard element in accounts of Rochberg's new direction after 1964. As a press release from his publisher puts it:

> 1964. His son Paul, a talented poet, dies aged 20. Following this, George finds that his grief and anger cannot be adequately expressed through serialism, which leads him, over the next few years, to return to tonality and abandon serialism as being devoid of emotion and unable to express fully the human condition.[23]

That such a pronouncement should come from the composer's publisher and not directly from the artist himself exemplifies both the willingness of recent composers to accept the aesthetics of self-expression and their reluctance to embrace it openly. Nevertheless, merely allowing for the plausibility of self-expression in the mid-1960s amounted to a rejection of modernist objectivity, at least in its most extreme forms. Critics, moreover, have responded accordingly, for composers invariably shape the perception of their music through their pronouncements, either about the art in general or their own art in particular.[24]

Rochberg has not been alone in his reluctance to openly embrace self-expression. John Corigliano (b. 1938) has been similarly averse to conceding the deeply subjective nature of his Symphony No. 1 (1989), even while acknowledging its origins in events of his personal life. Mark Adamo, writing in close collaboration with the composer, described the genesis of the work in this way:

> Corigliano had long resisted the notion of a contemporary symphony, both for its apparent historical redundancy . . . and for what he felt was its egotistical elevation of the composer's need to express himself over the needs of the performer or audiences. To him there was a pomposity, a subscription to the "masterpiece syndrome," built into the very form and nothing—neither person nor event—had hitherto sufficed to overcome his reluctance. Nothing, that is, until his closest friend for over twenty-five years, Sheldon Shkolnik, was diagnosed with AIDS.

At this point Adamo quotes Corigliano himself directly:

> The combination of the loss of so many friends—I stopped counting when I reached a hundred—and this other-worldly scene of most of society going about their business blithely unaware that so many around them were dying. . . . I felt like a Jew must have felt in Germany in the 1930s. . . . Meanwhile, I'm in residence in Chicago (with the Chicago Symphony Orchestra), and I owe them a piece, and all I can think about is all these friends, dying and dying, and suddenly the writing of a symphony became—well, just not possible—imperative, really. This just seemed an epic, epic tragedy to me, and I was feeling such staggering loss that a whole self-consciousness I had about this grand form just fell away. And it was no

longer about some ego shouting me-me-me for forty minutes. This was not a symphony for me but for my friends—those I had lost and the one I was losing.[25]

Corigliano's antipathy to writing to write a "me-me-me" work is thoroughly typical for composers of his generation; yet his insistence that the nature of the expression in his Symphony No. 1 is epic, even in the face of his acknowledgment that the direct motivation for it was personal, exemplifies the deep ambivalence of twentieth-century composers toward self-expression.

A similar ambivalence is evident in the pronouncements of such diverse figures as Luigi Nono (1924–90), Helmut Lachenmann (b. 1935), Arvo Pärt (b. 1935), and Wolfgang Rihm (b. 1952), all of whom have at times intimated—but only intimated—that their music is self-expressive. Nono, who like Rochberg began his career as an arch-formalist, also softened his stance toward self-expression later in life. His liner notes to Maurizio Pollini's recording of his . . . *sofferte onde serene* . . . (1976), for piano and magnetic tape, for example, allude to the recent death of a child in both musicians' families: "a harsh wind of death swept away 'the infinite smile of the waves' in my family and in Pollini's. This commonality was further joined by the sadness of the infinite smile of '. . . sofferte onde serene . . .' (suffered, serene waves). The dedication, 'To Maurizio and Marilisa Pollini,' signifies this as well."[26] Again, the acknowledgment of a direct connection between life and works is oblique, suggested rather than stated.

Helmut Lachenmann, who for a time studied with Nono, has embraced the idea of music as an image (*Abbild*) of the human condition but, typically for composers of his generation, has stopped short of claiming his works as an expression of *his* condition. "The composer"—Lachenmann is careful to use the third person here—"expresses himself" in "a creatively modificational interaction with the everyday" and in so doing "discovers himself anew as part of a more multifaceted reality than the merely bourgeois reality."[27] Lachenmann, like Copland before him, frames expression as an act of self-discovery rather than self-projection, even while failing to articulate the ways in which such a distinction might be perceptible to audiences.

The Estonian composer Arvo Pärt has similarly appealed to a process of self-discovery. In his acceptance speech for the International Bridge Prize of the European City of Görlitz in 2007, for example, he spoke of his search for "this precious island in the inner seclusion of our soul, . . . the 'place' where, over 2000 years ago, we were told that the Kingdom of God would be—inside us. . . . And so, I keep trying to stay on the path that searches for this passion-ately longed for 'magic island,' where all people—and for me, all sounds—can live together in love."[28] Pärt's marketing team has been careful to cultivate his public image as a deeply spiritual individual whose faith finds expression in his music. As Laura Dolp has pointed out, the techniques used to promote Pärt as a "modern monk, one who is devout yet non-partisan" have often been subtle, relying on visual cues as much as verbal ones.[29]

Wolfgang Rihm is an exceptional figure among contemporary composers in that he has never hesitated to speak about the emotional basis of his music. "I am, after all, a composer who composes with nerve-ends and not only with the pencil."[30] In his voluminous writings, as the musicologist Seth Brodsky points out, Rihm has repeatedly "declared his faith in the 'sub' of his subcon-scious."[31] Rihm described his Third String Quartet (1976), for example, titled *Im Innersten* (In the Innermost) as having

> intruded into the realm of what I was working on at the time without any preparation, broke it open, and enabled a breakout to the innermost. Thus: the expression of "deepest" and deep feelings to the point of that which is crude and brittle, just barely comprehensible. This makes this music understandable in a new way. It is either experienced directly or not at all.[32]

Yet things are never quite so simple with Rihm. Nine years later, he acknowledged that

> this title—"In the Innermost"—has been widely misunderstood, and this is a good thing. For I certainly did not choose it out of a sense of certainty, but rather out of an awareness that the only way to indicate sincerity at this time—1976—was to let oneself get involved with ambiguity.[33]

Rihm's equivocations about sincerity call into question the very premise itself even while claiming it. Such ambivalence is in no small part a recog-nition that the modern (and, for that matter, postmodern) self is at best a fragmented entity, at worst a fiction. For many composers, sincerity cannot be articulated without a question mark.

Indeed, perceived indicators of self-expression have taken on multiple and often contradictory forms since the 1920s. At times it is the very absence of any apparent connection between a composer's life and works that supports the notion of aesthetic distance itself as a form of self-expression. Stravinsky's *Symphony in C* offers a case in point. Almost every program note or commentary on it rehearses the turbulent backdrop of its genesis: soon after beginning work on it in the fall of 1938, Stravinsky learned of the death of his eldest daughter from tuberculosis, and years later he recalled: "I think it is no exaggeration to say that in the following weeks I myself survived only through my work on the *Symphony in C*—though I hasten to add that I did not seek to overcome my personal grief by 'expressing' or 'portraying' it 'in' music, and the listener in search of that kind of exploitation will search in vain, not only here but everywhere in my art."[34] Nor were his concerns at the time exclusively personal: in a radio interview broadcast in late December 1938, against a backdrop of international crises, he expressed deep pessimism about the future of humankind.[35] His wife, from whom he himself had contracted tuberculosis in 1937, would die of the same disease in March 1939, and while convalescing in a Swiss sanitarium in June 1939 he learned of the death of his mother. When war finally broke out in September 1939, Stravinsky began a second exile, leaving France by ship for New York. By this point he had completed only the first two of the symphony's planned four movements; he would finish the final two in the United States. As he would later observe, "I fear the symphony is divided down the middle."[36]

These contradictory statements—one denying, one acknowledging the effect of his life on his a particular work—capture the ambivalence of twentieth-century composers toward self-expression. If we are to believe the composer that family deaths, war, and exile found no manifestation in his works of the time, then the *Symphony in C* stands as a triumph of aesthetic sublimation, a monument to its creator's abilities of compartmentalization. There is, after all, nothing particularly lugubrious or dark about the work. If anything, it is bright and energetic, conveying an air of aesthetic detachment in keeping with its Neoclassical style. And it is precisely this disjuncture between the composer and his work that commentators have repeatedly lauded. Yet this in itself is a biographical interpretation of sorts. It is striking, moreover, that Stravinsky should have gone out of his way to point out the absence of personal connections in the case of this particular work, even while acknowledging the stylistic implications of its gestation on two different continents.

The music of György Ligeti (1923–2006) has raised similar expectations of a closer correlations between life and works. Ligeti himself acknowledged that his experience as a Jewish survivor of the Holocaust shaped his works to at least some extent, though not necessarily in ways the average listener might expect:

> One dimension of my music bears the imprint of a long time spent in the shadow of death both as an individual and as the member of a group. Not that it lends a tragic quality to my music, quite the opposite. Anyone who has been through horrifying experiences is not likely to create terrifying works of art in all seriousness. He is more likely to alienate.[37]

"Where is the Holocaust in all this?" asks Florian Scheding in a recent and thoughtful essay on Ligeti's music. The composer, he concludes, responded to the Holocaust not directly, with a specific work, as Schoenberg had in his *Survivor from Warsaw*, but through more indirect means that permeate his entire oeuvre. Wolfgang Marx, drawing on the work of Maria Cizmic, has recently expanded on this interpretation by applying theories of cultural trauma to explain the oblique artistic response of composers who, like Ligeti, have survived horrific, identity-threatening events. Marx enumerates the many techniques by which Ligeti creates a sense of alienation, including fragmentation, collage, allusion, parody, and irony, all of which taken together offer at least a partial explanation for the apparent disconnect between Ligeti's life and works. Yet as in the case of Stravinsky, the driving force behind such accounts is a search for a cause-and-effect relationship between life and works, so much so that the disconnect, paradoxically enough, itself becomes a form of connection: Ligeti's is a detached self-expressiveness.[38]

Critics have also assumed for the most part that whatever form of expressiveness they hear in the concert hall is sincere. "Sincere objectivity" may seem a contradiction in terms, but the sincerity in question nowadays is not so much one of emotions as one of purpose. "Serious music" (*ernste Musik*) is, after all, an earnest matter, and those few mid-century modernists who questioned this premise became objects of scorn in many quarters. Indeed, resistance to the music of John Cage during his lifetime fell basically along the divide of listeners who believed and those who did not believe that composers were fundamentally obligated to approach their art with a seriousness of purpose. That Cage's perceived insincerity might actually constitute a form of profound sincerity was beyond the imagination of those critics—and there were many of them—who rejected him as a charlatan. But Cage appeared on the scene at a time when listeners, most of whom were struggling to grasp the challenging new idioms of modernist music, craved at least some assurance that what they were hearing had been proffered as a serious—sincere—utterance, worthy of the efforts it might take to come to terms with it. Only gradually did audiences come to accept the idea that irony and playfulness might themselves be effective means to the end of articulating the human condition. Paradoxically, then, aesthetic distance has established itself as a form of sincere expression; it is no mere coincidence that the reputation of the frequently ironic Gustav Mahler enjoyed an enormous boom in the 1960s.

Perceptions of more conventional forms of self-expression endure in the discourse surrounding music that stands outside the notated tradition, such as jazz, blues, popular song, rock, and rap. These are repertoires transmitted primarily by aural means rather than a visual ones, that is, through performance and recordings as opposed to notation. As such, they lie outside Goehr's notion of the "work-concept" and elicit a very different kind of response from audiences: it is the performer who attracts our primary attention, not the composer, whose actual identity (if not the same as that of the performer) is often obscure in the mind of the average listener. Even when sung by someone else, it is Judy Garland we hear when we listen to "Somewhere Over the Rainbow," not Harold Arlen.

The roles of composer and performer merge with particular frequency in jazz. With its strong emphasis on improvisation, jazz has encouraged listeners to hear the inner self of its practitioners in ways that recall responses to eighteenth-century artists fantasizing at the keyboard. One early reviewer of Miles Davis's *Kind of Blue* (1959), for example, proclaimed that the album "is the soul of Miles Davis, and it's a beautiful soul."[39] Even in a jazz ensemble, a notated lead sheet may indicate who plays a solo and when, but those improvised (or quasi-improvised) moments are the raison d'être of any given performance. When John Coltrane reflects on "A Few of My Favorite Things," we attend to the presence of Coltrane, not of Richard Rodgers, the composer of the original melody that provides the point of departure for the artist.

Artists working in the aural tradition have encouraged the perception of their expressiveness as natural, sincere, and unstudied, often downplaying the many hours of study and practice essential to their livelihood.[40] Critics have followed their lead. The narrative—one might well call it a mythology—of personal revelation has been especially strong in the case of the blues. As Elijah Wald observes, "It is common to hail blues artists not for their technical skill or broad musical knowledge but rather for their 'authenticity.' By this standard, an unknown genius discovered in a Louisiana or Mississippi prison is by definition a deeper and more real bluesman than a million-selling star in a silk suit and a Cadillac." More often than not, however, as Wald points out, this perception is based on an illusion: "Hard as it is for the modern blues fan to accept, the artists we most admire often shared the mass tastes we despise, and dreamed not of enduring artistic reputations but of contemporary pop stardom."[41]

Popular song, rock, and rap are other genres in which self-expression—or, more precisely, the perception of self-expression—has played a crucial role, particularly in cases in which the songwriter and performer are one and the same. Examples abound. Shortly after the singer-songwriter Taylor Swift released the song "We Are Never Ever Getting Back Together" in August 2012, critics were quick to assume that it was a veiled self-commentary on her personal life, and so admirers and detractors alike immediately asked the inevitable question: to whom was this song directed? The headline for the story in the *New York Daily News* duly announced: "Taylor Swift Blasts Ex-Boyfriend in New Song, 'Never Ever Getting Back Together,'" but then added in a wry secondary headline: "Country Singer May Be Singing about Joe Jonas . . . or Taylor Lautner . . . or John Mayer . . . or Jake Gyllenhaal."[42]

This was not a new phenomenon. Goethe had experienced much the same thing almost two hundred years before. In notes to his own autobiography, he observed that "the poet transforms life into an image; the masses want to debase it into material." And in the poem "Geheimstes" (Most Secret), in his *West-östlicher Divan* (1819), he sardonically noted:

> We avidly track the trail,
> We, the anecdote hunters,
> To identify your lover.[43]

Neither Goethe nor Taylor Swift had any reason to be surprised at their followers' curiosity, however, for both had been at some pains to draw the public's attention to the autobiographical nature of their works. Small wonder that their audiences should respond accordingly.

Followers of rock and rap music have been particularly prone to hear their respective repertoires as inherently confessional. "The taint of inauthenticity," Theodore Gracyk has observed of rock, "appears when musicians present emotions that do not arise from their own lives." Gracyk sees the "Romantic mythology" of rock's disdain for the commercial side of the art as a symptom of the foundational assumption of the genre's emotional sincerity.

Simon Frith, in turn, has pointed out that the 1960s rockers perceived as most "authentic" were those who seemed to be performing for their own pleasure, not that of the audience.[44]

The presumption of rap as an essentially autobiographical genre came to the fore in the summer of 2015, when it was revealed that the artist Drake had employed ghostwriters—including a rival rapper, Meek Mill—to create at least some of his material. Drake's fans responded with a mixture of disappointment and outrage. What fueled the controversy was an underlying belief that rap is—or at least should be—a genuine reflection of lived experiences, not a performance of texts written by others.[45]

Artists who have reinvented themselves at some point in their careers (Bob Dylan, David Bowie, and Madonna, among others) have aroused a similar sense of disillusionment at various times from at least some of their followers. Dylan in particular was the object of intense outrage from those who felt he had sold out to commercialism when he made the switch from acoustic to electric guitar in 1965.[46] The vehemence of those denouncing him was driven in large part by a conviction that artists must create from within, untainted by outside influences such as money or fame, and that a personal identity, once it has found its expression in art, cannot change over time. Selves, by this reckoning, are immutable.

Nor is such disillusionment and outrage limited to repertoires in the aural tradition. When it was revealed in 2014 that a ghostwriter had crafted many of the most celebrated works of the Japanese composer Mamoru Samuragochi (b. 1963), including his Symphony No. 1 (*Hiroshima*), the public responded with anger and disbelief, in spite of Samuragochi's lengthy apologies, both in writing and in person. In a further twist, his ghostwriter revealed that Samuragochi had for years faked his own deafness in an attempt to appear more Beethovenesque.[47]

The habits of listening forged in the nineteenth century remain with us today. Even if we recognize expression as an objective construct, we continue to listen for the creative individual we perceive as being not only behind the music, but in it as well.

CONCLUSION
TRACKING COMETS

Writing a history of listening is in some respects a fool's errand: there are as many histories as there are listeners. And while we can generalize to a certain extent in describing the outward behaviors of audiences in the concert hall—applauding between movements or not, talking during performances or not, and so on—the inward responses of those listeners can vary widely according to place, time, and the work at hand. Even individual listeners can hear the same work in different ways at different times. And only a tiny fraction of these countless responses are ever committed to writing.

But listeners are not blank slates, and the responses they have set down in words are sufficient in number and scope to reveal broad changes in their conceptions of musical expression. Even before hearing a single note of music in the concert hall, listeners entertain assumptions (whether they realize it or not) about the relationship between composers' lives and works; those preconceptions, in turn, play a major role in determining the extent to which they hear music as a form of sonic autobiography. And these assumptions, as we have seen, changed radically and more than once, first in the years around 1830, and then again around 1920.

Yet assumptions, by their very nature, lie beneath what is actually articulated: they typically reveal themselves obliquely, often through metaphors and images. One particularly revealing pair of images that neatly captures the shift from objective to subjective expression appears in the 1845 memoirs of the noted Czech composer Wenzel Johann Tomaschek (1774–1850). In spite of having been on good personal terms with Beethoven, Tomaschek expresses decided ambivalence about his music.

> Even if the entire world thinks differently of him, I will not for that reason change my opinion, because for me the service in which I stand—the glorification of art—is too holy that I should speak against my own conviction. People who talk about Beethoven often get around to speaking of Mozart as well, with the latter getting short shrift. But they forget that those works by Beethoven that are adorned with more understanding and grace than

his later ones owe much to Mozart's distinctively rational form, and that they still make a pleasant impression on the listener. I have always hated comparisons, especially in the realm of art, but if one had to compare, then I would imagine Mozart's spirit as a sun that shines and warms without deviating from its lawful path. I would call Beethoven a comet that traces bold paths without subjecting itself to any system and whose appearance gives rise to all kinds of superstitious construals. Or: Mozart sends his eternally youthful morning rays of the morning sun directly to earth in order to illuminate and warm it, while Beethoven concentrates the glowing rays of the midday sun into a single point of combustion and draws in as well the shadows of the night to cool and comfort those for whom the burning blaze is intolerable.[1]

Mozart the sun, Beethoven the comet: the images are deeply revealing. Only four years younger than Beethoven, Tomaschek had come of age in an era of expressive objectivity. He lauds Mozart for having followed a prescribed, "lawful" orbit that warms and illuminates listeners. Beethoven, he acknowledges, had been able to achieve this same effect in his earlier works but at some point began to follow his own path, like that of a comet, combining in his music the heat of the noonday sun and its diametrical opposite, the shadows of night. And like comets, long considered omens of the future, Beethoven's works had attracted their own "superstitious" interpretations.

Tomaschek occupied a leading position in the musical life of Prague, yet he clearly realized that his verdict on Beethoven would not be widely shared. Already in his early seventies by the mid-1840s, he recognized that other listeners—almost all of them younger—had accepted it as their responsibility to track this musical comet's unconventional path. For those who, like Tomaschek, listened within the framework of rhetoric, Beethoven's later works must indeed have seemed unpredictable, erratic, and somehow portentous.

Beethoven the comet: the image also reminds us of why paradigms of any kind change in the first place. As Thomas Kuhn argued in his classic study *The Structure of Scientific Revolutions* (1962), prevailing paradigms of thought are rejected when they can no longer explain significant anomalies.[2] And the orbits of comets, appropriately enough—Halley's in particular, as it would come to be known—were among the unusual and seemingly inexplicable phenomena that had led Isaac Newton to develop the theories he would set down in his paradigm-shifting *Principia* of 1687.[3] In similar fashion,

Beethoven's works provoked the kind of cognitive crisis that precipitates the overthrow of an existing paradigm. Listeners could not accommodate his instrumental music within the prevailing paradigm of expressive objectivity: the trajectory of his music, like that of a comet, was too erratic to be explained yet challenging enough to compel interpretation. And once listeners began to regard expression as an outpouring of the creative self, they perceived Beethoven's music in a new and different way. Encouraged by composers who rose to prominence in the generation immediately afterward—Berlioz and Schumann in particular—audiences were soon hearing all instrumental music from a new perspective: that of the composer.

Nor was Tomaschek the first to have compared Beethoven to a comet: Amadeus Wendt, it will be recalled, had done so in 1831, a good fourteen years earlier. Wendt too had repeatedly voiced deep concern about the erratic and unpredictable nature of the composer's works. The excess of fantasy in Beethoven's music, he had declared in 1815, could "only lead to great aberrations." Sixteen years later he still believed that the composer's path went "against established law," but by that point Wendt had come to see this as a positive development, for Beethoven's music had laid down a "new law of its own," and "the course of this multifaceted spirit," as he concluded, "is the course of a hero."[4] At some point in the 1820s or early '30s, Wendt had come to accept the new paradigm of subjective expression; Tomaschek, ten years his senior, never did. Wendt was willing to follow the path of a comet and calculate its trajectory as best he could; Tomaschek continued to believe that the purpose of music was to warm his soul.

What, then, dislodged this paradigm so dramatically less than a century later, in the years around 1920? It never disappeared entirely, but it ceded its centrality by giving way to a more nuanced understanding of expression, one that restored the prestige of artifice to art. Hanslick's formalist aesthetics, rejected or ignored by composers of his own time, came into its own in the early decades of the new century. What had once been dismissed as hopelessly archaic—the idea of music as forms set in motion through sound—was now embraced as central to the very essence of the art. Composers and critics had come to realize that the paradigm of subjective expression could not by itself adequately account for the nature of musical expression.

Just as Newton had explained the motion of comets toward the end of the seventeenth century, theorists and composers working at the turn of the twentieth were able to demonstrate in increasing detail the technical, objective basis of music and in so doing demystify to at least some extent the nature of musical expression. The growing power of musical analysis at the hands of such figures as Hermann Kretzschmar, Hugo Riemann, Guido Adler, and Heinrich Schenker offered a powerful alternative to biographical interpretations. Composers themselves encouraged this approach, and listeners responded accordingly.

Yet no matter how well we understand what comets are and how they move, they continue to inspire awe. At some level they remain a mystery. We no longer interpret them as omens, but we experience them as something more than a combination of solids and gasses, their orbits as something more than manifestations of parabolic or hyperbolic equations. In the same manner, no amount of technical analysis will ever eradicate the aura of mystery that surrounds the creative process and its musical products. The dual or mixed paradigms of listening under which we operate today thus contribute to a decidedly more balanced approach to hearing expression, one that accords objectivity its place even while accommodating the subjective element that always goes into the creation of any work of art, including music.

Notes

Introduction

1. Stefan Kunze, ed., *Ludwig van Beethoven: Die Werke im Spiegel seiner Zeit* (Laaber: Laaber-Verlag, 1987). Given its focus on reviews of concerts and published music, even Kunze's anthology, for all its size, omits a good many relevant contemporaneous sources.
2. Ernst Ludwig Gerber, *Neues historisch-biographisches Lexikon der Tonkünstler*, 4 vols. (Leipzig: A. Kühnel, 1812–14), 1:316–17: "zum Ernste und zur Schwermuth."
3. See, for example, Susan McClary, "Constructions of Subjectivity in Schubert's Music," in *Queering the Pitch: The New Gay and Lesbian Musicology*, ed. Philip Brett, Elizabeth Wood, and Gary C. Thomas (New York: Routledge, 1994), 205–33; Naomi Cumming, *The Sonic Self: Musical Subjectivity and Signification* (Bloomington: Indiana University Press, 2000); Lawrence Kramer, *Franz Schubert: Sexuality, Subjectivity, Song* (Cambridge: Cambridge University Press, 1998); Albrecht von Massow, *Musikalisches Subjekt: Idee und Erscheinung in der Moderne* (Freiburg: Rombach, 2001); McClary, *Modal Subjectivities: Self-Fashioning in the Italian Madrigal* (Berkeley and Los Angeles: University of California Press, 2004); John Butt, "Bach's Passions and the Construction of Early Modern Subjectivities," in his *Bach's Dialogue with Modernity: Perspectives on the Passions* (Cambridge: Cambridge University Press, 2010), 36–96; Judith A. Peraino, *Giving Voice to Love: Song and Self-Expression from the Troubadours to Guillaume de Machaut* (New York: Oxford University Press, 2011); Michael L. Klein, *Music and the Crises of the Modern Subject* (Bloomington: Indiana University Press, 2015).
4. Michael P. Steinberg, *Listening to Reason: Culture, Subjectivity, and Nineteenth-Century Music* (Princeton, NJ: Princeton University Press, 2004), 9: "In question is not the subjectivity of the composer or of anyone outside the music itself. The subjectivity is of the music itself. . . . Musical subjectivity cannot therefore be absorbed into the subject-positions of the composer or the listener."
5. See, for example, Fred Maus, "Music as Drama," *Music Theory Spectrum* 10 (1988): 56–73; Maus, "Agency in Instrumental Music and Song," *College Music Symposium* 29 (1989): 31–43; Seth Monahan, "Action and Agency Revisited," *Journal of Music Theory* 57 (2013): 321–71; Rebecca Thumpston, "The Embodiment of Yearning: Towards a Tripartite Theory of Musical Agency," in *Music, Analysis, Experience*, ed. Costantino Maeder and Mark Reybrouck (Leuven: Leuven University Press, 2015), 331–48; Edward Klorman, *Mozart's Music of Friends: Social Interplay in the Chamber Works* (Cambridge: Cambridge University Press, 2016); Robert Hatten, *A Theory of Virtual Agency for Western Art Music* (Bloomington: Indiana University Press, 2018).

6. Goethe, *Dichtung und Wahrheit* (1811–14), in his *Werke: Hamburger Ausgabe*, 14 vols., ed. Erich Trunz et al. (Munich: Beck, 1981), 9:283: "Ein Bild, ein Gedicht . . . Bruchstücke einer grossen Konfession." Goethe, "Noch ein Wort für junge Dichter," the title supplied by Eckermann, first published posthumously (in 1833), in his *Werke*, 12:360: "denn sie sind an mir gewahr worden, daß, wie der Mensch von innen heraus leben, der Künstler von innen heraus wirken müsse, indem er, gebärde er sich wie er will, immer nur sein Individuum zutage fördern wird."

7. Goethe, *Werke*, 12:361: "poetischer Gehalt . . . ist Gehalt des eigenen Lebens . . . [D]en jungen Dichtern, sprech' ich hierüber folgendermaßen: . . . fragt euch nur bei jedem Gedicht, ob es ein Erlebtes enthalte und ob dies Erlebte euch gefördert habe." Goethe to Ludwig I of Bavaria, 14 April 1829, in Goethe, *Briefe*, 4 vols., ed. Karl Robert Mandelkow (Hamburg: Christian Wegner, 1962–67), 4:326: "Die Gabe der Dichtkunst hat das Eigne besonders darin, daß sie den Besitzer nötigt, sich selbst zu enthüllen. Dichterische Äußerungen sind unwillkürliche Bekenntnisse, in welchen unser Innres sich aufschließt."

8. See Andrew Bowie, *Aesthetics and Subjectivity: From Kant to Nietzsche*, 2nd ed. (Manchester: Manchester University Press, 2003); Mark Evan Bonds, *Music as Thought: Listening to the Symphony in the Age of Beethoven* (Princeton, NJ: Princeton University Press, 2006); and Tomas George McAuley, "The Impact of German Idealism on Musical Thought, 1781–1803" (Ph.D. diss., King's College London, 2013).

9. William Wordsworth, preface to his *Lyrical Ballads*, 2nd ed., 2 vols. (London: T. N. Longman and O. Rees, 1800), 1:xiv; ibid., 1:xxxiii–xxxiv.

10. Peter Gay, *The Naked Heart* (New York: W. W. Norton, 1995), 5, 3, 6; and Isaiah Berlin, *The Roots of Romanticism*, ed. Henry Hardy (Princeton, NJ: Princeton University Press, 1999), 95.

11. There are of course exceptions, instances in which composers write the music first and add words only later. Perhaps the most famous example of this is the aria "Drum beim Barte des Propheten," discussed by Mozart in a letter to his father dated 26 September 1781, in which he says that he had already written the music to it for his opera *Die Entführung aus dem Serail* before receiving a text for it from his librettist, Johann Gottlieb Stephanie. Even here, however, Mozart knew in advance the emotional import of the aria and had directed Stephanie to construct a text that would fit the music in terms of both content and prosody. From the perspective of the unsuspecting listener, then, the finished product remains a projection of the text, even in this atypical case. See Wolfgang Amadeus Mozart, *Briefe und Aufzeichnungen*, rev. ed., 7 vols., ed. Wilhelm A. Bauer, Otto Erich Deutsch, and Ulrich Konrad (Kassel: Bärenreiter, 2005), 3:162.

12. See, for example, Kramer, *Franz Schubert*; Berthold Hoeckner, "Poet's Love and Composer's Love," *Music Theory Online* 7, no. 5 (October 2001).

13. E. T. A. Hoffmann, "Recension: *Sinfonie . . . par Louis van Beethoven . . . Oeuvre 67*," *AmZ* 12 (4 July 1810): 633: "dass ihm Vocal-Musik, die unbestimmtes Sehnen nicht zulässt, sondern nur die durch Worte bezeichneten Affecte, als in dem Reich des Unendlichen empfunden, darstellt, weniger gelingt." Hoffmann, "Recension: *Ouverture d'Egmont etc. par L. van Beethoven . . . Op. 84 . . .*," *AmZ* 15 (21 July 1813): 480–81: "Man ist

sonst in beethovenscher Instrumental-Musik an eine reiche Ausbeute genialischer contrapunktischer Wendungen, kühner Ausweichungen u.s.w. gewöhnt: wie sehr der Meister aber mit seinem Reichthum hauszuhalten und ihn zu rechter Zeit zu spenden versteht, beweiset die hier in Rede stehende Composition, die, ohne im mindesten für sich selbst glänzen zu wollen, ganz dem Sinne des Dichters folgt, und sich seiner Tendenz anschmiegt. Rec. bemühte sich daher auch, die gelungene ästhetische Behandlung des, dem Componisten gegebenen Stoffs gehörig ins Licht zu stellen und zu würdigen."

14. Anonymous, review of *Sechs Gesänge mit Begleit. des Pianoforte . . . von L. van Beethoven . . . Oeuvr. 75, AmZ* 13 (28 August 1811): 593: "Hr. v. B. schreibt nichts, was nicht mehr oder weniger den Stempel eines originellen Geistes, eines tiefen Gefühls, einer eigenthümlichen Laune, und auch einer besondern Art der Ausarbeitung trüge; aber er braucht, um diese Vorzüge in recht vollem Maasse darzulegen, viele Mittel, und einen weiten, freyen Spielraum. Wo er in dieser Absicht beschränkt ist—sey es nun durch die Gattung, oder durch Worte, oder durch Bequemung nach geringen Fähigkeiten der Spieler u. dergl.—da ist es ihm selten ganz, öfters weniger, zuweilen gar nicht gelungen, sein eigenthümliches Innere darzulegen." Kunze, *Ludwig van Beethoven* (209), suggests Friedrich Rochlitz as the probable author of this review.

15. Anonymous, "Quatre symphonies pour l'orchestre, comp. par Wolfgang Amad. Mozart. Oeuvre 64," *AmZ* 1 (1 May 1799): 494: "Ein Tonkünstler kann in dieser Gattung [i.e., instrumental music] am mehresten Genie zeigen; denn nicht nur muss er hier ganz allein erfinden und sich selber allen Stoff geben, sondern er ist auch einzig und allein auf die Sprache der Töne eingeschränkt. Seine Gedanken haben ihre Bestimmtheit in sich selber, ohne von der Poesie unterstützt zu seyn."

16. On landscape painting as at once the most realistic and abstract of all the visual arts in the nineteenth century, see Charles Rosen and Henri Zerner, *Romanticism and Realism: The Mythology of Nineteenth-Century Art* (New York: Viking, 1984), 34–35.

17. See Rudolf Wittkower and Margot Wittkower, *Born under Saturn: The Character and Conduct of Artists* (London: Weidenfeld and Nicolson, 1963); and Frank Zöllner, " 'Ogni pittore dipinge sé': Leonardo da Vinci and 'Automimesis'," in *Der Künstler über sich in seinem Werk*, ed. Matthias Winner (Weinheim: VCH, 1992), 137–60.

18. See Celia Applegate, "How German Is It? Nationalism and the Idea of Serious Music in the Early Nineteenth Century," *19CM* 21 (1998): 274–96; Celia Applegate and Pamela Potter, eds., *Music and German National Identity* (Chicago: University of Chicago Press, 2002); and David Gramit, *Cultivating Music: The Aspirations, Interests, and Limits of German Musical Culture, 1770–1848* (Berkeley and Los Angeles: University of California Press, 2002).

19. Friedrich Rochlitz, "Den Freunden Beethovens," *AmZ* 29 (17 October 1827): 705–10. For further commentary on this document, see below, p. 128.

20. Joseph Fröhlich, "Recensionen: *Sinfonie, mit Schlusschor über Schillers Ode: 'An die Freude' . . . von Ludwig van Beethoven. . . . Erste Recension," *Cäcilia* 8 (1828): 236: "so dass man dieses Werk die *musikalisch-geschriebene Autobiographie Beethoven's* nennen könnte."

21. See, for example, the remarks on Op. 132 in Anonymous, "Soirées musicales de MM. Bohrer frères," *Revue musicale*, 2nd sér., 1 (1830): 213: "L'adagio, que Beethoven a écrit en actions de grâces, après sa guérison d'une longue maladie."

22. Julian Schmidt, *Geschichte der deutschen Nationalliteratur im neunzehnten Jahrhundert*, 2 vols. (Leipzig: Herbig, 1853), 2:410: "Bei Beethovens Symphonien haben wir das Gefühl, es handle sich um etwas ganz Anderes, als um den gewöhnlichen Wechsel von Lust und Schmerz, in welchem sich die wortlose Musik sonst bewegt. Wir ahnen den geheimnißvollen Abgrund einer geistigen Welt, und quälen uns um das Verständniß. . . . Wir wollen wissen, was den Tondichter so bis zur grenzenlosen Verzweiflung, bis zum ausgelassensten Jubel getrieben hat; wir wollen diesen geheimnißvoll schönen Zügen der Sphinx ein Verständniß abgewinnen."

23. Alfred Einstein, *Mozart: His Character, His Work*, trans. Arthur Mendel and Nathan Broder (New York: Oxford University Press, 1945), 255; Erich Schenk, *Wolfgang Amadeus Mozart: Sein Leben, seine Welt*, 2nd ed. (Vienna: Amalthea Verlag, 1975), 381: "schmerzlich resignierende Bekenntniswerke"; and Marius Flothuis, "K. 304," in Neal Zaslaw and William Cowdery, eds., *The Compleat Mozart* (New York: W. W. Norton, 1990), 290.

24. Théodore de Wyzewa, "À propos du centenaire de la mort de Joseph Haydn," *Revue des deux mondes* 79 (1909): 935–46. See Mark Evan Bonds, "Haydn's 'Cours complet de la composition' and the 'Sturm und Drang,'" in *Haydn Studies*, ed. Dean Sutcliffe (Cambridge: Cambridge University Press, 1998), 152–76.

25. Franz Liszt, "Marx und die Musik des neunzehnten Jahrhunderts," *NZfM* 42 (11 May 1855): 217–18: "daß der Künstler nicht blos die Form um der Form willen handhaben müsse, daß er in ihr nur die Stimme zu suchen habe, welche die Eindrücke seines innern Wesens kundgiebt: daß es für ihn demnach das Nothwendigste sei, diese seine Innerlichkeit zu erheben und zu eredeln, sie zu läutern und zu bereichern."

26. Susan B. Rosenbaum, *Professing Sincerity: Modern Lyric Poetry, Commercial Culture, and the Crisis in Reading* (Charlottesville: University Press of Virginia, 2007), 5.

27. Schoenberg to Kandinsky, 24 January 1911, in Arnold Schoenberg and Wassily Kandinsky, *Arnold Schönberg, Wassily Kandinsky: Briefe, Bilder und Dokumente einer aussergewöhnlichen Begegnung*, ed. Jelena Hahl-Koch (Salzburg: Residenz-Verlag, 1980), 21: "Und die Kunst gehört aber dem *Unbewußten!* Man soll *sich* ausdrücken! Sich *unmittelbar* ausdrücken! *Nicht aber seinen Geschmack oder seine Erziehung oder seinen Verstand, sein Wissen, sein Können. Nicht alle diese *nichtangeborenen* Eigenschaften. Sondern die *angeborenen*, die *triebhaften*." Translation from Schoenberg and Kandinksy, *Arnold Schoenberg, Wassily Kandinsky: Letters, Pictures, and Documents*, ed. Jelena Hahl-Koch, trans. John C. Crawford (London: Faber and Faber, 1984). Schoenberg, "Probleme des Kunstunterrichts" (1911), in his *"Stile herrschen, Gedanken siegen": Ausgewählte Schriften*, ed. Anna Maria Morazzoni (Mainz: Schott, 2007), 58: "Kunst kommt nicht vom Können, sondern vom Müssen." Translation from "Problems in Teaching Art," in his *Style and Idea: Selected Writings of Arnold Schoenberg*, ed. Leonard Stein (Berkeley and Los Angeles: University of California Press, 1975), 365.

28. Igor Stravinsky, *Chroniques de ma vie*, 2 vols. (Paris: Denoël et Steele, 1935), 1:116–17: "Car je considère la musique, par son essence, impuissante à exprimer quoi que ce soit: un sentiment, une attitude, un état psychologique, un phénomène de la nature, etc. . . . L'expression n'a jamais été la propriété immanente de la musique. La raison d'être de celle-ci n'est d'aucune façon conditionée par celle-là. Si, comme c'est presque toujours le cas, la musique paraît exprimer quelque chose, ce n'est qu'une illusion et non pas une réalité. C'est simplement un élément additionnel que, par une convention tacite et invétérée, nous lui avons prêté, imposé, comme une étiquette, un protocole, bref, une tenue et que, par accoutumance ou inconscience, nous sommes arrivée à confondre avec son essence." Ellipsis in the original. The translation is from the authorized but unattributed English translation, published as *An Autobiography* (New York: Simon & Schuster, 1936), 83–84. For further discussion of Stravinsky's commentaries on expression, see below, pp. 173 and 192.

29. Edward T. Cone, *The Composer's Voice* (Berkeley and Los Angeles: University of California Press, 1974), 5. Cone's theory of the compositional persona is discussed further below (p. 177).

30. See George Perle, *Style and Idea in the "Lyric Suite" of Alban Berg*, rev. ed. (Hillsdale, NY: Pendragon Press, 2001); and Michael Cherlin, "Memory and Rhetorical Trope in Schoenberg's String Trio," *JAMS* 51 (1998): 559–602.

31. For a brief but insightful overview of changing concepts of musical expression since antiquity, see Reinhard Kapp, "Zur Geschichte des musikalischen Ausdrucks," in *Beiträge zur Interpretationsästhetik und zur Hermeneutik-Diskussion*, ed. Claus Bockmaier (Laaber: Laaber-Verlag, 2009), 143–79.

32. Lydia Goehr, *The Imaginary Museum of Musical Works: An Essay in the Philosophy of Music*, rev. ed. (New York: Oxford University Press, 2007). On the implications of Goehr's work-concept on the perception of composers, see Michael Talbot, "The Work-Concept and Composer-Centredness," in *The Musical Work: Reality or Invention?* ed. Michael Talbot (Liverpool: Liverpool University Press, 2000), 168–86. See also below, p. 118.

33. Mary Hunter provides a valuable survey of subjectivity in performance in the late eighteenth and early nineteenth centuries in her " 'To Play as if from the Soul of the Composer': The Idea of the Performer in Early Romantic Aesthetics," *JAMS* 58 (2005): 357–98. On the mid- to late nineteenth century, see Karen Leistra-Jones, "Staging Authenticity: Joachim, Brahms, and the Politics of *Werktreue* Performance," *JAMS* 66 (2013), 397–436. See also below, pp. 194–96.

34. Carl Dahlhaus, *Ludwig van Beethoven: Approaches to his Music*, trans. Mary Whittall (Oxford: Clarendon Press, 1991), 1–10 ("Life and Work: The Biographical Method"); and Lewis Lockwood, *Beethoven: The Music and the Life* (New York: W. W. Norton, 2003), 15–21 ("Life and Works").

35. Lockwood, *Beethoven*, 19.

36. Scott Burnham, *Beethoven Hero* (Princeton, NJ: Princeton University Press, 1995), xvi.

37. Maynard Solomon, "Thoughts on Biography," in his *Beethoven Essays* (Cambridge, MA: Harvard University Press, 1988), 112.

Chapter 1

1. See Mark Evan Bonds, *Wordless Rhetoric: Musical Form and the Metaphor of the Oration* (Cambridge, MA: Harvard University Pres, 1991).

2. On the so-called doctrines of affections (*Affektenlehre*) and figures (*Figurenlehre*), see the relevant entries by George Buelow in *The New Grove Dictionary of Music and Musicians*, 29 vols., ed. Stanley Sadie (New York: Oxford University Press, 2001); and Dietrich Bartel, *Musica poetica: Musical-Rhetorical Figures in German Baroque Music* (Lincoln: University of Nebraska Press, 1997). On the decline of the *Figurenlehre* in the late eighteenth century, see Wolfgang Fuhrmann, "'Alle innern Gefühle hörbar hervor in die Luft gezaubert': Wilhelm Heinse und die Theorie des musikalischen Ausdrucks nach dem Verblassen der Figurenlehre," in *Musikalisches Denken im Labyrinth der Aufklärung: Wilhelm Heinses "Hildegard von Hohenthal,"* ed. Thomas Irvine, Wiebke Thormählen, and Oliver Wiener (Mainz: Are Edition, 2015), 33–73. On the related notion of the *loci topici* in music, see Danuta Mirka, ed., *The Oxford Handbook of Topic Theory* (New York: Oxford University Press, 2016).

3. The long history of conflict between rhetoric and philosophy goes back to Plato; see in particular his *Phaedrus* and *Gorgias*, as well as *Republic*, Books 2, 3, and 10.

4. Charles Avison, *An Essay on Musical Expression* (London: C. Davis, 1752), 61, 89.

5. Jean-Jacques Rousseau, "Expression," in his *Dictionnaire de musique* (Paris: Veuve Duchesne, 1768), 207–13. Joseph Martin Kraus takes a similar approach in his essay on expression ("Ausdruck") in his *Wahrheiten die Musik betreffend* (Frankfurt am Main: Eichenbergsche Erben, 1779), 96–117.

6. Mozart to Leopold Mozart, 3 July 1778, *Briefe und Aufzeichnungen*, 2:388–89: "Die Sinfonie fing an . . . und gleich mitten im Ersten Allegro war eine Passage die ich wohl wuste, daß sie gefallen müste; alle zuhörer wurden davon hingerissen—und war ein grosses applaudißement—weil ich aber wuste, wie ich sie schrieb, was das für einen Effect machen würde, so brachte ich sie auf die letzt noch einmahl an—da gings nun Da capo. das Andante gefiel auch, besonders aber das letzte Allegro—weil ich hörte, daß hier alle lezte Allegro wie die Ersten, mit allen instrumenten zugleich und meistens unisono anfangen, so fieng ichs mit die 2 violin allein piano nur 8 Tact an—darauf kamm gleich ein forte—mit hin machten die Zuhörer, | wie ichs erwartete | beym Piano sch—dann kamm gleich das forte—sie das Forte hören, und die hände zu klatschen war eins –ich gieng also gleich für freüde nach der Sinfonie ins Palais Royal—nahm ein guts gefrornes—bat den Rosenkranz, den ich versprochen hatte—und ging nach Haus."

7. Mozart to Leopold Mozart, 26 September 1781, *Briefe und Aufzeichnungen*, 3:162: "das, *drum beym Barte des Propheten* etc: ist zwar im nemlichen tempo, aber mit geschwinden Noten—und da sein zorn immer wächst, so muß—da man glaubt, die aria seye schon zu Ende—das allegro aßai—ganz in einem andern zeitmaas, und in einem andern Ton—eben den besten Effect machen; denn ein Mensch, der sich in einem so heftigen zorn befindet, überschreitet alle ordnung, Maas und Ziel, er kennt sich nicht—so muß sich auch die Musick nicht mehr kennen—weil aber die leidenschaften, heftig oder nicht, niemals bis zum Eckel ausgedrücket seyn müssen,

und die Musick, auch in der schaudervollsten Lage, das Ohr niemalen beleidigen, sondern doch dabey vergnügen muß, folglich allzeit Musick bleiben Muß, so habe ich keinen fremden ton zum F |: zum Ton der Aria:| sondern einen befreundten dazu, aber nicht den Nächsten, D minor, sondern den weitern, A minor, gewählt."

8. Carl Ditters von Dittersdorf, *Lebensbeschreibung* (Leipzig: Breitkopf & Härtel, 1801), 237: "*Kaiser*: Was sagen Sie zu Mozarts Komposition? *Ich*: Er ist unstreitig eins der größten Originalgenies, und ich habe bisher noch keinen Komponisten gekannt, der so einen erstaunlichen Reichthum von Gedanken besitzt. Ich wünschte, er wäre nicht so verschwenderisch damit. Er läßt den Zuhörer nicht zu Athem kommen; denn, kaum will man einem schönen Gedanken nachsinnen, so steht schon wieder ein anderer herrlicher da, der den vorigen verdrängt, und das geht immer in einem so fort, so daß man am Ende keine dieser Schönheiten im Gedächtniß aufbewahren kann."

9. Georg August Griesinger, *Biographische Notizen über Joseph Haydn* (Leipzig: Breitkopf & Härtel, 1810), 114: "'Ich setzte mich hin, fing an zu phantasiren, je nachdem mein Gemüth traurig oder fröhlich, ernst oder tändelnd gestimmt war. Hatte ich eine Idee erhascht, so ging mein ganzes Bestreben dahin, sie den Regeln der Kunst gemäß auszuführen und zu soutenirem. So suchte ich mir zu helfen, und das ist es, was vielen unserer neuern Komponisten fehlt; sie reihen ein Stückchen an das andere, sie brechen ab, wenn sie kaum angefangen haben: aber es bleibt auch nichts im Herzen sitzen, wenn man es angehört hat.'" On the translation of *Gemüt(h)* as "animus," with its implications of volition, see Monique Scheer, "Topographies of Emotion," in *Emotional Lexicons: Continuity and Change in the Vocabulary of Feeling, 1700–2000*, ed. Ute Frevert et al. (New York: Oxford University Press, 2014), 44–51. Avison had similarly complained decades before about themes that break off and remain undeveloped; see his *Essay on Musical Expression*, 39–40.

10. Horace, *Ars poetica*, in his *Satires, Epistles, Art of Poetry*, rev. ed., trans. H. Rushton Fairclough (Cambridge, MA: Harvard University Press, 1929), 459. On later interpretations of this much-discussed passage in regard to music, see Jürgen Stenzel, "'Si vis me flere . . .'—'Musa iocosa mea': Zwei poetologische Argumente in der deutschen Diskussion des 17. und 18. Jahrhunderts," *Deutsche Vierteljahrsschrift für Literaturwissenschaft und Geistesgeschichte* 48 (1974): 650–71; and Andreas Liebert, *Die Bedeutung des Wertesystems der Rhetorik für das deutsche Musikdenken im 18. und 19. Jahrhundert* (Frankfurt am Main: Peter Lang, 1993), 219–49.

11. Forkel, *Commentar über die 1777 gedruckte Abhandlung über "Die Theorie der Musik," insofern sie Liebhabern und Kennern nothwendig und nützlich ist*, manuscript, ca. 1780–85, Sibley Music Library, Eastman School of Music, Rochester, New York (Vault ML95.F721S38), [19]: "Jeder Gedanke, nimmt von dem eigenen Charakter desjenigen, der ihn denkt, ein gewisses Gepräge an, das nur einem allein, und keinem andern Individuo eigen seÿn kann. . . . So muß der Künstler seine musikalischen Gedanken so zu biegen und zu formen wissen, daß sie am Ende in ihrer vollen Verbindung seinen vorgesetzten Absichten entsprechen können." On Forkel's lectures, see Mark Evan Bonds, "Turning *Liebhaber* into *Kenner*: Johann Nikolaus Forkel's Lectures on the Art of Listening, ca. 1780–1785," in *The Oxford Handbook of*

Music Listening in the 19th and 20th Centuries, ed. Christian Thorau and Hansjakob Ziemer (New York: Oxford University Press, 2019), 145–62.

12. Amand Wilhelm Smith, *Philosophische Fragmente über die praktische Musik* (Vienna: Taubstummeninstitutsbuchdruckerey, 1787), 51: "Bach wird nie Dittersdorf, und Dittersdorf nie Bach werden." Ibid., 50: "Jeder sollte also seinen Hang studieren und demselben folgen." Ibid., 46–47: "Ein Compositeur muß ferner eine empfindsame Seele haben, welche sich leicht in verschiedene auch wechselweise entgegengesetzte Leidenschaften versetzen kann." Smith's treatise was listed in Mozart's estate: see Otto Erich Deutsch and Heinz Eibl, eds., *Mozart: Die Dokumente seines Lebens* (Kassel: Bärenreiter, 1961), 509.

13. Ignaz Theodor Ferdinand Cajetan Arnold, *Gallerie der berühmtesten Tonkünstler des achtzehnten und neunzehnten Jahrhunderts*, 2 vols. (Erfurt: Johann Karl Müller, 1810), 1:110–11: "Daß gewisse Gattungen der Kompositionen ihm vorzüglich entsprechen, liegt, so wie bei jedem andern Künstler in der Individualité seines persönlichen Karakters und dessen Einfluß auf den Künstlerkarakter. Frohsinn gelingt ihm im Durchschnitt mehr, als Schmerz und Verzweiflung."

14. Johann Mattheson, *Der vollkommene Capellmeister* (Hamburg: Herold, 1739), 16; ibid., 108 (section 64): "Denn niemand wird geschickt seyn, eine Leidenschafft in andrer Leute Gemüthern zu erregen, der nicht eben dieselbe Leidenschaft so kenne, als ob er sie selbst empfunden hätte, oder noch empfindet."

15. Ibid., 108 (section 65): "Zwar ist das keine Nothwendigkeit, daß ein musicalischer Setzer, wenn er z. E. ein Klagelied, ein Trauer-Stück, oder dergleichen zu Papier bringen will, auch dabey zu heulen und zu weinen afange: doch ist unumgänglich nöthig, daß er sein Gemüth und Herz gewisser maassen dem vorhabenden Affect einräume; sonst wird es ihm nur schlecht von statten gehen."

16. Avison, *Essay on Musical Expression*, 75.

17. Christian Friedrich Daniel Schubart, *Ideen zu einer Aesthetik der Tonkunst* (Vienna: J. V. Degen, 1806), 371: "Ein wahrer Capellmeister und Musikdirector . . . muss das Herz der Menschen tief studiert haben, um auf den Cordialnerven eben so sicher spielen zu können, wie auf seinem Lieblingsinstrumente." Although not published until 1806, Schubart's text dates from 1784–85.

18. William Duff, *An Essay on Original Genius* (London: Edward and Charles Dilly, 1767), 250, 251.

19. Quintilian, *Institutio oratoria*, trans. H. E. Butler, 4 vols. (Cambridge, MA: Harvard University Press, 1946), 2:433 (VI.ii.26–27).

20. Jean-Philippe Rameau, *Traité de l'harmonie* (Paris: Ballard, 1722), 143: "Un bon Musicien doit se livrer à tous les caracteres qu'il veut dépeindre; & comme un habile Comedien, se mettre à la place de celuy qui parle."

21. Heinrich Christoph Koch, *Versuch einer Anleitung zur Composition*, 3 vols. (Rudolstadt and Leipzig: Böhme, 1782–93), 2:94–96.

22. Johann Georg Sulzer, "Ausdruck in der Musik," in his *Allgemeine Theorie der schönen Künste*, 2 vols. (Leipzig: M. G. Weidemanns Erben und Reich, 1771–74), 1:109: "Der Ausdruck ist die Seele der Musik: ohne ihn ist sie blos ein angenehmes Spielwerk; durch ihn wird sie zur nachdrücklichsten Rede, die unwiderstehlich auf unser Herz

würket." The composer Johann Abraham Peter Schulz was Sulzer's musical collaborator for later entries in the *Allgemeine Theorie*. For the sake of bibliographic simplicity, the author of this and other collaborative entries on music in the *Allgemeine Theorie der schönen Künste* shall be referred to simply as "Sulzer."

23. Sulzer, "Ausdruck in der Musik," in his *Allgemeine Theorie der schönen Künste*, 1:109, 111: "Aber wie erlangt der Tonsetzer diese Zauberkraft, so gewaltig über unser Herz zu herrschen? ... Jedes Tonstück, es sey ein würklicher von Worten begleiteter Gesang oder nur für die Instrumente gesetzt, muß einen bestimmten Charakter haben und in dem Gemüte des Zuhörers Empfindungen von bestimmter Art erwecken. Es wäre töricht, wenn der Tonsetzer seine Arbeit anfangen wollte, ehe er den Charakter seines Stü[c]ks festgesetzt hat. ... Wenn er auch durch einen Zufall sein Thema erfunden oder wenn es ihm von ungefähr eingefallen ist, so untersuche er den Charakter desselben, damit er ihn auch bei der Ausführung beybehalten könne.

"Hat er den Charakter des Stü[c]ks festgesetzt, so muss er sich selbst in die Empfindung setzen, die er in andern hervor bringen will. Das beste ist, daß er sich eine Handlung, eine Begebenheit, einen Zustand vorstelle, in welchem sich dieselbe natürlicher Weise in dem Lichte zeiget, worin er sie vortragen will; und wenn seine Einbildungskraft dabey in das nöthige Feuer gesetzt worden, alsdenn arbeite er und hüthe sich irgend eine Periode, oder eine Figur einzumischen, die außer dem Charakter seines Stü[c]ks liegt."

24. For a similar account, see Carl Ludwig Junker, *Tonkunst* (Bern: Typographische Gesellschaft, 1777), 27–28: "Er [the composer] überlegt ... welche Empfindung er herfürbringen wolle; er setzt sich selbst zuerst in diese Empfindung hinein, denkt sich bey der ersten Fantasie, durchs mentale Bewußtweyn, den Mann dieser Leidenschaft, mit allen Bewegungen wie er ihn sah, und bestimmt denn, den Charackter seines Stücks."

25. Sulzer, "Gedicht," in his *Allgemeine Theorie der schönen Künste*, 1:43–34: "Die Dichtkunst hat mehr den lebhaften Ausdru[c]k des Gegenstands ihrer Vorstellung, als die besondere Wirkung, die er auf andre thun soll, zum Augenmerk. Der Dichter ist selbst lebhaft gerührt und von seinem Gegenstand in Leidenschaft, wenigstens in Laune gesetzt: er kann der Begierde, seine Empfindung zu äussern, nicht widerstehen; er wird hingerissen. Seine Hauptabsicht ist, den Gegenstand der ihn rührt, lebhaft zu schildern, und zugleich den Eindruck, den er davon empfindet, zu äussern: er redet, wenn ihm auch niemand zuhören sollte, weil ihn seine Empfindung nicht schweigen läßt. Er überläßt sich den Eindrücken, die seine Materie auf ihn macht, so sehr, daß man aus seinem Ton und aus seinem wenig überlegten Ausdruck merkt, er sey ganz von seinem Gegenstand eingenommen. Dieses giebt seiner Rede etwas ausserordentliches und phantastisches, dergleichen Menschen annehmen, die bey starken Empfindungen sich selbst vergessen, und selbst in Gesellschaft so reden und handeln, als wenn sie allein wären."

26. Sulzer, "Gedicht," in his *Allgemeine Theorie der schönen Künste*, 1:434: "Ohne merkliche Leidenschaft und Ueberwältigung von derselben, scheint natürlicher Weise kein Gedicht entstehen zu können. Nur itzt, da die Poesie zu einer gewöhnlichen Kunst worden ist, thut die Nachahmung dieses natürlichen Zustandes

das, was in dem Stande der bloßen Natur nur die starke Rührung thun würde. Daher sehen wir, dass die Dichter sich noch oft anstellen, als wenn sie auch wider ihren Willen getrieben würden, ihr Herz auszuschütten. Es ist damit, wie mit dem Tanz, der in seinem Ursprung nichts anders, als ein leidenschaftlicher, schwärmerischer Gang ist. Wilde Völker, bei denen noch nichts zur Kunst geworden, tanzen nie, als wenn sie in Leidenschaft gesetzt sind: aber wo das Tanzen zur Kunst geworden, da tanzt man auch mit kaltem Geblüte. Doch stellt man sich immer dabey an, als wenn irgend ein kräftiger Gegenstand diese phantastische Gemüthslage hervorgebracht habe. Daß so wohl Poesie als Tanz eine solche Faßung zum Grund haben, wird auch noch dadurch offenbar, dass beyde die Unterstützung der Musik bedürfen. Diese unterhält die Empfindung und reizet die schon aufgebrachte Einbildungskraft noch mehr. Sie wiegt das Gemüth in seiner eigenen Empfindung ein, daß der Dichter und Tänzer sich völlig vergessen und blos dem nachhängen, was sie empfinden. Aus dieser Entwicklung des Ursprungs der Poesie, läßt sich der wahre Charakter des Gedichts bestimmen."

27. B., "Die Künstler," *AmZ* 17 (22 March 1815): 195–96: "Bey den Schöpfern stehender Kunstwerke wechseln mit den Momenten der Begeisterung und des Enthusiasmus die des mechanischen Arbeitens, und der Künstler hält oft sein Gebilde in einer gewissen kalten Entfernung von sich. Dies ist beym Musiker nicht leicht der Fall. Er vermag nur durch eine fortwährende Wärme des Gefühls zu wirken, und nur sparsam darf er, um die Lücken der Begeisterung auszufüllen, uns mit blosser Kunstfertigkeit abfertigen.

   "Auch er muss, gleich den übrigen Künstlern des höhern Ranges, ganz aus seiner Individualität heraus treten, und sich alle Formen des Daseyns musikalisch aneignen können. Was er darstellt, in das muss sich der Quell seines innersten Gemüths ergiessen; jeder Ton muss gewissermassen der Ertrag seines ganzen Lebens seyn, und in der höchsten Täuschung muss er uns die höchste Wahrheit geben."

28. See George Winchester Stone, Jr., and George M. Kahrl, *David Garrick: A Critical Biography* (Carbondale: Southern Illinois University Press, 1979), chap. 2 ("Garrick and the Acting Tradition"); and Jean Benedetti, *David Garrick and the Birth of Modern Theatre* (London: Methuen, 2001). For a concise summary of the movement in Germany, see Theodore Ziolkowski, "Language and Mimetic Action in Lessing's *Miss Sara Sampson*," *Germanic Review* 40 (1965): 262–76.

29. See Joseph Roach, *The Player's Passion: Studies in the Science of Acting* (Newark: University of Delaware Press, 1985), 157.

30. Denis Diderot, *Paradoxe sur le comédien*, ed. Robert Abirached (Paris: Gallimard, 1994), 46: "C'est l'extrême sensibilité qui fait les acteurs médiocres; c'est la sensibilité médiocre qui fait la multitude des mauvais acteurs; et c'est le manque absolu de sensibilité qui prépare les acteurs sublimes." Translation from Diderot, *Selected Writings on Art and Literature*, trans. and ed. Geoffrey Bremner (Harmondsworth: Penguin, 1994), 108.

31. See James Harriman-Smith, "*Comédien*–Actor–*Paradoxe*: The Anglo-French Sources of Diderot's *Paradoxe sur le comédien*," *Theatre Journal* 67 (2015): 83–96. See also Earl R. Wasserman, "The Sympathetic Imagination in Eighteenth-Century Theories of

Acting," *Journal of English and Germanic Philology* 46 (1947): 264–72; and Richard Kramer, "Diderot's *Paradoxe* and C. P. E. Bach's *Empfindungen*," in *C. P. E. Bach Studies*, ed. Annette Richards (Cambridge: Cambridge University Press, 2006), 6–24.

32. Johann Joachim Quantz, *Versuch einer Anweisung die Flöte traversiere zu spielen* (Berlin: J. F. Voss, 1752), 107: "zu versetzen suchen." Ibid., 99.

33. Carl Philipp Emanuel Bach, *Versuch über die wahre Art das Clavier zu spielen*, 2 vols. (Berlin: C. F. Henning and G. L. Winter, 1753–62), 1:119: "aus der Seele muß man spielen, und nicht wie ein abgerichteter Vogel."

34. Bach, *Versuch*, 1:122: "Indem ein Musickus nicht anders rühren kan[n], er sey dann selbst gerührt; so muß er nothwendig sich selbst in alle Affecten setzen können, welche er bey seinen Zuhörern erregen will; er giebt ihnen seine Empfindungen zu verstehen und bewegt sie solchergestalt am besten zur Mit-Empfindung. Bey matten und traurigen Stellen wird er matt und traurig. Man sieht und hört es ihm an." See above, p. 31.

35. Bach, *Versuch*, 1:122: "Kaum, daß er einen [Affekt] stillt, so erregt er einen andern, folglich wechselt er beständig mit Leidenschaften ab."

36. Friedrich Wilhelm Marpurg, "Anmerkungen über den Anhang etc. des Herrn Weitzler," *Historisch-kritische Beiträge zur Aufnahme der Musik* 3 (1757): 120–21: "Der Ausführer soll empfinden, was der Componist empfunden hat. Er hat ihm seine Empfindung vorgeschrieben. Der Zuhörer soll in gleiche Empfindung gestzet werden. . . . "Muß sich der Ausführer nicht wie ein Schauspieler verhalten, und sich eine Zeitlang in diesen oder jenen Affect zu versetzen, und eben dahin, den Absichten des Componisten gemäß, seine Zuhörer zu versetzen . . . wissen? Er muß nicht der Bewegung der Seele folgen, die etwan in diesem Augenblicke würklich in ihm vorhanden ist. Er muß die vorgeschriebene Empfindung des Componisten annehmen. . . . Der Ausführer muß sich an die Stelle des Componisten setzten. Was bey diesem vorgegangen, muß bey jenem auch vorgehen."

37. The citations that follow in this paragraph are drawn from Hunter's insightful survey of sources from the late eighteenth and early nineteenth centuries in her "'To Play as if from the Soul of the Composer'."

38. Sulzer, "Vortrag (Musik)," in his *Allgemeine Theorie der schönen Künste*, 2:1252: " daß er gleichsam aus der Seele des Tonsetzers spielt." Schubart, *Ideen zu einer Ästhetik der Tonkunst*, 295: "Will ich eine Sonate von Bach vortragen, so muss ich mich so ganz in den Geist dieses grossen Mannes versenken, dass meine Ichheit wegschwindet und Bachisches Idiom wird."

39. Pierre Baillot, Pierre Rode, and Rodolphe Kreutzer, *Méthode du violon* (Paris: Au Magasin de musique, 1803), 479, quoted and translated in Hunter, "'To Play as if from the Soul'," 366: "Toute traduire, tout animer, faire passer dans l'âme de l'auditeur le sentiment que le compositeur avait dans la sienne."

40. E. T. A. Hoffmann, "Deux Trios . . . par Louis van Beethoven. Oeuvr. 70. . . ," *AmZ* 15 (3 March 1813): 153–54: "Der ächte Künstler lebt nur in dem Werke, das er in dem Sinne des Meisters aufgefasst hat, und nun vorträgt. Er verschmäht es, auf irgend eine Weise seine Persönlichkeit geltend zu machen."

41. François Fayolle, *Paganini et Bériot* (Paris: M. Legouest, 1831), 41; translation slightly modified from Hunter, "'To Play as if from the Soul'," 370–71: " Il [Baillot] possède

le génie de l'exécution, car il dépouille son *moi*, pour être, tour-à-tour, Haydn, Boccherini, Mozart et Beethoven."

42. See Rose Whyman, *The Stanislavsky System of Acting: Legacy and Influence in Modern Performance* (Cambridge: Cambridge University Press, 2008). Sanford Meisner and Dennis Longwell, *Sanford Meisner on Acting* (New York: Vintage, 1987), 15.

43. On the problem of translating mimesis as imitation, see Stephen Halliwell, *The Aesthetics of Mimesis: Ancient Texts and Modern Problems* (Princeton, NJ: Princeton University Press, 2002), 13–14. On mimesis in music of the late Enlightenment, see Wye J. Allanbrook, *The Secular Commedia: Comic Mimesis in Late Eighteenth-Century Music* (Berkeley and Los Angeles: University of California Press, 2014), esp. chap. 2.

44. Johann Elias Schlegel, "Abhandlung, daß die Nachahmung der Sache, der man nachahmet, zuweilen unähnlich werden müsse" (1745), in his *Aesthetische und dramaturgische Schriften*, ed. Johann von Antoniewicz (Heilbronn: Gebrüder Henninger, 1887), 96–105.

45. Charles Batteux, *Les beaux-arts réduits à un même principe* (Paris: Durand, 1746), 34: "C'est pour le même effet que ce même enthousiasme est nécessaire aux peintres & aux musiciens. Ils doivent oublier leur état; sortir d'eux-mêmes, & se mettre au milieu des choses qu'ils veulent représenter."

46. Batteux, *Les beaux-arts*, 15: "le portrait artificiel des passions humaines."

47. Thomas Twining, *Aristotle's Treatise on Poetry* (London: Payne and Son, 1789), 139–40.

48. Louis de Cahusac, "Expression (Opéra)," in *Encyclopédie, ou dictionnaire raisonné des sciences, des arts et des métiers, etc.*, 28 vols., ed. Denis Diderot and Jean le Rond d'Alembert (Paris: Le Breton et al., 1751–72), 6:315: "on n'imite point sans exprimer, ou plûtôt que l'expression est l'*imitation* même." Ibid., 6:316: "La musique est une imitation, & l'imitation n'est & ne peut être que l'*expression* véritable du sentiment qu'on veut peindre."

49. John Mainwaring, *Memoirs of the Life of the Late George Frideric Handel* (London: R. and J. Dodsley, 1760).

50. Franz Niemetschek, *Leben des k.k. Kapellmeisters Wolfgang Gottlieb Mozart, nach Originalquellen beschrieben* (Prague: Herrlische Buchhandlung, 1798); Johann Nikolaus Forkel, *Ueber Johann Sebastian Bachs Leben, Kunst und Kunstwerke* (Leipzig: Hoffmeister und Kühnel, 1802); and Pierre Louis Ginguené, *Notice sur la vie et les ouvrages de Nicolas Piccinni* (Paris: Veuve Panckoucke, 1800), 1.

Chapter 2

1. M. H. Abrams, *The Mirror and the Lamp: Romantic Theory and the Critical Tradition* (Oxford: Oxford University Press, 1953), 22.

2. Abrams, *The Mirror and the Lamp*, 3. The enormous influence of Abrams's study encouraged what Jerome J. McGann in 1983 called "an uncritical absorption in Romanticism's own self-representations"; see McGann, *The Romantic Ideology: A Critical Investigation* (Chicago: University of Chicago Press, 1983), 1. Subsequent

critics have taken note of this, and as Seamus Perry points out, it is Abrams's aesthetic "coordinates" that have made the most lasting impression in the field; see Perry, "New Impressions VII: *The Mirror and the Lamp*," *Essays in Criticism* 54 (2004): 260–82. See also Jonathan Culler, *The Pursuit of Signs: Semiotics, Literature, Deconstruction* (New York: Routledge, 2001), chap. 8 ("The Mirror Stage").

3. See Frederick Burwick, *Mimesis and Its Romantic Reflections* (University Park: Pennsylvania State University Press, 2001); Robert Alter, "Mimesis and the Motive for Fiction," *Tri-Quarterly* 42 (1978): 228-49; and Halliwell, *The Aesthetics of Mimesis*. Max Paddison, "Mimesis and the Aesthetics of Musical Expression," *Music Analysis* 29 (2010): 126-48, argues for the long afterlife of mimesis as it applies to music in the work of such diverse later writers as Schopenhauer, Hanslick, and Adorno.

4. Karl Philipp Moritz, *Über die bildende Nachahmung des Schönen* (Braunschweig: Schul-Buchhandlung, 1788). Halliwell, *The Aesthetics of Mimesis*, 359, points out that Schelling takes the same approach.

5. Ludwig Tieck, *Franz Sternbalds Wanderungen*, 2 vols. (Berlin: Johann Friedrich Unger, 1798), 2:125: "Denn was soll ich mit allen Zweigen und Blättern? mit dieser genauen Kopie der Gräser und Blumen? Nicht diese Pflanzen, nicht die Berge will ich abschreiben, sondern mein Gemüth, meine Stimmung, die mich gerade in diesem Momente regiert, will ich mir selber festhalten, und den übrigen Verständigen mittheilen."

6. August Wilhelm Schlegel, *Vorlesungen über schöne Litteratur und Kunst, erster Teil: Die Kunstlehre* (1801–2), ed. Jacob Minor (Heilbronn: Gebrüder Henninger, 1884), 91–92: " unabsichtlich, oft unfreywillig. . . . Das Wort Ausdruck ist dafür sehr treffend gewählt: das Innere wird gleichsam wie durch eine uns fremde Gewalt herausgedrückt; oder der Ausdruck ist ein von innen hervortretendes Gepräge des Äußern."

7. The enormous literature on changing conceptions of the self around this time includes Charles Taylor, *Sources of the Self: The Making of Modern Identity* (Cambridge: Cambridge University Press, 1989); Karl Ameriks and Dieter Sturma, eds., *The Modern Subject: Conceptions of the Self in Classical German Philosophy* (Albany: State University of New York Press, 1995); David E. Klemm and Günter Zöller, eds., *Figuring the Self: Subject, Absolute, and Others in Classical German Philosophy* (Albany: State University of New York Press, 1997); Jerrold Seigel, *The Idea of the Self: Thought and Experience in Western Europe since the Seventeenth Century* (Cambridge: Cambridge University Press, 2005); Raymond Martin and John Barresi, *The Rise and Fall of the Soul and Self: An Intellectual History of Personal Identity* (New York: Columbia University Press, 2006); and Andreas Reckwitz, *Das hybride Subjekt: Eine Theorie der Subjektkulturen von der bürgerlichen Moderne zur Postmoderne* (Weilerswist: Velbrück, 2006), esp. 204-42.

8. See Jan Goldstein, *The Post-Revolutionary Self: Politics and Psyche in France, 1750-1850* (Cambridge, MA: Harvard University Press, 2005); and Fritz Breithaupt, "Narcissism, the Self, and Empathy: The Paradox that Created Modern Literature," in *The Self as Muse: Narcissism and Creativity in the German Imagination, 1750-1830*, ed. Alexander Mathäs (Lewisburg, PA: Bucknell University Press, 2011), 42-43.

9. For overviews, see Lancelot L. Whyte, *The Unconscious before Freud* (New York: Basic Books, 1960); and Angus Nicholls and Martin Liebscher, eds., *Thinking the Unconscious: Nineteenth-Century German Thought* (Cambridge: Cambridge University Press, 2010), particularly the editors' introduction and the essays by Paul Bishop, Andrew Bowie, and Rüdiger Görner. See also Michael B. Buchholz and Günter Gödde, eds., *Das Unbewusste*, 3 vols. (Gießen: Psychosozial Verlag, 2005-6), esp. vol. 1, *Macht und Dynamik des Unbewussten: Auseinandersetzungen in Philosophie, Medizin und Psychoanalyse*; and Elke Völmicke, *Das Unbewusste im deutschen Idealismus* (Würzburg: Königshausen & Neumann, 2005). On parallel developments of psychology with literature and philosophy, see Matthew Bell, *The German Tradition of Psychology in Literature and Thought, 1700-1840* (Cambridge: Cambridge University Press, 2005); and Paul Bishop, *Analytical Psychology and German Classical Aesthetics: Goethe, Schiller, and Jung*, 2 vols. (London: Routledge, 2008).

10. For an excellent account of these developments in philosophy, see Bowie, *Aesthetics and Subjectivity*.

11. See Alexander M. Schlutz, *Mind's World: Imagination and Subjectivity from Descartes to Romanticism* (Seattle: University of Washington Press, 2009); and Udo Thiel, *The Early Modern Subject: Self-Consciousness and Personal Identity from Descartes to Hume* (Oxford: Oxford University Press, 2011).

12. David Hume, *A Treatise of Human Nature* (1738-40), ed. David Fate Norton and Mary J. Norton, 2 vols. (Oxford: Clarendon Press, 2007), 1:174.

13. Kant, *Prolegomena zu einer jeden künftigen Metaphysik, die als Wissenschaft wird auftreten können* (1783), in his *Gesammelte Schriften*, ed. Königlich-Preussische Akademie der Wissenschaften zu Berlin (Berlin: G. Reimer, 1902-), 4:260: "dogmatischer Schlummer."

14. *KdU*, section 49 (B193): "Die Einbildungskraft (als produktives Erkenntnisvermögen) ist nämlich sehr mächtig in Schaffung gleichsam einer anderen Natur aus dem Stoffe, den ihr die wirkliche gibt." Translation from Kant, *Critique of the Power of Judgment*, ed. Paul Guyer, trans. Paul Guyer and Eric Matthews (Cambridge: Cambridge University Press, 2000), 192. On the immediate and widespread impact of Kant's *Kritik der reinen Vernunft*, see Frederick Beiser, *The Fate of Reason: German Philosophy from Kant to Fichte* (Cambridge, MA: Harvard University Press, 1987).

15. See Richard Kearney, *The Wake of Imagination: Ideas of Creativity in Western Culture* (London: Hutchinson, 1988), esp. chap. 4 ("The Transcendental Imagination"); and Jane Kneller, *Kant and the Power of Imagination* (Cambridge: Cambridge University Press, 2007).

16. See Ameriks and Sturma, *The Modern Subject*; Manfred Frank, *Selbstgefühl* (Frankfurt am Main: Suhrkamp, 2002); and Karl Ameriks, "The Key Role of *Selbstgefühl* in Philosophy's Aesthetic and Historical Turns," *Critical Horizons* 5 (2004): 27-52.

17. David Wellbery, "The Transformation of Rhetoric," in *The Cambridge History of Literary Criticism*, vol. 5, *Romanticism*, ed. Marshall Brown (Cambridge: Cambridge University Press, 2000), 192. The paradox, as Wellbery points out, is that Kant himself moved within the conventions of rhetoric and at times even used its highly specialized terminology to support his arguments.

18. See Tobia Bezzola, *Die Rhetorik bei Kant, Fichte und Hegel: Ein Beitrag zur Philosophiegeschichte der Rhetorik* (Tübingen: Max Niemeyer, 1993).

19. Johann Gottlieb Fichte, *Grundlage der gesammten Wissenschaftslehre* (Leipzig: Christian Ernst Gabler, 1794); Friedrich Schiller, *Über die ästhetische Erziehung des Menschen in einer Reihe von Briefen* (1794–95), ed. Wolfgang Düsing (Munich: Hanser, 1981).

20. Friedrich Wilhelm Joseph Schelling, *System des transzendentalen Idealismus* (Tübingen: Cotta, 1800), 19: "das allgemeine Organon der Philosophie—und der Schlußstein ihres ganzen Gewölbes—die Philosophie der Kunst." Ibid., 475: "dass die Kunst das einzige wahre und ewige Organon zugleich und Document der Philosophie sey, welches immer und fortwährend aufs neue beurkundet, was die Philosophie äusserlich nicht darstellen kann, nämlich das Bewußtlose im Handeln und Produciren und seine ursprüngliche Identität mit dem Bewussten. Die Kunst ist ebendeswegen dem Philosophen das Höchste, weil sie ihm das Allerheiligste gleichsam öffnet, wo in ewiger und ursprünglicher Vereinigung gleichsam in Einer Flamme brennt, was in der Natur und Geschichte gesondert ist, und was im Leben und Handeln ebenso wie im Denken ewig sich fliehen muss." On the implications of Schelling's philosophy for the arts, see Rüdiger Görner, "The Hidden Agent of the Self: Towards an Aesthetic Theory of the Non-Conscious in German Romanticism," in Nicholls and Liebscher, *Thinking the Unconscious*, 121–39; and Andrew Bowie, "The Philosophical Significance of Schelling's Conception of the Unconscious," in Nicholls and Liebscher, *Thinking the Unconscious*, 57–86.

21. Georg Wilhelm Friedrich Hegel, *Vorlesungen über die Aesthetik*, ed. H. G. Hotho, 3 vols. (Berlin: Duncker & Humblot, 1835), 1:11: "eine Art und Weise, . . . das Göttliche, die tiefsten Interessen des Menschen, die umfassendsten Wahrheiten des Geistes zum Bewußtseyn zu bringen und auszusprechen."

22. Schiller, "Sprache," in *Musenalmanach für das Jahr 1797*, ed. Friedrich Schiller (Tübingen: Cotta, 1797), 177.

23. On *furor poeticus*, see Plato, *Ion* 533c; *Laws* 719c; *Phaedrus* 245a; and *Apology* 22c. On its applicability to literature of the late eighteenth and early nineteenth centuries, see Frederick Burwick, *Poetic Madness and the Romantic Imagination* (University Park: Pennsylvania State University Press, 1996). On its applicability to music, see Peter Kivy, *The Possessor and the Possessed: Handel, Mozart, Beethoven, and the Idea of Musical Genius* (New Haven, CT: Yale University Press, 2001). On Goethe, see Angus Nicholls, *Goethe's Concept of the Daemonic: After the Ancients* (Rochester, NY: Camden House, 2006).

24. See Jerome Hamilton Buckley, *The Turning Key: Autobiography and the Subjective Impulse since 1800* (Cambridge, MA: Harvard University Press, 1984), 15; Edward S. Reed, *From Soul to Mind: The Emergence of Psychology, from Erasmus Darwin to William James* (New Haven, CT: Yale University Press, 1997); and George Makari, *Soul Machine: The Invention of the Modern Mind* (New York: W. W. Norton, 2015). The turn from the sacred to the secular as a driving force of Romanticism lies at the heart of M. H. Abrams, *Natural Supernaturalism: Tradition and Revolution in Romantic Literature* (New York: W. W. Norton, 1971).

25. Edward Young, *Conjectures on Original Composition* (London: A. Millar and R. and J. Dodsley, 1759), 25. Young's works were quickly translated into German: see John Louis Kind, *Edward Young in Germany* (New York: Macmillan, 1906).

26. Young, *Conjectures on Original Composition*, 53–54.

27. On the role of genius in the arts in the late eighteenth century, see Penelope Murray, ed., *Genius: The History of an Idea* (Oxford: Basil Blackwell, 1989); Taylor, *Sources of the Self*, chap. 21 ("The Expressivist Turn"); Kivy, *The Possessor and the Possessed*; Jochen Schmidt, *Die Geschichte des Genie-Gedankens in der deutschen Literatur, Philosophie und Politik, 1750-1945*, 3rd ed., 2 vols. (Heidelberg: Universitätsverla g, 2004); and Roderick Cavaliero, *Genius, Power and Magic: A Cultural History of Germany from Goethe to Wagner* (London: Palgrave Macmillan, 2013).

28. *KdU*, section 47 (B184).

29. *KdU*, section 46 (B181), 193; ibid., section 49 (B198), 206.

30. *KdU*, section 46 (B181), 193: "Genie ist das Talent (Naturgabe) welches der Kunst die Regel gibt." Ibid., "Da das Talent, als angeborenes produktives Vermögen des Künstlers, selbst zur Natur gehört, so könnte man sich auch so ausdrücken: *Genie* ist die angeborene Gemütsanlage (*ingenium*), *durch welche* die Natur der Kunst die Regel gibt." Translations from Kant, *Critique of the Power of Judgment*, 186.

31. *KdU*, section 46 (B182), 194: "da es auch originalen Unsinn geben kann." Translation from Kant, *Critique of the Power of Judgment*, 186.

32. *KdU*, section 46 (B181), 193: "Denn eine jede Kunst setzt Regeln voraus, durch deren Grundlegung allererst ein Produkt, wenn es künstlich heißen soll, als möglich vorgestellt wird." Translation from Kant, *Critique of the Power of Judgment*, 186.

33. *KdU*, section 47 (B186), 197: "So gibt es doch keine schöne Kunst, in welcher nicht etwas Mechanisches, welches nach Regeln gefaßt und befolgt werden kann, und also etwas *Schulgerechtes* die wesentliche Bedingung der Kunst ausmachte." Ibid.: "Das Genie kann nur reichen *Stoff* zu Produkten der schönen Kunst hergeben; die Verarbeitung desselben und die *Form* erfordert ein durch die Schule gebildetes Talent, um einen Gebrauch davon zu machen, der vor der Urteilskraft bestehen kann." Ibid., section 50 (B203), 210: " bringt in ihrer gesetzlosen Freiheit nichts als Unsinn hervor." Translations from Kant, *Critique of the Power of Judgment*, 188, 189, 197.

34. Griesinger, *Biographische Notizen über Joseph Haydn*, 114: "Man erzählte Haydn, daß Albrechtsberger alle Quarten aus dem reinsten Satze verbannt wissen wolle. 'Was heißt das? erwiederte Haydn; die Kunst ist frey, und soll durch keine Handwerksfesseln beschränkt werden. Das Ohr, versteht sich ein gebildetes, muß entscheiden, und ich halte mich für befugt, wie irgend einer, hierin Gesetze zu geben. Solche Künsteleyen haben keinen Werth; ich wünschte lieber, daß es einer versuchte, einen wahrhaft *neuen* Menuet zu komponieren." For a review of this and other similar statements by Haydn, see Elaine Sisman, "Haydn, Shakespeare, and the Rules of Originality," in *Haydn and His World*, ed. Elaine Sisman (Princeton, NJ: Princeton University Press, 1997), 6–8.

35. Griesinger, *Biographische Notizen über Joseph Haydn*, 113: "Haydns ästhetischer Charakter war das Werk einer glücklichen Naturgabe und des anhaltenden Studiums. Wer ihn von seiner Kunst reden hörte, hätte in ihm den großen Künstler nicht

geahnet, und die Bemerkung Kants, 'daß der Urheber eines Produkts, welches er dem Genie verdankt, selbst nicht wisse, wie sich in ihm die Ideen dazu herbey finden, auch es nicht in seiner Gewalt habe, dergleichen nach Belieben oder planmäßig auszudenken, und andern in Vorschriften mitzutheilen, die sie in den Stand setzten, gleichmäßige Produkte hervorzubringen'." The passage Griesinger quotes (with slight emendations) is from Kant, *KdU*, section 46 (B182), 194.

36. *KdU*, section 50 (B203), 210: "Der Geschmack ist, so wie die Urteilskraft überhaupt, die Disziplin (oder Zucht) des Genies, beschneidet diesem sehr die Flügel und macht es gesittet oder geschliffen; zugleich aber gibt er diesem eine Leitung, worüber und bis wie weit es sich verbreiten soll, um zweckmäßig zu bleiben; und indem er Klarheit und Ordnung in die Gedankenfülle hineinbringt, macht er die Ideen haltbar, eines dauernden, zugleich auch allgemeinen Beifalls, der Nachfolge anderer und einer immer fortschreitenden Kultur fähig. Wenn also im Widerstreite beiderlei Eigenschaften an einem Produkte etwas aufgeopfert werden soll, so müßte es eher auf der Seite des Genies geschehen; und die Urteilskraft, welche in Sachen der schönen Kunst aus eigenen Prinzipien den Ausspruch tut, wird eher der Freiheit und dem Reichthum der Einbildungskraft als dem Verstande Abbruch zu tun erlauben." Translation from Kant, *Critique of the Power of Judgment*, 197.

37. Leopold Mozart to Maria Anna Mozart, 16 February 1785, in Mozart, *Briefe und Aufzeichnungen*, 3:373: "H: Haydn sagte mir: *ich sage ihnen vor gott, als ein ehrlicher Mann, ihr Sohn ist der größte Componist, den ich von Person und dem Nahmen nach kenne: er hat geschmack, und über das die größte Compositionswissenschaft.*"

38. See above, p. 24.

39. Christian Fürchtegott Gellert, *Von dem Einflusse der schönen Wissenschaften auf das Herz und die Sitten* (1756), in *Sammlung vermischter Schriften*, 2 vols. (Leipzig: M. G. Weidmanns Erben und Reich, 1766), 2:148: "Allein, was vermag das beste Genie ohne Unterricht, ohne Kunst, ohne Uebung? Was wird der größte Geist treffliches hervorbringen, wenn er noch nicht durch Wissenschaften gebildet, noch nicht mit einem Vorrathe schöner und nützlicher Gedanken ausgerüstet, mit einer Menge lebhafter Bilder ausgeschmückt, noch nicht mit den Schätzen der Sprache und des Ausdruckes bereichert ist?"

40. See Roger Paulin, *The Critical Reception of Shakespeare in Germany, 1682–1914: Native Literature and Foreign Genius* (Hildesheim: Georg Olms, 2003), as well as the repeated references to Shakespeare throughout Matthias Luserke-Jaqui, ed., *Handbuch Sturm und Drang*, ed. (Boston: Walter de Gruyter, 2017).

41. Christoph Martin Wieland, "Einige Nachrichten von den Lebens-Umständen des Herrn Willhelm Shakespear," in William Shakespeare, *Theatralische Werke, aus dem Englischen übersetzt von Herrn Wieland*, 8 vols. (Zurich: Orell, Gebner, 1762–66), 8:8: "eine Regelmäßigkeit, eine Correction und Vollendung gegeben haben, die ihm itzt mangelt; aber mit allen diesen Vortheilen würde er nicht mehr Shakespear gewesen seyn; nicht mehr der ursprüngliche Genie, der Sohn der Phantasie ... dessen wilde Töne, gleich dem Waldgesang der freyen Nachtigall, die antwortenden Sayten unsers Herzens schneller und tiefer rühren, als das angelehrte künstliche Lied des eingebauerten Canarienvogels."

42. Goethe, "Zum Shakespeares-Tag" (1771), in his *Werke*, 12:225: "Es schien mir die Einheit des Orts so kerkermäßig ängstlich, die Einheiten der Handlung und der Zeit lästige Fesseln unsrer Einbildungskraft."

43. Mary Sue Morrow, *German Music Criticism in the Late Eighteenth Century: Aesthetic Issues in Instrumental Music* (Cambridge: Cambridge University Press, 1997), 99–133.

44. Steven Lukes, *Individualism* (New York: Harper & Row, 1973), 1.

45. On *Bildung*, see Walter Horace Bruford, *The German Tradition of Self-Cultivation: Bildung from Humboldt to Thomas Mann* (Cambridge: Cambridge University Press, 1975); and Rebekka Horlacher, *The Educated Subject and the German Concept of Bildung: A Comparative Cultural History* (New York: Routledge, 2016.)

46. Taylor, *Sources of the Self*, 376. See also Seigel, *The Idea of the Self*; and Gerald Izenberg, *Impossible Individuality: Romanticism, Revolution, and the Origins of Modern Selfhood* (Princeton, NJ: Princeton University Press, 1992).

47. See Robert C. Solomon, *Continental Philosophy since 1750: The Rise and Fall of the Self* (Oxford: Oxford University Press, 1988).

48. August Wilhelm Schlegel, "Über das Verhältnis der schönen Kunst zur Natur," *Prometheus* 5, no. 6 (1808): 15: "Wo aber soll der Künstler seine erhabene Meisterin, die schaffende Natur, finden, um sich mit ihr gleichsam zu berathen, da sie in keiner äusseren Erscheinung enthalten ist? In seinem eigenen Innern, im Mittelpunkte seines Wesens durch geistige Anschauung kann er es nur, oder nirgends. Die Astrologen haben den Menschen Mikrokosmus, die kleine Welt, genannt, was sich philosophisch sehr gut rechtfertigen läßt. . . . Die Klarheit nun, der Nachdruck, die Fülle, die Allseitigkeit, womit sich das Weltall in einem menschlichen Geiste abspiegelt, und womit sich wiederum dieses Abspiegeln in ihm spiegelt, bestimmt den Grad seiner künstlerischen Genialität, und setzt ihn in den Stand, eine Welt in der Welt zu bilden. Man könnte die Kunst daher auch definieren als die durch das Medium eines vollendeten Geistes hindurchgegangene, für unsre Betrachtung verklärte und zusammengedrängte Natur."

49. Novalis [Friedrich von Hardenberg], "Teplitzer Fragment 82" (ca. 1797–98), in his *Schriften*, ed. Paul Kluckhohn and Richard Samuel, 2nd ed. (Stuttgart: W. Kohlhammer, 1977), 2:610: "ein ächter Ausfluß der *Persönlichkeit*." Johann Gottlieb Fichte, "Versuch einer neuen Darstellung der Wissenschaftslehre," *Philosophisches Journal* 5 (1797): 6: "Merke auf dich selbst: kehre deinen Blick von allem, was dich umgiebt, ab, und in dein Inneres; ist die erste Foderung, welche die Philosophie an ihren Lehrling thut. Es ist von nichts, was außer dir ist, die Rede, sondern lediglich von dir selbst."

50. For overviews of the general change in attitudes toward emotions that began around the middle of the eighteenth century, see Thomas Dixon, *From Passions to Emotions: The Creation of a Secular Psychological Category* (Cambridge: Cambridge University Press, 2003), chaps. 3 and 4; and Ute Frevert, *Emotions in History— Lost and Found* (New York: Central European Press, 2011), esp. chap. 3 ("Finding Emotions"). These changes are further reflected in the semantics of such terms as "sympathy," "empathy," "pity," and the like, as detailed in Ute Frevert et al., eds.,

Emotional Lexicons: Continuity and Change in the Vocabulary of Feeling, 1700–2000 (New York: Oxford University Press, 2014).

51. Hume, *A Treatise of Human Nature*, 1:266–67. On the implications of this position, see Elijah Millgram, "Was Hume a Humean?" *Hume Studies* 21 (1995): 75–93.

52. Jean-Jacques Rousseau, *Les confessions* (1782), ed. Jacques Voisine (Paris: Classiques Garnier, 2011), 3: "Je forme une entreprise qui n'eut jamais d'exemple et dont l'exécution n'aura point d'imitateur. Je veux montrer à mes semblables un homme dans toute la vérité de la nature; et cet homme ce sera moi.

"Moi seul. Je sens mon cœur et je connais les hommes. Je ne suis fait comme aucun de ceux que j'ai vus; j'ose croire n'être fait comme aucun de ceux qui existent. Si je ne vaux pas mieux, au moins je suis autre." Translation from Rousseau, *The Confessions*, trans. J. M. Cohen (Harmondsworth: Penguin, 1953), 17.

53. See Francis Mariner, "From Portraiture to Reverie: Rousseau's Autobiographical Framing," *South Atlantic Review* 57 (1992): 15–31.

54. On the transformative role of Goethe's autobiography within the long history of the genre, see Karl Joachim Weintraub, *The Value of the Individual: Self and Circumstance in Autobiography* (Chicago: University of Chicago Press, 1978), chap. 13; and Gay, *The Naked Heart*, chap. 2 ("Exercises in Self-Definition").

55. See Downing A. Thomas, *Music and the Origins of Language: Theories from the French Enlightenment* (Cambridge: Cambridge University Press, 1995).

56. Sulzer, "Nachahmung," in his *Allgemeine Theorie der schönen Künste*; see above, p. 30.

57. See Matthew Gelbart, *The Invention of "Folk Music" and "Art Music": Emerging Categories from Ossian to Wagner* (Cambridge: Cambridge University Press, 2007).

58. Plato, *Republic*, 401d–402a, trans. G. M. A. Grube, rev. C. D. C. Reeve, in Plato, *Complete Works*, ed. John M. Cooper (Indianapolis: Hackett, 1997), 1038.

59. Sulzer, "Singen," in his *Allgemeine Theorie der schönen Künste*, 2:1075: "Worte, die für sich nur einen schwachen Eindruck machen würden, können, wenn sie gesungen werden, zur Sprache des Herzens werden, und eine ganze Vesammlung in Rührung setzen."

60. Johann Gottfried Herder, *Ideen zur Philosophie der Geschichte der Menschheit*, 4 vols. (Riga and Leipzig: Johann Friedrich Hartknoch, 1784–91), 2:235: "die Empfindungen unseres Herzens aber blieben in unserer Brust vergraben, wenn der melodische Strom sie nicht in sanften Wellen zum Herzen des andern hinüber brächte. Auch darum also hat der Schöpfer die Musik der Töne zum Organ unsrer Bildung gewählt; eine Sprache für die Empfindung, eine Vater- und Mutter- Kindes- und Freundessprache."

61. Novalis, "Anekdoten 226," in his *Schriften*, 2:574: "Der Musiker nimmt das Wesen seiner Kunst aus sich, auch nicht der leiseste Verdacht von Nachahmung kann ihn treffen."

62. Hegel, *Vorlesungen über die Aesthetik*, 3:192: "die Melodie, dieß reine Ertönen des Innern, ist die eigenste Seele der Musik."

63. Richard Wagner, *Das Kunstwerk der Zukunft* (Leipzig: Otto Wigand, 1850), 68: "Das Organ des Herzens aber ist der *Ton*; seine künstlerische bewußte Sprache, die *Tonkunst*."

64. Lionel Trilling, *Sincerity and Authenticity* (Cambridge, MA: Harvard University Press, 1972), 2, 6.

65. See Christine Roulston, *Virtue, Gender, and the Authentic Self in Eighteenth-Century Fiction: Richardson, Rousseau, and Laclos* (Gainesville: University of Florida Press, 1998), chap. 1. See also Leon Guilhamet, *The Sincere Ideal: Studies on Sincerity in Eighteenth-Century English Literature* (Montreal: McGill–Queen's University Press, 1974).

66. Rousseau, *The Confessions*, 506.

67. Jean-Jacques Rosseau, *Julie ou La nouvelle Héloïse*, ed. René Pomeau (Paris: Classiques Garnier, 2012), 740–41: "Ce n'est que dans le monde qu'on apprend à parler avec énergie. Premièrement, parce qu'il faut toujours dire autrement et mieux que les autres, et puis que, forcé d'affirmer à chaque instant ce qu'on ne croit pas, d'exprimer des sentiments qu'on n'a point, on cherche à donner à ce qu'on dit un tour persuasif qui supplée à la persuasion intérieure . . . la passion, pleine d'elle même, s'exprime avec plus d'abondance que de force; elle ne songe même pas à persuader; elle ne soupçonne pas qu'on puisse douter d'elle." The translation here is from J.-J. Rousseau, *Julie, or The New Heloise*, trans. and ed. Philip Stewart and Jean Vaché (Hanover, NH: University Press of New England, 1997), 9–10.

68. Johann Peter Eckermann, *Gespräche mit Goethe in den letzten Jahren seines Lebens* (1836–48), ed. Heniz Schlaffer, in Goethe, *Sämtliche Werke nach Epochen seines Schaffens: Münchner Ausgabe*, 21 vols., ed. Karl Richter et al. (Munich: Carl Hanser, 1985), 19:489–90: "Das ist auch so ein Geschöpf, sage Goehte, das ich gleich dem Pelikan mit dem Blute meines eigenen Herzens gefüttert habe. Es ist darin so viel Innerliches aus meiner eigenen Brust." Goethe, *Dichtung und Wahrheit*, in his *Werke*, 9:587–88: "ziemlich unbewußt, einem Nachtwandler ähnlich. . . . Ich fühlte mich, wie nach einer Generalbeichte, wieder froh und frei, und zu einem neuen Leben berechtigt."

69. Abrams, *The Mirror and the Lamp*, 84–88.

70. Sulzer, "Lyrisch," in his *Allgemeine Theorie der schönen Künste*, 2:726–27: "Das lyrische Gedicht hat, selbst da, wo es die Rede an einen andern wendet, gar viel von der Natur des empfindungsvollen Selbstgespräches. . . . Wo andre Dichter aus Ueberlegung sprechen, das spricht der Lyrische blos aus Empfindung."

71. Sulzer, "Originalwerk," in his *Allgemeine Theorie der schönen Künste*, 2:864: "Man siehet leicht, wieviel Vorzüge diese Originale vor den Werken, die es nicht sind, haben müssen: sie sind wahre Aeußerungen des Genies; da die andern Schilderungen verstellter nicht würklich vorhandener Empfindungen sind. Jene lassen uns allemal die Natur, diese nur die Kunst sehen. Ein Dichter der von einem Gegenstand bis zur lyrischen Begeisterung gerührt worden, und denn singt, weil er der Begierde das was er fühlt auszudrüken, nicht wiederstehen kann, dichtet eine Originalode, die ein wahrer Abdruck des Zustandes seines Gemüths ist. Ein andermal aber fodern außer der Kunst liegende Veranlassungen eine Ode; oder er selbst stellt sich vor, er sey in einem Fall, in eine Lage, darin er nicht ist, sucht Empfindungen hervor, die dem Fall natürlich sind, die er aber nicht würklich hat, und in dieser angenommenen Stellung dichtet er. Da muß freylich ein ganz anderes Werk entstehen, das uns mehr die Kunst,

als die Natur sehen läßt. Ein solches Werk ist etwas betrügerisches, damit man uns, blos um die Kunst zu zeigen, hintergehen will." On the tradition of German lyric poetry as a reflection of poets' personal experiences, see in particular Michael Feldt, *Lyrik als Erlebnislyrik: Zur Geschichte eines Literatur-und Mentalitätstypus zwischen 1600 und 1900* (Heidelberg: Carl Winter, 1990); and Karl S. Guthke, *Die Entdeckung des Ich: Studien zur Literatur* (Tübingen: A. Francke, 1993).

72. Werther's letter of 22 May in Goethe, *Die Leiden des jungen Werthers* (1774), in his *Werke*, 6:13: "Ich kehre in mich selbst zurück und finde eine Welt!"

73. Eckermann, *Gespräche mit Goethe* (29 January 1826), 19:155: "Solange er bloß seine wenigen subjektiven Empfindungen ausspricht, ist er noch keiner zu nennen; aber sobald er die Welt sich anzueignen und auszusprechen weiß, ist er ein Poet."

74. Anne Louise Germaine de Staël-Holstein, *De l'Allemagne*, 3 vols. (Paris: H. Nicolle, 1813), 1:252: "que l'artiste doit conserver son sang-froid pour agir plus fortement sur l'imagination de ses lecteurs: peut-être n'auroit-il pas eu cette opinion dans sa première jeunesse."

75. Katrin Kohl, "No Escape? Goethe's Strategies of Self-Projection and Their Role in German Literary Historiography," *Goethe Yearbook* 16 (2009): 176.

76. August Wilhelm Schlegel, *Vorlesungen über dramatische Kunst und Literatur* (1801-04), in A. W. Schlegel, *Sämmtliche Werke*, 16 vols., ed. Eduard Böcking, 3rd ed. (Leipzig: Weidmann, 1846-48), 5:39: "Das lyrische Gedicht ist der musikalische Ausdruck von Gemüthsbewegungen durch die Sprache. Das Wesen der musikalischen Stimmung besteht darin, daß wir irgend eine Regung, sei sie nun an sich erfreulich oder schmerzlich, mit Wohlgefallen festzuhalten, ja innerlich zu verewigen suchen." Ibid., 5:48: "der innigste Ausdruck unsers ganzen Wesens."

77. Hegel, *Vorlesungen über die Aesthetik*, 3:323: "Ihr Inhalt ist das Subjektive, die innere Welt, das betrachtende, empfindende Gemüth, das . . . sich deshalb . . . das Sich Aussprechen des Subjekts zur einzigen Form und zum letzten Ziel nehmen kann."

78. William Wordsworth, *The Poetical Works of Wordsworth*, ed. Paul Sheats (Boston: Houghton Mifflin, 1982), 91–93, 570.

79. Abrams, *The Mirror and the Lamp*, 22–23.

80. Wordsworth, *Lyrical Ballads*, 3rd ed., 2 vols. (London: T. N. Longman and O. Rees, 1802), xxviii.

81. David Perkins, *Wordsworth and the Poetry of Sincerity* (Cambridge, MA: Harvard University Press, 1964), 81. Perkins, *Wordsworth*, and Kenneth R. Johnston, *The Hidden Wordsworth: Poet, Lover, Rebel, Spy* (New York: W. W. Norton, 1998), demonstrate convincingly that Wordsworth, for one, did not in fact write his poems in this way.

82. Byron to Thomas Moore, 5 July 1821, in George Gordon Byron, *Byron's Letters and Journals*, ed. Leslie A. Marchand, 13 vols. (Cambridge, MA: Harvard University Press, 1973–82), 8:146. Shelley, "A Defence of Poetry" (1821), in his *Essays, Letters from Abroad, Translations and Fragments*, ed. Mary Wollstonecraft Shelley, 2 vols. (London: Edward Moxon, 1840), 53. Keats to J. H. Reynolds, 9 April 1818, in John Keats, *Selected Letters*, ed. Grant Scott, rev. ed. (Cambridge, MA: Harvard University Press, 2002), 113.

83. François-Auguste Chateaubriand, *Génie du Christianisme*, 4 vols. (Paris: Migneret, 1802), 2:18: "Les grands écrivains ont mis leur histoire dans leurs ouvrages. On ne peint bien que son propre coeur, en l'attribuant à un autre, et la meilleure partie du génie se compose de souvenirs."

84. André Chénier, *Élégie XXI*, in his *Oeuvres posthumes*, ed. D. Ch. Robert (Paris: Guillaume, 1826), 192: "L'Art des transports de l'âme est un faible interprète; / L'Art ne fait que des vers: le cœur seul est poète. / Sous sa fécondité le génie opprimé / Ne peut garder l'ouvrage en sa tête formé . . . / Son coeur dicte: il écrit. A ce maître divin / Il ne fait qu'obéir, et que prêter sa main."

85. See Peter Martin, *Edmond Malone, Shakespearean Scholar: A Literary Biography* (Cambridge: Cambridge University Press, 1995), 47–48. On the tradition of interpreting the sonnets through biography, see Abrams, *The Mirror and the Lamp*, 246–49.

86. August Wilhelm Schlegel, *Vorlesungen über dramatische Kunst und Literatur*, in his *Sämmtliche Werke*, 5:174: "Sie schildern ganz augenscheinlich wirkliche Lagen und Stimmungen des Dichters, sie machen uns mit den Leidenschaften des Menschen bekannt, ja sie enthalten auch sehr merkwürdige Geständnisse über seine jugendlichen Verirrungen."

87. William Wordsworth, "Scorn Not the Sonnet" (1827), in Wordsworth, *Poetical Works*, 2:305; and Wordsworth, "Essay Supplementary to the Preface," in his *Poems . . . with Additional Poems, a New Preface, and a Supplementary Essay*, 2 vols. (London: Longman, Hurst, Rees, Orme, and Brown, 1815), 352. On Heine and Emerson, see James Shapiro, "Unravelling Shakespeare's Life," in *On Life-Writing*, ed. Zachary Leader (New York: Oxford University Press, 2015), 7–24.

88. On the relationship between the rise of lyric poetry and the decline of rhetoric, see Gerhard Kaiser, *Geschichte der deutschen Lyrik von Goethe bis Heine: Ein Grundriß in Interpretationen*, 3 vols. (Frankfurt am Main: Suhrkamp, 1988), 1:188–212.

89. Shelley, "A Defence of Poetry," 1:14. On Shelley's belief in the strong musical qualities of poetry, see Jessica K. Quillin, *Shelley and the Musico-Poetics of Romanticism* (Farnham, Surrey: Ashgate, 2012).

90. Thomas Babington Macaulay, review of John Milton, *A Treatise on Christian Doctrine . . . translated from the original by Charles R. Sumner*, *Edinburgh Review* 42 (1825): 313, 307.

91. John Stuart Mill, "What Is Poetry?" (1833), in his *Essays on Poetry*, ed. F. Parvin Sharpless (Columbia: University of South Carolina Press, 1976), 12. On the idea of lyric poetry in particular as private, see Herbert F. Tucker, "Dramatic Monologue and the Overhearing of Lyric," in his *Lyric Poetry: Beyond the New Criticism* (Ithaca: Cornell University Press, 1985), 226–43.

92. On the decline of rhetoric as a model of poetics in the decades around 1800, see Manfred Fuhrmann, *Rhetorik und öffentliche Rede: Über die Ursachen des Verfalls der Rhetorik im ausgehenden 18. Jahrhundert* (Konstanz: Universitätsverlag, 1983); and Rüdiger Campe, "Umbrüche und Wandlungen der Rhetorik," in *Die Wende von der Aufklärung zur Romantik, 1760–1820: Epoche im Überblick*, ed. Horst Albert Glaser and György Mihály Vajda (Amsterdam and Philadelphia: John Benjamins, 2000), 589–612.

Chapter 3

1. For purposes of linguistic simplicity, *fantasia* serves here to encompass other genres that at different times and places were perceived as more or less improvisatory, such as the capriccio and (especially in earlier times) the toccata. While some writers insisted on various degrees of distinction among these genres, they all agreed on the centrality of musical freedom and the predominance (or apparent predominance) of fantasy in all of them. See Gretchen Wheelock, "Mozart's Fantasy, Haydn's Caprice: What's in a Name?," in *The Century of Bach and Mozart: Perspectives on Historiography, Composition, Theory and Performance*, ed. Sean Gallagher and Thomas Forrest Kelly (Cambridge, MA: Harvard University Department of Music, 2008), 317–41.

2. Rousseau, "Fantasie," in his *Dictionnaire de musique*, 215: "Pièce de Musique Instrumentale qu'on éxecute en la composant."

3. On the eighteenth century's cult of musical solitude, see Laurenz Lütteken, *Das Monologische als Denkform in der Musik zwischen 1760 und 1785* (Tübingen: Niemeyer, 1998), 266–86; and Annette Richards, *The Free Fantasia and the Musical Picturesque* (Cambridge: Cambridge University Press, 2001), 155.

4. Johann Friedrich Reichardt, *Briefe eines aufmerksamen Reisenden die Musik betreffend*, 2 vols. (Frankfurt am Main and Leipzig: n. p., 1774–76), 1:15: "Seine ganze Seele ist dabey in Arbeit."

5. Bach, *Versuch*, 1:123–24: "... Fantasien, welche nicht in auswendig gelernten Passagien oder gestohlnen Gedancken bestehen, sondern aus einer guten musikalischen Seele herkommen müssen, das Sprechende, das hurtig Ueberraschende von einem Affeckte zum andern."

6. H. 300, in F♯ minor, originally for solo keyboard, later arranged for keyboard and violin and given its distinctive title as H. 536. See Sara Gross Ceballos, "Sympathizing with *C. P. E. Bachs Empfindungen*," *Journal of Musicology* 34 (2017): 1–31.

7. Matthew Head, "C. P. E. Bach 'in tormentis': Gout Pain and Body Language in the Fantasia in A Major, H. 278 (1782)," *Eighteenth-Century Music* 13 (2016): 211–34. Wolfgang Wiemer has argued that the Fantasia in C minor, H. 75, follows the formal outlines of a funeral oration and for this reason could be heard as a lamentation on the death of this father; see Wiemer, "Carl Philipp Emanuel Bach Fantasie in c-Moll—ein Lamento auf den Tod des Vaters?" *Bach-Jahrbuch* 74 (1988): 163–77.

8. Charles Burney, *The Present State of Music in Germany, the Netherlands, and United Provinces*, 2 vols. (London: T. Becket, 1773), 2:269–70.

9. Matthias Claudius to Heinrich Wilhelm von Gerstenberg, early October 1768, in Carl Philipp Emanuel Bach, *Briefe und Dokumente: Kritische Gesamtausgabe*, ed. Ernst Suchalla, 2 vols. (Göttingen: Vandenhoeck & Ruprecht, 1994), 1:164: "Sein Adagiospiel kann ich nicht besser beschreiben, als wenn ich Sie an einen Redner zu denken ganz gehorsamst ersuche, der seine Reden nicht auswendig gelernt hat, sondern von dem Inhalt seiner Rede ganz voll ist, gar nicht eilt, etwas herauszubringen, sondern ganz ruhig eine Welle nach der andern aus der Fülle seiner Seele herausströmen läßt, ohne an der Art der Herausströmung zu künsteln."

10. See Eugene Helm, "The 'Hamlet' Fantasy and the Literary Element in C. P. E. Bach's Music," *MQ* 58 (1972): 277–96; and Tobias Plebuch, "Dark Fantasies of the Dawn of the Self: Gerstenberg's Monologues for C. P. E. Bach's C minor Fantasia," in *C. P. E. Bach Studies*, ed. Annette Richards (Cambridge: Cambridge University Press, 2006), 25–66.

11. Friedrich Rochlitz, "Der Besuch im Irrenhaus," *AmZ* 6 (1804): 645–54, 661–72, 677–85, 693–706. See Richards, *The Free Fantasia*, 145–49; and Deirdre Loughridge, "Magnified Vision, Mediated Listening and the 'Point of Audition' of Early Romanticism," *18th-Century Music* 10 (2013): esp. 197–202.

12. On the problematic nature of the term *improvisation* and its derivatives, see Leo Treitler, "Speaking of the I-Word," *AfMw* 72 (2015): 1–18; Richard Kramer, "Improvisatori. Improvisiren. Improviser...," *AfMw* 73 (2016): 2–8.

13. See Martin Kaltenecker, "The 'Fantasy-Principle': Improvisation between Imagination and Oration in the Eighteenth Century," in *Beyond Notes: Improvisation in Western Music of the Eighteenth and Nineteenth Centuries*, ed. Rudolf Rasch (Turnhout: Brepols, 2011), 17–34.

14. Carl Friedrich Cramer, review of Carl Philipp Emanuel Bach, *Claviersonaten und freye Fantasien ... Fünfte Sammlung* (1785), *Magazin der Musik* 2 (5 August 1786), 872: "Der Kenner wird aber doch aus den gegenwärtigen Fantasien schon sehen können, wie die Manier des Componisten hierinn beschaffen sey, durch welche besondere Wege er von einer Tonart in die andere bald langsam hinschleicht, bald gleichsam einen *salto mortale* hinüberspringt, wie er die kühnen Ausweichungen vorbereitet, und die *Tempi* ändert, so wie es sein Genius in der freyen Fantasie für gut findet."

15. Heinrich Christoph Koch, "Fantasie," in his *Musikalisches Lexikon* (Frankfurt am Main: Johann André, 1802). Carl Czerny, *Die Kunst des Vortrags der ältern und neuen Claviercompositionen ... Supplement (oder 4ter Theil) zur grossen Pianoforte-Schule, Op. 500* (Vienna: Diabelli, 1846), 70: "Diese sehr geistreiche Fantasie gibt ein treues Bild von der Art, wie er zu improvisieren pflegte, wenn er kein bestimmtes Thema durchführen wollte, und daher sich seinem Genie in Erfindung immer neuer Motive überliess."

16. Johann Christoph Gottsched, *Versuch einer critischen Dichtkunst*, 4th ed. (Leipzig: Breitkopf & Härtel, 1751), 108. The Viennese commentator Amand Wilhelm Smith would use the same imagery in talking specifically about musical composition: see his *Philosophische Fragmente* (1787), 45.

17. Griesinger, *Biographische Notizen über Joseph Haydn*, 114 (see above, p. 24).

18. The only compositions Haydn labeled "Fantasia" are the Fantasia in C Major, Hob. XVII:4, for keyboard, and the second movement of the String Quartet in E♭ Major, Op. 76, No. 6. On the audible residue of fantasizing in Haydn's notated works, see James Webster, "The Rhetoric of Improvisation in Haydn's Keyboard Music," in *Haydn and the Performance of Rhetoric*, ed. Tom Beghin and Sander M. Goldberg (Chicago: University of Chicago Press, 2007), 172–212.

19. Michael Johann Friedrich Wiedeburg, *Der sich selbst informirende Clavierspieler*, 3 vols. (Leipzig: Waisenhaus, 1765–75), 3:776: "Weil das Fantasiren nichts anders ist,

als ein Componiren ohne viel Bedenken und künstliches langes Nachsinnen . . . so kann ein Anfänger diese Uebung viel und oft treiben, daß er nemlich neue Melodien zu Gesängen macht, die er hernach auf allerley Art variiren kann."

20. Johann Wilhelm Hertel, *Autobiographie* (1783), ed. Erich Schenk (Graz: Hermann Böhlaus Nachfolger, 1957), 58: "Er . . . griff auf demselben [i.e., the keyboard] nicht viel mehr als unzusammenhangende Sätze und Ackorde, die jedem andern zu hören allezeit würden unverständlich, unerträglich gewesen seyn. Hierdurch feuerte er nach gerade aber seine ganze Seele dergestalt an, daß man ihm beynahe täglich ansehen konnte, ob er ein *allegro* oder *adagio* im Kopf hatte." Ibid., "mit aller Kaltblütigkeit." Johann Nepomuk Hummel (1778–1837) described a similar process to Johann Christian Lobe at some point between 1819 and 1837, during Hummel's time in Weimar; see Lobe, *Aus dem Leben eines Musikers* (Leipzig: J. J. Weber, 1859), 75–76. I am grateful to David Trippett for calling this passage to my attention.

21. Christian Gottlob Neefe, "Ueber die musikalische Wiederholung," *Deutsches Museum* 2 (1776): 748: "Was würden wir dann für Ungeheuer von musikalischen Stücken bekommen, wenn man nur Ideen zu Ideen ohne Beziehung auf einander häufen, wenn man nur eine zügellose Phantasie und nicht zugleich Herz und Verstand arbeiten lassen wollte. Kein Zuhörer würde mehr eine Musik fassen und empfinden können."

22. Koch, "Bizarria," in his *Musikalisches Lexikon*, 259: "eine Art von Fantasie, in welcher der Spieler sich vorzüglich einer eigenen Laune überläßt." On the connection of the bizarre and the fantastic in music in the late eighteenth century, see Richards, *The Free Fantasia*, 36.

23. Heinrich Christoph Koch, "Fantasie," in his *Kurzgefasstes Handwörterbuch der Musik* (Leipzig: Johann Friedrich Hartknoch, 1807), 146–47: "Chaos von Bildern und Begriffen"; "man setzt jederzeit die Mitwirkung des Verstandes voraus, durch welchen diese Bilder und Begriffe gewählt, geordnet und an einander gereihet werden."

24. See in particular Hans Heinrich Eggebrecht, "Das Ausdrucksprinzip im musikalischen Sturm und Drang," *Deutsche Vierteljahrsschrift für Literaturwissenschaft und Geistesgeschichte* 29 (1955): 323–49, which extrapolates the perception of musical self-expression back to the early 1770s but does so exclusively on the basis of eighteenth-century commentaries about the genre of the fantasia.

25. Bonn, Beethoven-Haus, MH 75 (SBH 691), f. 3–4: "Man fantasirt eigentlich nur, wenn man gar nicht acht giebt, was man spielt, so—würde man auch am besten, wahrsten fantasiren öffentlich—sich ungezwungen überlassen, eben was einem gefällt." Transcription from Elaine Sisman, "After the Heroic Style: *Fantasia* and the 'Characteristic' Sonatas of 1809," *Beethoven Forum* 6 (1998): 76, who cites in turn Helmut Aloysius Löw, "Die Improvisation im Klavierwerk L. van Beethovens" (Ph.D. diss., Saarland, 1962), 12. Note that *sich überlassen*—to yield, to give oneself over to something—is the same verb Czerny would later use to describe Beethoven's improvisations.

26. Louis Baron de Trémont [i.e., Louis-Philippe-Joseph Girod de Vienney], writing in the 1840s, transcribed in *Beethoven aus der Sicht seiner Zeitgenossen in Tagebüchern, Briefen, Gedichten und Erinnerungen*, ed. Klaus Martin Kopitz and Rainer Cadenbach,

2 vols. (Munich: G. Henle, 2009), 2:1006: "Lorsqu'il était bien disposé le jour fixé pour son improvisation, il etait sublime. C'était de l'inspiration, de l'entraînement, de beaux chants et une harmonie franche, parce que, dominé par le sentiment musical, il ne songeait pas, comme la plume a la main, a chercher des effets; ils se produisaient d'eux mêmes sans divagation."

27. For a summary of differing views on the authorship of this text (generally thought to be by the poet Christoph Kuffner), see Kurt Dorfmüller, Norbert Gertsch, and Julia Ronge, eds., *Ludwig van Beethoven: Thematisch-bibliographisches Werkverzeichnis*, 2 vols. (Munich: G. Henle, 2014). 1:498–99.

28. Ignaz Theodor Ferdinand Cajetan Arnold, "Recension: *Phantasie für das Pianoforte, mit Begleitung des ganzen Orchesters und Chor, in Musik gesetzt . . . von Louis van Beethoven, 80stes Werk*," *AmZ* 14 (6 May 1812): 307–11: "Wenn die Phantasie der eigentliche Culminationspunkt des aus sich selbst schaffenden Genius ist, der hier sein eigenes Seelengemälde zeichnet und die Form der Kunst zum blossen Reflectirspiegel seines Innern macht, aus dem die Fülle in Klarheit vortritt: so muss dem Kunstfreunde ein solches Werk um so schätzbarer seyn, je reiner sich in ihm der Genius des Schöpfers selbst, und ohne fremde Beyhülfe, ohne Zwang irgend einer aufgegebenen Form, darstellen kann. Die Phantasie ist der Monolog des Künstlers, in dem er das Eigene, Selbstempfundene rein ausspricht, während er sich zu den gegebenen Formen—zum Oratorium, zur Oper, u.s.f.—nur dialogisirend verhalten, das heisst, nur das geben kann, wozu ihn die gebotenen Formen veranlassen. . . . So sind im Gegentheil in der freyen Phantasie alle Fesseln gebrochen und der Genius des Künstlers ist in seine Urrechte—älter, als die Formen—wieder eingesetzt, als Schöpfer, als Herrscher, im Reich der Klänge. Benu[t]zte jeder Künstler diesen Wink—oder richtiger, gewöhnte sich der Genius der meisten Künstler minder an die Formen und verstände sich auf seine eigne Geistesemancipation ins Reich der Freyheit: so würde jede Phantasie—vorausgesetzt, der Künstler sey wirklich der Selbstdenkenden und nicht der Nachahmenden einer—eine wahre Selbstbiographie, und der hellste Blick in sein schaffendes Innere seyn, aus dem man sein Walten und Wirken beschauen, sich gleichsam in seine Gedankenwerkstätte schleichen könnte. . . . Nächst dem Studium der Kunst, ist hier eine reichhaltige Menge psychologischer Züge von Beethovens Künstlercharakter niedergelegt." The attribution of this review to Arnold is from Kunze, *Ludwig van Beethoven*, 673.

29. Adolph Bernhard Marx, "Erstes grosses Konzert im Winterhalbenjahre 1825–26, in Berlin," *BAmZ* 2 (9 November 1825): 366: "Nun, diese Symphonie ist gleichsam seine musikalische Karakteristik. Er ist es, der am Pianoforte fantasirt, aus Nacht und Licht seine Ideen webt, bis sich an seinem Geiste die Klänge der Instrumente beseelen, eines nach dem andern in den Reigen tritt und von seinem Feuer zuletzt das ganze Orchester und der ihm eingewebte Chor der menschlichen Stimmen erbrauset."

30. Adolph Bernhard Marx, "Recensionen: Symphonie mit Schlusschor . . . von Ludwig van Beethoven, 125tes Werk," *BAmZ* 3 (22 November 1826): 373: "Zweimal hat Beethoven, sicherlich, ohne sich dessen bewußt zu sein, seine eigene künstlerische Individualität zum Inhalt eines Kunstwerkes erhoben."

31. Anonymous, "Recensionen: *Trois Sonates pour le Clavecin ou Pianoforte, comp.* . . . *par Louis van Beethoven. Oeuv. 10* . . . ," *AmZ* 2 (9 October 1799): 25–26: "Phantasie, wie sie Beethoven in nicht gemeinem Grade hat . . . ist etwas sehr Schä[t]zbares und eigentlich Unentbehrliches für einen Komponisten, der in sich die Weihe zu einem grössern Künstler fühlt und der es verschmäht, flach und überpopulär zu schreiben, vielmehr etwas aufstellen will, das inneres kräftiges Leben habe und auch den Kenner zur öftern Wiederholung seines Werkes einlade. Allein in allen Künsten giebt es ein Ueberladen, das von zu vielem und häufigem Wirkungsdrange und Gelehrthun herrührt, wie es eine Klarheit und Anmuth giebt, die bey aller Gründlichkeit und Mannigfaltigkeit der Komposition . . . gar wohl bestehen kann. Rec., der Hrn. v. Beethoven, nachdem er sich an seine Manier nach und nach mehr zu gewöhnen versucht hat, mehr zu schätzen anfängt, als vorher, kann daher den Wunsch nicht unterdrücken . . . dass es diesem phantasiereichen Komponisten gefallen möge, sich durchweg bey seinen Arbeiten von einer gewissen Oekonomie leiten zu lassen, die allemal dankbarer als das Gegentheil ist. Es sind wohl wenige Künstler, denen man zurufen muss: spare deine Schätze und gehe haushälterisch damit um! denn nicht viele sind überreich an Ideen und sehr gewandt in Kombinationen derselben! Es ist also weniger direkter Tadel, was Hrn. v. B. hier treffen soll, als vielmehr ein wohlgemeynter Zuruf, der, wenn er auf der einen Seite allerdings tadelt, auf der andern immer etwas Ehrenvolles behält."

32. Anonymous, "Nachrichten   . . . Wien, d. 28. Jan.," *AmZ* 7 (13 February 1805): 321: "Diese lange, für die Ausführung äusserst schwierige Komposition ist eigentlich eine sehr weit ausgeführte, kühne und wilde Phantasie. Es fehlt ihr gar nicht an frappanten und schönen Stellen, in denen man den energischen, talentvollen Geist ihres Schöpfers erkennen muss: sehr oft aber scheint sie sich ganz ins Regellose zu verlieren . . . Ref. gehört gewiss zu Hrn. v. Beethovens aufrichtigsten Verehrern; aber bey dieser Arbeit muss er doch gestehen, des Grellen und Bizarren allzuviel zu finden, wodurch die Uebersicht äusserst erschwert wird und die Einheit beynahe ganz verloren geht."

33. A. G., "Conservatoire Impérial de Musique, Ier. et IIme. excercises des éleves," *Les tablettes de Polymnie* 2 (20 March 1811): 310–11: "Après avoir pénétré l'ame d'une douce mélancolie, il la déchire aussi-tôt par un amas d'accords barbares. Il me semble voir renfermer ensemble des colombes et des crocodilles." Though often attributed to the composer Giuseppe Cambini, this notice is signed simply "A. G."

34. Anonymous, review of *Quatuor pour 2 Violons, Viola, et Violoncelle, par L. van Beethoven* . . . *Oeuvr. 74, AmZ* 13 (22 May 1811): 349: "Die grossen Quartetten . . . athmen aber einen ganz andern Geist. Der Verf. hat sich hier ohne Rücksicht den wunderbarsten und fremdartigsten Einfällen seiner originellen Phantasie hingegeben, das Unähnlichste phantastisch verbunden, und fast alles mit einer . . . tiefen und schweren Kunst behandelt."

35. Ibid., 351: "Der geringe melodische Zusammenhang, und das humoristische Hin- und Herschweifen von einem Einfall zum andern, geben ihm mehr das Ansehn einer freyen Phantasie, als eines geregelten Ganzen. . . . Beethovens Genius bedarf unserer Lobreden nicht, und wird schwerlich auf unsere Wünsche achten. Doch

wenn der Künstler—er sey Dichter oder Tonsetzer—sich, unbekümmert um Einheit und Reinheit des Effects, *nur* seinem subjectiven Phantasiespiel glaubt hingeben zu dürfen, um das Schöne zu schaffen: so darf der kunstliebende Empfänger sich an die objective Einheit und Schönheit des Products allein halten, und anzeigen, was ihm darin den reinen, vollen Genuss gestört habe. Schreiber dieses gesteht mit der ihm zur Natur gewordenen Aufrichtigkeit, die Pflicht ist, in der Kunst, wie im Leben, und mit der Ueberzeugung, dass die Freunde der freundlichen Kunst mit ihm gleich denken: *er könne nicht wünschen, dass die Instrumental-Musik sich in diese Art und Weise verliere.*"

36. Johann Nikolaus Forkel, *Allgemeine Geschichte der Musik*, 2 vols. (Leipzig: Schwickert, 1788–1801), 1:61–62. Friedrich Rochlitz, "Über den zweckmässigen Gebrauch der Mittel der Tonkunst," *AmZ* 8 (2 October 1805): 6: "weit weniger wirksam."

37. *Neues Zeitungs- und Conversations-Lexikon oder Handwörterbuch*, 8 vols. (Vienna: Schrämbl, 1812–14), 1:161, transcribed in Kopitz and Cadenbach, *Beethoven aus der Sicht seiner Zeitgenossen*, 1:257: "Diese Fülle, diese Neuheit, dieser Reichthum an Ideen, diese Kunst, mit welcher er alle seine Compositionen durchführt, sind in der That bewunder[n]swert, obgleich man nicht in Abrede seyn kann, daß er sich vielleicht vom Fluge seiner Fantasie bisweilen zu sehr verleiten läßt und seine Zuhörer in oft unverständliche Regionen hinführt." On the infiltration of fantasialike elements into other genres of composition, see Peter Schleuning, *Die freie Fantasie: Ein Beitrag zur Erforschung der klassischen Klaviermusik* (Göppingen: A. Kümmerle, 1973), 358–68; and Sisman, "After the Heroic Style," 67–96.

38. Giuseppe Carpani, *Le Haydine ovvero Lettere su la vita et le opere del celebre maestro Giuseppe Haydn* (Milan: Buccinelli, 1812), 253: "Fu chiesto una volta ad Haydn da un mio amico, che gli sembrasse di questo giovine compositore. Rispose il vecchio con tutta la sincerità. 'Le prime sue cose mi piacquero assai, ma le ultime confesso che non le capisco. Mi pare sempre che scriva delle fantasie.'" I am grateful to Elaine Sisman for calling this passage to my attention.

39. Amadeus Wendt, "Gedanken über die neuere Tonkunst, und van Beethovens Musik, namentlich dessen Fidelio," *AmZ* 17 (1815): 385: "allein es steht eben darum auch an der Gränze der Musik und der Kunst." On Wendt as a critic for the *AmZ*, see Robin Wallace, *Beethoven's Critics: Aesthetic Dilemmas and Resolutions during the Composer's Lifetime* (Cambridge: Cambridge University Press, 1986), 26–35.

40. Wendt, "Gedanken über die neuere Tonkunst," 385–86: "Der musikalischen Phantasie wird am meisten die Sünde gegen Form und Regel verziehen, wenn ein grosser Geist in ihr waltet; sie ist ein köstliches Product, wenn sie die technische Sicherheit des Meisters absicht[s]los, doch überall an den Tag legt. Aber diesen Charakter der Phantasie auf andere Tonstücke überzutragen, und so die *musikal. Phantasie in dem Gebiete der Tonwelt herrschend machen*, kann nur zu grossen Verirrungen führen. Ueberschwenglicher Reichthum der Ideen und eine unversiegbare Originalität kann sich dabei offenbaren, aber Klarheit, Verständlichkeit und Ordnung, wodurch das Kunstwerk, ein Werk nicht der augenblicklichen Stimmung, sondern des fortgesetzten Genusses wird, wird ihm oft fehlen. Hier ist es, wo ich auch von Beethovens *grossen Verirrungen* spreche, denn ich habe nicht den Zweck, sein

Lobredner zu werden, wozu ich mich weder berufen noch befugt fühle, sondern seinen Einfluss auf die neueste Tonkunst, und seinen Charakter nach Vermögen und Einsicht unbefangen zu würdigen.

"Viele Werke Beethovens, z.B. mehrere seiner Symphonien, Sonaten, können nur als *musikalische Phantasien* gefasst und gewürdigt werden. In ihnen verliert auch der aufmerksame Zuhörer den Grundgedanken oft ganz aus den Augen; er findet sich in einem herrlichen Labyrinthe, wo auf allen Seiten üppiges Gebüsch und wunderseltne Blumen den Blick auf sich ziehen, doch ohne den Faden in die ruhige Heymath wieder zu gewinnen; des Künstlers Phantasie fliesst unaufhaltsam weiter fort, Ruhepuncte sind selten gewährt, und der Eindruck, welchen das Frühere machte, wird durch das Spätere nicht selten ausgetilgt; der Grundgedanke ist ganz verschwunden, oder schimmert nur aus dunkler Ferne in dem Flusse der bewegten Harmonie hervor." Wayne Senner, in *The Critical Reception of Beethoven's Compositions by his German Contemporaries*, ed. Wayne M. Senner, Robin Wallace, and William Meredith, 2 vols. (Lincoln: University of Nebraska Press, 1999–2001), 2:199, translates "der musikalischen *Phantasie*" at the beginning of this passage as "musical fantasy," whereas the subsequent reference to "other musical works" and the explicit evocation of the genre of the fantasia in the passage immediately preceding, as well as in the one immediately following, point to a preferable rendition of the word here as *fantasia*, that is, as a specific genre of music.

41. Wendt, "Gedanken über die neuere Tonkunst," 389: "wenn er *überall* die Ehre der Tonkunst mehr, als die Ehre *seiner* Kunst bestrebte."

42. Diary entry of 16 June 1816 in *Schubert: Die Dokumente seines Lebens*, ed. Otto Erich Deutsch (Kassel: Bärenreiter, 1964), 45: "[die] Bizarrerie . . . welche bey den meisten Tonsetzern jetzt zu herrschen pflegt, u. einem unserer größten deutschen Künstler beynahe allein zu verdanken ist, von dieser Bizzarrerie, welche das Tragische mit dem Komischen, das Angenehme mit dem Widrigen, das Heroische mit Heulerey, das Heiligste mit dem Harlequin vereint, verwechselt, nicht unterscheidet."

43. Ernst Ludwig Gerber to Christian Heinrich Rinck, 1817 or 1818, quoted in Friedrich Noack, "Eine Briefsammlung aus der ersten Hälfte des 19. Jahrhunderts," *AfMw* 4 (1953): 326: "Endlich scheint es mir, als ob die Phantasie, als Despot, die unumschränkte Herrschaft über die Musik an sich gerissen habe. Freilich läßt sich keine Musik ohne Phantasie denken; nur muß sie durch Geschmack und Vernunft zweckmäßig geregelt seyn. Aber jetzt sind an keine Formen, an keine Schranken der Phantasie mehr zu denken. Alles geht obenaus und nirgend an; je toller, je besser! je wilder, je bizarrer, desto neumodischer und effectvoller; das ist ein unaufhörliches Haschen nach fremden Tonarten und Modulationen, nach unharmonischen Ausweichungen, nach ohrenzerreißenden Dissonanzen und nach chromatischen Gängen, ohne Erholung und Aufhören für den Zuhörer. Auf solche Weise hören und spielen wir aber nichts, als lauter Phantasien. Unsere Sonaten sind Phantasien, unsere Ouvertüren sind Phantasien und selbst unsere Sinfonien, wenigstens die von Beethoven und Konsorten, sind Phantasien. Rechnet man nun noch den Unfug und den Kampf, den die Instrumente unter und gegen einander treiben, so bleibt es dem Laien unmöglich, Vergnügen von solchem Charivari zu finden."

44. Amadeus Wendt, *Über die Hauptperioden der schönen Kunst oder die Kunst im Laufe der Weltgeschichte* (Leipzig: J. A. Barth, 1831), 307: "Seine feurige, erfinderische Phantasie entwickelt einen Reichthum von Ideen.... Die Symphonie ist ihm vielmehr eine ausgebildete *Orchesterphantasie* im wahren Sinne des Worts. Er ist Feind von Wiederholungen, immer groß in der fortschreitenden Bewegung;—und scheint diese Bewegung dem bestehenden Gesetze zu widersprechen, so stellt sie, wie die Bahn eines Kometen, ein neues Gesetz auf. Das Wandeln dieses vielgestaltigen Geistes ist Heldengang."

45. In his later (1822) translation of Thomas Busby's *General History of Music*, Michaelis noted that "one could call Haydn the [Laurence] Sterne of music"; see Busby, *Allgemeine Geschichte der Musik*, ed. and trans. Christian Friedrich Michaelis, 2 vols. (Leipzig: Baumgartner, 1821–22), 2:457: "Man könnte Joseph Haydn vielleicht den musikalischen *Sterne* nennen." See also Mark Evan Bonds, "Haydn, Laurence Sterne, and the Origins of Musical Irony," *JAMS* 44 (1991): 57–91.

46. Christian Friedrich Michaelis, "Ueber das Humoristische oder Launige in der musikalischen Komposition," *AmZ* 9 (1807): 725: "Die Musik ist humoristisch, wenn die Komposition mehr die Laune des Künstlers, als die strenge Ausübung des Kunstsystems verräth." A partial English translation of the essay is available in Peter Le Huray and James Day, eds., *Music and Aesthetics in the Eighteenth and Early-Nineteenth Centuries* (Cambridge: Cambridge University Press, 1981), 291–92.

47. Michaelis, "Ueber das Humoristische oder Launige," 725–26: "Die musikalischen Gedanken sind dann von einer ganz eigenen, ungewohnten Art; sie folgen nicht so auf einander, wie man etwa nach einem gewissen Herkommen, oder nach dem natürlichen Gange der Harmonie und Modulation vermuthen sollte, sondern überraschen durch ganz unerwartete Wendungen und Uebergänge, durch ganz neue, sonderbar zusammengesetzte Figuren."

48. Michaelis, "Ueber das Humoristische oder Launige," 726: "Der humoristische Komponist . . . setzt sich über das Hergebrachte hinweg, und ohne die Regeln der Harmonie zu verletzen, ja oft bey der feinsten Ausübung kontrapunktischer Künste." Ibid., 727: " aus den üblichen Formeln der Komposition . . . wie die Einfälle eines launigen oder humoristischen Erzählers, der das Fremdartigste verbindet und in seiner sonderbaren Gemüthsstimmung auch den bekanntesten Dingen ein neues Ansehen giebt, und . . . mit einer gewagten Freymüthigkeit seinen Gedanken freyen Lauf lässt." Ibid., 728: "Die humoristische Musik ist bald komisch und naiv, bald ernsthaft und erhaben."

49. Michaelis, "Ueber das Humoristische oder Launige," 727: "Die humoristische Musik ist entweder witzig und von heiterm, pleaisantem Charakter, oder sie ist im Ganzen mehr ernsthaft und trägt die Spuren einer eigensinnigen Laune, einer Gemüthsstimmung, in der sich die Empfindungen sonderbar durchkreuzen und die Phantasie nicht ganz frey spielen kann. Selten trifft man diese Gattungen völlig rein an."

50. Michaelis, "Ueber das Humoristische oder Launige," 728: "Das, was ich hier unter Capriccio verstehe, führt bey unsern Komponisten auch oft den Namen *Phantasie* und besonders *freye Phantasie*." Koch, in his *Musikalisches Lexicon* of 1802, had

earlier attributed the unconventional features of the capriccio to the composer's *Laune* ("Capriccio, Caprice," 305–6).

51. Michaelis, "Ueber das Humoristische oder Launige," 728: "Die scherzhaft-humoristische Musik verräth die Abischt, wirklich zu erheitern und zu belustigen; der Komponist bewegt sich darin freyer, als in der entgegengesetzten Gattung [i.e., the Capriccio], und ob er gleich seine subjektive Individualität ausdrückt, so thut er es doch an einem von ihm selbst gewählten Gegenstande, an einem gewissen anziehenden oder drolligen Thema, das er auf eigene Manier bald variirt, bald mit andern Sätzen in Kontrast bringt."

52. Michaelis, "Ueber das Humoristische oder Launige," 728: "Denn in diesem [i.e., the Capriccio] scheint der Komponist zu sehr von dem Eigensinn seiner Laune, von den Eigenheiten seiner jetzigen Gemüthsstimmung abzuhängen, als dass er sich einen bestimmten Zweck, die Zuhörer zu unterhalten, und ihre Sympathie durch fassliche Regelmässigkeit zu gewinnen, vorsetzen könnte. Er scheint nur durch innern Drang getrieben, sich so zu zeigen, wie er jetzt ist, den sonderbaren Gang und Wechsel seiner Empfindungen und Einfälle darzustellen."

53. Michaelis, "Ueber das Humoristische oder Launige," 728–29: "Bey den alten Komponisten war das Humoristische etwas sehr Seltenes, weil sie sich gern an die strenge Regelmässigkeit banden, und ihre Imagination noch nicht so leicht den kühnen Schwung nahm, der sie über das Hergebrachte erhob. Händels ideenreiches Genie gehörte vielleicht zu den vorzüglichsten, die einen freyeren Flug wagten und der Musik bisweilen den interessanten Ausdruck des Launigen gaben. Hingegen ist unsere neueste Musik grossentheils humoristisch, besonders seitdem Joseph Haydn, als der grösste Meister in dieser Gattung, vorzüglich in seinen originellen Sinfonieen und Quartetten, den Ton dazu angab. J. Seb. Bach neigte sich oft schon zu dieser Manier, hielt sich aber immer noch durch seine kunstreiche Harmonie in Schranken. Auch K. Ph. Eman. Bach komponirte nicht selten im launigen Stil: aber Haydn that es zuerst mit dem allgemeinen Effekt, und weckte eine Menge berühmter Tonkünstler der neuesten Zeit, in diesem Charakter zu schreiben. Dem reichhaltigen Genie Mozarts war auch das Humoristische nicht fremd, allein er schien im Ganzen mehr zum Ernsthaften und Erhabenen, als zum Komischen und Naiven gestimmt zu seyn, und, so sehr er auch in scherzhafter Laune zu komponiren wusste, verweilte er doch nicht lange dabey, oder ging gern zum Grossen und Imposanten oder zum Innigen und Rührenden über. Ganz vorzüglich scheinen sich Duetten, Quartetten und Quintetten für verschiedene Instrumente zum launigen Stil zu eignen, und nicht nur Haydn sondern auch Pleyel, Viotti, Rode, Kreu[t]zer, Clementi und Beethoven haben in ihren Kompositionen eine reiche Quelle jenes Humors fliessen lassen, der bey den einen mehr zum schalkhaften Scherz, bey den andern mehr zum schwärmerischen Ernst sich hinneigt."

54. Carl Ludwig Junker, *Zwanzig Componisten: Eine Skizze* (Bern: Typographische Gesellschaft, 1776), 66: "Aber man nenne mir auch nur ein einziges Produkt von Hayden, wo Laune nicht immer merklicher Zug wäre? Man wird keines finden." See also Wolfgang Fuhrmann, "Haydn und sein Publikum: Die Veröffentlichung eines Komponisten, ca. 1750-1815" (Habilitationsschrift, Bern, 2010), 392–99. I am grateful to Dr. Fuhrmann for providing me a copy of his text.

55. Jean Paul, *Vorschule der Ästhetik*, 2 vols. (Hamburg: Friedrich Perthes, 1804), 1:191: "Daher spielt bei jedem Humoristen das Ich die erste Rolle." Ibid., 1:193: "Da im Humor das Ich parodisch heraustritt."

56. Jean Paul, *Vorschule der Ästhetik*, 2nd ed., 2 vols. (Stuttgart and Tübingen: J. G. Cotta, 1813), 1:253–54: "So spricht z. B. *Sterne* mehrmals lang und erwägend über gewisse Begebenheiten, bis er endlich entscheidet: es sey ohnehin kein Wort davon wahr. Etwas der Keckheit des vernichtenden Humors ähnliches, gleichsam einen Ausdruck der Welt-Verachtung kann man bei mancher Musik, z. B. der Haydnschen, vernehmen, welche ganze Tonreihen durch eine fremde vernichtet und zwischen Pianissimo und Fortissimo, Presto und Andante wechselnd stürmt." The comment on Sterne was new to the second edition of the *Vorschule* (1813); the comments on Haydn had appeared in the first edition of the *Vorschule* (1804), 1:189.

57. Tieck, as quoted in Rudolf Köpke, *Ludwig Tieck: Erinnerungen aus dem Leben des Dichters nach dessen mündlichen und schriftlichen Mittheilungen*, 2 vols. (Leipzig: F. A. Brockhaus, 1855), 2:236–37: "die besondere und eigenthümliche Art und Weise Jemandes, sein eigenstes Wesen, zu bezeichnen. Mitunter ist es auch was wir wo[h]l Laune nennen. Im Humor paaren sich Spaß und Ernst miteinander, wie z. B. bei Sterne."

58. See Elisabeth Eleonore Bauer, "Beethoven—unser musikalischer Jean Paul: Anmerkungen zu einer Analogie," in *Beethoven: Analecta varia*, ed. Heinz-Klaus Metzger and Rainer Riehn (Munich: edition text + kritik, 1987): 83–105.

59. Gotthold Ephraim Lessing, *Laokoon* (1766) in his *Werke*, ed. Jost Perfahl, vol. 2 (Munich: Winkler, 1969), chap. 17.

60. Lessing, *Hamburgische Dramaturgie, Sechsunddreissigstes Stück* (1 September 1767), in his *Werke*, 2:425–26: "Und wie schwach muss der Eindruck sein, den das Werk gemacht hat, wenn man in ebendem Augenblicke auf nichts begieriger ist, als die Figur des Meisters dagegenzuhalten? Das wahre Meisterstück, dünkt mich, erfüllet uns so ganz mit sich selbst, dass wir des Urhebers darüber vergessen; dass wir es nicht als das Produkt eines einzeln Wesens, sondern der allgemeinen Natur betrachten. . . . Die Täuschung muss sehr schwach sein, man muss wenig Natur, aber desto mehr Kunstelei empfinden, wenn man so neugierig nach dem Künstler ist." On the role of illusion in Lessing's aesthetics, see Armand Nivelle, *Kunst- und Dichtungstheorien zwischen Aufklärung und Klassik*, 2nd ed. (Berlin: Walter de Gruyter, 1971), 94–102. On Lessing's indebtedness in this area to earlier aestheticians, particularly Baumgarten, Meier, and Mendelssohn, see chap. 2 of David E. Wellbery, *Lessing's "Laocoon": Semiotics in the Age of Reason* (Cambridge: Cambridge University Press, 1984).

61. Johann Gebhard Ehrenreich Maass, "Ueber die Instrumentalmusik," *Neue Bibliothek der schönen Wissenschaften* 48 (1792): 23: "Die beste Kunst des Komponisten ist, so zu komponiren, daß man gar keine Kunst merke." Maass (1766–1823) was a professor of philosophy at Halle and the author of several supplementary essays on music for Sulzer's *Allgemeine Theorie der schönen Künste*.

62. Amadeus Wendt, "Ueber Beethovens neueste Symphonie," *Leipziger Kunstblatt für gebildete Kunstfreunde, insbesondere für Theater und Musik* 1 (14 February

1818): 280: "Der durch sonderbare Sprünge schon längst bekannte Humor des genialen Componisten erreicht hier eine so kecke Höhe, daß der Zuhörer mehr lächelt, als fühlt, und die Frage sich kaum unterdrücken läßt, wohin soll die Kunst der Töne nun noch kommen, wenn jeder eigensinnige Einfall eines Componisten das Gesetz der Tonfolge durchbrechen, und den Faden der Melodie abbrechen darf, wo es ihm beliebt,—kurz, wenn die Kunst der, oft gesuchten, Laune eines Individuums zum willkührlichen Spiele dienen darf, sey diese auch mit allem Glanze des Talents und der Uebung ausgestattet? ... Zwar kann man sich auch an das Sonderbare gewöhnen, je öfter man es hört. ... Ich will auch gern zugeben, daß man ein tiefes Kunstwerk erst allmählich ganz durchdringt. Aber das erste, unbefangene Anschauen und Anhören gibt uns gemeiniglich den richtigen Totaleindruck, den ich hier bei Wiederholung nur bestätigt fand. ... Der erste und vor allen der letzte Satz hat alle oben angedeutete Mängel der Beethoven'schen Musik und—*dieser* Zeit." Wendt was a frequent contributor to this short-lived (1817–18) journal; this review is not included in Kunze, *Ludwig van Beethoven*.

63. The one notable exception is the finale of the Symphony No. 45 in F# Minor ("Farewell"), discussed below (p. 161).

64. See Furhmann, "Haydn und sein Publikum."

65. See Mark Evan Bonds, "Irony and Incomprehensibility: Beethoven's 'Serioso' String Quartet in F Minor, Op. 95, and the Path to the Late Style," *JAMS* 70 (2017): 285–356.

66. Lockwood, *Beethoven*, 329.

67. Adolph Bernhard Marx, *Ludwig van Beethoven: Leben und Schaffen*, 2nd ed., 2 vols. (Berlin: Otto Janke, 1863), 2:317: "So müssen wir doch gestehen, eine bestimmte Idee des Ganzen, oder auch nur einheitvolle psychologische Entwickelung nicht gefunden zu haben; gern wollen wir annehmen, dass die Schuld in uns liegt."

68. Vincent d'Indy, *Cours de composition musicale*, ed. Auguste Sérieyx and Guy de Lioncourt, 3 vols. (Paris: Durand, 1903–50), 2:241: "une Coda ¢ en FA, sans intérêt ni utilité d'aucune sorte ... un exemple de 'ce qu'il ne faut pas faire'?" Walter Willson Cobbett, *Cobbett's Cyclopedic Survey of Chamber Music*, 2 vols. (Oxford: Oxford University Press; London: Humphrey Milford, 1929–30), 1:97.

69. Basil Lam, *Beethoven String Quartets 2* (London: British Broadcasting Corporation, 1975), 10–11; David Wyn Jones, "Beethoven and the Viennese Legacy," in *The Cambridge Companion to the String Quartet*, ed. Robin Stowell (Cambridge: Cambridge University Press, 2003), 221; William Kinderman, *Beethoven*, 2nd ed. (New York: Oxford University Press, 2009), 316, 171; and Daniel K. L. Chua, *Absolute Music and the Construction of Meaning* (Cambridge: Cambridge University Press, 1999), 108.

70. Carl Czerny, "Further Recollections of Beethoven," *Cock's Musical Miscellany*, vol. 1, no. 6 (2 August 1852): 65–66, transcribed in Kopitz and Cadenbach, *Beethoven aus der Sicht seiner Zeitgenossen*, 1:215. The German version in Czerny's *Erinnerungen aus meinem Leben*, ed. Walter Kolneder (Strasbourg: P. H. Heitz, 1968), 44–47, cannot be traced back to Czerny himself and is presumably a translation from the English.

71. For a more detailed discussion of Op. 95, see Bonds, "Irony and Incomprehensibility."

72. August Wilhelm Schlegel, *Vorlesungen über dramatische Kunst und Literatur*, in his *Sämmtliche Werke*, 5:198: "Die Ironie bezieht sich aber bei'm Shak[e]speare nicht bloß auf die einzelnen Charakter, sondern häufig auf das Ganze der Handlung. Die meisten Dichter . . . nehmen Partei, und verlangen von den Lesern blinden Glauben. . . . Je eifriger diese Rhetorik ist, desto leichter verfehlt sie ihren Zweck. Auf jeden Fall werden wir gewahr, daß wir die Sache nicht unmittelbar, sondern durch das Medium einer fremden Denkart erblicken. Wenn hingegen der Dichter zuweilen durch eine geschickte Wendung die weniger glänzende Kehrseite der Münze nach vorne dreht, so setzt er sich mit dem auserlesenen Kreiß der Einsichtsvollen unter seinen Lesern oder Zuschauern in ein verstohlnes Einverständniß; er zeigt ihnen, daß er ihre Einwendungen vorhergesehen und im voraus zugegeben habe; daß er nicht selbst in dem dargestellten Gegenstande befangen sei, sonder frei über ihm schwebe, und daß er den schönen, unwiderstehlich anziehenden Schein, den er selbst hervorgezaubert, wenn er anders wollte, unerbittlich vernichten könnte."

73. Arnold, *Gallerie der berühmtesten Tonkünstler*, 1:109–10: "Es giebt keinen musikalischen Gedanken, sey er auch noch so einfältig oder bunt, der nicht durch Verkehrungen, Zertheilungen, Versetzungen und Aehnlichkeiten interessant würde. Die Sicherheit und Gewandtheit in den Künsten des Kontrapunkts, von einer nie erschöpften Gedankenquelle unterhalten, führen das Ohr unvermuthet in Wildnisse und Tiefen, wohin es einer so sichern Leitung gern folgt und immer dafür reichlich belohnt wird. Haydn macht es wie ein schlauer Redner, der, wenn er uns zu etwas überreden will, von einem allgemein als wahr anerkannten Satze ausgeht, den jeder einsieht, jeder begreifen muß, bald aber diesen Satz so geschickt zu wenden versteht, daß er uns zu allen überreden kann, wozu er will, und wärs zum Gegentheil des aufgestellten Satzes. Seine Musik geht dem Gehöre glatt ein, weil wir wähnen etwas Leichtfaßliches, schon Vernommenes zu vernehmen; allein bald finden wir, daß es nicht das wird, nicht das ist, was wir glaubten, daß es sey, daß es werden sollte; wir hören etwas neues und staunen über den Meister, der so schlau Unerhörtes uns unter dem Anstrich des Allbekannten zu bieten wußte. Eben diese liebenswürdige Popularité giebt seinen Kompositionen bei aller Fülle von Harmonieaufwand und Instrumentazion eine so unendliche Klarheit, Allgemeinfaßlichkeit und Verständlichkeit, daß wir mit Leichtigkeit das Schwerste vernehmen."

74. The phrase "eine dunkle Künstlichkeit oder eine künstliche Dunkelheit" appears in an anonymous review of the Op. 10 piano sonatas in *AmZ* 2 (9 October 1799): 25.

75. Letter of August–September 1796, *BGA* no. 22, 1:32: "Wenn mich auch nur einige verstehen, so bin ich zufrieden."

76. Triest, "Bemerkungen über die Ausbildung der Tonkunst in Deutschland im achtzehnten Jahrhundert," 407. For further commentary on Triest's remarks about Haydn, see Mark Evan Bonds, "Rhetoric versus Truth: Listening to Haydn in the Age of Beethoven," in *Haydn and the Performance of Rhetoric*, ed. Sander Goldberg and Tom Beghin (Chicago: University of Chicago Press, 2007), 109–28. See also Elaine Sisman, "Haydn's Career and the Idea of the Multiple Audience," in *The Cambridge Companion to Haydn*, ed. Caryl Clark (Cambridge: Cambridge University Press,

2005), 3–16; and Wolfgang Fuhrmann, "Originality as Market Value: Remarks on the Fantasia in C Hob. XVII:4 and Haydn as Musical Entrepreneur," *Studia Musicologica* 51 (2010): 303–16.

77. Albert Christoph Dies, *Biographische Nachrichten von Joseph Haydn* (Vienna: Camesina, 1810), 75: " 'Meine Sprache versteht man durch die ganze Welt.' "

78. Mozart to Leopold Mozart, 28 December 1782, in Mozart, *Briefe und Aufzeichnungen*, 3:245–46: "die Conzerten sind eben das Mittelding zwischen zu schwer, und zu leicht—sind sehr Brillant—angenehm in die ohren—Natürlich ohne in das leere zu fallen—hie und da—können auch *kenner allein satisfaction erhalten*—doch so—daß die *nicht-kenner damit zufrieden* seyn müssen, ohne zu wissen warum."

79. Joseph II's alleged statement ("gewaltig viel Noten lieber Mozart!") was first reported by Niemetschek, *Leben des k.k. Kapellmeisters Wolfgang Gottlieb Mozart*, 23. A***, "Wien, den 29sten Januar, 1787," *Magazin der Musik* 2 (1787): 1274: "doch wohl zu stark gewürzt."

80. Beethoven to Johann Andreas Streicher, 16 September 1824, *BGA* no. 1875, 5:364: "und [weil] es bey Bearbeitung dieser großen Messe meine Hauptabsicht war, sowohl bey den Singenden als bey den Zuhörenden, Religiöse Gefühle zu erwecken und dauernd zu machen."

81. Johann Friedrich Reichardt, *Vertraute Briefe, geschrieben auf einer Reise nach Wien und den oesterreichischen Staaten zu Ende des Jahres 1808 und zu Anfang 1809*, 2 vols. (Amsterdam: Kunst- und Industrie-Comptoir, 1810), 1:231–32: "Es war mir sehr interessant, in dieser Folge zu beobachten, wie die drei echten Humoristen das Genre, so jeder nach seiner individuellen Natur, weiter ausgebildet haben. Haydn erschuf es aus der reinen, hellen Quelle seiner lieblichen, originellen Natur. An Naivetät und heitrer Laune bleibt er daher auch immer der Einzige. Mozarts kräftigere Natur und reichere Phantasie griff weiter um sich, und sprach in manchem Satz das Höchste und Tiefste seines innern Wesens aus; er war auch selbst mehr executirender Virtuose und muthete daher den Spielern weit mehr zu; setzte auch mehr Werth in künstlich durchgeführte Arbeit, und baute so auf Haydns lieblich phantastisches Gartenhaus seinen Pallast. Be[e]thoven hatte sich früh schon in diesem Pallast eingewohnt, und so blieb ihm nur, um seine eigene Natur auch in eignen Formen auszudrücken, der kühne, trotzige Thurmbau, auf den so leicht keiner weiter etwas setzen soll, ohne den Hals zu brechen." This passage was later excerpted in the *AmZ* 12 (7 February 1810): 289, and in Johann Aloys Schlosser, *Ludwig van Beethoven: Leben und Schaffen* (Prague: Buchler, Stephani und Schlosser, 1828), 90–91n.

82. Hoffmann, "Recension: *Sinfonie . . . par Louis van Beethoven . . . Oeuvre 67*, 633–34: "Er trennt sein Ich von dem innern Reich der Töne und gebietet darüber als unumschränkter Herr."

83. On Hoffmann's indebtedness to other aspects of eighteenth-century music criticism, see Morrow, *German Music Criticism*, 156–57.

84. Anonymous, "Beethoven und Jean Paul!—Mozart und Göthe!—Eine Paral[l]ele," *Minerva: Ein Beiblatt zum Allgemeinen musikalischen Anzeiger* (Frankfurt) 1 (1826): 134–35: "Beethoven, ohne Zweifel der genialste Tonsetzer unserer Zeit, der seinen Genius wie einen Sclaven beherrscht."

85. Friedrich August Kanne, "Akademie, des Lud. van Beethoven," *Allgemeine musikalische Zeitung mit besonderer Rücksicht auf den österreichischen Kaiserstaat* 8 (5 June 1824): 149: "erhabene Besonnenheit."

86. E. T. A. Hoffmann, "Beethovens Instrumentalmusik" (1813), *Fantasiestücke in Callot's Manier*, in his *Sämtliche Werke*, 2/1, ed. Hartmut Steinecke (Frankfurt am Main: Deutscher Klassiker Verlag, 1993), 54–55: "Den musikalischen Pöbel drückt Beethovens mächtiger Genius; er will sich vergebens dagegen auflehnen. . . . Wie ist es aber, wenn nur *Eurem* schwachen Blick der innere tiefe Zusammenhang jeder Beethovenschen Komposition entgeht? Wenn es nur an *Euch* liegt, daß Ihr des Meisters, dem Geweihten verständliche, Sprache nicht versteht, wenn Euch die Pforte des innersten Heiligtums verschlossen blieb?"

87. Karl Blum, "Miscellen," *AmZ* 16 (8 June 1814): 396: "Dank Dir, grosser herrlicher Künstler, dass Du uns aus der Tiefe Deines reichen Gemüths dieses Werk dichtetest." The attribution to Blum is from Kunze, *Ludwig van Beethoven*, 673.

88. Blum, "Miscellen," 810: "Aber welcher Andere der jetzt lebenden Tonsetzer vermag wo[h]l im Gegentheil, so wie er, selbst aus Harmonie die tiefste, innigste Empfindung widerhallen zu lassen? Seine Seele gleicht dem Meere: ist es ruhig, dann spiegelt sich der Himmel, sammt allen Gestirnen in seinen Fluthen; aber haucht der allmächtige Odem der Natur über dasselbe, dann wogt es auch, und bricht sich schäumend und brandend an dem Gestade. So auch bey *ihm*. Ist seine Seele ruhig und still: dann brechen freundlich leuchtende Stra[h]len nach allen Richtungen in unendlicher Fülle daraus hervor, und eine Wunderwelt wird uns erschlossen bey ihrem magischen Schimmer. Doch ist der innerste Kern seines Wesens von feindlichen Kräften bewegt: dann freylich stürzen nur Wogen der Harmonie, donnernd und brandend, neben und über einander, dahin; aber selbst in diesen Orkan tönt oft ein leiser Himmelsklang hinein, der auf Frieden deutet, auf Beschwichtigung des Sturms."

89. Blum, "Miscellen," 505–6: "In den Werken der grössten Dichter ist eine, oft nur leise über dem Ganzen schwebende, oft aber auch schneidend hervorbrechende Ironie, dem sinnig Aufmerksamen leicht bemerkbar. Ich erinnere hier, statt aller Andern, nur an Shak[e]speare, Cervantes und Göthe. Beethovens Compositionen sind, auch von dieser Seite, noch lange nicht genug beachtet; und doch wird eben nur hieraus manches *scheinbar* Herbe und Fremdartige bey ihm, als köstlich und nothwendig erkannt. Ueber vielen seiner vortrefflichsten Productionen schwebt, bald leise, bald aber auch schneidend und furchtbar, diese echt poetische Ironie."

90. Friedrich Schlegel, "Über Goethes Meister" (1798), in *KFSA*, 2:137: "die Ironie, die über dem ganzen Werke schwebt."

91. Ibid., 138: "Dieser sich selbst belächelnde Schein von Würde und Bedeutsamkeit."

92. Ibid., 133: "Man lasse sich also dadurch, daß der Dichter selbst die Personen und die Begebenheiten so leicht und so launig zu nehmen, den Helden fast nie ohne Ironie zu erwähnen, und auf sein Meisterwerk selbst von der Höhe seines Geistes herabzulächeln scheint, nicht täuschen, als sei es ihm nicht der heiligste Ernst." On the widespread perception of *Wilhelm Meisters Lehrjahre* as ironic, see Ernst Behler, *Studien zur Romantik und zur idealistischen Philosophie* (Paderborn: Schöningh, 1988), 57–58.

93. Adam Müller, "Die Lehre vom Gegensatze" (1804), in his *Kritische, ästhetische und philosophische Schriften*, ed. Walter Schroeder and Werner Siebert, 2 vols. (Berlin: Luchterhand, 1967), 2:238: "An gegensätzischer Kunst, an der besonnenen Umwechslung der algebraischen Zeichen, in der Gestalt welches möglichen Gegensatzes sie auch auftreten können, also an fester Beweglichkeit, an wahrer Ironie, an Weltreichtum wissen wir ihm [Goethe] keinen Meister an die Seite zu setzen."

94. Jean Paul cites these figures repeatedly under the rubric of "Humorische Totalität" in his *Vorschule der Ästhetik*, 2nd ed., 1:237–47. On irony in the works of Goethe, see Hans-Egon Hass, "Über die Ironie bei Goethe," in *Ironie und Dichtung*, ed. Albert Schaefer (Munich: C. H. Beck, 1970), 59–83; and Ellis Dye, *Love and Death in Goethe: One and Double* (Rochester, NY: Camden House, 2004), esp. chap. 11 ("Truth. Paradox. Irony.").

95. Anonymous, "Recension: *Sonate für Pianoforte und Violin, von Ludwig van Beethoven. 96tes Werk*," *AmZ* 19 (26 March 1817): 228: "weil Künstler eben *seiner* Art ihr Innerstes, wie dies zu jeder Zeit sich gestaltet, in ihren Werken aussprechen, und mithin zu schliessen wäre, der treffliche B. sey selbst jetzt zufrieden, freundlich und heiter."

96. Anonymous, "Nachrichten: Leipzig," *AmZ* 19 (21 May 1817): 361: "dass nämlich eben das Eigenste an Beethoven (wie das an Jean Paul) nur darum so hinreisse, weil es sein Eigenstes, das Selbstgeschaffne seiner innersten, gewaltigen, und vom Haus aus originellen Natur ist."

97. L. Poundie Burstein, "'Lebe wohl tönt überall' and a 'Reunion after So Much Sorrow': Beethoven's Op. 81a and the Journeys of 1809," *MQ* 93 (2010): 366–413.

98. Burstein, "'Lebe wohl tönt überall,'" 368.

99. Beethoven to Ries, 5 March 1818, *BGA* no. 1247, 4:178: "durch meine unglückliche Verbindung mit diesem Erzherzog bin ich beynahe an den *Bettelstab gebracht*, darben kann ich nicht sehn, geben muß ich, so können sie nach denken, wie ich bey dieser Lage noch mehr Leide!"

100. See Mark Evan Bonds, "The Court of Public Opinion: Haydn, Mozart, Beethoven," in *Beethoven und andere Hofmusiker seiner Generation*, ed. Birgit Lodes, Elisabeth Reisinger, and John D. Wilson (Bonn: Beethoven-Haus, 2018), 7–24.

101. Beethoven to Breitkopf & Härtel, 28 February 1812, *BGA* no. 555, 2:245–46: "für heute kann ich nichts weiter als das nöthigste schreiben, Gute Laune sagen sie leuchtete aus meinem Briefe, der Künstler muß oft sich in alle werfen können, und so kann auch diese erkünstelt gewesen seyn, ich bin es eben jezt nicht, das Ereigniß mit dem Erzherzog Rudolf hat fatale Folgen für mich, wenn mir nur der Himmel Geduld giebt, bis ich die Fremde erreicht, so bin ich wieder im Stande mich selbst in mir selbst zu finden."

102. Staatsbibliothek zu Berlin—Preußischer Kulturbesitz, Musikabteilung, Mus. ms. autogr. Beethoven 1, dating from sometime between April 1819 and March 1820; see Dorfmüller, Gertsch, and Ronge, *Ludwig van Beethoven*, 1:797. "Von Herzen" is to be understood here not in the plural, but rather as an idiomatic expression of the singular.

103. Birgit Lodes, "'Von Herzen—möge es wieder—zu Herzen gehn!' Zur Widmung von Beethovens *Missa solemnis*," in *Altes im Neuen: Festschrift Theodor Göllner zum 65. Geburtstag*, ed. Bernd Edelmann und Manfred Hermann Schmid (Tutzing: Hans Schneider, 1995), 295-306.

104. Wilhelm von Lenz, *Beethoven: Eine Kunststudie*, 4 vols. (Kassel: Ernst Balde; Hamburg: Hoffmann & Campe, 1855-60), 4:145.

105. Alexander Wheelock Thayer, *Ludwig van Beethovens Leben*, 5 vols., ed. Hermann Deiters and Hugo Riemann (Leipzig: Breitkopf & Härtel, 1901-8), 5:130: "Wenn ich dann und wann versuche meinen aufgeregten Gefühlen in Tönen eine Form zu geben—ach, dann find ich mich schrecklich getäuscht." Stumpff's account survives in a copy made by Thayer and published in Thayer, *Ludwig van Beethovens Leben*, 5:122-31. The terminus post quem for Stumpff's original notation of Beethoven's alleged statement is evident from internal details: he relates an event first reported by Schindler in 1840 that occurred before Stumpff's arrival in Vienna; Seyfried's earlier report of the same incident, published in 1832, neglects a key detail transmitted by Schindler and repeated by Stumpff.

106. Karl Holz to Wilhelm von Lenz, 16 July 1857, quoted in Lenz, *Beethoven*, 4:217: "Für ihn war die Krone aller Quartettsätze und sein Lieblingsstück, die *Cavatine* Es ¾ aus dem B Quartett. Er hat sie wirklich unter Thränen der Wehmuth komponirt, und gestand mir, daß noch nie seine eigene Musik einen solchen Eindruck auf ihn hervorgebracht habe, und daß selbst das Zurückempfinden dieses Stückes, ihm immer neue Thränen koste."

107. On the deeply problematic implications of this attitude, see Nicholas Cook, "The Other Beethoven: Heroism, the Canon, and the Works of 1813-14," *19CM* 27 (2003): 3-24; Nicholas Mathew, *Political Beethoven* (Cambridge: Cambridge University Press, 2013); and John David Wilson, "Beethoven's Popular Style: *Der glorreiche Augenblick* and the Art of Writing for the Galleries," in *Beethoven und der Wiener Kongress (1814/15): Bericht über die vierte New Beethoven Research Conference Bonn, 10. bis 12. September 2014*, ed. Bernhard R. Appel et al. (Bonn: Beethoven-Haus, 2016), 219-88.

108. Beethoven to Schotts Söhne, 10 March 1824, *BGA* no. 1787, 5:278: "wie gern würde ich ihr dienen, was mein geringes Indiwiduum anbelangt, fühlte ich nicht den mir angebohrnen größern Beruf durch werke mich der welt zu offenbaren."

109. See Bonds, "The Court of Public Opinion."

Chapter 4

1. On the relationship of the two in language, see the essays by Peter L. Oesterreich ("Homo rhetoricus," 49-58) and Daniel M. Gross ("Listening Culture," 59-73) in *Culture and Rhetoric*, ed. Ivo Strecker and Stephen Tyler (New York: Berghahn Books, 2009). On the cultural context of "rhetorical listening" in the eighteenth century, see Martin Kaltenecker, *L'oreille divisée: Les discours sur l'écoute musicale aux XVIIIe et XIXe siècles* (Paris: Éditions MF, 2010), 29-78.

2. See Frieder Zaminer, "Über die Herkunft des Ausdrucks 'Musik verstehen,'" in *Musik und Verstehen: Aufsätze zur semiotischen Theorie, Ästhetik und Soziologie der musikalischen Rezeption*, ed. Peter Faltin and Hans-Peter Reinecke (Cologne: Arno Volk, 1973), 314–19.

3. E. T. A. Hoffmann, "Ueber einen Ausspruch Sacchini's, und über den sogenannten Effect in der Musik," *AmZ* 16 (20 July 1814): 482: "Nur *das* Tongedicht, das wahr und kräftig aus dem Innern hervorging, dringt wieder ein in das Innere des Zuhörers. Der Geist versteht nur die Sprache des Geistes." Ibid., 485: "Dies ist . . . der wahrhaftige Effect des aus dem Innern hervorgegangenen Tongedichts." First published anonymously in the *AmZ*, the essay soon found its way into Hoffmann's *Kreisleriana*. On the neologism of *Tondichter* around the turn of the nineteenth century, see Peter Jost, "Vom Musicus zum Tondichter: Wandlungen des Komponisten-Bildes um 1800," in *Aufbrüche—Fluchtwege: Musik in Weimar um 1800*, ed. Helen Geyer and Thomas Radecke (Cologne: Böhlau, 2003), 73–84.

4. Amadeus Wendt, "Ausdruck in der Musik," *Cäcilia* 4 (1826): 173–74: "Der Ausdruck findet überall da Statt, wo von Äusserung eines *Innern* die Rede ist. Der Ausdruck setzt also voraus ein Inneres, und dies ist in der Kunst die Beschaffenheit des darzustellenden Gegenstandes, insofern er von dem Künstler angeschaut und so eigentümlich empfunden wird. Der Künstler stellt uns daher mit dem Gegenstande seinen inneren Zustand dar, und die Natur der schönen Kunst verlangt, dass das Äussere dem Inneren angemessen sey, mithin das allgemeine Darstellungsmittel einer Kunst auch wirklich zum Ausdrucksmittel werde. Sonach hängt der Ausdruck in der Kunst zuerst ab von der Empfindung des Stoffes. Wie die Seele des Künstlers ihren Gegenstand innerlich wahrnimmt, so soll er auch äusserlich erscheinen; und so muss einer geistreichen Darstellung, die sich in der Ausführung eines Stoffes kund thut, auch eine geistreiche Auffassung vorhergehen. Ist diese Darstellung mehr an die besondere Beschaffenheit des Gegenstandes gebunden, der durch sie treu und anschaulich geschildert wird, so pflegt man auch den Ausdruck *charakteristisch* zu nennen, und vom Charakteristischen überhaupt zu sprechen; dagegen andrerseits der Ausdruck oft mehr *subjectiv* ist, das heisst, den Gemüthszustand des Künstlers, der durch den Gegenstand erweckt worden ist, unmittelbar darstellt. Der wahre Ausdruck umfasst Beides."

5. Carl Borromäus von Miltitz, "Ueber musikalische Begeisterung," *AmZ* 36 (2 April 1834): 216: "das gelungene Werk ist das Werk des Augenblicks der Begeisterung, di prima intenzione."

6. Franz Anton Nüsslein, *Lehrbuch der Kunstwissenschaft zum Gebrauche bei Vorlesungen* (Landshut: Philipp Krüll, 1819), 103: "Die Musik ist in der Tiefe des menschlichen Gemüthes gegründet." Ibid.: "Da die Musik Widerhall des Innern ist."

7. Hegel, *Vorlesungen über die Aesthetik*, 3:143–44: "daß die Musik . . . sich darauf beschränken muß, die Innerlichkeit dem Innern faßbar zu machen . . . so dass ihr diese subjektive Innigkeit selbst zu ihrem eigentlichen Gegenstande wird." Ibid., 3:192; see above, p. 52.

8. For a particularly lucid explication of this point, see Bowie, *Aesthetics and Subjectivity*, 227–38.

9. Byron to Miss Milbanke, 10 November 1813, in *Byron's Letters and Journals*, 3:179. Victor Hugo, "Note ajoutée à la l'édition définitive," in his *Notre-Dame de Paris*, 2 vols. (Paris: Eugène Hugues, 1832), 1:3: "jaillir d'un seul jet."

10. Alphonse de Lamartine, *avertissement* to his *Harmonies poétiques et religieuses* (Paris: Charles Gosselin, 1830), 7–8: "Voici quatre livres de poésies écrites comme elles ont été senties, sans liaison, sans suite, sans transition apparente . . . ; poésies réelles et non feintes, qui sentent moins le poète que l'homme même, révélation intime et involontaire de ses impressions de chaque jour, pages de sa vie intérieure inspirées tantôt par la tristesse, tantôt par la joie, par la solitude ou par le monde, par le désespoir ou l'espérance, dans ses heures de sècheresse ou d'enthousiasme, de prière ou d'aridité." On the centrality of sincerity in nineteenth-century French literature and criticism, see Henri Peyre, *Literature and Sincerity* (New Haven, CT: Yale University Press, 1963).

11. John Keble, "Life of Sir Walter Scott" (1838), in his *Occasional Papers and Reviews* (Oxford and London: James Parker, 1877), 8.

12. Thomas Carlyle, review of J. G. Lockhart, *The Life of Robert Burns*, *Edinburgh Review* 48 (1828): 274.

13. Matthew Arnold, "The Study of Poetry" (1880), in his *Essays in Criticism: Second Series* (London: Macmillan, 1888), 48.

14. Leo Tolstoy, "What Is Art?" (1896), trans. Aylmer Maude (New York: Thomas Crowell, 1899), 43, 133, 134. On the history of the concept of sincerity in general, see R. Jay Magill, Jr., *Sincerity* (New York: W. W. Norton, 2012).

15. Wassily Kandinsky, *Über das Geistige in der Kunst, insbesondere in der Malerei*, 3rd ed. (Munich: Piper, 1912), 69: "Sein offenes Auge soll auf sein inneres Leben gerichtet werden und sein Ohr soll dem Munde der inneren Notwendigkeit stets zugewendet sein. Dann wird er zu jedem erlaubten Mittel und ebenso leicht zu jedem verbotenen Mittel greifen. Dieses ist der einzige Weg, das Mystischnotwendige zum Ausdruck zu bringen. Alle Mittel sind heilig, wenn sie innerlich-notwendig sind. Alle Mittel sind sündhaft, wenn sie nicht aus der Quelle der inneren Notwendigkeit stammen." On the influence of Tolstoy's aesthetics on Kandinsky, see Vincent Tomas, "Kandinsky's Theory of Painting," *British Journal of Aesthetics* 9 (1969): 20–24.

16. See David Gramit, "Selling the Serious: The Commodification of Music and Resistance to It in Germany, circa 1800," in *The Musician as Entrepreneur, 1700–1914: Managers, Charlatans, and Idealists*, ed. William Weber (Bloomington: Indiana University Press, 2004), 81–101; and Christina Bashford and Roberta Montemorra Marvin, eds., *The Idea of Art Music in a Commercial World, 1800–1930* (Woodbridge: Boydell Press, 2016).

17. See David Minden Higgins, *Romantic Genius and the Literary Magazine: Biography, Celebrity and Politics* (London: Routledge, 2005); Tom Mole, ed., *Romanticism and Celebrity Culture, 1750–1850* (Cambridge: Cambridge University Press, 2009); and Antoine Lilti, *The Invention of Celebrity, 1750–1850*, trans. Lynn Jeffress (Cambridge: Polity, 2017).

18. For multiple examples of this, from Fauré to Dukas to Debussy, see Carlo Caballero, *Fauré and French Musical Aesthetics* (Cambridge: Cambridge University Press, 2001), chap. 1.

19. Edgar Allan Poe, "The Philosophy of Composition," *Graham's Magazine* 28 (April 1846): 163.

20. Edmund Gosse, "The Sonnets from the Portuguese," in his *Critical Kit-Kats* (New York: Dodd, Mead, 1903), 11. Tolstoy, "What Is Art?" 134. For a defense of the moral principles behind authenticity, see Charles Taylor, *The Ethics of Authenticity* (Cambridge, MA: Harvard University Press, 1992).

21. See Charles S. Brauner, "Irony in the Heine Lieder of Schubert and Schumann," *MQ* 67 (1981): 261–81. More recent publications on irony in music include Michael Cherlin, *Varieties of Musical Irony: From Mozart to Mahler* (Cambridge: Cambridge University Press, 2017); and Bonds, "Irony and Incomprehensibility."

22. On irony in Mahler in particular, see Julian Johnson, *Mahler's Voices: Expression and Irony in the Songs and Symphonies* (New York: Oxford University Press, 2009).

23. On the relation of allusion to irony, see Christopher Reynolds, *Motives for Allusion: Context and Content in Nineteenth-Century Music* (Cambridge, MA: Harvard University Press, 2003), 68–87, 164–65.

24. See Bezzola, *Die Rhetorik bei Kant, Fichte und Hegel*; and Matthias Schöning, *Ironieverzicht: Friedrich Schlegels theoretische Konzepte zwischen "Athenäum" und "Philosophie des Lebens"* (Paderborn: Ferdinand Schöningh, 2002).

25. See Bonds, "Irony and Incomprehensibility," 337–39.

26. See Bonds, *Music as Thought*, chaps. 1 and 2.

27. Jacques-Auguste Delaire, "Des innovations en musique," *Revue musicale*, 2. sér., 1 (20 February 1830): 70–71: "Vivant isolé, il s'est replié sur lui-même, il est descendu dans le fond de son être pour étudier les mouvemens de sa vie intérieure tranquille ou agitée; aussi tous ses ouvrages sont une traduction de ses sentimens, de ses émotions; il y a mis toutes ses haines, toutes ses douleurs, toutes ses colères, toutes ses vengeances, toutes ses rêveries de bonheur. Là, toutes ses impressions se peignent comme dans un miroir magique, et lui-même est l'enchanteur qui nous dévoile ces mystères. . . .C'est un volcan qui mugit, c'est une lave qui coule et brûle tout sur son passage!!"

28. See James H. Johnson, *Listening in Paris: A Cultural History* (Berkeley and Los Angeles: University of California Press, 1996); and Thorau and Ziemer, *The Oxford Handbook of Music Listening in the 19th and 20th Centuries*.

29. Anonymous, "Wien: Musikalisches Tagebuch vom Monat März," *AmZ* 28 (1826): 310–11: "Aber den Sinn des fugirten Finale wagt Ref. nicht zu deuten: für ihn war es unverständlich, wie Chinesisch. Wenn die Instrumente in den Regionen des Süd- und Nordpols mit ungeheuern Schwierigkeiten zu kämpfen haben, wenn jedes derselben anders figurirt und sie sich *per transitum irregularem* unter einer Unzahl von Dissonanzen durchkreuzen, wenn die Spieler, gegen sich selbst misstrauisch, wohl auch nicht ganz rein greifen, freylich, dann ist die babylonische Verwirrung fertig."

30. Ibid., 311: "Doch wollen wir damit nicht voreilig absprechen: vielleicht kommt noch die Zeit, wo das, was uns beym ersten Blicke trüb und verworren erschien, klar und wohlgefälligen Formen erkannt wird."

31. S., "Tonstücke für 2 Violinen, Alto und Violoncello," *Allgemeine Musikzeitung zur Beförderung der theoretischen und praktischen Tonkunst* 1 (10 November 1827): 303–4: "leidenschaftliche Anhänger."

32. On this phenomenon in literature, see Brian Tucker, *Reading Riddles: Rhetorics of Obscurity from Romanticism to Freud* (Lewisburg, PA: Bucknell University Press, 2011). On music, see Holly Watkins, *Metaphors of Depth in German Musical Thought: From E. T. A. Hoffmann to Arnold Schoenberg* (Cambridge: Cambridge University Press, 2011).

33. Richard Taruskin, "Resisting the Ninth," *19CM* 12 (1989): 248; and Gustav Mahler to Anna von Mildenburg, 1 July 1896, in Mahler, *Briefe*, ed. Herta Blaukopf, 2nd ed. (Vienna: Paul Zsolnay, 1996), 190: "Die Menschen werden einige Zeit an den Nüssen zu knacken haben, die ich ihnen vom Baume schüttle."

34. Georg von Weiler, "Ueber den Geist und das Auffassen der Beethoven'schen Musik," *Cäcilia* 9 (1828): 46: "das *Unbegreifliche*. . .hat seine Begründung in der *Unendlichkeit* des dichterischen Genius."

35. Anonymous, "Nachrichten: Wien," *AmZ* 30 (13 February 1828): 107–8: "Allmählig fangen wir nun an, den Faden dieses kunstreichen Tongewebes entwirren zu lernen; immer deutlicher treten die wundersamen Umrisse hervor, und kaum dürften ein paar Jährchen ins Land gegangen seyn, so wird dieses Riesenwerk eben so allgemein erkannt und verstanden werden, wie seine Vorgänger, die auch bey ihrem Entstehen gleich ägyptischen Hieroglyphen verschrieen waren."

36. Anonymous, "Noch ein Wort über Beethoven," *Allgemeine Musikzeitung zur Beförderung der theoretischen und praktischen Tonkunst* 2 (1 March 1828): 143: " '. . . die auch bei ihrem Entstehen gleich ägyptischen *Hieroglyphen* (mit Recht!) verschrieen waren.' Was soll man zu einem solchen Urtheil sagen? Man muss verstummen, wenn man siehet, dass es Menschen gibt, deren blinde Vergötterung so weit gehet, dass sie eine Rhapsodie in Schutz nehmen, welche bisher noch Niemand verstanden hat, und welche sie selbst erst in *einigen Jahren* zu verstehen hoffen? Ist es denn der Zweck der Tonkunst, *ägyptische Hieroglyphen* zu entziffern? Soll sie, statt Vergnügen zu gewähren, eine peinliche Arbeit des Verstandes werden? Soll Ohr und Herz dabei leer ausgehen?—Und wie Viel sind der Menschen, welche— wenn es anders möglich ist—ein solches Problem zu lösen vermögen? Ist die wahre Musik nur für Wenige in die Tiefen der Mystik eingeweihete, oder für alle gebildete Menschen bestimmt?—Doch, es verlohnt sich der Mühe nicht, mehr über die Thorheit derer zu sagen, welche alles *Gefühl* verläugnen, um einer Afterkunst zu huldigen, welche gleich der Algebra blos den Kopf beschäftiget und das Herz erstarren läßt."

37. See Matthew Riley, *Musical Listening in the German Enlightenment: Attention, Wonder and Astonishment* (Aldershot: Ashgate, 2004); and Bonds, *Music as Thought*.

38. Friedrich Schlegel, "Lyceums-Fragment 112" (1797), in *KFSA*, 2:161: "Der analytische Schriftsteller beobachtet den Leser, wie er ist; danach macht er seinen Kalkül, legt seine Maschinen an, um den gehörigen Effekt auf ihn zu machen. Der synthetische Schriftsteller konstruiert und schafft sich einen Leser, wie er sein soll; er denkt sich denselben nicht ruhend und tot, sondern lebendig und entgegenwirkend. Er läßt das, was er erfunden hat, vor seinen Augen stufenweise werden, oder er lockt ihn es selbst zu erfinden. Er will keine bestimmte Wirkung auf ihn machen, sondern er tritt mit ihm in das heilige Verhältnis der innigsten Symphilosophie oder Sympoesie."

39. On the concept of *Symphilosophie*, see Izenberg, *Impossible Individuality*, 65–66, 113–15, and Michael N. Forster and Kristin Gjesdal, eds., *The Oxford Handbook of German Philosophy in the Nineteenth Century* (Oxford: Oxford University Press, 2015), 29–33. Terry Pinkard, in his *German Philosophy, 1760–1860: The Legacy of Idealism* (Cambridge: Cambridge University Press, 2002), 147, deftly translates the term as "sympathetic communal philosophizing."

40. Novalis, *Vermischte Bemerkungen und Blüthenstaub* (1798), in his *Schriften*, 2:470: "Der wahre Leser muß der erweiterte Autor seyn." Friedrich Schlegel, *Philosophische Lehrjahre* (1796–1806), in *KFSA*, 18:106: "Die wahre Kritik ein Autor in der 2t Potenz."

41. On the close relationship between irony and incomprehensibility from the Enlightenment to the present, see Eckhard Schuhmacher, *Die Ironie der Unverständlichkeit: Johann Georg Hamann, Friedrich Schlegel, Jacques Derrida, Paul de Man* (Frankfurt am Main: Surhkamp, 2000).

42. Gary Handwerk, "Romantic Irony," in *The Cambridge History of Literary Criticism*, vol. 5, *Romanticism*, ed. Marshall Brown (Cambridge: Cambridge University Press, 2000), 217.

43. For a detailed account of this development, see Robert S. Leventhal, *The Disciplines of Interpretation: Lessing, Herder, Schlegel and Hermeneutics in Germany, 1750–1800* (Berlin and New York: Walter de Gruyter, 1994). On Friedrich Schlegel's forerunners in this area, see John A. McCarthy, *Crossing Boundaries: A Theory and History of Essay Writing in German, 1680–1815* (Philadelphia: University of Pennsylvania Press, 1989), esp. chap. 8 ("The Dialectic Muse Soars I: Essayistic Prose, 1750–1790").

44. "Über die Unverständlichkeit," *KFSA*, 2: 371–72: "und es bleibt nun nichts zu wünschen übrig, als daß einer unsrer vortrefflichen Komponisten die meinige würdig finden mag, ihr eine musikalische Beglietung zu geben. Schöneres gibt es nichts auf der Erde, als wenn Poesie und Musik in holder Eintracht zur Veredlung der Menschheit wirken." For an English translation of the complete essay, see Friedrich Schlegel, *Friedrich Schlegel's "Lucinde" and the Fragments*, trans. Peter Firchow (Minneapolis: University of Minnesota Press, 1971), 259–71. On Schlegel's essay, see Cathy Comstock, "'Transcendental Buffoonery': Irony as Process in Schlegel's 'Über die Unverständlichkeit," *Studies in Romanticism* 26 (1987): 445–64; Marike Finlay, *The Romantic Irony of Semiotics: Friedrich Schlegel and the Crisis of Representation* (Berlin: Mouton de Gruyter, 1988), 183–259; Elizabeth Millán-Zaibert, *Friedrich Schlegel and the Emergence of Romantic Philosophy* (Albany: State University of New York Press, 2007), 165–70; and Madleen Podewski, "Konzeptionen des Unverständlichen um und nach 1800: Friedrich Schlegel und Heinrich Heine," in *Krisen des Verstehens um 1800*, ed. Sandra Heinen and Harald Nehr (Würzburg: Königshausen & Neumann, 2004), 55–73.

45. August Wilhelm Schlegel, "Etwas über William Shakespeare bey Gelegenheit Wilhelm Meisters," *Die Horen*, 4. Stück (1796): 66: "die Unergründlichkeit der schaffenden Natur, deren Ebenbild er [i.e., genius] im Kleinen ist."

46. August Wilhelm Schlegel, "Allgemeine Übersicht des gegenwärtigen Zustandes der deutschen Literatur" (1803), in his *Vorlesungen über schöne Litteratur und Kunst*,

erster Teil, 69–70: "Eben auf dem Dunkel, worein sich die Wurzel unsers Daseyns verliert, auf dem unauslöslichen Geheimniß beruht der Zauber des Lebens, dieß ist die Seele aller Poesie."

47. Schiller to Goethe, 2 July 1796, in Goethe, *Briefwechsel zwischen Schiller und Goethe in den Jahren 1794 bis 1805*, ed. Manfred Beetz, vol. 8.1 of Goethe, *Sämtliche Werke nach Epochen seines Schaffens*: "Ruhig und tief, klar und doch unbegreiflich wie die Natur."

48. See Hermann Beisler, "Die Unergründlichkeit des Werks und die Unendlichkeit der Interpretation," in *Theorie der Interpretation vom Humanismus bis zur Romantik: Rechtswissenschaft, Philosophie, Theologie*, ed. Jan Schröder (Stuttgart: Steiner, 2001), 217–48; and Tucker, *Reading Riddles*, 27. See also Bernd Brunemeier, *Vieldeutigkeit und Rätselhaftigkeit: Die semantische Qualität und Kommunikativitätsfunktion des Kunstwerks in der Poetik und Ästhetik der Goethezeit* (Amsterdam: B. R. Grüner, 1983).

49. See Watkins, *Metaphors of Depth in German Musical Thought*.

50. On the relevance of Schleiermacher's theory of hermeneutics to musical analysis in the early nineteenth century, see Ian Bent, "General Introduction," in *Music Analysis in the Nineteenth Century*, ed. Ian Bent, 2 vols. (Cambridge: Cambridge University Press, 1993–94), 2:1–27; and Bent, "Plato—Beethoven: A Hermeneutics for Nineteenth-Century Music?" *Indiana Theory Review* 16 (1995): 1–33.

51. Hoffmann, "Beethovens Instrumentalmusik," 54–55. For the original German, see above, p. 236.

52. Leventhal, *Disciplines of Interpretation*, 30–31.

53. See Leventhal, *Disciplines of Interpretation*, 13–14; and Gerhard Kurz, "Alte, neue, altneue Hermeneutik: Überlegungen zu den Normen romantischer Hermeneutik," in Heinen and Nehr, *Krisen des Verstehens um 1800*, 31–54.

54. Leventhal, *Disciplines of Interpretation*, 300.

55. Ernst Behler, "What It Means to Understand an Author Better than He Understood Himself: Idealistic Philosophy and Romantic Hermeneutics," in *Literary Theory and Criticism: Festschrift Presented to René Wellek in Honor of his Eightieth Birthday*, ed. Joseph P. Strelka, 2 vols. (Bern: Peter Lang, 1984), 1:75.

56. Johann Gottfried Herder, *Vom Erkennen und Empfinden der menschlichen Seele* (Riga: Johann Friedrich Hartknoch, 1778), 56–57: "Man sollte jedes Buch als den Abdruck einer lebendigen Menschenseele betrachten können. . . . Das Leben eines Autors ist der beste Commentar seiner Schriften, wenn er nehmlich treu und mit sich selbst Eins ist. . . . Jedes Gedicht, zumal ein ganzes, großes Gedicht, ein Werk der Seele und des Lebens, ist ein gefährlicher Verräther seines Urhebers, oft, wo dieser am wenigsten sich zu verrathen glaubte. . . . Wo es der Mühe lohnt, ist dies lebendige Lesen, diese Divination in die Seele des Urhebers das einzige Lesen und das tiefste Mittel der Bildung. . . . Solches Lesen ist Wetteifer, Heuristik; wir klimmen mit auf schöpferische Höhen oder entdecken den Irrthum und die Abweichung in ihrer Geburtsstätte. Je mehr man den Verfasser lebendig kennt und mit ihm gelebt hat, desto lebendiger wird dieser Umgang."

57. Friedrich Schleiermacher, *Hermeneutik und Kritik* (1838), ed. Manfred Frank (Frankfurt am Main: Suhrkamp, 1977), 78: "Ebenso ist jede Rede immer nur zu

verstehen aus dem ganzen Leben, dem sie angehört, d.h. da jede Rede nur als Lebensmoment des Redenden in der Bedingtheit aller seiner Lebensmomente erkennbar ist, und dies nur aus der Gesamtheit seiner Umgebungen, wodurch seine Entwicklung und sein Fortbestehen bestimmt werden, so ist jeder Redende nur verstehbar durch seine Nationalität und sein Zeitalter."

58. Schleiermacher, *Hermeneutik und Kritik*, 85–90.

59. Schleiermacher, *Hermeneutik und Kritik*, 94: "Die Aufgabe ist auch so auszudrücken, 'die Rede zuerst ebensogut und dann besser zu verstehen als ihr Urheber.' Denn weil wir keine unmittelbare Kenntnis dessen haben, was in ihm ist, so müssen wir vieles zum Bewußtsein zu bringen suchen, was ihm unbewußt bleiben kann."

60. Thomas Carlyle, review of *Jean Paul Friedrich Richter's Leben . . .* by Heinrich Doering, *Edinburgh Review* 46 (1827): 191.

61. Abrams, *The Mirror and the Lamp*, 248. For a survey of efforts by other critics to delineate the inner selves of authors through their works, see chap. 9, "Literature as a Revelation of Personality."

62. Carlyle, review of *Jean Paul Friedrich Richter's Leben*, 190.

63. Thomas Carlyle, "Thoughts on History," *Fraser's Magazine* 2 (1830): 414. Carlyle, *On Heroes, Hero-Worship, and the Heroic in History* (1841), ed. David R. Sorensen and Brent E. Kinser (New Haven, CT: Yale University Press, 2013), 41. See also Eric Bentley, *A Century of Hero-Worship: A Study of the Idea of Heroism in Carlyle and Nietzsche, with Notes on Wagner, Spengler, Stefan George, and D. H. Lawrence*, 2nd ed. (Boston: Beacon Press, 1957).

64. Raphael Georg Kiesewetter, *Geschichte der europäisch-abendländischen oder unsrer heutigen Musik* (Leipzig: Breitkopf & Härtel, 1834). On the broader context of Kiesewetter's history of music, see Jim Samson, "The Great Composer," in *The Cambridge History of Nineteenth-Century Music*, ed. Jim Samson (Cambridge: Cambridge University Press, 2002), 259–84; and Gundula Kreuzer, "*Heilige Trias, Stildualismus*, Beethoven: On the Limits of Nineteenth-Century Germanic Music Historiography," in *The Invention of Beethoven and Rossini: Historiography, Analysis, Criticism*, ed. Nicholas Mathew and Benjamin Walton (Cambridge: Cambridge University Press, 2013), 66–95.

65. John Ruskin, *The Queen of the Air* (London: Smith, Elder, 1869), 119–20.

66. See above, Introduction n. 6.

67. E. T. A. Hoffmann, "Recension: *Messa a quattro voci . . . da Luigi van Beethoven . . .* ," *AmZ* 15 (16 June 1813): 392: "aus seinem Innersten hervorgegangen." Hoffmann, "Alte und Neue Kirchenmusik," *AmZ* 16 (14 September 1814): 612: "Er hat indessen in einem einzigen Kirchenwerke sein Inneres aufgeschlossen."

68. Georg von Nissen, *Biographie W. A. Mozarts* (Leipzig: Breitkopf und Härtel, 1828), 627. On the subsequent perception of the Requiem as an autobiographical work, see Cliff Eisen, "Mozart, das Requiem und die Biographie der Romantik," in *Mozart: Experiment Aufklärung im Wien des ausgehenden 18. Jahrhunderts*, ed. Herbert Lachmayer (Ostfildern: Hatje Cantz, 2006), 807–21.

69. Gottfried Weber, "Über die Echtheit des Mozartschen Requiem," *Cäcilia* 3 (1825): 205: "ja kaum wirklich ein Werk von Mozart zu nennen ist." For an overview

of the controversy, see Simon Keefe, *Mozart's Requiem: Reception, Work, Completion* (Cambridge: Cambridge University Press, 2012), 44–57.

70. Goehr, *The Imaginary Museum of Musical Works.*

71. Franz Stoepel, "P.S. des Uebersetzers," in Anonymous, "Ueber den gegenwärtigen Zustand der Musik in London," *Münchener Allgemeine Musik-Zeitung* 1 (3 November 1827): 80: "Was ist denn auch einer Symphonie von Beethoven, Mozart, oder gar von *Haydn* abzuhören? Das ist Musik, und nichts als Musik, Ton, und nichts als Ton; da kommen keine Liebesgeschichten mit etlichen feinen Intriguen, oder ein lockerer *Don Juan*, oder ein durchtriebener *Figaro* d'rin vor; kurz, es ist langweilig. Viele sonst recht vernünftige Leute sagen zwar, dass man sich eben dabei unendlich viel denken könne, dass eben in solchen Werken das reiche Seelenleben jener grossen Männer am schönsten, in ewig neuen Bildern, sich ausspreche und zeige, dass gerade in solchen Werken die reinste und reichste Poesie walte u. s. w.; aber wir glauben, dass das schönste Kunstwerk das ist, wobei man am wenigsten, oder noch lieber gar nichts zu denken braucht, wo einem die gebratenen Tauben so zu sagen ins—." The last sentence alludes to the saying "Eine gebratene Taube fliegt nicht ins Maul," literally, "A roasted pigeon doesn't fly into one's mouth," or in other words, that which satisfies does not appear magically and fully formed on its own but instead requires effort.

Chapter 5

1. August Kuhn, as quoted in Elisabeth Eleonore Bauer, *Wie Beethoven auf den Sockel kam: Die Entstehung eines musikalischen Mythos* (Stuttgart: J. B. Metzler, 1992), 60: "von einem geistvollen, in E. T. A. Hoffmanns Darstellungsweise und Kunstansichten tief eingedrungenen jungen Manne."

2. Marx, "Erstes grosses Konzert," 366: "Beethovens herrliche Fantasie [Op. 80] wird den in ihr wohnenden grossen Geist einem Theil der Zuhörer gewiss noch nicht geoffenbaret haben. Wie ist es auch möglich, dass ein Werk, das in einem grossen Künstler Wochen, vielleicht Monate bedurfte, um zu reifen, das aus einer neuen Idee hervorgegangen ist, neue Seiten unsers Innern aufsucht, um uns mit neuen Anklängen, neuen Ahnungen und Anschauungen zu berühren, dass das von einer gemischten Versammlung gleichsam im Vorübergehen erhascht werde? Man muss gewohnt und geübt sein, dem Geistesflug des Künstlers in jede Gestaltung zu folgen, oder man muss so viel Pietät für Kunstschöpfungen und soviel Selbstkenntniss haben, dass man zu einem Werke, in dem sich Neues und Gutes auch nur ahnen lässt, mehrmals zurückkehrt und alle vorgefassten Meinungen und Grundsätze einstweilen aufzugeben bereit ist, um das Neue ungestört auf sich wirken und ihm Zeit zu lassen, sich uns vollkommen zu entfalten. Wer dies verschmäht, der ist ein übel unterrichteter Beurtheiler aller vorschreitenden Werke und raubt sich selbst den Genuss an ihnen und der Fortbildung der Kunst in ihnen. Die Werke, die sofort allgemein angenommen und beliebt werden, sind eben die wertlosesten; denn jener Erfolg beweiset, dass sie nur Hergebrachtes, längst und allgemein Bekanntes enthalten."

3. Adolph Bernhard Marx, "Recensionen: Sonate für das Pianoforte von Ludwig van Beethoven. 110tes Werk," *BAmZ* 1 (10 March 1824): 87–90.

4. Marx, "Recensionen. Sonate . . . 110tes Werk," 87: "Es ist ein erhebender Anblick, menschliche Kraft gegen ein mächtiges Mißgeschick kämpfen und siegen zu sehen.—Einen solchen Kampf besteht Beethovens Genius. Taubheit hat ihn jeder lebendigeren Mittheilung beraubt. Unter den Hunderttausenden der Kaiserstadt lebt er abgeschieden, einsam. Ihm ist der frohlockende Ruf der Freude, der Ausdruck der Liebe und Verehrung verstummt; seine Hand gleitet über die Saiten und er vernimmt nicht die Akkorde, die Alles entzücken. Welch ein harter Schlag für den Tondichter, das Ohr zu verlieren, den Sinn verschlossen zu sehen, der ihm der entwickeltste war, der seinem Geiste die reichste Nahrung gab!"

5. Marx, "Recensionen. Sonate . . . 110tes Werk," 87: "Beethoven hat die Kraft gehabt, in diesem Ringen zu bestehen und ist gekräftigter und erhoben aus dem Kampfe hervorgegangen. Je mehr sich ihm die Aussenwelt verschloss, desto tiefer wandte er sich in sein Inneres zurück. . . . Immer reiner löset er seine Aufgabe, immer reicher werden für den, der ihn versteht, seine Gaben—immer verschlossener werden seine Werke denen, die eben sein eigenstes Wesen nie aufzufassen verstanden."

6. Marx, "Recensionen: Sonate . . . 110tes Werk," 87: "Die vorliegende Sonate scheint ein solcher Erguss aus dem innersten Herzen zu sein. Man höre endlich auf, ein Kunstwerk wie ein todtes Produkt zu behandeln. Man glaube es erst dann zu verstehen, wenn man seinen Sinn in der Seele des Schaffenden wiedergefunden und nachgewiesen hat.

    "Die Klage des Einsamen ist das erste Allegro . . . voll des zartesten Ausdruckes der Wehmuth, reizend in Anmuth und Majestät."

7. Marx, "Recensionen: Sonate . . . 110tes Werk," 88: "Wenn der Gesang wie in Seufzern erstorben, wenn das Saitenspiel verklungen ist, folgt ein seltsam wildes Allegro molto (Fmoll 2/4), in das sich unerwartet die Melodie eines wüsten allgemein bekannten Volkliedes einwebt, das dann eben so unerwartet mit einem zarten Nachklang schliesst. 'Das alles,'—scheint uns der Künstler zu erzählen—'die kleinlichen Freuden, bei denen sich der Mensch um seine Zeit und um erhebendere betrügt, die wüste Lust, in deren Rausche so manches Leben verspielt wird, haben nie Macht über mich gehabt. Wie leerer Wind sind sie mir vorübergesauset (Trio Des-dur) und (Koda) so hat es sein sollen und müssen.'"

8. Marx, "Recensionen: Sonate . . . 110tes Werk," 88: "Wer nicht . . . ahnet, dass Beethoven hier sein innerstes Herz—und wie schmerzlich—öffnen will, wer in dem Gesange des Arioso . . . in der weinenden zweiten Stimme am Schlusse nicht die Klage des tief verwundeten, verwaiseten Herzens vernimmt: für den ist Beethoven ewig stumm, der wird auch mich nie verstehen."

9. Adolph Bernhard Marx, "Als Recension der Sonate Op. 111 von L. van Beethoven . . . Brief eines Recensenten an den Redakteur," *BAmZ* 1 (17 March 1824): 95–99.

10. Marx, "Als Recension der Sonate Op. 111," 97: "Ich verschone Ew. Wohlgeboren mit der Dithyrambe, in die sich Edward ergoss nach langem Schweigen, wie er seufzte, nun sei Beethoven gestorben und sein Riesengeist sei vor die Menschen getreten und habe gesprochen: ihr habt mich nie erkannt; schaut auf, das war mein mächtiges Leben, diese Schmerzen haben mich geläutert, diese Lichtblicke aus Elisium, diese

Klänge aus der seeligen Jugendzeit haben mich gestärkt, das zagende Herz erquickt—
und nun sterbe ich. 'Ja, er ist gestorben!' rief Edward aus und vergeblich fragte ich, ob
die Nachricht zuverlässig genug für Ihre Zeitung wäre."

11. Marx, "Als Recension der Sonate Op. 111," 98: "Welcher Künstler gäbe auch etwas
anderes, als was er in sich erlebt?"

12. Marx, "Als Recension der Sonate Op. 111," 99: "Trost ist für die Schwachen. Die
heilige Kunst belehrt uns, indem sie zeigt und vorempfinden lässt, was getragen
werden muss; sie stärkt uns, indem sie die erwachenden Kräfte in unsrer Brust uns
bekannt macht; sie erhebt uns, indem sie, wie die Natur, selbst im Untergange den
Aufgang, das neue Leben, im Ende des Endlichen das Ewige zeigt."

13. Ludwig Rellstab, "Ueber Beethovens neuestes Quartett," *BAmZ* 2 (25 May 1825): 165–
66. In the journal's table of contents, the essay is listed as "Den Zeitgenossen grosser
Künstler—Beethoven's" (For the Contemporaries of Great Artists—Beethoven's).

14. On the circumstances surrounding the premiere of Op. 127, see John M. Gingerich,
"Ignaz Schuppanzigh and Beethoven's Late Quartets," *MQ* 93 (2010): 450–513.

15. Rellstab, "Ueber Beethovens neuestes Quartett," 166: "Das ganze Werk [Op. 127] ist
der Ausdruck der edelsten Seele, des reinsten Eifers für die Kunst selbst, nirgend eine
Spur, dass etwas um eines andern willen da sei, als um sich selbst. Der Genius wollte
sich nur selbst verwirklichen—das andre war gleichgültig, war nichts. Und so sollen
wir es auch hinnehmen. Solche Werke können und dürfen nicht anders sein. Was
uns auch darin fremd, dunkel, verworren erscheinen mag, es hat seine Klarheit und
Nothwendigkeit in der Seele des Schaffenden, und dort müssen wir Belehrung suchen.
Wer es vermag, sich in die Seele des Mannes zu denken, der seit vierzehn leidenvollen
Jahren einsam in der Welt des Lebens und der Freude steht, wer es vermag, sich ohne
den Sinn zu denken, aus dem uns der edelste reinste Genuss des Geistes entspringt;
wer begreift, daß selbst der gewaltigste Genius endlichen Bestimmungen unterliegt
und unterliegen muß: der wird auch wünschen, daß selbst einem Beethoven die
Erinnerung des Ohrs schwächer werden, die lebendigen Farben der Töne nach und
nach erblassen müssen. So steht manches wohl in seiner himmlischen Phantasie
anders, als in unserm irdisch schwer vernehmendem Ohr; und ohne uns ein Recht,
eine Stimme anzumassen, mögen wir in Demuth zurücktreten und sagen, daß ein
Genius, der eine wesentliche Aenderung und Störung in seiner Organisation gelitten
hat, auch anders erzeugen und schaffen muß, als der, der noch in der frischen
lebendigen Welt der Sinne mächtig und unverletzt steht und wandelt. Und was uns
daher fremd und unbegreiflich erscheint, das wollen wir nicht voreilig angreifen,
sondern anerkennen, dass, wo keine genaue Gemeinschaft des Maasses ist, auch
keine richtige Würdigung statt finden kann.—Niemand aber glaube aus dem
Gesagten, daß etwa deswegen das neueste Werk Beethovens mit unserer Auffassung
inkommensurabel wäre. Nein, Dank dem Himmel, es ist noch Verbindung genug
zwischen ihm und uns, dass wir eine gemeinsame Sprache für unsere Empfindungen
haben, wenn sie auch nicht in ihren letzten und feinsten Beziehungen überall
verständlich ist—und wo wäre denn das, *streng genommen*, nur bei zwei Menschen
der Fall?—Und in dieser Sprache hat Beethoven wunderwürdig und in's Tiefste
ergreifend zu uns geredet. Es ist ein ernstes Wort, das er zu uns spricht, es sind die

gefassten Aeusserungen bekämpften Leids einer tief verwundeten, aber eben so stark hoffenden Seele, es ist der männliche Schmerz eines Laokoon, der durch das ganze Werk mit geheimen Fäden sich selbst da noch hindurchschlingt, wo es in einem tiefen Scherzo sich selbst zu verspotten scheint und eben darum um so tiefer und erschütternder unsere Brust ergreift.—Du hoher Genius, der Du uns so göttlich segensreich beschenkst, solltest Du allein der Leidende sein? Nein, aus solchem Born quillt ewige Stärkung und Erhebung, und Du wirst Dich selbst halten und trösten und erheben, wenn auch nie wieder der Lichtstral süßer Töne, die du wunderbar erschaffest, in die stumme lautlose Nacht deines irdischen Lebens dringt."

16. Christian Gottlob Rebs, "Ueber mehrere Musikaufführungen in Leipzig," *BAmZ* 3 (28 June 1826): 203–4, 213–17, 225–28, 248–49. Kunze's transcription (*Ludwig van Beethoven*, 487–92) omits an important passage from the first installment of this review. Although unsigned, the review is attributed to Rebs in the volume's table of contents.

17. Rebs, "Ueber mehrere Musikaufführungen in Leipzig," 204: "Die Erscheinung eines solchen Egoismus kann klein und widrig sein, wo es dem Komponisten an Kraft der Phantasie und des Gefühls gebricht, und leere Künstelei sich an die Stelle der Kunst setzen will. . . . [E]s kann aber auch einen Egoismus geben, der mit prometheïscher Kühnheit auftritt und den Ossa auf den Pelion thürmt, um die Götter in ihren Wohnsitzen zu finden. Ein solcher Gigant—ich muss meine Meinung unbefangen bekennen—erscheint mir Beethoven in dieser letzten Symphonie. . . . Er stösst durch seine Kraft eben so oft feindlich ab, als er anzieht und erfreut, er spannt, betäubt und ermüdet . . . und das Alles—wie es scheint, will er so. Ich spreche hier aber—will ich wohl bemerken—nur den Gesammteindruck aus, welchen dieses Werk nach zwei mit ungemeinem Fleisse von unseren Orchester vorbereiteten Aufführungen auf mich machte; ich will einem solchen Meister und seinem Werke gegenüber keinen Anspruch auf ein Urtheil machen; ich verlange blos, dass der, der es kennen gelernt hat, den Eindruck, den er auf ihn macht, uneingenommen mit dem hier ausgesprochenen vergleiche, ohne noch etwa auf des Meisters persönliche Verhältnisse hinzublicken."

18. Rebs, "Ueber mehrere Musikaufführungen in Leipzig," 214: "Manches ist minder Resultat einer innern objektiven Nothwendigkeit, als der Willkühr einer kecken Laune—so daß das Ganze in seinem Karakter sich der Phantasie und dem Capriccio annähert."

19. Anonymous, "Felix Mendelssohn-Bartholdy, in Stettin," *BAmZ* 4 (14 March 1827): 86: "Dass Beethoven in dieser aufgeregten Stimmung komponirte, sich wenigstens in sie hinein versetzte, leidet wohl keinen Zweifel. . . . Welcher glatte und polirte Künstler giebt auf eine so natürliche Art sein Ich der Welt preis, wie Beethoven es in diesem Finale that?"

20. Rochlitz, "Den Freunden Beethovens," 705–10. We know from Schindler's biography of Beethoven that he had sent a copy of the document to Rochlitz, along with a renewed request to collaborate on a biography of the composer. Rochlitz describes his reaction to it in a letter to Schindler dated 3 October 1827; see Anton Schindler, *Biographie von Ludwig van Beethoven* (Münster: Aschendorff, 1840), 6.

21. Rochlitz, "Den Freunden Beethovens," 706: "feindselig, störrisch oder misanthropisch"; ibid., "einen Sinn, den ich einst in der grössten Vollkommenheit besass, in einer Vollkommenheit, wie ihn wenige von meinem Fache gewiss haben noch gehabt haben."

22. Rochlitz, "Den Freunden Beethovens," 707: "nahe ich mich einer Gesellschaft, so überfällt mich eine heisse Ängstlichkeit, indem ich befürchte, in Gefahr gesetzt zu werden, meinen Zustand merken zu lassen . . . welche Demüthigung, wenn jemand neben mir stand und von weitem eine Flöte hörte und ich nichts hörte, oder jemand den Hirten singen hörte, und ich nichts hörte, solche Ereignisse brachten mich nahe an Verzweiflung, es fehlte wenig, und ich endigte selbst mein Leben—nur sie die Kunst, sie hielt mich zurück, ach es dünkte mir unmöglich, die Welt eher zu verlassen, bis ich das alles hervorgebracht, wozu ich mich aufgelegt fühlte, und so fristete ich dieses elende Leben—wahrhaft elend . . . Geduld—so heisst es, sie muss ich nun zur Führerin wählen . . . schon in meinem 28. Jahre gezwungen, Philosoph zu werden, es ist nicht leicht, für den Künstler schwerer als für irgend jemand—Gottheit, du siehst herab auf mein Innres, du kennst es, du weisst, dass Menschenliebe und Neigung zum Wohlthun drin hausen, o Menschen, wenn ihr einst dieses leset, so denkt, dass ihr mir unrecht gethan, und der Unglückliche, er tröste sich, einen seines Gleichen zu finden, der trotz allen Hindernissen der Natur doch noch alles gethan, was in seinen Vermögen stand, um in die Reihe würdiger Künstler und Menschen aufgenommen zu werden." The transcription here follows that of the original publication in the *AmZ*. For a critical edition of the complete text, see *BGA* no. 106, 1:121–25. For a translation of the complete text, see Solomon, *Beethoven*, 151–54.

23. Rochlitz, "Den Freunden Beethovens," 709: "für meine Brüder *Carl* und [blank space] nach meinem Tode zu lesen und zu vollziehen." There has been much speculation as to why Beethoven did not name his other brother, Nikolaus Johann, and left a blank space instead; see Solomon, *Beethoven*, 155–57.

24. See, for example, Solomon, *Beethoven*, 157–62; Lockwood, *Beethoven*, 115–22; and Joseph N. Straus, *Extraordinary Measures: Disability in Music* (New York: Oxford University Press, 2011), chap. 2 ("Musical Narratives of Disability Overcome: Beethoven's Deafness").

25. Anonymous, "Aus Beethovens Testament, als Beytrag zu seiner Biographie," *Allgemeine Theaterzeitung und Unterhaltungsblatt* 20 (6 November 1827): 541–42; Anonymous, "Memoir of Beethoven," *Quarterly Musical Magazine and Review* 9 (1827): 266–68; Beethoven, "Beethoven's Will," *The Harmonicon*, n.s. 6 (January 1828): 6–7; and Anonymous, "Literary Intelligence: Beethoven," *Philadelphia Monthly Magazine* 2 (15 April 1828): 60–61 (my thanks to Molly Barnes for pointing out this last source). The document appeared in Dutch as Ludwig van Beethoven, "Eigenhandige brief van den onlangs overleden' vermaarden componist Ludwig van Beethoven, onder zijne nagelatene papieren gevonden," *Vaderlandsche Letteroefeningen* 2 (1828): 94–96; and in French in François-Joseph Fétis's translation of Ignaz Ritter von Seyfried's *Ludwig van Beethoven's Studien im Generalbasse, Contrapuncte und in der Compositionslehre* (Vienna: Tobias Haslinger, 1832) as *Études de Beethoven: Traité d'harmonie et de composition*, 2 vols. (Paris: Maurice Schlesinger, 1833) 1:25–28.

26. Seyfried, *Ludwig van Beethoven's Studien im Generalbasse*, separately paginated "Anhang," 28–32, and *Études de Beethoven*, 1:25–28. For a detailed survey of Beethoven's compositional studies that takes into account their historiography, see Julia Ronge, *Beethovens Lehrzeit: Kompositionsstudien bei Joseph Haydn, Johann Georg Albrechtsberger und Antonio Salieri* (Bonn: Beethoven-Haus, 2011).

27. Beethoven, "Testament de Louis Beethoven, d'après le texte original," *Le Voleur*, 2nd ser., 6 (20 April 1833): 341–42; Castil-Blaze [François-Henri-Joseph Blaze], "Beethoven (Ludwig van)," in his *Dictionnaire de la conversation, et de la lecture*, 52 vols. (Paris: Belin-Mandar, 1832–39), 5:171–72.

28. Fröhlich, "Recensionen: *Sinfonie, mit Schlusschor* ... ," 234, 236: "zu *einem vollendeten Seelengemälde*"; "so dass man dieses Werk die *musikalisch-geschrieben Autobiographie Beethoven's* nennen könnte."

29. Adolph Bernhard Marx, "Beurtheilungen: Quatuor pour 2 Violons, Alto et Violoncelle par L. v. Beethoven. Oeuvr. 135 ... ," *BAmZ* 6 (1829): 169: "Der Inhalt der letzten Werke scheint innigst an die Subjektivität und an die besondre Lage Beethovens geknüpft; man begreift, wie dieser Ideengang einem kalt abgeschlossenen, nur aussen verweilenden Betrachter als Verwirrung und Verirrung erscheinen kann,—während sich in die Brust des theilnehmenden, nachfühlenden Freundes die tiefste innigste Seele des Tondichters in allem Reichthum seiner Empfindungen, Erinnerungen und Schmerzen ergiesst."

30. Alfred Julius Becher, "Correspondenz: Köln," *NZfM* 2 (13 March 1834): 85: "der gewaltige Beethoven, der Höhepunkt der gegenwärtigen Musik-Periode und der größte Tondichter aller Zeiten, hat die ganze Fülle seiner Gefühle, den ganzen Reichthum seiner Ideen in seine Symphonieen strömend ausgegossen"; "[die] Ausprägung wirklicher Ideen und selbstbewußter Geisteszustände in Tönen, im Gegensatze zur bloßen Schilderung von Situationen."

31. Adolph Bernhard Marx, "Louis van Beethoven: Esquisse biographique," *Gazette musicale de Paris* 1 (21 December 1834): 409: "Une page de son histoire intime nous est fournie par sa sonate (quasi fantaisie, en ut mineur no 2, œuv. 27), écrite par lui au moment où il se trouva déçu dans un tendre sentiment auquel il fut obligé de renoncer. Ceux dont le cœur ressent pour Beethoven cette sympathie sans laquelle les arts en général ne sauraient être bien compris, reconnaîtront facilement dans la sonate œuv. 3 [*sic*] et dans d'autres de ses ouvrages de pareilles manifestations de sentimens déterminés et les dispositions de l'âme du compositeur au moment où il écrivait, alors même qu'il n'a pas eu soin d'avertir le public de ces dispositions par des suscriptions expresses comme celles que portent l'œuvre 81—26, son avant-dernier quatuor et quelques autres de ses compositions." The references to Op. 81[a] and Op. 26 are to piano sonatas that contain specific inscriptions; the "penultimate" string quartet is presumably Op. 132, with its "Heiliger Dankgesang." Marx appears to have written this essay specifically for the *Gazette musicale de Paris*, on whose masthead he is listed as a corresponding editor. He would make similar if less extreme comments on the "Moonlight" Sonata in his later and better-known *Beethoven* (1859), which is the source cited in Lawrence Kramer, "Hands On, Lights Off: The 'Moonlight' Sonata and the Birth of Sex at the Piano," in his *Musical Meaning: Toward a Critical History* (Berkeley and Los Angeles: University of California Press, 2002), 29–50.

32. Bettina Brentano von Arnim, *Goethes Briefwechsel mit einem Kinde*, 3 vols. (Berlin: F. Dümmler, 1835), 2:192: "und so fühlt Beethoven sich auch, als Begründer einer neuen sinnlichen Basis im geistigen Leben"; ibid., 2:192–93: "'und die Welt muß ich verachten, die nicht ahnt, daß Musik höhere Offenbarung ist als alle Weisheit und Philosophie.'"

33. Bettina Brentano von Arnim, "Drei Briefe von Beethoven," *Athenaeum für Wissenschaft, Kunst und Leben* 1 (1839): 1–7. Anonymous, "Vermischtes," *NZfM* 10 (25 June 1839): 204; Schindler, *Biographie von Ludwig van Beethoven*, 81–84. On the publication and reception of these letters, see Heinz Härtl, *"Drei Briefe von Beethoven": Genese und Frührezeption einer Briefkomposition Bettina von Arnims* (Bielefeld: Aisthesis, 2016); Ursula Härtl, "Carl Röhlings Bild *Beethoven und Goethe in Teplitz*," *Neue Zeitung für Einsiedler: Mitteilungen der Internationalen Arnim-Gesellschaft* 10–11 (2010–11): 28–33; and Helga Lühning, "'…an diesem geht die ganze Welt auf und nieder': Bettine Brentano zwischen Beethoven und Goethe," in *Goethe und die Musik*, ed. Walter Hettche and Rolf Selbmann (Würzburg: Königshausen & Neumann, 2012), 145–65.

34. Ernst Ortlepp, *Beethoven: Eine phantastische Charakteristik* (Leipzig: Johann Friedrich Hartknoch, 1836), 45: "'Du wirst ihn vollenden!' erwiederte Haydn, 'und er wird noch nach tausend Jahren tönen! Ich bringe Dir die Weihe und die Kraft dazu vom Himmel, daß Deine letzte Schöpfung Alles enthalte, was noch unausgesprochen in den tiefsten Tiefen Deiner Seele lag, daß sie ein Bild werde Deines heiligsten Selbst, anfangs unverstanden und verworfen, dann geahnet und angestaunt, später gefaßt und geliebt, und endlich bewundert und gepriesen in ewige Zeiten!'"

35. Ortlepp, *Beethoven*, 55: "'Ja,' rief er aus, 'sie sollen nun einmal, ehe ich sterbe, Alles erfahren, was mir auf der Seele gelegen; ich will ihn mit gewaltigen Strichen hinmalen den großen Kampf des Weltenschmerzes mit der Weltenlust . . . so sollen sie doch sehen, daß ich mich siegreich erhebe über das irdische Leid gleich einem gen Himmel ragenden Kolosse!'" On the figure of Beethoven in nineteenth-century fiction, see Sieghard Brandenburg, "Künstlerroman und Biographie: Zur Entstehung des Beethoven-Mythos im 19. Jahrhundert," in *Beethoven und die Nachwelt*, ed. Helmut Loos, 65–80 (Bonn: Beethoven-Haus, 1986); and Egon Voss, "Das Beethoven-Bild der Beethoven-Belletrisik: Zu einigen Beethoven-Erzählungen des 19. Jahrhunderts," both in *Beethoven und die Nachwelt*, ed. Helmut Loos (Bonn: Beethoven-Haus, 1986), 65–80 and 81–94, respectively.

36. Chrétien Urhan, "Feuilleton, Revue musicale. Musique. Premier concert du Conservatoire.—Symphonie avec choeur de Beethoven," *Le Temps*, 25 January 1838, as quoted in David B. Levy, "Early Performances of Beethoven's Ninth Symphony: A Study of Five Cities" (Ph.D. diss., University of Rochester, Eastman School of Music, 1980), 323: "Sa symphonie avec choeur résume *la vie toute entière* de Beethoven . . . ; il a déposé là le secret de toute son existence intérieure et des diverses transformations de son âme. C'est sa biographie morale!" For further commentary on this review, see Ora Frishberg Saloman, *Listening Well: On Beethoven, Berlioz, and Other Music Criticism in Paris, Boston, and New York, 1764–1890* (New York: Peter Lang, 2009), 71–93.

37. Joseph d'Ortigue, "Du mouvement et de la résistance en musique," *Revue de Paris*, 5 June 1841, in d'Ortigue, *Écrits sur la musique, 1827–1846*, ed. Sylvia L'Écuyer (Paris: Société française de musicologie, 2003), 235: "C'est dans le silence et pour ainsi dire dans le tête à tête de la confidence qu'il me dévoile les secrets de son coeur, qu'il me fait le long récit de ses souffrances, de ses joies, de ses passions; . . . langage mystérieux . . . qui pénètre jusqu'à la moelle des os, qui remue jusqu'aux dernières fibres de son être."

38. Schlosser, *Ludwig van Beethoven*, trans. Reinhard G. Pauly as *Beethoven: The First Biography*, ed. Barry Cooper (Portland, OR: Amadeus Press, 1996). The title page bears the date 1828, but in his introduction to Pauly's translation, Cooper makes a convincing case that the work was actually published in September 1827.

39. Schlosser, *Ludwig van Beethoven*, 41: "Schmerzen, die durch eine Täuschung seines Herzens veranlaßt worden [footnote: "Diese Leiden sprachen sich in allen damals erschienenen Werken Beethovens sehr deutlich aus."] vergrößerten die Unzufriedenheit mit seinen Verhältnissen." Ibid., 83: "Wenn eine Vermuthung erlaubt ist, so scheint der Charakter mehrerer Werke aus dieser Zeit auf einen Gemüthszustand hinzuweisen, der durch etwas Außerordentliches bestimmt war, und auf den ich oben schon hingedeutet habe."

40. Schlosser, *Ludwig van Beethoven*, 83–84: "in ihrer Verbindung von erinnernden und weissagenden Tönen stellt sie die innere Geschichte des Künstlers dar." Ibid., 84: "die wehmüthige Trauer des darauf folgenden Andante wird gehoben durch einen Blick voll Hoffnung in die Unendlichkeit; im nächsten Allegro hört man den hereinbrechenden Sturm des Schicksals, bis mit dem Eintritte des Finale jeder irdische Druck abfällt und der siegende Geist sich aufschwingt in den sonnenklaren Aether ewiger Freyheit."

41. Franz Wegeler and Ferdinand Ries, *Biographische Notizen über Ludwig van Beethoven* (Koblenz: K. Bädeker, 1838). The "Biographische Notizen" appended to Ignaz Seyfried's *Ludwig van Beethoven's Studien* (1832) had included valuable documentary evidence but provided only a brief prose summary of Beethoven's life; see above, p. 131.

42. Beethoven to Franz Gerhard Wegeler, 6 November 1801, in Wegeler and Ries, *Biographische Notizen*, 41: "Ich will dem Schicksal in den Rachen greifen; ganz niederbeugen soll es mich gewiß nicht."

43. Wegeler and Ries, *Biographische Notizen*, 27: "Ich lebe nur in meinen Noten. . . . So wie ich jetzt schreibe, mache ich oft drei, vier Sachen zugleich."

44. Wegeler and Ries, *Biographische Notizen*, 78. Remarkably, Berlioz had reported this story as early as 1829, at least in its outlines and without identifying his sources, though this seems to have gone otherwise unnoticed in the literature on Beethoven: see Berlioz, "Biographie étrangères: Beethoven," *Le Correspondant*, 11 August 1829, reproduced in Berlioz, *Critique musicale, 1823–1863*, ed. H. Robert Cohen, Yves Gérard, et al. (Paris: Buchet/Chastel, 1996–), 1:53.

45. Daniel Brenner, *Anton Schindler und sein Einfluss auf die Beethoven-Biographie* (Bonn: Beethoven-Haus, 2013), offers a comprehensive review of the influence of Schindler's Beethoven biography on the reception of the composer and his music.

46. Schindler, *Biographie von Ludwig van Beethoven*, 7: "es handelt sich hauptsächlich darum, zu zeigen: *unter welchen Umständen und in welchen Lebensverhältnissen Beethoven so Grosses und Unvergängliches schuf*—folglich um Thatsachen, deren grössten Theil man an Ort und Stelle und dazu noch an der Seite dieses grossen Mannes mit erlebt haben muss, um deren grössere oder geringere Einwirkung auf sein ganzes Seyn richtig bemessen zu können."

47. Schindler, *Biographie von Ludwig van Beethoven*, 29: "ächte Künstlerseele"; ibid., "Zeigt sich diese eigene Weltanschauung doch, bald mehr, bald weniger, in jedem seiner Werke."

48. Schindler, *Biographie von Ludwig van Beethoven*, 34: "Welcher Genius hätte wohl die Cis-moll Phantasie geschrieben ohne eine solche Liebe? und nur im Vorübergehen sey es hier gesagt: es war die Liebe zu jener Giulietta, der dieses phantasiereiche Werk gewidmet ist, die ihn dabei inspirirte." A. B. Marx had made a similar suggestion in 1834 (see above, p. 132) without providing a specific name. Elsewhere in his biography, Schindler identified Giulietta Guicciardi as Beethoven's Immortal Beloved.

49. Schindler, *Biographie von Ludwig van Beethoven*, 63–66.

50. Schindler, *Biographie von Ludwig van Beethoven*, 241: "So pocht das Schicksal an die Pforte!" The more common English translation—"Thus fate knocks at the door"—is far too gentle. On the resonance of this anecdote in the subsequent reception of the symphony, see Brenner, *Anton Schindler*, 293–304. Beate Angelika Kraus, "Beethoven and the Revolution: The View of the French Musical Press," in *Music and the French Revolution*, ed. Malcolm Boyd (Cambridge: Cambridge University Press, 1992), 305, points out that the German émigré critic Heinrich (Henri) Panofka had in fact publicly transmitted the essence of Schindler's comments from a conversation with him some three years before. In this telling, Beethoven (according to Schindler, via Panofka) is said to have sung the opening motif and added, "Das sind die Worte des Schicksals" ("These are the words of fate"). See Panofka, "Correspondence particulière," *Revue et Ggazette musicale de Paris* 4 (27 August 1837): 391.

51. Schindler, *Biographie von Ludwig van Beethoven*, 45: "Das Schicksal setzt sich in seinem Ohre fest, und versagt ihm Wort und Ton zu hören." Ibid., 240: "spricht sich hier an Ort und Stelle ein Kampf mit dem Schicksal aus."

52. Peter Cornelius, review of Richard Würst, *Preis-Sinfonie*, Op. 21, NZfM 41 (8 December 1854): 258: "Vom Laien ... bis zum feinsten Kenner ... hat jeder Zuhörer Beethovenscher Schöpfungen das Bewußtsein, daß aus denselben ein Mehr, ein andres spricht als aus Haydn und Mozart, und man sucht sich auf den verschiedensten Wegen Rechenschaft davon zu geben. Man nennt es Tiefe, Humor, Subjektivität; man vergleicht ihn mit Shakespeare, Jean Paul, Byron. Wir unsererseits suchen für dies besondere in Beethoven eine Erklärung darin, daß wir sein ganzes großes und ernstes Leben uns wie in geistigen Geburtswehen begriffen vorstellen, den Geburtswehen des *bestimmten Gedankens, ausgesprochen durch die Sprache der Töne.*"

53. Lenz, *Beethoven*, 1:160: "Das Postscriptum des Briefes lese man im Trio des Scherzo der Sinfonia eroica, wo die schwellenden Klänge der ... Hörner in der schmachtenden Sekunde zusammentreten, um von einer namenlosen Liebe zu reden. Hier lebt Julia, hier verkörpert sich die edelste Leidenschaft." Ibid., 4:19–20.

54. Alexandre Oulibicheff, *Beethoven: Ses critiques et ses glossateurs* (Leipzig: Brockhaus; Paris: Jules Gavelot, 1857), 197: "Rien de plus émouvant que ce drame, extrait des profondeurs de la conscience et que nul n'aurait pu écrire avec autant de vérité et de grandeur, que l'homme qui en fut tout ensemble l'auteur et le héros."

55. Oulibicheff, *Beethoven*, 262: "ce que je cherche surtout dans les oeuvres de Beethoven, c'est Beethoven lui-même, le plus intime de son moi." Ibid., 263: "la mélancolie Beethovénien." On the possible autobiographical implications of this movement, see Elaine Sisman, "Music and the Labyrinth of Melancholy: Traditions and Paradoxes in C. P. E. Bach and Beethoven," in *The Oxford Handbook of Music and Disability Studies*, ed. Blake Howe, Stephanie Jensen-Moulton, Neil Lerner, and Joseph Straus (New York: Oxford University Press, 2016), 590–617.

56. Adolph Bernhard Marx, *Ludwig van Beethoven: Leben und Schaffen*, 2 vols. (Berlin: Otto Janke, 1859), 2:102: "Die Symphonie . . . öffnet uns, wie jede seiner Dichtungen, Beethovens Seele und lässt da inne werden, was die Rückkehr in den Schooß des Naturlebens ihm gegeben hat."

57. Marx, *Ludwig van Beethoven* (1859), 2:210: "O Nachtgebet! In dir ruhte Beethovens Seele."

58. Adolph Bernhard Marx, *Die alte Musiklehre im Streit mit unserer Zeit* (Leipzig: Breitkopf & Härtel, 1841), 50–54.

59. August Wilhelm Ambros, *Culturhistorische Bilder aus dem Musikleben der Gegenwart* (Leipzig: Heinrich Matthes, 1860), 184: "Alles, was in ihm lebt—das Höchste und Tiefste—will er in Musik und durch Musik aussprechen."

60. Ambros, *Culturhistorische Bilder*, 9: "daß wir uns mit der Frage an ihn wenden möchten, *was* ihn denn so bewegt habe. . . . Wir interessiren uns nicht mehr für die *Tondichtung* allein—wir interessiren uns auch für den *Tondichter*. Wir stehen demzufolge bei Beethoven fast schon auf demselben Standpunkte, wie bei Göthe—wir betrachten seine Werke als den Commentar zu seinem Leben—wiewohl man bei beiden großen Männern den Satz auch umkehren und eben so richtig sagen könnte, daß wir ihr Leben als Commentar zu ihren Werken betrachten."

61. Ambros, *Culturhistorische Bilder*, 184–85: "Organismen voll unsterblichen Lebens."

62. Ludwig Nohl, *Beethovens Leben*, 4 vols. (Vienna: Hermann Markgraf, 1864–77), 2:197: "Sie ist einer der leidenschaftlichsten Ergüsse seines schmerzlich erregten, fast grollenden Innern."

63. Nohl, *Beethovens Leben*, 2:170: "die Zeit des Leidens und der Entsagung." Ibid., 2:171: "Den besten Commentar zu der hart andrängenden Verzweiflung wie zu der sanften Melancholie der D-moll-Sonate aber bildet eben jenes Testament." Ibid., 2:171–74.

64. John Sullivan Dwight, "The Intellectual Influence of Music," *Atlantic Monthly* 26 (19 November 1870), 615. I am grateful to Molly Barnes for calling this passage to my attention.

65. Richard Wagner, *Beethoven* (Leipzig: E. W. Fritzsch, 1870), 29: "Da es ganz unmöglich ist, das eigentliche Wesen der Beethovenschen Musik besprechen zu wollen, ohne sofort in den Ton der Verzückung zu verfallen . . . wollen wir . . . uns zunächst immer wieder der persönliche Beethoven zu fesseln haben, als der Focus der Lichtstrahlen

der von ihm ausgehenden Wunderwelt." Ibid, 39: "Das Bild eines Lebenstages unseres Heiligen."

66. The text was first published (though not in its entirety) in Ludwig Nohl, *Die Beethoven-Feier und die Kunst der Gegenwart* (Vienna: Wilhelm Braumüller, 1871), 52–74.

67. Ludwig van Beethoven, *Beethovens Tagebuch: 1812–1818*, ed. Maynard Solomon, 2nd ed. (Bonn: Beethoven-Haus, 2005), 29–30: "Du darfst nicht *Mensch* seyn, *für dich nicht, nur für andre*; für dich gibt's kein Glück mehr als in dir selbst in deiner Kunst—o Gott! gib mir Kraft, mich zu besiegen, mich darf ja nichts an das Leben fesseln." Translation from Maynard Solomon, "Beethoven's *Tagebuch*," in his *Beethoven Essays*, 246. Solomon's essay includes a concise history of the text, which was transmitted through various copies of Beethoven's original, now lost.

68. Beethoven, *Beethovens Tagebuch*, 30: "Die genaue Zusammenhaltung mehrerer Stimmen hindert im Großen das Fortschreiten einer zur anderen." Translation from Solomon, "Beethoven's *Tagebuch*," 247.

69. Anonymous, review of *Dix Thémes [sic] Russes, Ecossoie et Tyroliens . . . par Louis van Beethoven, AmZ* 23 (15 August 1821): 568.

70. Gustav Nottebohm, *Ein Skizzenbuch von Beethoven* (Leipzig: Breitkopf & Härtel, 1865), 7–8: "Wir suchen es in Beethoven, dem Künstler, selbst; in der Einheit seines ganzen Wesens und Geistes; in der Harmonie seiner Seelenkräfte."

71. The two types of genius and their relationship to music are addressed in Kivy, *The Possessor and the Possessed*. See also Cavaliero, *Genius, Power and Magic*.

72. Mozart's actual working methods are now known to have been not nearly so effortless. See in particular Ulrich Konrad, *Mozarts Schaffensweise: Studien zu den Werkautographen, Skizzen und Entwürfen* (Göttingen: Vandenhoeck & Ruprecht, 1992).

73. Douglas Johnson, "Beethoven Scholars and Beethoven's Sketches," *19CM* 2 (1978): 6. On the history of sketch studies in general, see Friedmann Sallis, *Music Sketches* (Cambridge: Cambridge University Press, 2015), chap. 2. On Beethoven's sketches specifically, see Douglas Johnson, Alan Tyson, and Robert Winter, *The Beethoven Sketchbooks: History, Reconstruction, Inventory* (Berkeley and Los Angeles: University of California Press, 1985); and for a recent survey, Lewis Lockwood, "Beethoven's Sketches: The State of our Knowledge," http://www.bu.edu/beethovencenter/beethovens-sketches-the-state-of-our-knowledge/.

74. Paul Bekker, *Beethoven* (Berlin and Leipzig: Schuster & Loeffler, 1911), 78: "Die Wucht seiner Empfindungen vernichtet alle eindämmenden Regeln der Etikette. Eine Seele offenbart ihre letzten Geheimnisse. Eine Persönlichkeit, durchwühlt von elementaren Stürmen, läßt alle Schleier fallen und ruft ihr eigenes Erleben mit rücksichtsloser Offenheit der staunenden Menschheit entgegen. Keine von außen kommende Anregung kann Beethoven tiefere Impulse geben, als er aus sich selbst empfängt. So erhebt er dieses Selbst zum Objekt der künstlerischen Darstellung und wählt als Medium der Mitteilung die Sprache, in deren Zauberformeln er alles ausspricht, was Menschen denken und fühlen können: die wortlose Instrumentalmusik." Bekker makes similar assertions about various specific works, e.g., Op. 53 (p. 141), Op. 18, No. 4 (pp. 383–84), and works of the year 1809 in general (p. 401).

75. See Alessandra Comini, "The Visual Beethoven: Whence, Why, and Whither the Scowl?" in *Beethoven and His World*, ed. Scott Burnham and Michael P. Steinberg (Princeton, NJ: Princeton University Press, 2000), 287–312; and more generally, Comini, *The Changing Image of Beethoven: A Study in Mythmaking*, rev. ed. (Santa Fe, NM: Sunstone Press, 2008).

76. Anton Schindler, "Das ähnlichste Bildniss Beethovens: Schreiben an den Redacteur," *AmZ* 37 (14 January 1835): 17–25. The ascription to Schindler is from the volume's table of contents.

77. Ludwig Rellstab, *Beethoven: Ein Bild der Erinnerung aus meinem Leben* (1854), transcribed in Kopitz and Cadenbach, *Beethoven aus der Sicht seiner Zeitgenossen*, 2:682: "Nichts drückte jene Schroffheit, jene stürmerische Fessellosigkeit aus, die man seiner Physiognomie geliehen, um sie in Uebereinstimmung mit seinen Werken zu bringen."

78. George Grove, *Beethoven and His Nine Symphonies* (London: Novello, 1896), 140.

79. See Sanna Pederson, "Beethoven and Masculinity," in *Beethoven and His World*, ed. Scott Burnham and Michael P. Steinberg (Princeton, NJ: Princeton University Press, 2000), 313–31.

80. Hans Heinrich Eggebrecht, *Zur Geschichte der Beethoven-Rezeption*, 2nd ed. (Laaber: Laaber-Verlag, 1994), 56: "Erlebensmusik" and "Biographischer Gehalt der Musik (Einheit von Leben und Werk)."

Chapter 6

1. See Hans Lenneberg, "Revising the History of the Miniature Score," *Notes* 45 (1988): 258–61.

2. For a study of the role of biography in the historiography of music that is at once both detailed and wide-ranging, see Melanie Unseld, *Biographie und Musikgeschichte: Wandlungen biographischer Konzepte in Musikkultur und Musikhistoriographie* (Cologne: Böhlau, 2014).

3. For an inventory, see Willi Kahl, *Selbstbiographien deutscher Musiker des XVIII. Jahrhunderts* (Cologne: Staufen, 1948).

4. See Maria Loh, *Still Lives: Death, Desire, and the Portrait of the Old Master* (Princeton, NJ: Princeton University Press, 2015), 19–20.

5. See William Weber, *The Rise of Musical Classics in Eighteenth-Century England: A Study in Canon, Ritual, and Ideology* (Oxford: Clarendon Press, 1992).

6. Goethe, *Dichtung und Wahrheit*, in his *Werke*, 9:9: "Denn dieses scheint die Hauptaufgabe der Biographie zu sein, den Menschen in seinen Zeitverhältnissen darzustellen, und zu zeigen, inwiefern ihm das Ganze widerstrebt, inwiefern es ihm begünstigt, wie er sich eine Welt- und Menschenansicht daraus gebildet, und wie er sie, wenn er Künstler, Dichter, Schriftsteller ist, wieder nach außen abgespiegelt."

7. Anonymous, "Ueber den Verein der Musikfreunde in Wien und das damit verbundene Conservatorium," *AmZ* 35 (13 November 1833): 757–65; and Otto Biba, "Nachrichten über Joseph Haydn, Michael Haydn und Wolfgang Amadeus Mozart in der Sammlung

handschriftlicher Biographien der Gesellschaft der Musikfreunde in Wien," in *Studies in Music History Presented to H. C. Robbins Landon on His Seventieth Birthday*, ed. Otto Biba and David Wyn Jones (London: Thames & Hudson, 1996), 152–64.

8. François-Joseph Fétis, "Analyse critique: *Épisode de la vie d'un artiste: Grand Symphonie fantastique* par Hector Berlioz," *Revue musicale* 9 (1 February 1835): 34: "Devenu journaliste, il insinua à ses lecteurs . . . la foi en son nom." Fétis's essay was translated into German and republished in full in *NZfM* 2 (19 and 23 June 1835): 197–98, 201–2.

9. Anonymous, review of *XIVe Nocturne . . . par John Field*, *AmZ* 38 (20 July 1836): 472: "Ist es doch, als ob des Meisters Seele so völlig kindlich geblieben wäre, wie sie es sonst war, als wäre das Leben mit seinen Erfahrungen wie ein Schatten spurlos an ihr vorübergegangen."

10. Berlioz to Humbert Ferrand, 16 April 1830, in Berlioz, *Correspondance générale*, 1:319: "mon roman, ou plutôt mon histoire, dont il ne vous est pas difficile de reconnaître le héros." Ibid., 1:306: "ma grande symphonie (Épisode de la vie d'un artiste), où le développement de mon infernale passion doit être peint."

11. See Francesca Brittan, "Berlioz and the Pathological Fantastic: Melancholy, Monomania, and Romantic Autobiography," *19CM* 29 (2006): 211–39; and Brittan, *Music and Fantasy in the Age of Berlioz* (Cambridge: Cambridge University Press, 2017.

12. Victor Hugo, "Littérature: *Eloa ou La soeur des anges . . .par Le comte Alfred de Vigny . . .*" (1824), in *La muse française, 1823–1824: Édition critique*, ed. Jules Marsan, 2 vols. (Paris: Société nouvelle de Librairie et d'Édition, 1909), 248: "Ce n'est point réellement aux *sources d'Hippocrène*, à *la fontaine de Castalie*, ni même au *ruisseau du Permesse*, que le poète puise le génie; mais tout simplement dans son âme et dans son coeur."

13. Ferdinand Hiller, "Hector Berlioz," *Westermann's illustrirte deutsche Monats-Hefte* 45 (1878–79): 554–55: "Was ihn mehr als billig beherrschte, war die andauernde Betrachtung seiner selbst, seiner leidenschaftlichen Empfindungen, seines ganzen Thun und Treibens. Er gehörte zu den Menschen, denen es ein Bedürfnis ist, vor sich selber immer interessant zu erscheinen—dem Geringsten, was sie thun, fühlen, leiden, dem Guten und Schlimmen, was ihnen widerfährt, eine erhöhte Bedeutung zu geben, und doch machte er nicht den Eindruck, eitel zu sein, was um so bemerkenswerther ist, als er viel und fast ausschließlich von sich sprach. Nicht als ob er nicht Gott und die Welt, Musik und Dichtung, Menschen und Länder ins Bereich seiner Ergießungen gezogen hätte—aber er blieb stets, um mich echt deutsch auszudrücken, subjectiv im allerhöchsten Grade."

14. D. Kern Holoman, *Berlioz* (Cambridge, MA: Harvard University Press, 1989), 137.

15. Joseph d'Ortigue, "Galerie biographique des artistes français et étrangers: Hector Berlioz," *Revue de Paris* 45 (23 December 1832), 289: "Tous ces détails biographiques . . . sont ici indispensables pour l'intelligence de cette composition extraordinaire. Il n'est pas possible aujourd'hui de juger une oeuvre sérieuse isolément, c'est-à-dire, si l'on ne remonte de fil en fil jusqu'à l'homme même, et si l'on ne tient aucun compte des circonstances dans lesquelles l'auteur est placé. . . . Il faut se demander ce que l'artiste a ressenti."

16. Joseph d'Ortigue, "Grand concert dramatique de M. Berlioz," *Gazette musicale de Paris* 2 (10 May 1833): 159–61. D. Kern Holoman, *Berlioz* (Cambridge, MA: Harvard University Press, 1989), 137, points out that Berlioz provided d'Ortigue with much of the material for this biographical profile.

17. Heinrich Panofka, "Aus Paris: Ueber Berlioz und seine Kompositionen," *NZfM* 2 (17 February and 3 March 1835): 67: "Ehe wir nun an eine genauere Schilderung dieser Werke, namentlich der Symphonieen gehen, scheint es zu ihrem besseren Verständnisse nöthig, einige Notizen über das vielfach interessante Leben dieses Künstlers zu geben."

18. Panofka, "Aus Paris," 68–69: "Diese Symphonie ist ein Drama. Sie ist der leidenschaftliche Erguß des Jünglingherzens, den Berlioz uns durch Musik ausdrückt; sie ist eine Epoche seines Lebens, die er uns durch Töne wiedergibt." Panofka identifies Harriet Smithson by name as the inspiration for the work.

19. Fétis, "Analyse critique: *Épisode de la vie d'un artiste*," 33–35.

20. Robert Schumann, "'Aus dem Leben eines Künstlers': Phantastische Symphonie in 5 Abtheilungen von Hector Berlioz," *NZfM* 3 (1 July 1835): 2: "So gehört Berlioz mehr zu den Beethovenschen Charakteren, deren Kunstbildung mit ihrer Lebensgeschichte genau zusammenhängt, wo mit jedem veränderten Moment in dieser ein anderer Augenblick in jener auf- und niedergeht."

21. Ibid., 50: "Es besitzt der Mensch eine eigene schöne Scheu vor der Arbeitsstätte des Genius: er will gar nichts wissen, wie ja auch die Natur eine gewisse Zartheit bekundet, indem sie ihre Wurzeln mit Erde überdeckt. Verschließe sich also der Künstler mit seinen Wehen; wir würden schreckliche Dinge erfahren, wenn wir bei allen Werken bis auf den Grund ihrer Entstehung sehen könnten."

22. Berlioz, *Les soirées de l'orchestre* (Paris: Michel Lévy frères, 1852), 276: "J'ouvre toute grande ma porte. . . . Entre, entre, sois la bienvenue, fière mélodie! . . . Dieu! qu'elle est noble et belle! . . . Où donc Beethoven a-t-il trouvé ces milliers de phrases, toutes plus poétiquement caractérisées les unes que les autres, et toutes différentes, et toutes originales, et sans avoir même entre elles cet air de famille qu'on retrouve dans celles des grands maîtres renommés pour leur fécondité? Et quels développements ingénieux! Quels mouvements imprévus! . . . Comme il vole à tire d'ailes, cet aigle infatigable; comme il plane et se balance dans son ciel harmonieux! ... Il s'y plonge, il s'y perd, il monte, il redescend, il disparaît . . . puis il revient à son point de départ, l'œil plus brillant, l'aile plus forte, impatient du repos, frémissant, altéré de l'infini. . . ." Ellipses in the original. The translation is from Berlioz, *Evenings in the Orchestra*, trans. Charles E. Roche (New York: Knopf, 1929), 236–37. Berlioz's original critique had appeared the year before in the *Journal des débats politiques et littéraires*; see Berlioz, *Critique musicale*, 7:490.

23. See, for example, John Daverio, "Schumann's 'Im Legendenton' and Friedrich Schlegel's 'Arabeske'," *19CM* 11 (1987): 150–63; Daverio, "Reading Schumann by Way of Jean Paul and His Contemporaries," *College Music Symposium* 30 (1990): 28–45; Leon Botstein, "History, Rhetoric, and the Self: Robert Schumann and Music Making in German-Speaking Europe, 1800–1860," in *Schumann and His World*, ed. R. Larry Todd (Princeton, NJ: Princeton University Press, 1994); Yael Braunschweig,

"Biographical Listening: Intimacy, Madness and the Music of Robert Schumann" (Ph.D. diss., University of California, Berkeley, 2013); and John MacAuslan, *Schumann's Music and E. T. A. Hoffmann's Fiction* (Cambridge: Cambridge University Press, 2016).

24. See Uwe Schweikert, "Das literarische Werk: Lektüre, Poesie, Kritik und poetische Musik," in *Schumann Handbuch*, ed. Ulrich Tadday (Stuttgart: J. B. Metzler, 2006), 123.

25. Robert Schumann, "Etuden für das Pianoforte," *NZfM* 11 (15 October 1839): 121: "Sein eigenes Leben steht in seiner Musik."

26. Robert Schumann to Carl Koßmaly, 5 May 1843, in Schumann, *Robert Schumanns Briefe: Neue Folge*, ed. F. Gustav Jansen, 2nd ed. (Leipzig: Breitkopf und Hartel, 1904), 227: "Mit einiger Scheu lege ich Ihnen ein Paquet älterer Compositionen von mir bei. Sie werden, was unreif, unvollendet an ihnen ist, leicht entdecken. Es sind meistens Wiederspiegelungen meines wildbewegten früheren Lebens; Mensch und Musiker suchten sich immer gleichzeitig bei mir auszusprechen; es ist wohl auch noch jetzt so, wo ich mich freilich und auch meine Kunst mehr beherrschen gelernt habe. Wie viele Freuden und Leiden in diesem kleinen Häuflein Noten zusammen begraben liegen, Ihr mitfühlendes Herz wird das herausfinden."

27. David Ferris, "Public Performance and Private Understanding: Clara Wieck's Concerts in Berlin," *JAMS* 56 (2003): 351–408; and Anthony Newcomb, "Schumann and the Marketplace: From Butterflies to Hausmusik," in *Nineteenth-Century Piano Music*, 2nd ed., ed. R. Larry Todd (New York: Routledge, 2004), 258–315.

28. Franz Brendel, "Robert Schumann mit Rücksicht auf Mendelssohn-Bartholdy und die Entwicklung der modernen Tonkunst überhaupt," *NZfM* 22 (30 April 1845): 145.

29. Ernst von Elterlein [Ernst Gottschald], "Robert Schumann's zweite Symphonie: Zugleich mit Rücksicht auf andere, insbesondere Beethoven's Symphonien," *NZfM* 32 (1850): 137–39, 141–42, 145–48, 157–59. On Gottschald's essay in general, see Anthony Newcomb, "Once More 'Between Absolute and Program Music': Schumann's Second Symphony," *19CM* 7 (1984): 233–50.

30. von Elterlein, "Robert Schumann's zweite Symphonie," 138: "noch mitten im befremdeter Einsamkeit befangen." Ibid., 138: "*seine* innerste Seele, welche fest und unerschütterlich die Feuerprobe . . . besteht." Ibid., 137–38: "das *sieggekrönte* Ringen der besonderen Individualität nach ihrer innigsten Verschmelzung mit der geistigen Allgemeinheit in der alle egoistischen Schranken vernichtet sind, Schranken, welche die einzelnen Geister von einander trennten, die sich nun als Gleiche lieben, denn sie wohnen im Reiche der Freiheit, Gleichheit und Brüderlichkeit."

31. von Elterlein, "Robert Schumann's zweite Symphonie," 138: "denn der Künstler hat 'gewollt,' 'gelitten' und 'gehandelt.'"

32. Schumann to Georg Dietrich Otten, 2 April 1849, in Hermann Erler, *Robert Schumann's Leben: Aus seinen Briefen geschildert*, 2 vols. (Berlin: Ries & Erler, 1887), 2:73: "Die Symphonie schrieb ich im December 1845 noch halb krank; mir ist's als müßte man ihr dies anhören. Erst im letzten Satz fing ich an mich wieder zu fühlen; wirklich wurde ich auch nach Beendigung des ganzen Werkes wieder wohler. Sonst aber, wie gesagt, erinnert sie mich an eine dunkle Zeit."

33. Joseph von Wasielewski, *Robert Schumann: Eine Biographie*, 2 vols. (Dresden: Rudolph Kunze, 1858), 2:236: "'Ich skizzirte sie, als ich physisch noch sehr leidend war; ja ich kann wohl sagen, es war gleichsam der Widerstand des Geistes, der hier sichtbar influirt hat, und durch den ich meinen Zustand zu bekämpfen suchte. Der erste Satz ist voll dieses Kampfes und in seinem Charakter sehr launenhaft widerspenstig.'"

34. La Mara [Ida Marie Lipsius], *Musikalische Studienköpfe* (Leipzig: Weißbach, 1868), 168: "In jeder einzelnen derselben hat Schumann ein Stück seines Selbst niedergelegt, darum ist auch sein Schaffen untrennbar von seinem Sein und Leben, untrennbarer vielleicht als dasjenige irgend eines Meisters."

35. Albert Tottmann, *Kurzgefaßter Abriß der Musikgeschichte von der ältesten Zeit bis auf die Gegenwart*, 2 vols. (Leipzig: Otto Lenz, 1883), 2:156: "Wo Mendelssohn zu uns spricht, überall zeigt er sich als Meister der Form, als klar denkender, ästhetischer Geist, als ein glänzender Redner in Tönen, dessen farbenreiche, schwunghafte Diktion sofort Ohr und Herz aller Hörer gewinnt. Schumann dagen schrieb mit Herzblut. Wie Beethoven, so schuf auch er bei seiner in sich gekehrten Natur nichts, was er nicht im Innersten der Seele empfunden und durchlebt hatte." Tottmann's comments echo in many respects those expressed by Franz Brendel in his 1845 essay on the two composers while they were both still alive, "Robert Schumann mit Rücksicht auf Mendelssohn-Bartholdy."

36. Anonymous, "Contemporary Musical Composers, Frederic Chopin," *Athenæum* 740 (1 January 1842): 18. For further commentary on this and similar responses to Chopin and his music, see Jeffrey Kallberg, "Chopin's March, Chopin's Death," *19CM* 25 (2001): 3–26.

37. Wilhelm von Lenz, *Die grossen Pianoforte-Virtuosen unserer Zeit aus persönlicher Bekanntschaft* (Berlin: B. Behr, 1872), 86: "Die Mazurken von Chopin sind das Tagebuch seiner seelischen Reisen auf den politisch-socialen Gebieten sarmatischer Traumwelt!" "Sarmatia" refers to the region between the Vistula and Volga Rivers.

38. James William Davison, *An Essay on the Works of Frederic Chopin* (London: Wessel and Stapleton, 1843), 4; punctuation amended. On Davison's vacillating attitude toward Chopin's music, see Charles Reid, *The Music Monster: A Biography of James William Davison, Music Critic of "The Times" of London, 1846–78* (London: Quartet Books, 1984).

39. See, for example, Barbara Milewski, "Chopin's Mazurkas and the Myth of the Folk," *19CM* 23 (1999): 113–35; Jolanta T. Pekacz, "Deconstructing a 'National Composer': Chopin and Polish Exiles in Paris, 1831–49," *19CM* 24 (2000): 161–72; and Jeffrey Kallberg, "Hearing Poland: Chopin and Nationalism," in *Nineteenth-Century Piano Music*, ed. R. Larry Todd, 2nd ed. (New York: Routledge, 2004), 221–57.

40. Franz Liszt, *F. Chopin* (Paris: M. Escudier, 1852), 106: "Il épancha son âme dans ses compositions comme d'autres l'épanchent dans la prière: y versant toutes ces effusions du coeur, ces tristesses inexprimées, ces regrets indicibles, que les âmes pieuses versent dans leurs entretiens avec Dieu. Il disait dans ses oeuvres ce qu'elles ne disent qu'à genoux: ces mystères de passion et de douleur qu'il a été permis à l'homme de comprendre sans parole, parce qu'il ne lui a pas été donné de les exprimer en paroles."

Translation from Franz Liszt, *The Life of Chopin*, trans. Martha Walker Cook, 4th ed. (Boston: O. Ditson, 1863), 113. On contemporaneous perceptions of Chopin's music as an expression of his presumed nationalistic sentiments, see Angelika Varga-Behrer, *"Hut ab, ihr Herren, ein Genie": Studien zur Chopin-Rezeption in der zeitgenössischen Musikpresse Deutschlands und Frankreichs* (Mainz: Schott, 2010).

41. See Halina Goldberg, "Chopin's Oneiric Soundscapes and the Role of Dreams in Romantic Culture," in *Chopin and His World*, ed. Jonathan D. Bellman and Halina Goldberg (Princeton, NJ: Princeton University Press, 2017), 15–43.

42. See above, p. 12.

43. Adolph Bernhard Marx, *Ludwig van Beethoven* (1859), 1:257: "[Beethoven] hatte mit lebensleeren Abstraktionen nichts zu schaffen; Leben zu schaffen, Leben aus seinem Leben, war sein Beruf, wie aller Künstler." Marx points out in a footnote to this passage that he had treated this issue more extensively in his earlier *Ueber Malerei in der Tonkunst: Ein Maigruß an die Kunstphilosophen* (Berlin: G. Fink, 1828), esp. pp. 47–52.

44. For a survey of this ongoing debate, see Mark Evan Bonds, *Absolute Music: The History of an Idea* (New York: Oxford University Press, 2014), 129–249.

45. Eduard Hanslick, *Vom Musikalisch-Schönen: Ein Beitrag zur Revision der Ästhetik der Tonkunst* (Leipzig: Rudolph Weigel, 1854), 55: "Streng ästhetisch können wir von irgend einem Thema sagen: es *klinge* stolz oder trübe, nicht aber: es sei ein Ausdruck der stolzen oder trüben Gefühle des Componisten." Emphasis in the original. On the residue of Hanslick's legal training in his writings about music, see Anthony Pryer, "Hanslick, Legal Processes, and Scientific Methodologies: How Not to Construct an Ontology of Music," in *Rethinking Hanslick: Music, Formalism, and Expression*, ed. Nicole Grimes, Siobhán Donovan, and Wolfgang Marx (Rochester, NY: University of Rochester Press, 2013), 52–69.

46. Hanslick, *Vom Musikalisch-Schönen*, 55, 57: "Was der gefühlvolle und was der geistreiche Componist bringt, der graziöse oder der erhabene, ist zuerst und vor Allem *Musik* (objectives Gebilde). Principiell untergeordnet bleibt das *subjective* Moment immer, nur wird es nach Verschiedenheit der Individualität in ein verschiedenes Größenverhältniß zu dem objectiven treten. Man vergleiche vorwiegend subjective Naturen, denen es um Aussprache ihrer gewaltigen oder sentimentalen Innerlichkeit zu thun ist (Beethoven, Spohr), im Gegensatz zu klar Formenden (Mozart, Mendelssohn). Ihre Werke werden sich von einander durch unverkennbare Eigenthümlichkeiten unterscheiden, und als Gesammtbild die Individualität ihrer Schöpfer abspiegeln, doch wurden sie alle, die einen wie die andern, als selbstständiges Schöne, rein musikalisch um ihretwillen erschaffen, und erst innerhalb der Grenzen dieses künstlerischen Bildens mehr oder weniger subjectiv ausgestattet. Ins Extrem gesteigert, läßt sich daher wohl eine Musik denken, welche *blos* Musik, aber keine, die *blos* Gefühl wäre. . . . In der *Composition* eines Musikstückes findet daher eine Entäußerung des eigenen, persönlichen Affectes nur insoweit statt, als es die Grenzen einer vorherrschend objectiven, formenden Thätigkeit zulassen."

47. Hanslick, *Vom Musikalisch-Schönen*, 45: "Die ästhetische Untersuchung weiß nichts und darf nichts wissen von den persönlichen Verhältnissen und der geschichtlichen

Umgebung des Componisten, nur was das Kunstwerk selbst ausspricht, wird sie hören und glauben. Sie wird demnach in *Beethoven*'s Symphonien, auch ohne Namen und Biographie des Autors zu kennen, ein Stürmen, Ringen, unbefriedigtes Sehnen, kraftbewußtes Trotzen herausfinden, allein daß der Componist republikanisch gesinnt, unverheirathet, taub gewesen, und all' die andern Züge, welche der Kunsthistoriker beleuchtend hinzuhält, wird jene nimmermehr aus den Werken lesen und zur Würdigung derselben verwerthen dürfen."

48. Edmund Gurney, *The Power of Sound* (London: Smith, Elder, 1880), 347.

49. See Nicholas Vaszonyi, *Richard Wagner: Self-Promotion and the Making of a Brand* (Cambridge: Cambridge University Press, 2010).

50. Richard Wagner, *Drei Operndichtungen nebst einer Mittheilung an seine Freunde als Vorwort* (Leipzig: Breitkopf und Härtel, 1852), 62: "Mein Verfahren war neu; es war mir aus meiner innersten Stimmung angewiesen, von dem Drange zur Mittheilung dieser Stimmung aufgenöthigt."

51. Richard Wagner to Mathile Wesendonck, 10 April 1860, in Wagner, *Sämtliche Briefe*, ed. Werner Breig (Wiesbaden: Breitkopf & Härtel, 1967–), 12:117: "dass unser Eines nicht rechts noch links, nicht vorwärts noch rückwärts sieht, Zeit und Welt uns gleichgültig ist, und nur Eines uns bestimmt, die Noth der Entladung unsres Inneren."

52. Richard Wagner, *Oper und Drama*, 3 vols. (Leipzig: J. J. Weber, 1852), 2:179: "Das ursprünglichste Aeußerungsorgan des innern Menschen ist . . . die Tonsprache." Wagner, *Das Kunstwerk der Zukunft*, 80: "Seelenbedürfnisse."

53. Wagner, "Ein Brief von Richard Wagner über Franz Liszt," *NZfM* 46 (10 April 1857): 163: "Wenn wir einen großen Künstler lieben, so sagen wir daher hiermit, daß wir dieselben individuellen Eigenthümlichkeiten, die ihm jene schöpferische Anschauung ermöglichten, in die Aneignung der Anschauung selbst mit einschließen. . . . Vertraut nur, und Ihr werdet erstaunen, was Ihr durch Euer Vertrauen gewinnt!"

54. See Raymond Knapp, "'*Selbst dann bin ich die Welt*': On the Subjective-Musical Basis of Wagner's *Gesamtkunstwelt*," *19CM* 29 (2005): 142–60. On the perception of composers as mediators of universal wisdom, see below, p. 106.

55. Friedrich von Hausegger, *Die Musik als Ausdruck*, 2nd ed. (Vienna: C. Konegen, 1887), 170: "Der Künstler schafft unbewußt, und alle die überraschenden Übereinstimmungen seines Tongebildes mit in den Ausdrucks-Apparaten herrschenden Bewegungen sind nicht Ergebniß der Beobachtung, sondern Product eines unmittelbaren in ihm wach gewordenen Dranges nach Ausdruck."

56. Tchaikovsky to Sergei Taneyev, 27 March 1878, quoted in Alexandra Orlova, *Tchaikovsky: A Self-Portrait*, trans. R. M. Davison (Oxford: Oxford University Press, 1990), 121. On the *Pathétique* Symphony, see Heinz von Loesch, "Tschaikowskys *Pathétique*: Lebenssymphonie oder schwules Bekenntniswerk? Ein kurzer kommentierter Literaturbericht," in *Musik und Biographie: Festschrift für Rainer Cadenbach*, ed. Cordula Heymann-Wentzel and Johannes Laas (Würzburg: Königshausen & Neumann, 2004), 344–51.

57. There can be little doubt that Mahler was aware of Bauer-Lechner playing the role of Eckermann to Mahler's Goethe; see Morten Solvik and Stephen Hefling, "Natalie

Bauer-Lechner on Mahler and Women: A Newly Discovered Document," *MQ* 97 (2014): 12–65; and Leon Botstein, "Second Thoughts: The Genre of Biography and Natalie Bauer-Lechner as Witness," *MQ* 97 (2014): 1–11.

58. Natalie Bauer-Lechner, *Gustav Mahler in den Erinnerungen von Natalie Bauer-Lechner*, rev. ed., ed. Herbert Killian and Knud Martner (Hamburg: Karl Dieter Wagner, 1984), 26: "Meine beiden Symphonien erschöpfen den Inhalt meines ganzen Lebens: es ist Erfahrenes und Erlittenes, was ich darin niedergelegt habe, Wahrheit und Dichtung in Tönen. Und wenn einer gut zu lesen verstünde, müßte ihm in der Tat mein Leben darin durchsichtig erscheinen."

59. Mahler to Arthur Seidl, 17 February 1897, in Mahler, *Briefe*, 223: "Nur wenn ich erlebe, 'tondichte' ich—nur, wenn ich tondichte, erelebe ich!"

60. For a thorough review of the evidence, see Seth Monahan, "'I Have Tried to Capture You . . . ': Rethinking the 'Alma' Theme from Mahler's Sixth Symphony," *JAMS* 64 (2011): 119–78.

61. Letter of 29 August 1912, quoted in Michael Kennedy, *Portrait of Elgar*, 2nd ed. (London: Oxford University Press, 1982), 254.

62. Arnold Schoenberg, "Vortrag über Gustav Mahler" (1912; revised 1948) in his *"Stile herrschen, Gedanken siegen,"* 77: "In Wirklichkeit giebt es für den Künstler nur ein Größtes, das er anstrebt: sich auszudrücken. Gelingt das, dann ist das Größte gelungen, das dem Künstler gelingen kann; daneben ist alles andere klein, denn darin ist alles andere enthalten." Translation from Schoenberg, "Gustav Mahler," in his *Style and Idea*, 454.

63. From an exhibit at the Arnold Schönberg Center, Vienna, transcribed from an otherwise unidentified 1937 interview: "Ich schreibe, was ich in meinem Herzen fühle—und was schließlich aufs Papier kommt, hat zunächst jede Faser meines Körpers durchlaufen." See https://www.schoenberg.at/images/.../pf_gedanke_041013.pdf.

64. Schoenberg, "Probleme des Kunstunterrichts" (1911), in his *"Stile herrschen, Gedanken siegen,"* 59: "Ein Ausdrucksinhalt will sich verständlich machen, seine Bewegung bringt eine Form hervor. Ein Vulkan bricht aus, die Verwüstungen wirken ornamental, ein Dampfkessel explodiert; die Gegenstände, die er von sich schleudert, kommen an Stellen zu liegen, die aus den Spannungsverhältnissen, den Gewichten, Abständen und Widerständen genau zu berechnen wären. Allerdings kann man auch die Gegenstände so herumlegen, daß sie den ordnenden Sinn einer Explosion und das Temperament der Abstände und Gewichte vortäuschen. Aber das ist doch ein Unterschied. . . . [D]ann macht hier etwas aus, ob ein Ornament einen Dampfkessel, der explodiert, oder einen Tapezierer, der arrangiert, zum Autor hat. . . . Es ist zwecklos, die Indizien eines Vulkanausbruches zu arrangieren, weil der Kundige auf den ersten Blick sieht, daß da nur ein Spirituskocher gewütet hat. . . . Aber uns und ihnen wäre mehr gedient, wenn sie uns etwas Wahres von ihren Erbärmlichkeiten erzählten, dort, wo sie im Leben versagen." Translation from Schoenberg, "Problems of Teaching Art," in his *Style and Idea*, 367.

65. Bartók to Márta Ziegler, 4 February 1909, quoted in translation from the "Private Life" section of the website http://www.zti.hu/bartok/exhibition/en_P2.htm, Bartók

Archives of the Hungarian Academy of Sciences Institute for Musicology, 2004–5, accessed 17 July 2019.

66. Ludwig Speidel, *Fremden-Blatt*, 25 January 1893, 7–8, as quoted in Elizabeth Way Sullivan, "Conversing in Public: Chamber Music in Vienna, 1890–1910" (Ph.D. diss., University of Pittsburgh, 2001), 129.

67. "... in Töne übersetztes Stück Herzensgeschichte," *Deutsche Zeitung*, 7 February 1893, 1, as quoted in Sullivan, "Conversing in Public," 128. Sandra McColl, *Music Criticism in Vienna, 1896–1897: Critically Moving Forms* (Oxford: Clarendon, 1996), 21–22, 24, suggests that the unnamed reviewer is Theodor Helm. For other Viennese reviews of chamber music from this time that link composers' lives to their works, see chap. 5 of Sullivan, "Conversing in Public."

68. See Constantin Floros, *Johannes Brahms, "Free but Alone": A Life for a Poetic Music*, trans. Ernest Bernhardt-Kabisch (Frankfurt am Main: Peter Lang, 2010).

69. Max Kalbeck, *Johannes Brahms*, 4 vols. (Vienna: Wiener Verlag, 1904–14).

70. The relevant passages in Kalbeck's biography are cited in Floros, *Johannes Brahms*, 42–44.

71. On the reception of the *Ode triomphale*, see Annegret Fauser, *Musical Encounters at the 1889 Paris World's Fair* (Rochester, NY: University of Rochester Press, 2005), 129–38. On the reception of Holmès's music in general, see Jann Pasler, "The Ironies of Gender, or Virility and Politics in the Music of Augusta Holmès," *Women & Music* 2 (1998): 1–25.

72. Anonymous, "A New Opera in New York," *Musical Courier* 46, no. 11 (18 March 1903): 12. On Smyth's career in general, see Jane A. Bernstein, "'Shout, Shout, Up with Your Song!' Dame Ethel Smyth and the Changing Role of the British Woman Composer," in *Women Making Music*, ed. Jane Bowers and Judith Tick (Urbana: University of Illinois Press, 1985), 304–24.

73. Louis de Romain, *Essais de critique musicale* (Paris: Alphonse Lemarre, 1890), 144: "Ici, nous sommes en présence d'une page écrite avec une indiscutable autorité, d'une oeuvre forte et virile, trop virile même, et c'est le reproche que je serais tenté de lui adresser. J'ai presque regretté, pour mon compte, de n'y point trouver davantage ce cachet de grâce et de douceur qui rentre dans la nature de la femme et dont elle possède si bien tous les secrets."

74. See Marcia Citron, *Gender and the Musical Canon* (Urbana: University of Illinois Press, 2000).

75. For a survey of various accounts, see James Webster, *Haydn's "Farewell" Symphony and the Idea of Classical Style: Through-Composition and Cyclic Integration in his Instrumental Music* (Cambridge: Cambridge University Press, 1991), 113–16; and Mark Evan Bonds, "Life, Liberty, and the Pursuit of Happiness: Revolutionary Ideals in Narratives of the 'Farewell' Symphony," in *Joseph Haydn und die "neue Welt": Bericht über das Symposium der Internationalen Joseph Haydn Privatstiftung Eisenstadt . . . vom 13. bis 15. September 2011*, ed. Walter Reicher (Vienna: Hollitzer, 2019), 283–301.

76. Nicolas Étienne Framery, *Notice sur Joseph Haydn* (Paris: Barba, 1810), 15–22.

77. Joseph Haydn to Marianne von Genzinger, 8 January 1791, in Haydn, *Gesammelte Briefe und Aufzeichnungen*, ed. Dénes Bartha (Kassel: Bärenreiter, 1965), 250–51.

78. Otto Jahn, *W. A. Mozart*, 2nd ed., 2 vols. (Leipzig: Breitkopf & Härtel, 1867), 2:107: "es kann nur als ein fertiges aufgefaßt und genossen werden." This comment does not appear in the work's first edition (1856–59).

79. Piotr Ilich Tchaikovsky to Nadezhda von Meck, 13 April 1878, in Tchaikovsky, *"To My Best Friend": Correspondence between Tchaikovsky and Nadezhda von Meck, 1876–1878*, trans. Galina von Meck, ed. Edward Garden and Nigel Gotteri (Oxford: Clarendon Press, 1993), 238.

80. Ferruccio Busoni, "Was gab uns Beethoven?" *Die Musik* 15, no. 1 (1922): 20: "Das Menschliche tritt mit Beethoven zum erstenmal als Hauptargument in die Tonkunst." For many similar assertions by others, see Eggebrecht, *Zur Geschichte der Beethoven-Rezeption*, esp. 78–83.

81. Friedrich Rochlitz, "Noch einige Kleinigkeiten aus Mozarts Leben, von seiner Witwe mitgeteilt," *AmZ* 1 (11 September 1799): 854–55; and Vincent Novello and Mary Novello, *A Mozart Pilgrimage, Being the Travel Diaries of Vincent and Mary Novello in the Year 1829*, ed. Rosemary Hughes (London: Novello, 1955), 112.

82. Edward Holmes, *The Life of Mozart* (New York: Harper & Brothers, 1845), 239.

83. Wolfgang Hildesheimer, *Mozart* (1977), trans. Marion Faber (New York: Farrar, Straus and Giroux, 1982), 165.

84. Alexandre Oulibicheff, *Nouvelle biographie de Mozart*, 3 vols. (Moscow: August Semen, 1843), 3:16: "Preuve que Mozart savait s'émouvoir et s'échauffer quand il le voulait, autant et plus que personne."

85. Otto Jahn, *W. A. Mozart*, 4 vols. (Leipzig: Breitkopf & Härtel, 1856–59), 4:63: "größere Tiefe und Bedeutung."

86. Ludwig Nohl, *Mozart* (Stuttgart: Friedrich Bruckmann, 1863), 386: "des tiefen Zwiespaltes." Ibid., 425: "verräth manches von den tiefen Bewegungen seiner Seele." Ibid., 193–94: "Das energische Ringen mit sich selbst . . . ist das geistige Abbild jener Kämpfe zwischen Pflicht und Neigung, die Wolfgang damals durchführte." Ibid., 193: "In der That kann uns nichts so sehr eine sichere Kunde geben von der Seelenstimmung, in der Mozart damals lebte, als diese Sonate."

87. Karen Painter, "W. A. Mozart's Beethovenian Afterlife: Biography and Musical Interpretation in the Twilight of Idealism," in *Late Thoughts: Reflections on Artists and Composers at Work*, ed. Karen Painter and Thomas Crow (Los Angeles: Getty Research Institute, 2006), 117–43. For a penetrating critique of the long-standing fascination with Mozart's minor-mode works, see Wye J. Allanbrook, "Tunes and the Comedy of Closure," in *On Mozart*, ed. James M. Morris (Washington, DC: Woodrow Wilson Center Press; Cambridge: Cambridge University Press, 1994), 169–86.

88. Julian Rushton, *Mozart* (Oxford: Oxford University Press, 2006), 62.

89. Hans-Georg Nägeli, *Vorlesungen über Musik, mit Berücksichtigung der Dilettanten* (Stuttgart and Tübingen: Cotta, 1826), 194–95, 32. Hanslick, *Vom Musikalisch-Schönen*, 32: "tönend bewegte Formen." On the long-standing conception of music as sounding form, which extends back to antiquity, see Bonds, *Absolute Music*.

90. See Bernd Sponheuer, *Musik als Kunst und Nicht-Kunst: Untersuchungen zur Dichotomie von "hoher" und "niederer" Musik im musikästhetischen Denken zwischen Kant und Hanslick* (Kassel: Bärenreiter, 1987); and Applegate, "How German Is It?"

91. See the essays in Christian Thorau and Hansjakob Ziemer, eds., *The Oxford Handbook of Music Listening in the 19th and 20th Centuries* (New York: Oxford University Press, 2019).

92. See Johnson, *Listening in Paris*.

93. See Christian Thorau, *Semantisierte Sinnlichkeit: Studien zu Rezeption und Zeichenstruktur der Leitmotivtechnik Richard Wagners* (Stuttgart: Steiner, 2003); and Thorau, " 'What Ought to Be Heard': Touristic Listening and the Guided Ear," in *The Oxford Handbook of Music Listening in the 19th and 20th Centuries,* ed. Christian Thorau and Hansjakob Ziemer (New York: Oxford University Press, 2019), 207–28.

94. Hermann Kretzschmar, *Führer durch den Konzertsaal,* 3 vols. (Leipzig: Liebeskind, 1887–90); and Kretzschmar, "Anregungen zur Förderung musikalischer Hermeneutik," *Jahrbuch der Musikbibliothek Peters* 9 (1902): 47–66.

95. See Thorau, *Semantisierte Sinnlichkeit,* 161–67.

96. Sulzer, "Symphonie," in his *Allgemeine Theorie der schönen Künste*; and Philipp Gäng, *Aesthetik oder allgemeine Theorie der schönen Künste und Wissenschaften* (Salzburg: Waisenhausbuchhandlung, 1785), 184: "Ein witziges, launigtes [*sic*] Gedicht, eine kleine tändelnde Musik etc. etc. können uns vortref[f]lich gefallen, ohne daß wir dabey eine besondre Neigung, oder einen Affekt in der Seele spüren; dieß sind also blos gefallende Schönheiten." Koch, "Divertimento," in his *Musikalisches Lexikon,* 440: "Sie haben mehrentheils keinen bestimmten Charakter, sondern sind bloß Tongemälde, die mehr auf die Ergötzung des Ohres, als auf den Ausdruck einer bestimmten Empfindung mit ihren Modifikationen, Anspruch machen."

97. Gustav Schilling, *Franz Liszt: Sein Leben und Wirkung, aus nächster Beschauung dargestellt* (Stuttgart: A. Stoppani, 1844), 1: "Daß eine Kunst der Seele unsere Musik sei, hat längst den allgemeinsten Glauben und keinerlei Widerspruch mehr gefunden, und glücklich ist dadurch alles Spiel der Töne zur bloßen Lust und Unterhaltung untergegangen in dem Begriffe alltäglicher Musikmacherei."

Chapter 7

1. Oscar Wilde, "The True Function of Criticism," *The Nineteenth Century* 28 (1890): 452.

2. T. S. Eliot, "Tradition and the Individual Talent," in his *The Sacred Wood: Essays on Poetry and Criticism* (New York: Knopf, 1921), 47–48, 52–53.

3. See Victor Erlich, "Limits of the Biographical Approach," *Comparative Literature* 6 (1954): 130–37; and Catherine Gallagher, "The History of Literary Criticism," *Daedalus* 126 (1997): 133–53.

4. José Ortega y Gasset, *La deshumanización del arte* (1925), ed. Valeriano Bozal (Madrid: Espasa-Calpe, 1987), 68: "Desde Beethoven a Wagner el tema de la música fue la expresión de sentimientos personales. El artista mélico componía grades

edificios sonoros para alojar en ellos su autobiografía. No había otra manera de goce estético que la contaminación. . . . El arte no puede consistir en el contagio psíquico, porque éste es un fenómeno inconsciente y el arte ha de ser todo plena claridad, mediodía de intelección." Ibid., 71: "Era forzoso extirpar de la música los sentimientos privados, purificarla en una ejemplar objetivación. Esta fue la hazaña de Debussy. Desde él es posible oír música serenamente, sin embriaguez y sin llantos. . . . Debussy deshumanizó la música y por ello data de él la nueva era del arte sonoro." The translation is from *The Dehumanization of Art and Other Essays on Art, Culture, and Literature*, trans. Helen Weyl, 2nd ed. (Princeton, NJ: Princeton University Press, 1968), 26, 29-30.

5. Ferruccio Busoni, "Junge Klassizität" (1920), in Busoni, *Von der Einheit der Musik* (Berlin: Max Hesse, 1922), 278-79: "die Abstreifung des '*Sinnlichen*' und die *Entsagung gegenüber dem Subjektivismus* (der Weg zur Objektivität—das Zurücktreten des Autors gegenüber dem Werke—ein reinigender Weg, ein harter Gang, eine Feuer- und Wasserprobe), die Wiedereroberung der Heiterkeit (Serenitas): nicht die Mundwinkel Beethovens, und auch nicht das 'befreiende Lachen' Zarathustras, sondern das Lächeln des Weisen, der Gottheit und—*absolute* Musik. Nicht Tiefsinn und Gesinnung und Metaphysik; sondern:—Musik durchaus, destilliert, niemals unter der Maske von Figuren und Begriffen, die anderen Bezirken entlehnt sind."

6. Louise Varèse, *Varèse: A Looking-Glass Diary* (New York: W. W. Norton, 1972), 228, quoting program notes her husband had written for a performance of his *Intégrales* in New York City in 1925.

7. Heinz Tiessen, *Zur Geschichte der jüngsten Musik (1913-1928): Probleme und Entwicklungen* (Mainz: Melosverlag, 1928), 60: "die musikalische Substanz um ihre Entfaltung aus sich selbst."

8. Aaron Copland, "Carlos Chávez—Mexican Composer," in *American Composers on American Music: A Symposium*, ed. Henry Cowell (Stanford, CA: Stanford University Press, 1933), 102-3.

9. Igor Stravinsky, "Some Ideas about My Octuor," *Arts* 6, no. 1 (January 1924): 5. On the complicated history of this text, see Jürg Stenzl, "Igor Strawinskys Manifest von 1924," in his *Auf der Suche nach Geschichte(n) der musikalischen Interpretation* (Würzburg: Köngishausen & Neumann, 2012), 71-91.

10. Nadia Boulanger, "Concerts Koussevitsky," *Le monde musical*, November 1923, 365: "Dans cette oeuvre, Stravinsky apparaît sous son jour de constructeur, de géomètre. . . . Nulle transposition, toute est musique, purement." For a translation of the complete portion of the review dealing with the Octet, see Scott Messing, *Neoclassicism in Music: From the Genesis of the Concept through the Schoenberg/ Stravinsky Polemic* (Rochester, NY: University of Rochester Press, 1996), 133.

11. Stravinsky, *Chroniques de ma vie*, 1:116-17: "Car je considère la musique, par son essence, impuissante à *exprimer* quoi que ce soit: un sentiment, une attitude, un état psychologique, un phénomène de la nature, etc. . . . *L'expression* n'a jamais été la propriété immanente de la musique. La raison d'être de celle-ci n'est d'aucune façon conditionée par celle-là. Si, comme c'est presque toujours le cas, la musique paraît exprimer quelque chose, ce n'est qu'une illusion et non pas une réalité. C'est simplement

un élément additionnel que, par une convention tacite et invétérée, nous lui avons prêté, imposé, comme une étiquette, un protocole, bref, une tenue et que, par accoutumance ou inconscience, nous sommes arrivée à confondre avec son essence." Ellipsis in the original. The translation is from the authorized but unattributed English translation, published as *An Autobiography* (New York: Simon & Schuster, 1936), 83–84.

12. Paul Hindemith, *A Composer's World* (Cambridge, MA: Harvard University Press, 1952), 36.

13. John Keats to Richard Woodhouse, 27 October 1818, in Keats, *Selected Letters*, 194–95.

14. See Drummond Bone, "The Emptiness of Genius: Aspects of Romanticism," in *Genius: The History of an Idea*, ed. Penelope Murray (Oxford: Basil Blackwell, 1989), 113–27. For an insightful analysis of this idea in the realm of music in the nineteenth century, see Francesca Brittan, "Liszt, Sand, García, and the Contrebandier: Intersubjectivity and Romantic Authorship," *Journal of the American Liszt Society* 65 (2014): 65–94.

15. Alfred Heuß, "Allerlei Zeitgemäßes," *NZfM* 95 (1928): 276: "was solls mit Strawinsky, dem internationen Musik-Chamäleon"; and Olivier Messiaen, "Le rhythme chez Igor Strawinsky," *Revue musicale* 191 (May 1939): 91: "Strawinsky, le musicien-caméléon, l'homme aux mille et un styles, nous a légué un trésor rythmique très 'un,' quit suit une courbe parfaite, progressant ... de sa première à sa dernière oeuvre."

16. Donal J. Henahan, "Current Chronicle: United States, Chicago," *MQ* 53 (1967): 246; and Alan Gilbert, "Alan Gilbert on This Program," program notes for New York Philharmonic concerts of 26–28 January 2012 (New York: New York Philharmonic, 2012).

17. Theodor Adorno, *Philosophie der neuen Musik* (1949) (Frankfurt am Main: Suhrkamp, 1978), 166: "Das Verbot des Pathos im Ausdruck ereilt die kompositorische Spontaneität selber: das Subjekt, das musikalisch nicht länger etwas von sich aussagen soll, hört damit auf, eigentlich zu 'produzieren,' und begnügt sich mit dem hohlen Echo der objektiven musikalischen Sprache, die nicht seine eigen mehr ist." Translation from Adorno, *Philosophy of New Music*, ed. and trans. Robert Hullot-Kentor (Minneapolis: University of Minnesota Press, 2006), 134.

18. Claire Taylor-Jay cites numerous other instances of commentators who find a consistent "voice" throughout the works not only of Stravinsky but also of Ernst Krenek and Kurt Weill, all of whom are perceived to have made major stylistic shifts at various points in their careers. See her "The Composer's Voice? Compositional Style and Criteria of Value in Weill, Krenek and Stravinsky," *Journal of the Royal Musical Association* 134 (2009): 85–111.

19. Mozart to Leopold Mozart, 7 February 1778, in Mozart, *Briefe und Aufzeichnungen*, 2:265: "das ist gewis das mir gar nicht bang wäre, denn ich kann so ziemlich, wie sie wissen, alle Art und styl vom Compositions annehmen und nachahmen."

20. Anonymous, "Recension: Musée musical des Clavicinistes. Museum für Claviermusik. Erstes Heft, enthält: *Sonate (in A-dur) für das Pianoforte (Hammer-Clavier) von Ludwig van Beethoven, 101tes Werk*," *Allgemeine musikalische Zeitung mit besonderer Rücksicht auf den österreichischen Kaiserstaat* 1 (27 February 1817): 66.

21. Friedrich Schlegel, "Lyceums-Fragment 55" (1797), *KFSA*, 2:154: "Ein recht freier und gebildeter Mensch müßte sich selbst nach Belieben philosophisch oder philologisch, kritisch oder poetisch, historisch oder rhetorisch, antik oder modern stimmen können, ganz willkürlich, wie man ein Instrument stimmt, zu jeder Zeit, und in jedem Grade."

22. Cone, *The Composer's Voice*, 2; and Wayne C. Booth, *The Rhetoric of Fiction* (Chicago: University of Chicago Press, 1961). See in particular Booth's bibliographies for "'The Author's Objectivity and the 'Second Self'" in the book's second edition (Chicago: University of Chicago Press, 1983), 478–80, with an updated supplementary bibliography on pp. 511–12.

23. Cone, *The Composer's Voice*, 85.

24. Cone, *The Composer's Voice*, 93, 85. On *Harold en Italie* as a personal projection of the composer's self, see Oliver Vogel, "Berlioz als Harold: Ein romantisches Selbstporträt im Zeichen des Liberalismus," *Mf* 68 (2015): 136–64.

25. Arthur Schopenhauer, *Parerga und Paralipomena*, 2 vols., ed. Gerd Haffmans (Zurich: Haffmans, 1988), 2:381: "was die Töne in ihrer allgemeinen, bilderlosen Sprache des Herzens besagen." Ibid., 2:380: "die heilige, geheimnißvolle, innige Sprache der Töne."

26. Arthur Schopenhauer, *Die Welt als Wille und Vorstellung*, 2 vols., ed. Gerd Haffmans (Zurich: Haffmans, 1988), 1:344: "der Komponist offenbart das innerste Wesen der Welt und spricht die tiefste Weisheit aus, in einer Sprache, die seine Vernunft nicht versteht; wie eine magnetische Somnambule Aufschlüsse giebt über Dinge, von denen sie wachen keinen Begriff hat. Daher ist in einem Komponisten, mehr als in irgend einem andern Künstler, der Mensch vom Künstler ganz getrennt und unterschieden."

27. Bauer-Lechner, *Gustav Mahler*, 59: "Wahres Entsetzen faßt mich an, wenn ich sehe, wohin das führt, welcher Weg der Musik vorbehalten ist, und daß mir das schreckliche Amt geworden, Träger dieses Riesenwerkes zu sein. Heute ist mir, wie einem manchmal durch eigenes Erleben etwas längst Gekanntes aufleuchtet und offenbar wird, plötzlich blitzartig aufgegangen: Christus auf dem Ölberg, der den Leidenskelch bis zur Neige leeren mußte und—wollte. Wem dieser Kelch bestimmt ist, der kann und will ihn nicht zurückweisen, doch muß ihn zu Zeiten eine Todesangst überkommen, wenn er denkt, was ihm noch bevorsteht. Solch ein Gefühl habe ich im Hinblick auf diesen Satz und in der Voraussicht dessen, was ich deshalb werde leiden müssen, um gewiß nicht mehr zu erleben, daß er erkannt und anerkannt werden wird."

28. Friedrich Nietzsche, *Zur Genealogie der Moral* (1887), in his *Sämtliche Werke*, 15 vols., ed. Giorgio Colli and Mazzino Montinari (Munich: Deutscher Taschenbuch Verlag, 1980), 5:346: "dieser Bauchredner Gottes."

29. Igor Stravinsky and Robert Craft, *Expositions and Developments* (Garden City, NY: Doubleday, 1962), 169.

30. See Bonds, *Absolute Music*, 252–62.

31. In addition to Schenker's many analyses of Beethoven's music, see Hans Mersmann, *Beethoven: Die Synthese der Stile* (Berlin: Julius Bard, 1922); Fritz Cassirer, *Beethoven*

und die Gestalt (Berlin and Leipzig: Deutsche Verlags-Anstalt, 1925); and Walter Riezler, *Beethoven* (Berlin and Zurich: Atlantis, 1936).

32. Guido Adler, *Methode der Musikgeschichte* (Leipzig: Breitkopf & Härtel, 1919), 110: "die wichtigste ideelle Vereinheitlichung." On the relationship of musical biography and hermeneutics in twentieth-century musical scholarship, see Hermann Danuser, "Biographik und musikalische Hermeneutik: Zum Verhältnis zweier Disziplinen der Musikwissenschaft," in *Neue Musik und Tradition: Festschrift für Rudolf Stefan zum 65. Geburtstag*, ed. Josef Kuckertz et al. (Laaber: Laaber-Verlag, 1990), 571–601; Jolanta T. Pekacz, introduction to *Musical Biography: Towards New Paradigms*, ed. Jolanta T. Pekacz (Aldershot: Ashgate, 2006); Christopher Wiley, "Re-Writing Composers' Lives: Critical Historiography and Musical Biography" (Ph.D. diss., Royal Holloway, University of London, 2008); and Unseld, *Biographie und Musikgeschichte*.

33. Hermann Abert, "Über Aufgaben und Ziele der musikalischen Biographie," in his *Gesammelte Schriften und Vorträge*, ed. Friedrich Blume (Halle: Niemeyer, 1929), 575: "auch sonst hören wir immer wieder die Ansicht, dass hinter jedem guten Tonstück ein bedeutender Lebensvorgang stehen müsse. Heutzutage gilt sehr häufig das gerade Gegenteil, nämlich der Satz, dass das Leben eines Künstlers mit seiner Kunst überhaupt nichts zu tun habe."

34. Pierre Boulez, "'Sonate, Que me Veux-tu?,'" trans. David Noakes and Paul Jacobs, *Perspectives of New Music* 1, no. 2 (1963): 44.

35. Joseph N. Straus, "Stravinsky the Serialist," in *The Cambridge Companion to Stravinsky*, ed. Jonathan Cross (Cambridge: Cambridge University Press, 2003), 172.

Chapter 8

1. Arnold Schmitz, *Das romantische Beethovenbild: Darstellung und Kritik* (Berlin and Bonn, 1927; rpt., Darmstadt: Wissenschaftliche Buchgesellschaft, 1978), 178: "Im romantischen Beethovenbild ist nicht der echte Beethoven dargestellt, sondern der Typus des romantischen Künstlers. Es ist mit Farben gemalt, die aus der Palette der romantischen Philosophie stammen, die aber nicht der geschichtlichen Wirklichkeit entsprechen." On Schmitz's work as a turning point in the reception of Beethoven, see Eggebrecht, *Zur Geschichte der Beethoven-Rezeption*, 21–23; and Helmut Loos, "Arnold Schmitz as Beethoven Scholar: A Reassessment," *Journal of Musicological Research* 32 (2013): 150–62.

2. Hermann Abert, "Beethoven zum 26. März 1927," *Die Musik* 19 (1927): 386: "Unter den jüngeren Leuten . . . macht sich bereits eine gereizte Stimmung gegen Beethoven fühlbar; sie finden sein Pathos gewaltsam, überspannt, ja unerträglich und seinen scharfen Subjektivismus geradezu ein Verhängnis für die Kunst. Alle Anzeichen deuten darauf hin, daß neuerdings in der Geschichte der Beethovenschen Kunst ein neues Blatt aufgeschlagen wird."

3. Felix Joachimson, "Beethoven in der Meinung der jungen Musiker: Eine Rundfrage," *Die literarische Welt* 12, no. 3 (25 March 1927): 3–4.

4. J. W. N. Sullivan, *Beethoven: His Spiritual Development* (New York: Knopf, 1927), viii.

5. Sullivan, *Beethoven*, 55.

6. Sullivan, *Beethoven*, 114–15.

7. Solomon, *Beethoven*; Solomon, *Beethoven Essays*, esp. "Thoughts on Biography," 101–15; and Solomon, *Late Beethoven: Music, Thought, Imagination* (Berkeley and Los Angeles: University of California Press, 2003). The quotation is from "Thoughts on Biography," 112.

8. Jan Swafford, *Beethoven: Anguish and Triumph* (New York: Houghton Mifflin Harcourt, 2014), 556, 557.

9. Edward T. Cone, "Schubert's Promissory Note: An Exercise in Musical Hermeneutics," *19CM* 5 (1982): 233–41.

10. Cone, "Schubert's Promissory Note," 240–41.

11. For further commentary on Cone's reading, including biographical sources not cited by Cone that would seem to support his interpretation, see Kramer, *Musical Meaning*, 18–28.

12. See Maynard Solomon, "Franz Schubert and the Peacocks of Benvenuto Cellini," *19CM* 12 (1989): 193–206, and "Schubert: Music, Sexuality, Culture," special issue, *19CM* 17, no. 1 (1993) entitled The debate would continue in such publications as McClary, "Constructions of Subjectivity in Schubert's Music"; Kramer, *Franz Schubert*; and Jeffrey Kallberg, "Sex, Sexuality, and Schubert's Piano Music," in *Historical Musicology: Sources, Methods, Interpretations*, ed. Stephen A. Crist and Roberta Montemorra Marvin (Rochester, NY: University of Rochester Press, 2004), 219–31. The controversy as a whole is summarized from a more recent perspective in Geoffrey Block, *Schubert's Reputation from His Time to Ours* (Hillsdale, NY: Pendragon Press, 2017), 285–320.

13. James Webster, "Music, Pathology, Sexuality, Beethoven, Schubert," *19CM* 17 (1993): 91. Webster's reference to Dahlhaus is specifically to the opening two chapters of the latter's *Ludwig van Beethoven: Approaches to His Music*.

14. See Laurel E. Fay, *Shostakovich: A Life* (New York: Oxford University Press, 2000), 217–20. Shostakovich derives the motive D–S–C–H from D. Schostakowich, his name in German transliteration, with "S" derived from E♭ ("Es" in German) and "H" from B♮. This device also appears in the Tenth Symphony (1957). On the Eighth Quartet in particular, see David Fanning, *Shostakovich: String Quartet No. 8* (Aldershot: Ashgate, 2004).

15. Shostakovich to Isaak Glikman, 19 July 1960, quoted in Wendy Lesser, *Music for Silenced Voices: Shostakovich and His Fifteen Quartets* (New Haven, CT: Yale University Press, 2011), 145–46.

16. On the difficulty of interpreting the self-expressive nature of Shostakovich's music (and music in general), see Gregory Karl and Jenefer Robinson, "Shostakovich's Tenth Symphony and the Musical Expression of Cognitively Complex Emotions," *Journal of Aesthetics and Art Criticism* 53 (1995): 401–15; and Marina Frolova-Walker, "'Music Is Obscure': Textless Soviet Works and Their Phantom Programmes," in *Representation in Western Music*, ed. Joshua S. Walden (Cambridge: Cambridge University Press, 2013), 47–63.

17. Lesser, *Music for Silenced Voices*, 3, 142–53. See also Sarah Reichardt, *Composing the Modern Subject: Four String Quartets by Dmitri Shostakovich* (Aldershot: Ashgate, 2008).

18. Aaron Copland, *Music and Imagination* (Cambridge, MA: Harvard University Press, 1952), 40–41.

19. Marx, *Ludwig van Beethoven* (1859), 1:124: "Diese Einkehr in die eigene Brust, dies sinnige Betrachten seiner selbst, das die Frage 'Wer bin Ich?' auf den Lippen trägt, kann nur im stillen Adagio beantwortet werden." On the broader context of Marx's comment, see Margaret Notley, "Late Nineteenth-Century Chamber Music and the Cult of the Classical Adagio," *19CM* 23 (1999): 33–61.

20. See Alan Gillmor, "The Apostasy of George Rochberg," *Intersections* 29 (2009): 32–48.

21. George Rochberg, "Notes by the Composer" (to the Octet, 1980), in Joan DeVee Dixon, *George Rochberg: A Bio-Bibliographic Guide to his Life and Works* (Stuyvesant, NY: Pendragon Press, 1992), 103–4.

22. George Rochberg, *The Aesthetics of Survival: A Composer's View of Twentieth-Century Music*, rev. ed. (Ann Arbor: University of Michigan Press, 2004); George Rochberg and Istvan Anhalt, *Eagle Minds: Selected Correspondence of Istvan Anhalt and George Rochberg, 1961–2005*, ed. Alan M. Gillmor (Waterloo, Ontario: Wilfrid Laurier University Press, 2007); and Guy Freedman, "Metamorphosis of a 20th-Century Composer," *Music Journal* 34, no. 3 (1976): 12–13, 34.

23. Theodore Presser Company, *George Rochberg: Composer Scrapbook* (King of Prussia, PA: Theodore Presser, 2013), 4. https://issuu.com/theodorepresser/docs/scrapbook_rochberg

24. For an excellent account of this phenomenon in the form of two case studies, see Judy Lochhead, "Refiguring the Modernist Program for Hearing: Steve Reich and George Rochberg," in *The Pleasure of Modernist Music*, ed. Arved Ashby (Rochester, NY: University of Rochester Press, 2004), 325–44.

25. Mark Adamo, *John Corigliano: A Monograph* (Todmorden: Arc Music, 2000), 21–22. Ellipses in the original.

26. Luigi Nono, liner notes to his . . . *sofferte onde serene* . . . , DG 2531 004 (Polydor, 1979): "un duro vento di morte spazzò 'l'infinito sorriso delle onde' nella famiglia mia e in quella dei Pollini. Questa comunanza ci accumunò ancor più nella tristezza dell'infinito sorriso di . . . sofferte onde serene. . . .' La dedica: A Maurizio e a Marilisa Pollini significa anche questo."

27. Helmut Lachenmann, "Musik als Abbild vom Menschen" (1984), in his *Musik als existentielle Erfahrung: Schriften, 1966–1995*, ed. Josef Häusler, 2nd ed. (Wiesbaden: Breitkopf & Härtel, 2004), 115: "In solchem kreativ veränderndem Umgang mit dem Gewohnten drückt der Komponist sich aus und entdeckt er sich selbst neu als Teil einer vielschichtigeren als bloß der unmittelbaren bürgerlichen Wirklichkeit."

28. Arvo Pärt, "Acceptance Speech for the International Bridge Prize of the European City of Görlitz" (2007), in *The Cambridge Companion to Arvo Pärt*, ed. Andrew Shenton (Cambridge: Cambridge University Press, 2012), 201.

29. Laura Dolp, "Arvo Pärt in the Marketplace," in *The Cambridge Companion to Arvo Pärt*, ed. Andrew Shenton (Cambridge: Cambridge University Press, 2012), 177–92.

For an examination of Pärt's music from an Orthodox Christian perspective, see Peter C. Bouteneff, *Arvo Pärt: Out of Silence* (Yonkers, NY: St. Vladimir's Seminary Press, 2015).

30. Quoted in Seth Brodsky, "Two Ways of Dealing with Wolfgang Rihm," *Musical Times* 145, no. 1888 (2004): 58.

31. Brodsky, "Two Ways of Dealing with Wolfgang Rihm," 68.

32. Wolfgang Rihm, "'Im Innersten,' Drittes Streichquartett (1976)," in his *Ausgesprochen: Schriften und Gespräche*, ed. Ulrich Mosch, 2 vols. (Winterthur: Amadeus, 1997), 2:303: "Ohne Vorbereitung brach es in die Welt meiner damaligen Arbeit ein, brach diese auf und ermöglichte mir einen Ausbruch ins Innerste. Also: Ausdruck 'tiefster' und tiefer Empfindungen bis zum Ungeschliffenen und Brüchigen, gerade noch Verstehbaren. Das macht diese Musik auf neue Weise verständlich. Sie wird entweder direkt erfahren oder gar nicht."

33. Rihm, "'Im Innersten,'" 2:304: "Dieser Titel—'Im Innersten'—ist viel mißverstanden worden, und das ist gut so. Denn ich wählte ihn sicher nicht aus einer Sicherheit heraus. Wohl aber aus dem Bewußtsein, daß nur ein Sich-Einlassen auf das Mißverständliche zu dieser Zeit—1976—Ehrlichkeit bedeutete."

34. Igor Stravinsky and Robert Craft, *Themes and Episodes* (New York: Knopf, 1966), 41.

35. See the interview with Serge Moreux, 24 December 1938, transcribed in Eric Walter White, *Stravinsky: The Composer and His Works*, 2nd ed. (Berkeley and Los Angeles: University of California Press, 1979), 585–87.

36. Igor Stravinsky, liner notes to *Stravinsky Conducts* (Columbia MS6548, 1963).

37. Claude Samuel and Péter Várnai, eds., *György Ligeti in Conversation with Péter Várnai, Josef Häusler, Claude Samuel, and Himself* (London: Eulenberg, 1983), 21.

38. Florian Scheding, "Where Is the Holocaust in All This? György Ligeti and the Dialectics of Life and Work," in *Dislocated Memories: Jews, Music, and Postwar German Culture*, ed. Tina Frühauf and Lily Hirsch (New York: Oxford University Press, 2014), 205–21. Wolfgang Marx, "Ligeti's Musical Style as Expression of Cultural Trauma," in *György Ligeti's Cultural Identities*, ed. Amy Bauer and Márton Kerékfy (New York: Routledge, 2018), 74–91.

39. *Down Beat*, 1 October 1959, 28, as quoted in Jeremy Yudkin, "The Naming of Names: 'Flamenco Sketches' or 'All Blues'? Identifying the Last Two Tracks on Miles Davis's Classic Album *Kind of Blue*," *MQ* 95 (2012): 15.

40. See Paul F. Berliner, *Thinking in Jazz: The Infinite Art of Improvisation* (Chicago: University of Chicago Press, 1994); and James O. Young and Carl Matheson, "The Metaphysics of Jazz," *Journal of Aesthetics and Art Criticism* 58 (2000): 125–33.

41. Elijah Wald, *Escaping the Delta: Robert Johnson and the Invention of the Blues* (New York: Amistad, 2004), xiii–xiv.

42. Ethan Sacks, "Taylor Swift Blasts Ex-Boyfriend in New Song, 'Never Ever Getting Back Together,' from Upcoming Album 'Red,'" *New York Daily News*, 14 August 2012. http://www.nydailynews.com/entertainment/music-arts/taylor-swift-releases-new-song-back-upcoming-album-red-article-1.1135999#ixzz23d1E6O8k accessed 5 June 2018. Ellipses in the original.

43. Goethe, *Paralipomena* to *Dichtung und Wahrheit*, ed. Peter Sprengel, in his *Sämtliche Werke nach Epochen seines Schaffens: Münchner Ausgabe*, 16:847: "Der

Dichter verwandelt das Leben in ein Bild / Die Menge will das Bild wieder zu Stoff erniedrigen." Ibid., "Geheimstes," in his *Werke*, 2:33: "Wir sind emsig, nachzuspüren, / Wir, die Anekdotenjäger, / Wer dein Liebchen sei."

44. Theodore Gracyk, *Rhythm and Noise: An Aesthetics of Rock* (Durham, NC: Duke University Press, 1996), 224. Simon Frith, "Rock and the Politics of Memory," in *The 60s without Apology*, ed. Sohnya Sayres et al. (Minneapolis: University of Minnesota Press, 1984), 66.

45. Travis M. Andrews, "Drake, Meek Mill and Their Bitter Feud about Ghostwriting in Hip-Hop," *Washington Post*, 26 May 2016. Matthew R. Hodgman, "Class, Race, Credibility, and Authenticity within the Hip-Hop Music Genre," *Journal of Sociological Research* 4 (2013): 402–13.

46. Elijah Wald, *Dylan Goes Electric! Newport, Seeger, Dylan, and the Night that Split the Sixties* (New York: Dey Street, 2015).

47. Martin Fackler, "In Japan, a Beloved Deaf Composer Appears to Be None of the Above," *New York Times*, 6 February 2014, A1.

Conclusion

1. Wenzel Johann Tomaschek [Václav Jan Tomášek], *Selbstbiographie* (1845), transcribed in Kopitz and Cadenbach, *Beethoven aus der Sicht seiner Zeitgenossen*, 2:988–89: "Möge die ganze Welt anders über ihn denken, ich werde deßhalb meine Meinung über ihn nie ändern; denn der Dienst, in dem ich für die Verherrlichung der Kunst stehe, ist mir zu heilig, als daß ich gegen meine Ueberzeugung sprechen sollte. Viele, wenn sie von Beethoven sprechen, sind gleich bei Mozart, wo der Letzte immer das Kürzere zieht, sie vergessen aber, daß des Ersten Werke, welche mit mehr Verständniß und Grazie ausgestattet sind, als seine spätern Werke, diese Vorzüge gerade der vernünftigen von Mozart ausgeprägten Form verdanken, und noch immer einen wohlthuenden Eindruck auf den Zuhörer machen. Ich hasse von jeher alle Vergleichungen, vorzüglich aber im Gebiete der Kunst; doch wenn schon verglichen sein soll, so denke ich mir Mozarts Geist als eine Sonne, die leuchtet und erwärmt, ohne ihre gesetzmäßige Bahn zu verlassen; Beethoven nenne ich einen Komet, der kühne Bahnen bezeichnet ohne sich einem System zu unterordnen, dessen Erscheinen zu allerlei abergläubischen Deutungen Anlaß giebt. Oder: Mozart sendet seine ewig jungen Morgenstrahlen der Morgensonne gleich zur Erde, sie zu erhellen, und zu erwärmen, Beethoven sammelt die glühenden Strahlen der Mittagssonne in einem Brennpunkt zusammen, sammelt auch die Schatten der Nacht, die zu kühlen und zu laben, denen die brennende Gluth unerträglich."

2. Thomas Kuhn, *The Structure of Scientific Revolutions*, 3rd ed. (Chicago: University of Chicago Press, 1996).

3. See J. A. Ruffner, "Newton's Propositions on Comets: Steps in Transition, 1681–84," *Archive for History of Exact Sciences* 54 (2000): 259–77.

4. See above, p. 73.

Bibliography

A***. "Wien, den 29sten Januar, 1787." *Magazin der Musik* 2 (1787): 1273–74.

Abert, Hermann. "Beethoven zum 26. März 1927." *Die Musik* 19 (1927): 385–88.

Abert, Hermann. "Über Aufgaben und Ziele der musikalischen Biographie." In his *Gesammelte Schriften und Vorträge*, 562–88. Edited by Friedrich Blume. Halle: Niemeyer, 1929.

Abrams, M. H. *The Mirror and the Lamp: Romantic Theory and the Critical Tradition.* Oxford: Oxford University Press, 1953.

Abrams, M. H. *Natural Supernaturalism: Tradition and Revolution in Romantic Literature.* New York: W. W. Norton, 1971.

Adamo, Mark. *John Corigliano: A Monograph.* Todmorden: Arc Music, 2000.

Adler, Guido. *Methode der Musikgeschichte.* Leipzig: Breitkopf & Härtel, 1919.

Adorno, Theodor. *Philosophie der neuen Musik* (1949). Frankfurt am Main: Suhrkamp, 1978.

Adorno, Theodor. *Philosophy of New Music.* Edited and translated by Robert Hullot-Kentor. Minneapolis: University of Minnesota Press, 2006.

Allanbrook, Wye J. *The Secular Commedia: Comic Mimesis in Late Eighteenth-Century Music.* Berkeley and Los Angeles: University of California Press, 2014.

Allanbrook, Wye J. "Tunes and the Comedy of Closure." In *On Mozart*, 169–86. Edited by James M. Morris. Washington, DC: Woodrow Wilson Center Press; Cambridge: Cambridge University Press, 1994.

Alter, Robert. "Mimesis and the Motive for Fiction." *Tri-Quarterly* 42 (1978): 228–49.

Ambros, August Wilhelm. *Culturhistorische Bilder aus dem Musikleben der Gegenwart.* Leipzig: Heinrich Matthes, 1860.

Ameriks, Karl. "The Key Role of *Selbstgefühl* in Philosophy's Aesthetic and Historical Turns." *Critical Horizons* 5 (2004): 27–52.

Ameriks, Karl, and Dieter Sturma, eds. *The Modern Subject: Conceptions of the Self in Classical German Philosophy.* Albany: State University of New York Press, 1995.

Andrews, Travis M. "Drake, Meek Mill and Their Bitter Feud about Ghostwriting in Hip-Hop." *Washington Post*, 26 May 2016.

Anonymous. "Aus Beethovens Testament, als Beytrag zu seiner Biographie." *Allgemeine Theaterzeitung und Unterhaltungsblatt* 20 (6 November 1827): 541–42.

Anonymous. "Beethoven und Jean Paul! Mozart u. Göthe! Eine Paral[l]ele." *Minerva: Ein Beiblatt zum Allgemeinen musikalischen Anzeiger* (Frankfurt) 1 (25 October 1826): 134–35.

Anonymous. "Contemporary Musical Composers, Frederic Chopin." *Athenaeum*, no. 740 (1 January 1842): 18–19.

Anonymous. "Felix Mendelssohn-Bartholdy, in Stettin." *BAmZ* 4 (14 March 1827): 83–87.

Anonymous. "Literary Intelligence: Beethoven." *Philadelphia Monthly Magazine* 2 (15 April 1828): 60–61.

Anonymous. "Memoir of Beethoven." *Quarterly Musical Magazine and Review* 9 (1827): 264–78.

Anonymous. "Nachrichten: Leipzig." *AmZ* 19 (21 May 1817): 353–65.

Anonymous. "Nachrichten: Wien." *AmZ* 30 (13 February 1828): 105–11.

Anonymous. "Nachrichten... Wien, d. 28. Jan." *AmZ* 7 (13 February 1805): 319–23.

Anonymous. "A New Opera in New York." *Musical Courier* 46, no.11 (18 March 1903): 12.

Anonymous. "Noch ein Wort über Beethoven." *Allgemeine Musikzeitung zur Beförderung der theoretischen und praktischen Tonkunst* 2 (1 March 1828): 142–43.

Anonymous. "Quatre symphonies pour l'orchestre, comp. par Wolfgang Amad. Mozart. Oeuvre 64." *AmZ* 1 (1 May 1799): 494–96.

Anonymous. "Recension: Musée musical des Clavicinistes. Museum für Claviermusik. Erstes Heft, enthält: *Sonate (in A-dur) für das Pianoforte (Hammer-Clavier) von Ludwig van Beethoven, 101tes Werk.*" *Allgemeine musikalische Zeitung mit besonderer Rücksicht auf den österreichischen Kaiserstaat* 1 (27 February 1817): 66.

Anonymous. "Recension: *Sonate für Pianoforte und Violin, von Ludwig van Beethoven. 96tes Werk.*" *AmZ* 19 (26 March 1817): 228–29.

Anonymous. "Recensionen: *Trois Sonates pour le Clavecin ou Pianoforte, comp. . . . par Louis van Beethoven. Oeuv. 10 . . . .*" *AmZ* 2 (9 October 1799): 25–29.

Anonymous, Review of *XIVe Nocturne . . . par John Field. AmZ* 38 (20 July 1836): 471–72.

Anonymous. Review of *Dix Thémes [sic] Russes, Ecossoie et Tyroliens . . . par Louis van Beethoven. AmZ* 23 (15 August 1821): 567–69.

Anonymous. Review of *Quatuor pour 2 Violons, Viola, et Violoncelle, par L. van Beethoven . . . Oeuvr. 74. AmZ* 13 (22 May 1811): 349–51.

Anonymous. Review of *Sechs Gesänge mit Begleit. des Pianoforte . . . von L. van Beethoven . . . Oeuvr. 75. AmZ* 13 (28 August 1811): 593–595.

Anonymous. Review of *Trois Sonates pour le Clavecin ou Pianoforte, comp. . . . par Louis van Beethoven. Oeuv. 10 . . . " AmZ* 2 (9 October 1799): 25–29.

Anonymous, "Soirées musicales de MM. Bohrer frères." *Revue musicale*, 2nd ser., 1 (1830): 212–15.

Anonymous. "Ueber den Verein der Musikfreunde in Wien und das damit verbundene Conservatorium." *AmZ* 35 (13 November 1833): 757–65.

Anonymous. "Vermischtes." *NZfM* 10 (25 June 1839): 204.

Anonymous. "Wien: Musikalisches Tagebuch vom Monat März." *AmZ* 28 (1826): 301–4, 309–15.

Applegate, Celia. "How German Is It? Nationalism and the Idea of Serious Music in the Early Nineteenth Century." *19CM* 21 (1998): 274–96.

Applegate, Celia, and Pamela Potter, eds. *Music and German National Identity*. Chicago: University of Chicago Press, 2002.

Arnim, Bettina Brentano von. "Drei Briefe von Beethoven." *Athenaeum für Wissenschaft, Kunst und Leben* 1 (1839): 1–7.

Arnim, Bettina Brentano von. *Goethes Briefwechsel mit einem Kinde*. 3 vols. Berlin: Ferdinand Dümmler, 1835.

Arnold, Ignaz Theodor Ferdinand Cajetan. *Gallerie der berühmtesten Tonkünstler des achtzehnten und neunzehnten Jahrhunderts*. 2 vols. Erfurt: Johann Karl Müller, 1810.

Arnold, Ignaz Theodor Ferdinand Cajetan. "Recension: *Phantasie für das Pianoforte, mit Begleitung des ganzen Orchesters und Chor, in Musik gesetzt... von Louis van Beethoven, 80stes Werk.*" *AmZ* 14 (6 May 1812): 307–11.

Arnold, Matthew. "The Study of Poetry" (1880). In his *Essays in Criticism: Second Series*, 1–55. London: Macmillan, 1888.

Avison, Charles. *An Essay on Musical Expression*. London: C. Davis, 1752.

B. "Die Künstler." *AmZ* 17 (22 March 1815): 193–96.

Bach, Carl Philipp Emanuel. *Briefe und Dokumente: Kritische Gesamtausgabe*. Edited by Ernst Suchalla. 2 vols. Göttingen: Vandenhoeck & Ruprecht, 1994.

Bach, Carl Philipp Emanuel. *Versuch über die wahre Art das Clavier zu spielen*. 2 vols. Berlin: C. F. Henning and G. L. Winter, 1753–62.

Bartel, Dietrich. *Musica poetica: Musical-Rhetorical Figures in German Baroque Music*. Lincoln: University of Nebraska Press, 1997.

Bartók Archives of the Hungarian Academy of Sciences Institute for Musicology, 2004–2005. "Bartók Virtual Exhibition: Private Life." http://www.zti.hu/bartok/exhibition/en_P2.htm

Bashford, Christina, and Roberta Montemorra Marvin, eds. *The Idea of Art Music in a Commercial World, 1800–1930*. Woodbridge: Boydell Press, 2016.

Batteux, Charles. *Les beaux-arts réduits à un même principe*. Paris: Durand, 1746.

Bauer, Elisabeth Eleonore. "Beethoven—unser musikalischer Jean Paul: Anmerkungen zu einer Analogie." In *Beethoven: Analecta varia*, 83–105. Edited by Heinz-Klaus Metzger and Rainer Riehn. Munich: edition text + kritik, 1987.

Bauer, Elisabeth Eleonore. *Wie Beethoven auf den Sockel kam: Die Entstehung eines musikalischen Mythos*. Stuttgart: J. B. Metzler, 1992.

Bauer-Lechner, Natalie. *Gustav Mahler in den Erinnerungen von Natalie Bauer-Lechner* (1923). Rev. ed. Edited by Herbert Killian and Knud Martner. Hamburg: K.D. Wagner, 1984.

Becher, Alfred Julius. "Correspondenz: Köln." *NZfM* 2 (13 and 17 March 1834): 84–86, 89–90.

Beethoven, Ludwig van. *Beethovens Tagebuch: 1812–1818*. Edited by Maynard Solomon. 2nd ed. Bonn: Beethoven-Haus, 2005.

Beethoven, Ludwig van. "Beethoven's Will." *The Harmonicon*, n.s. 6 (January 1828): 6–7.

Beethoven, Ludwig van. "Eigenhandige brief van den onlangs overleden' vermaarden componist Ludwig van Beethoven, onder zijne nagelatene papieren gevonden." *Vaderlandsche Letteroefeningen* 2 (1828): 94–96.

Beethoven, Ludwig van. "Testament de Louis Beethoven, d'après le texte original." *Le Voleur*, 2nd ser. 6 (20 April 1833): 341–42.

Behler, Ernst. *Studien zur Romantik und zur idealistischen Philosophie*. Paderborn: Schöningh, 1988.

Behler, Ernst. "What It Means to Understand an Author Better than He Understood Himself: Idealistic Philosophy and Romantic Hermeneutics." In *Literary Theory and Criticism: Festschrift Presented to René Wellek in Honor of his Eightieth Birthday*, 2 vols, 1:69–92. Edited by Joseph P. Strelka. Bern: Peter Lang, 1984.

Beiser, Frederick. *The Fate of Reason: German Philosophy from Kant to Fichte*. Cambridge, MA: Harvard University Press, 1987.

Beisler, Hermann. "Die Unergründlichkeit des Werks und die Unendlichkeit der Interpretation." In *Theorie der Interpretation vom Humanismus bis zur Romantik: Rechtswissenschaft, Philosophie, Theologie*, 217–48. Edited by Jan Schröder. Stuttgart: Steiner, 2001.

Bekker, Paul. *Beethoven*. Berlin and Leipzig: Schuster & Loeffler, 1911.

Bell, Matthew. *The German Tradition of Psychology in Literature and Thought, 1700–1840*. Cambridge: Cambridge University Press, 2005.

Benedetti, Jean. *David Garrick and the Birth of Modern Theatre*. London: Methuen, 2001.

Bent, Ian. "General Introduction." In *Music Analysis in the Nineteenth Century*, 2 vols., 2:1–27. Edited by Ian Bent. Cambridge: Cambridge University Press, 1993–94.

Bent, Ian. "Plato—Beethoven: A Hermeneutics for Nineteenth-Century Music?" *Indiana Theory Review* 16 (1995): 1–33.

Bentley, Eric. *A Century of Hero-Worship: A Study of the Idea of Heroism in Carlyle and Nietzsche, with Notes on Wagner, Spengler, Stefan George, and D. H. Lawrence.* 2nd ed. Boston: Beacon Press, 1957.

Berlin, Isaiah. *The Roots of Romanticism.* Edited by Henry Hardy. Princeton, NJ: Princeton University Press, 1999.

Berliner, Paul F. *Thinking in Jazz: The Infinite Art of Improvisation.* Chicago: University of Chicago Press, 1994.

Berlioz, Hector. *Correspondance génerale.* Edited by Pierre Citron. Paris: Flammarion, 1972–.

Berlioz, Hector. *Critique musicale.* Edited by H. Robert Cohen, Yves Gérard, et al. Paris: Buchet/Chastel, 1996–.

Berlioz, Hector. *Evenings in the Orchestra.* Translated by Charles E. Roche. New York: Knopf, 1929.

Berlioz, Hector. *Les soirées de l'orchestre.* Paris: Michel Lévy frères, 1852.

Bernstein, Jane A. "'Shout, Shout, Up with Your Song!' Dame Ethel Smyth and the Changing Role of the British Woman Composer." In *Women Making Music,* 304–24. Edited by Jane Bowers and Judith Tick. Urbana: University of Illinois Press, 1985.

Bezzola, Tobia. *Die Rhetorik bei Kant, Fichte und Hegel: Ein Beitrag zur Philosophiegeschichte der Rhetorik.* Tübingen: Max Niemeyer, 1993.

Biba, Otto. "Nachrichten über Joseph Haydn, Michael Haydn und Wolfgang Amadeus Mozart in der Sammlung handschriftlicher Biographien der Gesellschaft der Musikfreunde in Wien." In *Studies in Music History Presented to H. C. Robbins Landon on His Seventieth Birthday,* 152–64. Edited by Otto Biba and David Wyn Jones. London: Thames & Hudson, 1996.

Bishop, Paul. *Analytical Psychology and German Classical Aesthetics: Goethe, Schiller, and Jung.* 2 vols. London: Routledge, 2008.

Block, Geoffrey. *Schubert's Reputation from His Time to Ours.* Hillsdale, NY: Pendragon Press, 2017.

Blum, Karl. "Miscellen." *AmZ* 16 (1814): 394–96, 794–95, 810–11.

Bonds, Mark Evan. *Absolute Music: The History of an Idea.* New York: Oxford University Press, 2014.

Bonds, Mark Evan. "The Court of Public Opinion: Haydn, Mozart, Beethoven." In *Beethoven und andere Hofmusiker seiner Generation,* 7–24. Edited by Birgit Lodes, Elisabeth Reisinger, and John D. Wilson. Schriften zur Beethoven-Forschung, vol. 29: Musik am Bonner kurfürstlichen Hof, vol. 1. Bonn: Beethoven-Haus, 2018.

Bonds, Mark Evan. "Haydn, Laurence Sterne, and the Origins of Musical Irony." *JAMS* 44 (1991): 57–91.

Bonds, Mark Evan. "Haydn's 'Cours complet de la composition' and the 'Sturm und Drang.'" In *Haydn Studies,* 152–76. Edited by Dean Sutcliffe. Cambridge: Cambridge University Press, 1998.

Bonds, Mark Evan. "Irony and Incomprehensibility: Beethoven's 'Serioso' String Quartet in F Minor, Op. 95, and the Path to the Late Style." *JAMS* 70 (2017): 285–356.

Bonds, Mark Evan. "Life, Liberty, and the Pursuit of Happiness: Revolutionary Ideals in Narratives of the 'Farewell' Symphony." In *Joseph Haydn und die "neue Welt": Bericht über das Symposium der Internationalen Joseph Haydn Privatstiftung Eisenstadt . . . vom 13. bis 15. September 2011,* 283–301. Edited by Walter Reicher. Eisenstädter Haydn Berichte, 11. Vienna: Hollitzer, 2019.

Bonds, Mark Evan. *Music as Thought: Listening to the Symphony in the Age of Beethoven.* Princeton, NJ: Princeton University Press, 2006.

Bonds, Mark Evan. "Rhetoric versus Truth: Listening to Haydn in the Age of Beethoven." In *Haydn and the Performance of Rhetoric*, 109–28. Edited by Sander Goldberg and Tom Beghin. Chicago: University of Chicago Press, 2007.

Bonds, Mark Evan. "Turning *Liebhaber* into *Kenner*: Johann Nikolaus Forkel's Lectures on the Art of Listening, ca. 1780–1785." In *The Oxford Handbook of Music Listening in the 19th and 20th Centuries*, 145–62. Edited by Christian Thorau and Hansjakob Ziemer. New York: Oxford University Press, 2019.

Bonds, Mark Evan. *Wordless Rhetoric: Musical Form and the Metaphor of the Oration.* Cambridge, MA: Harvard University Press, 1991.

Bone, Drummond. "The Emptiness of Genius: Aspects of Romanticism." In *Genius: The History of an Idea*, 113–27. Edited by Penelope Murray. Oxford: Basil Blackwell, 1989.

Booth, Wayne C. *The Rhetoric of Fiction.* Chicago: University of Chicago Press, 1961.

Booth, Wayne C. *The Rhetoric of Fiction.* 2nd ed. Chicago: University of Chicago Press, 1983.

Botstein, Leon. "History, Rhetoric, and the Self: Robert Schumann and Music Making in German-Speaking Europe, 1800–1860." In *Schumann and His World*, 3–46. Edited by R. Larry Todd. Princeton, NJ: Princeton University Press, 1994.

Botstein, Leon. "Second Thoughts: The Genre of Biography and Natalie Bauer-Lechner as Witness." *MQ* 97 (2014): 1–11.

Bouteneff, Peter C. *Arvo Pärt: Out of Silence.* Yonkers, NY: St. Vladimir's Seminary Press, 2015.

Boulanger, Nadia. "Concerts Koussevitsky." *Le monde musical*, November 1923, 365–67.

Boulez, Pierre. " 'Sonate, Que me Veux-tu?' " Translated by David Noakes and Paul Jacobs. *Perspectives of New Music* 1, no. 2 (1963): 32–44.

Bowie, Andrew. *Aesthetics and Subjectivity: From Kant to Nietzsche.* 2nd ed. Manchester: Manchester University Press, 2003.

Bowie, Andrew. "The Philosophical Significance of Schelling's Conception of the Unconscious." In *Thinking the Unconscious: Nineteenth-Century German Thought*, 57–86. Edited by Angus Nicholls and Martin Liebscher. Cambridge: Cambridge University Press, 2010.

Brandenburg, Sieghard. "Künstlerroman und Biographie: Zur Entstehung des Beethoven-Mythos im 19. Jahrhundert." In *Beethoven und die Nachwelt*, 65–80. Edited by Helmut Loos. Bonn: Beethoven-Haus, 1986.

Brauner, Charles S. "Irony in the Heine Lieder of Schubert and Schumann." *MQ* 67 (1981): 261–81.

Braunschweig, Yael. "Biographical Listening: Intimacy, Madness and the Music of Robert Schumann." Ph.D. diss., University of Califonia, Berkeley, 2013.

Breithaupt, Fritz. "Narcissism, the Self, and Empathy: The Paradox that Created Modern Literature." In *The Self as Muse: Narcissism and Creativity in the German Imagination, 1750–1830*, 39–57. Edited by Alexander Mathäs. Lewisburg, PA: Bucknell University Press, 2011.

Brendel, Franz. "Robert Schumann mit Rücksicht auf Mendelssohn-Bartholdy und die Entwicklung der modernen Tonkunst überhaupt." *NZfM* 22 (1845): 63–67, 81–83, 89–92, 113–15, 121–23, 145–47, 149–50.

Brenner, Daniel. *Anton Schindler und sein Einfluss auf die Beethoven-Biographik.* Bonn: Beethoven-Haus, 2013.

Brittan, Francesca. "Berlioz and the Pathological Fantastic: Melancholy, Monomania, and Romantic Autobiography." *19CM* 29 (2006): 211–39.

Brittan, Francesca. "Liszt, Sand, García, and the Contrebandier: Intersubjectivity and Romantic Authorship." *Journal of the American Liszt Society* 65 (2014): 65–94.

Brittan, Francesca. *Music and Fantasy in the Age of Berlioz.* Cambridge: Cambridge University Press, 2017.

Brodsky, Seth. "Two Ways of Dealing with Wolfgang Rihm." *Musical Times* 145, no. 1888 (2004): 57–71.

Brunemeier, Bernd. *Vieldeutigkeit und Rätselhaftigkeit: Die semantische Qualität und Kommunikativitätsfunktion des Kunstwerks in der Poetik und Ästhetik der Goethezeit.* Amsterdam: B. R. Grüner, 1983.

Bruford, Walter Horace. *The German Tradition of Self-Cultivation: Bildung from Humboldt to Thomas Mann.* London: Cambridge University Press, 1975.

Buchholz, Michael B., and Günter Gödde, eds. *Das Unbewusste.* 3 vols. Gießen: Psychosozial Verlag, 2005–6.

Buckley, Jerome Hamilton. *The Turning Key: Autobiography and the Subjective Impulse since 1800.* Cambridge, MA: Harvard University Press, 1984.

Burney, Charles. *The Present State of Music in Germany, the Netherlands, and United Provinces.* 2 vols. London: T. Becket, 1773.

Burnham, Scott. *Beethoven Hero.* Princeton, NJ: Princeton University Press, 1995.

Burstein, L. Poundie. " 'Lebe wohl tönt überall' and a 'Reunion after So Much Sorrow': Beethoven's Op. 81a and the Journeys of 1809." *MQ* 93 (2010): 366–413.

Burwick, Frederick. *Mimesis and Its Romantic Reflections.* University Park: Pennsylvania State University Press, 2001.

Burwick, Frederick. *Poetic Madness and the Romantic Imagination.* University Park: Pennsylvania State University Press, 1996.

Busoni, Ferruccio. "Junge Klassizität" (1920). In Busoni, *Von der Einheit der Musik,* 275–79. Berlin: Max Hesse, 1922.

Busoni, Ferruccio. "Was gab uns Beethoven?" *Die Musik* 15, no. 1 (1922): 19–23.

Busby, Thomas. *Allgemeine Geschichte der Musik.* 2 vols. Edited and translated by Christian Friedrich Michaelis. Leipzig: Baumgartner, 1821–22.

Butt, John. "Bach's Passions and the Construction of Early Modern Subjectivities." In his *Bach's Dialogue with Modernity: Perspectives on the Passions,* 36–96. Cambridge: Cambridge University Press, 2010.

Byron, George Gordon, Lord. *Byron's Letters and Journals.* Edited by Leslie A. Marchand. 13 vols. Cambridge, MA: Harvard University Press, 1973–82.

Caballero, Carlo. *Fauré and French Musical Aesthetics.* Cambridge: Cambridge University Press, 2001.

Cahusac, Louis de. "Expression (Opéra)." In *Encyclopédie, ou dictionnaire raisonné des sciences, des arts et des métiers, etc.* 28 vols. 6:315–18. Edited by Denis Diderot and Jean le Rond d'Alembert. Paris: Le Breton et al., 1751–72.

Campe, Rüdiger. "Umbrüche und Wandlungen der Rhetorik." In *Die Wende von der Aufklärung zur Romantik, 1760–1820: Epoche im Überblick,* 589–612. Edited by Horst Albert Glaser and György M. Vajda. Amsterdam and Philadelphia: John Benjamins, 2000.

Carlyle, Thomas. *On Heroes, Hero-Worship, and the Heroic in History* (1841). Edited by David R. Sorensen and Brent E. Kinser. New Haven, CT: Yale University Press, 2013.

Carlyle, Thomas. Review of *Jean Paul Friedrich Richter's Leben* . . . by Heinrich Doering. *Edinburgh Review* 46 (1827): 176–95.

Carlyle, Thomas. Review of J. G. Lockhart, *The Life of Robert Burns. Edinburgh Review* 48 (1828), 269–312.

Carlyle, Thomas. "Thoughts on History." *Fraser's Magazine* 2 (1830): 413–18.

Carpani, Giuseppe. *Le Haydine ovvero Lettere su la vita et le opere del celebre maestro Giuseppe Haydn.* Milan: Candido Buccinelli, 1812.

Cassirer, Fritz. *Beethoven und die Gestalt.* Berlin and Leipzig: Deutsche Verlags-Anstalt, 1925.

Castil-Blaze [François-Henri-Joseph Blaze]. "Beethoven (Ludwig van)." *Dictionnaire de la conversation, et de la lecture.* 52 vols. 5:167–72. Paris: Belin-Mandar, 1832–39.

Cavaliero, Roderick. *Genius, Power and Magic: A Cultural History of Germany from Goethe to Wagner.* London: Palgrave Macmillan, 2013.

Ceballos, Sara Gross. "Sympathizing with *C. P. E. Bachs Empfindungen.*" *Journal of Musicology* 34 (2017): 1–31.

Chateaubriand, François-Auguste. *Génie du Christianisme.* 4 vols. Paris: Migneret, 1802.

Chénier, André. *Oeuvres posthumes.* Edited by D. Ch. Robert. Paris: Guillaume, 1826.

Cherlin, Michael. "Memory and Rhetorical Trope in Schoenberg's String Trio." *JAMS* 51 (1998): 559–602.

Cherlin, Michael. *Varieties of Musical Irony: From Mozart to Mahler.* Cambridge: Cambridge University Press, 2017.

Chua, Daniel K. L. *Absolute Music and the Construction of Meaning.* Cambridge: Cambridge University Press, 1999.

Citron, Marcia. *Gender and the Musical Canon.* Urbana: University of Illinois Press, 2000.

Cobbett, Walter Willson. *Cobbett's Cyclopedic Survey of Chamber Music.* 2 vols. Oxford: Oxford University Press; London: Humphrey Milford, 1929–30.

Comini, Alessandra. *The Changing Image of Beethoven: A Study in Mythmaking.* Rev. ed. Santa Fe, NM: Sunstone Press, 2008.

Comini, Alessandra. "The Visual Beethoven: Whence, Why, and Whither the Scowl?" In *Beethoven and His World*, 287–312. Edited by Scott Burnham and Michael P. Steinberg. Princeton, NJ: Princeton University Press, 2000.

Comstock, Cathy. "'Transcendental Buffoonery': Irony as Process in Schlegel's 'Über die Unverständlichkeit'." *Studies in Romanticism* 26 (1987): 445–64.

Cone, Edward T. *The Composer's Voice.* Berkeley and Los Angeles: University of California Press, 1974.

Cone, Edward T. "Schubert's Promissory Note: An Exercise in Musical Hermeneutics." *19CM* 5 (1982): 233–41.

Cook, Nicholas. "The Other Beethoven: Heroism, the Canon, and the Works of 1813–14." *19CM* 27 (2003): 3–24.

Copland, Aaron. "Carlos Chávez—Mexican Composer." In *American Composers on American Music: A Symposium*, 102–6. Edited by Henry Cowell. Stanford, CA: Stanford University Press, 1933.

Copland, Aaron. *Music and Imagination.* Cambridge, MA: Harvard University Press, 1952.

Cornelius, Peter. Review of Richard Würst, *Preis-Sinfonie*, Op. 21. *NZfM* 41 (8 December 1854): 257–59.

Cramer, Carl Friedrich. Review of Carl Philipp Emanuel Bach, *Claviersonaten und freye Fantasien , , , Fünfte Sammlung* (1785). *Magazin der Musik* 2 (5 August 1786): 869–72.

Culler, Jonathan. *The Pursuit of Signs: Semiotics, Literature, Deconstruction.* New York: Routledge, 2001.

Cumming, Naomi. *The Sonic Self: Musical Subjectivity and Signification.* Bloomington: Indiana Unviersity Press, 2000.

Czerny, Carl. *Die Kunst des Vortrags der ältern und neuen Claviercompositionen . . . Supplement (oder 4ter Theil) zur grossen Pianoforte-Schule, Op. 500.* Vienna: Diabelli, 1846.

Dahlhaus, Carl. *Ludwig van Beethoven: Approaches to His Music.* Translated by Mary Whittall. Oxford: Clarendon Press, 1991.

Danuser, Hermann. "Biographik und musikalische Hermeneutik: Zum Verhältnis zweier Disziplinen der Musikwissenschaft." In *Neue Musik und Tradition: Festschrift für Rudolf Stefan zum 65. Geburtstag,* 571–601. Edited by Josef Kuckertz et al. Laaber: Laaber-Verlag, 1990.

Daverio, John. "Reading Schumann by Way of Jean Paul and His Contemporaries." *College Music Symposium* 30/2 (1990): 28–45.

Daverio, John. "Schumann's 'Im Legendenton' and Friedrich Schlegel's 'Arabeske'." *19CM* 11 (1987): 150–63.

Davison, James William. *An Essay on the Works of Frederic Chopin.* London: Wessel and Stapleton, 1843.

Delaire, Jacques-Auguste. "Des innovations en musique." *Revue musicale,* 2. sér., 1 (20 February 1830): 65–75.

Deutsch, Otto Erich, and Heinz Eibl, eds. *Mozart: Die Dokumente seines Lebens.* Kassel: Bärenreiter, 1961.

Deutsch, Otto Erich, and Heinz Eibl, eds. *Schubert: Die Dokumente seines Lebens.* Kassel: Bärenreiter, 1964.

Diderot, Denis. *Paradoxe sur le comédien.* Edited by Robert Abirached. Paris: Gallimard, 1994.

Diderot, Denis. *Selected Writings on Art and Literature.* Translated and edited by Geoffrey Bremner. Harmondsworth: Penguin, 1994.

Dies, Albert Christoph. *Biographische Nachrichten von Joseph Haydn.* Vienna: Camesina, 1810.

Dittersdorf, Carl Ditters von. *Lebensbeschreibung.* Leipzig: Breitkopf & Härtel, 1801.

Dixon, Thomas. *From Passions to Emotions: The Creation of a Secular Psychological Category.* Cambridge: Cambridge University Press, 2003.

Dolp, Laura. "Arvo Pärt in the Marketplace." In *The Cambridge Companion to Arvo Pärt,* 177–92. Edited by Andrew Shenton. Cambridge: Cambridge University Press, 2012.

Dorfmüller, Kurt, Norbert Gertsch, and Julia Ronge, eds. *Ludwig van Beethoven: Thematisch-bibliographisches Werkverzeichnis.* Munich: G. Henle, 2014.

Duff, William. *An Essay on Original Genius.* London: Edward and Charles Dilly, 1767.

Dwight, John Sullivan. "The Intellectual Influence of Music." *Atlantic Monthly* 26 (19 November 1870): 614–25.

Dye, Ellis. *Love and Death in Goethe: One and Double.* Rochester, NY: Camden House, 2004.

Eckermann, Johann Peter. *Gespräche mit Goethe in den letzten Jahren seines Lebens* (1836–48). Edited by Heinz Schlaffer. In Johann Wolfgang von Goethe, *Sämtliche Werke nach Epochen seines Schaffens: Münchner Ausgabe,* 19. Munich: Carl Hanser, 1986.

Eggebrecht, Hans Heinrich. "Das Ausdrucksprinzip im musikalischen Sturm und Drang." *Deutsche Vierteljahrsschrift für Literaturwissenschaft und Geistesgeschichte* 29 (1955): 323–49.

Eggebrecht, Hans Heinrich. *Zur Geschichte der Beethoven-Rezeption.* 2nd ed. Laaber: Laaber-Verlag, 1994.

Eliot, T. S. "Tradition and the Individual Talent." In his *The Sacred Wood: Essays on Poetry and Criticism*, 42–53. New York: Knopf, 1921.

Erlich, Victor. "Limits of the Biographical Approach." *Comparative Literature* 6 (1954): 130–37.

Einstein, Alfred. *Mozart: His Character, His Work.* Translated by Arthur Mendel and Nathan Broder. New York: Oxford University Press, 1945.

Eisen, Cliff. "Mozart, das Requiem und die Biographie der Romantik." In *Mozart: Experiment Aufklärung im Wien des ausgehenden 18. Jahrhunderts*, 807–21. Edited by Herbert Lachmayer. Ostfildern: Hatje Cantz, 2006.

Elterlein, Ernst von [Ersnet Gottschald]. "Robert Schumann's zweite Symphonie: Zugleich mit Rücksicht auf andere, insbesondere Beethoven's Symphonien." *NZfM* 32 (1850), 137–39, 141–42, 145–48, 157–59.

Erler, Hermann. *Robert Schumann's Leben: Aus seinen Briefen geschildert.* 2 vols. Berlin: Ries & Erler, 1887.

Fackler, Martin. "In Japan, a Beloved Deaf Composer Appears to Be None of the Above." *New York Times*, 6 February 2014.

Fanning, David. *Shostakovich: String Quartet No. 8.* Aldershot: Ashgate, 2004.

Fauser, Annegret. *Musical Encounters at the 1889 Paris World's Fair.* Rochester, NY: University of Rochester Press, 2005.

Fay, Laurel E. *Shostakovich: A Life.* New York: Oxford University Press, 2000.

Fayolle, François. *Paganini et Bériot.* Paris: M. Legouest, 1831.

Feldt, Michael. *Lyrik als Erlebnislyrik: Zur Geschichte eines Literatur- und Mentalitätstypus zwischen 1600 und 1900.* Heidelberg: Carl Winter, 1990.

Ferris, David. "Public Performance and Private Understanding: Clara Wieck's Concerts in Berlin." *JAMS* 56 (2003): 351–408.

Fétis, François-Joseph. "Analyse critique: *Épisode de la vie d'un artiste: Grand Symphonie fantastique* par Hector Berlioz." *Revue musicale* 9 (1 February 1835): 33–35.

Fichte, Johann Gottlieb. *Grundlage der gesammten Wissenschaftslehre.* Leipzig: Christian Ernst Gabler, 1794.

Fichte, Johann Gottlieb. "Versuch einer neuen Darstellung der Wissenschaftslehre." *Philosophisches Journal* 5 (1797): 1–49.

Finlay, Marike. *The Romantic Irony of Semiotics: Friedrich Schlegel and the Crisis of Representation.* Berlin: Mouton de Gruyter, 1988.

Flothuis, Marius. "K. 304." In *The Compleat Mozart*, 290. Edited by Neal Zaslaw and William Cowdery. New York: W. W. Norton, 1990.

Floros, Constantin. *Johannes Brahms, "Free but Alone": A Life for a Poetic Music.* Translated by Ernest Bernhardt-Kabisch. Frankfurt am Main: Peter Lang, 2010.

Forkel, Johann Nikolaus. *Allgemeine Geschichte der Musik.* 2 vols. Leipzig: Schwickert, 1788–1801.

Forkel, Johann Nikolaus. *Commentar über die 1777 gedruckte Abhandlung über Die Theorie der Musik, insofern sie Liebhabern und Kennern nothwendig und nützlich ist; zum Gebrauch akademischer Vorlesungen entworfen von Johahnn Nic. Forkel.*

Manuscript, ca. 1780, Sibley Music Library, Eastman School of Music, Vault ML95.F721S38

Forkel, Johann Nikolaus. *Ueber Johann Sebastian Bachs Leben, Kunst und Kunstwerke.* Leipzig: Hoffmeister und Kühnel, 1802.

Forster, Michael N., and Kristin Gjesdal, eds. *The Oxford Handbook of German Philosophy in the Nineteenth Century.* Oxford: Oxford University Press, 2015.

Framery, Nicolas Étienne. *Notice sur Joseph Haydn.* Paris: Barba, 1810.

Frank, Manfred. *Selbstgefühl.* Frankfurt am Main: Suhrkamp, 2002.

Frevert, Ute. *Emotions in History—Lost and Found.* New York: Central European Press, 2011.

Frevert, Ute, et al., eds. *Emotional Lexicons: Continuity and Change in the Vocabulary of Feeling 1700–2000.* New York: Oxford University Press, 2014.

Freedman, Guy. "Metamorphosis of a 20th-Century Composer." *Music Journal* 34, no. 3 (1976): 12–13, 34.

Frith, Simon. "Rock and the Politics of Memory." In *The 60s without Apology,* 59–69. Edited by Sohnya Sayres et al. Minneapolis: University of Minnesota Press, 1984.

Fröhlich, Joseph. "Recensionen: *Sinfonie, mit Schlusschor über Schillers Ode: 'An die Freude'. . . von Ludwig van Beethoven. . . .* Erste Recension." *Cäcilia* 8 (1828): 231–56.

Frolova-Walker, Marina. "'Music Is Obscure': Textless Soviet Works and Their Phantom Programmes." In *Representation in Western Music,* 47–63. Edited by Joshua S. Walden. Cambridge: Cambridge University Press, 2013.

Fuhrmann, Manfred. *Rhetorik und öffentliche Rede: Über die Ursachen des Verfalls der Rhetorik im ausgehenden 18. Jahrhundert.* Konstanz: Universitätsverlag, 1983.

Fuhrmann, Wolfgang. "'Alle innern Gefühle hörbar hervor in die Luft gezaubert': Wilhelm Heinse und die Theorie des musikalischen Ausdrucks nach dem Verblassen der Figurenlehre." In *Musikalisches Denken im Labyrinth der Aufklärung: Wilhelm Heinses "Hildegard von Hohenthal,"* 33–73. Edited by Thomas Irvine, Wiebke Thormählen, and Oliver Wiener. Mainz: Are Edition, 2015.

Fuhrmann, Wolfgang. "Haydn und sein Publikum: Die Veröffentlichung eines Komponisten, ca. 1750–1815." Habilitationsschrift, Bern, 2010.

Fuhrmann, Wolfgang. "Originality as Market Value: Remarks on the Fantasia in C Hob. XVII:4 and Haydn as Musical Entrepreneur." *Studia Musicologica* 51 (2010): 303–16.

G., A. "Conservatoire Impérial de Musique, Ier. et IIme. excercises des éleves." *Les tablettes de Polymnie* 2 (20 March 1811): 308–11.

Gäng, Philipp, *Aesthetik oder allgemeine Theorie der schönen Künste und Wissenschaften.* Salzburg: Waisenhausbuchhandlung, 1785.

Gallagher, Catherine. "The History of Literary Criticism." *Daedalus* 126 (1997): 133–53.

Gay, Peter. *The Naked Heart.* New York: W. W. Norton, 1995.

Gelbart, Matthew. *The Invention of "Folk Music" and "Art Music": Emerging Categories from Ossian to Wagner.* Cambridge: Cambridge University Press, 2007.

Gellert, Christian Fürchtegott. *Von dem Einfluss der schönen Wissenschaften* (1756). In his *Sammlung vermischter Schriften,* 2:146–59. 2 vols. Leipzig: M. G. Weidmanns Erben und Reich, 1766.

Gerber, Ernst Ludwig. *Neues historisch-biographisches Lexikon der Tonkünstler.* 4 vols. Leipzig: A. Kühnel, 1812–14.

Gilbert, Alan. "Alan Gilbert on This Program." New York Philharmonic Orchestra Program for 26–28 January, 2012.

Gillmor, Alan. "The Apostasy of George Rochberg." *Intersections* 29 (2009): 32–48.

Gingerich, John M. "Ignaz Schuppanzigh and Beethoven's Late Quartets." *MQ* 93 (2010): 450–513.

Ginguené, Pierre Louis. *Notice sur la vie et les ouvrages de Nicolas Piccinni*. Paris: Veuve Panckoucke, 1800.

Goehr, Lydia. *The Imaginary Museum of Musical Works: An Essay in the Philosophy of Music*. Rev. ed. New York: Oxford University Press, 2007.

Goethe, Johann Wolfgang von. *Briefe*. 4 vols. Edited by Karl Robert Mandelkow. Hamburg: Christian Wegner, 1962–67.

Goethe, Johann Wolfgang von. *Sämtliche Werke nach Epochen seines Schaffens: Münchner Ausgabe*, 21 vols. Edited by Karl Richter et al. Munich: Carl Hanser, 1985.

Goethe, Johann Wolfgang von. *Werke: Hamburger Ausgabe*. 14 vols. Edited by Erich Trunz et al. Munich: Beck, 1981.

Goldberg, Halina. "Chopin's Oneiric Soundscapes and the Role of Dreams in Romantic Culture." In *Chopin and His World*, 15–43. Edited by Jonathan D. Bellman and Halina Goldberg. Princeton, NJ: Princeton University Press, 2017.

Goldstein, Jan. *The Post-Revolutionary Self: Politics and Psyche in France, 1750–1850*. Cambridge, MA: Harvard University Press, 2005.

Görner, Rüdiger. "The Hidden Agent of the Self: Towards an Aesthetic Theory of the Non-Conscious in German Romanticism." In *Thinking the Unconscious: Nineteenth-Century German Thought*, 121–39. Edited by Angus Nicholls and Martin Liebscher. Cambridge: Cambridge University Press, 2010.

Gosse, Edmund. "The Sonnets from the Portuguese." In his *Critical Kit-Kats*, 1–17. New York: Dodd, Mead, 1903.

Gottsched, Johann Christoph. *Versuch einer critischen Dichtkunst*. 4th ed. Leipzig: Breitkopf & Härtel, 1751.

Gracyk, Theodore. *Rhythm and Noise: An Aesthetics of Rock*. Durham, NC: Duke University Press, 1996.

Gramit, David. *Cultivating Music: The Aspirations, Interests, and Limits of German Musical Culture, 1770–1848*. Berkeley and Los Angeles: University of California Press, 2002.

Gramit, David. "Selling the Serious: The Commodification of Music and Resistance to it in Germany, circa 1800." In *The Musician as Entrepreneur, 1700–1914: Managers, Charlatans, and Idealists*, 81–101. Edited by William Weber. Bloomington: Indiana University Press, 2004.

Griesinger, Georg August. *Biographische Notizen über Joseph Haydn*. Leipzig: Breitkopf & Härtel, 1810.

Grove, George. *Beethoven and His Nine Symphonies*. London: Novello, 1896.

Guilhamet, Leon. *The Sincere Ideal: Studies on Sincerity in Eighteenth-Century English Literature*. Montreal: McGill–Queen's University Press, 1974.

Gurney, Edmund. *The Power of Sound*. London: Smith, Elder, 1880.

Guthke, Karl S. *Die Entdeckung des Ich: Studien zur Literatur*. Tübingen: A. Francke, 1993.

Halliwell, Stephen. *The Aesthetics of Mimesis: Ancient Texts and Modern Problems*. Princeton, NJ: Princeton University Press, 2002.

Handwerk, Gary. "Romantic Irony." In *The Cambridge History of Literary Criticism*, vol. 5, *Romanticism*, 203–25. Edited by Marshall Brown. Cambridge: Cambridge University Press, 2000.

Hanslick, Eduard. *Vom Musikalisch-Schönen: Ein Beitrag zur Revision der Ästhetik der Tonkunst*. Leipzig: Rudolph Weigel, 1854.

Harriman-Smith, James. "*Comédien–Actor–Paradoxe*: The Anglo-French Sources of Diderot's *Paradoxe sur le comédien.*" *Theatre Journal* 67 (2015): 83–96.

Härtl, Heinz. "*Drei Briefe von Beethoven*": *Genese und Frührezeption einer Briefkomposition Bettina von Arnims*. Bielefeld: Aisthesis, 2016.

Härtl, Ursula. "Carl Röhlings Bild *Beethoven und Goethe in Teplitz.*" *Neue Zeitung für Einsiedler: Mitteilungen der Internationalen Arnim-Gesellschaft* 10–11 (2010–11): 28–33.

Hass, Hans-Egon. "Über die Ironie bei Goethe." In *Ironie und Dichtung*, 59–83. Edited by Albert Schaefer. Munich: C. H. Beck, 1970.

Hatten, Robert. *A Theory of Virtual Agency for Western Art Music*. Bloomington: Indiana University Press, 2018.

Hausegger, Friedrich von. *Die Musik als Ausdruck*. 2nd ed. Vienna: C. Konegen, 1887.

Haydn, Joseph. *Gesammelte Briefe und Aufzeichnungen*. Edited by Dénes Bartha. Kassel: Bärenreiter, 1965.

Head, Matthew. "C. P. E. Bach 'in tormentis': Gout Pain and Body Language in the Fantasia in A Major, H278 (1782)." *Eighteenth-Century Music* 13 (2016): 211–34.

Hegel, Georg Friedrich Wilehlm. *Vorlesungen über die Aesthetik*. Edited by H. G. Hotho. 3 vols. Berlin: Duncker & Humblot, 1835–38.

Helm, Eugene. The 'Hamlet' Fantasy and the Literary Element in C. P. E. Bach's Music." *MQ* 58 (1972): 277–96.

Henahan, Donal J. "Current Chronicle: United States, Chicago." *MQ* 53 (1967): 246–50.

Herder, Johann Gottfried. *Ideen zur Philosophie der Geschichte der Menschheit*. 4 vols. Riga and Leipzig: Johann Friedrich Hartknoch, 1784–91.

Herder, Johann Gottfried. *Vom Erkennen und Empfinden der menschlichen Seele*. Riga: Johann Friedrich Hartknoch, 1778.

Hertel, Johann Wilhelm. *Autobiographie* (1783). Edited by Erich Schenk. Graz: Hermann Böhlaus Nachfolger, 1957.

Heuß, Alfred. "Allerlei Zeitgemäßes." *NZfM* 95 (1928): 275–78.

Higgins, David Minden. *Romantic Genius and the Literary Magazine: Biography, Celebrity and Politics*. London: Routledge, 2005.

Hildesheimer, Wolfgang. *Mozart*. Translated by Marion Faber. New York: Farrar, Straus and Giroux, 1982.

Hiller, Ferdinand. "Hector Berlioz." *Westermann's illustrirte deutsche Monats-Hefte* 45 (1878–79): 554–93.

Hindemith, Paul. *A Composer's World: Horizons and Limitations*. Cambridge, MA: Harvard University Press, 1952.

Hodgman, Matthew R. "Class, Race, Credibility, and Authenticity within the Hip-Hop Music Genre." *Journal of Sociological Research* 4 (2013): 402–13.

Hoeckner, Berthold. "Poet's Love and Composer's Love." *Music Theory Online* 7, no. 5 (October 2001).

Hoffmann, E. T. A. "Alte und neue Kirchenmusik." *AmZ* 16 (1814): 577–84, 593–603, 611–19.

Hoffmann, E. T. A. "Beethovens Instrumentalmusik" (1813). In his *Fantasiestücke in Callot's Manier*. In his *Sämtliche Werke*, 2/1. Edited by Hartmut Steinecke. Frankfurt am Main: Deutscher Klassiker Verlag, 1993.

Hoffmann, E. T. A. "Deux Trios . . . par Louis van Beethoven. Oeuvr. 70. . . ." *AmZ* 15 (3 March 1813): 141–54.

Hoffmann, E. T. A. "Recension: *Messa a quattro voci . . . da Luigi van Beethoven. . . .*" *AmZ* 15 (1813): 389–97, 408–14.

Hoffmann, E. T. A. "Recension: *Ouverture d'Egmont etc. par L. van Beethoven . . . Op. 84. . . .*" *AmZ* 15 (21 July 1813): 473–81.

Hoffmann, E. T. A. "Recension: *Sinfonie . . . par Louis van Beethoven . . . Oeuvre 67 . . .*" *AmZ* 12 (1810): 630–42, 652–59.

Hoffmann, E. T. A. "Ueber einen Ausspruch Sacchini's, und über den sogenannten Effect in der Musik." *AmZ* 16 (20 July 1814): 477–85.

Holoman, D. Kern. *Berlioz.* Cambridge, MA: Harvard University Press, 1989.

Holmes, Edward. *The Life of Mozart.* New York: Harper & Brothers, 1845.

Horace. *Satires, Epistles, Art of Poetry.* Rev. ed. Translated by H. Rushton Fairclough. Cambridge, MA: Harvard University Press, 1929.

Horlacher, Rebekka. *The Educated Subject and the German Concept of* Bildung: *A Comparative Cultural History.* New York: Routledge, 2016.

Hugo, Victor. "Littérature: *Eloa ou La soeur des anges . . . par Le comte Alfred de Vigny . . .*" (1824). In *La muse française, 1823–1824: Édition critique.* Edited by Jules Marsan, 2 vols., 2:247–58. Paris: Société nouvelle de Librairie et d'Édition, 1909.

Hugo, Victor. *Notre-Dame de Paris.* 2 vols. Paris: Eugène Hugues, 1832.

Hume, David. *A Treatise of Human Nature* (1738–40). Edited by David Fate Norton and Mary J. Norton. 2 vols. Oxford: Clarendon Press, 2007.

Hunter, Mary. "'To Play as if from the Soul of the Composer': The Idea of the Performer in Early Romantic Aesthetics." *JAMS* 58 (2005): 357–98.

d'Indy, Vincent. *Cours de composition musicale.* Edited by Auguste Sérieyx and Guy de Lioncourt. 3 vols. Paris: Durand, 1903–50.

Izenberg, Gerald. *Impossible Individuality: Romanticism, Revolution, and the Origins of Modern Selfhood.* Princeton, NJ: Princeton University Press, 1992.

Jahn, Otto. *W. A. Mozart.* 4 vols. Leipzig: Breitkopf & Härtel, 1856–59.

Jahn, Otto. *W. A. Mozart.* 2 vols. 2nd ed. Leipzig: Breitkopf & Härtel, 1867.

Joachimson, Felix. "Beethoven in der Meinung der jungen Musiker: Eine Rundfrage." *Die literarische Welt* 12, no. 3 (25 March 1927): 3–4.

Johnson, Douglas. "Beethoven Scholars and Beethoven's Sketches." *19CM* 2 (1978): 3–17.

Johnson, Douglas, Alan Tyson, and Robert Winter. *The Beethoven Sketchbooks: History, Reconstruction, Inventory.* Berkeley and Los Angeles: University of California Press, 1985.

Johnson, James H. *Listening in Paris: A Cultural Hisory.* Berkeley and Los Angeles: University of California Press, 1996.

Johnson, Julian. *Mahler's Voices: Expression and Irony in the Songs and Symphonies.* New York: Oxford University Press, 2009.

Johnston, Kenneth R. *The Hidden Wordsworth: Poet, Lover, Rebel, Spy.* New York: W. W. Norton, 1998.

Jost, Peter. "Vom Musicus zum Tondichter: Wandlungen des Komponisten-Bildes um 1800." In *Aufbrüche—Fluchtwege: Musik in Weimar um 1800,* 73–84. Edited by Helen Geyer and Thomas Radecke. Cologne: Böhlau, 2003.

Junker, Carl Ludwig. *Tonkunst.* Bern: Typographische Gesellschaft, 1777.

Junker, Carl Ludwig. *Zwanzig Componisten: Eine Skizze.* Bern: Typographische Gesellschaft, 1776.

Kahl, Willi. *Selbstbiographien deutscher Musiker des XVIII. Jahrhunderts.* Cologne: Staufen, 1948.

Kallberg, Jeffrey. "Chopin's March, Chopin's Death." *19CM* 25 (2001): 3–26.

Kallberg, Jeffrey. "Hearing Poland: Chopin and Nationalism." In *Nineteenth-Century Piano Music,* 221–57. Edited by R. Larry Todd. 2nd ed. New York: Routledge, 2004

Kallberg, Jeffrey. "Sex, Sexuality, and Schubert's Piano Music." In *Historical Musicology: Sources, Methods, Interpretations*, 219–31. Edited by Stephen A. Crist and Roberta Montemorra Marvin. Rochester, NY: University of Rochester Press, 2004.

Kaiser, Gerhard. *Geschichte der deutschen Lyrik: Ein Grundriß in Interpretationen.* 3 vols. Frankfurt am Main: Suhrkamp, 1988.

Kalbeck, Max. *Johannes Brahms.* 4 vols. Vienna: Wiener Verlag, 1904–14.

Kaltenecker, Martin. "The 'Fantasy-Principle': Improvisation between Imagination and Oration in the Eighteenth Century." In *Beyond Notes: Improvisation in Western Music of the Eighteenth and Nineteenth Centuries*, 17–34. Edited by Rudolf Rasch. Turnhout: Brepols, 2011.

Kaltenecker, Martin. *L'oreille divisée: Les discours sur l'écoute musicale aux XVIIIe et XIXe siècles.* Paris: Éditions MF, 2010.

Kandinsky, Wassily. *Über das Geistige in der Kunst, insbesondere in der Malerei.* 3rd ed. Munich: Piper, 1912.

Kanne, Friedrich August. "Akademie, des Lud. van Beethoven." *Allgemeine Musikalische Zeitung, mit besonderer Rücksicht auf den österreichischen Kaiserstaat* 8 (1824): 149–51, 157–60, 173–74.

Kant, Immanuel. *Critique of the Power of Judgment.* Edited by Paul Guyer. Translated by Paul Guyer and Eric Matthews. Cambridge: Cambridge University Press, 2000.

Kant, Immanuel. *Gesammelte Schriften.* Edited by the Königlich-Preussische Akademie der Wissenschaften zu Berlin. Berlin: G. Reimer, 1902–.

Kant, Immanuel. *Kritik der Urteilskraft* (1790). Edited by Heiner F. Klemme. Hamburg: Felix Meiner, 2001.

Kapp, Reinhard. "Zur Geschichte des musikalischen Ausdrucks." In *Beiträge zur Interpretationsästhetik und zur Hermeneutik-Diskussion*, 143–79. Edited by Claus Bockmaier. Laaber: Laaber-Verlag, 2009.

Karl, Gregory, and Jenefer Robinson. "Shostakovich's Tenth Symphony and the Musical Expression of Cognitively Complex Emotions." *Journal of Aesthetics and Art Criticism* 53 (1995): 401–15.

Kearney, Richard. *The Wake of Imagination: Ideas of Creativity in Western Culture.* London: Hutchinson, 1988.

Keats, John. *Selected Letters.* Rev. ed. Edited by Grant Scott. Cambridge, MA: Harvard University Press, 2002.

Keble, John. "Life of Sir Walter Scott." In his *Occasional Papers and Reviews*, 1–80. Oxford and London: James Parker, 1877.

Keefe, Simon. *Mozart's Requiem: Reception, Work, Completion.* Cambridge: Cambridge University Press, 2012.

Kennedy, Michael. *Portrait of Elgar.* 2nd ed. London: Oxford University Press, 1982.

Kiesewetter, Raphael Georg. *Geschichte der europäisch-abendländischen oder unsrer heutigen Musik.* Leipzig: Breitkopf & Härtel, 1834.

Kind, John Lewis. *Edward Young in Germany.* New York: Macmillan, 1906.

Kinderman, William. *Beethoven.* 2nd ed. New York: Oxford University Press, 2009.

Kivy, Peter. *The Possessor and the Possessed: Handel, Mozart, Beethoven, and the Idea of Musical Genius.* New Haven, CT: Yale University Press, 2001.

Klemm, David E., and Günter Zöller, eds. *Figuring the Self: Subject, Absolute, and Others in Classical German Philosophy.* Albany: State University of New York Press, 1997.

Klein, Michael L. *Music and the Crises of the Modern Subject.* Bloomington: Indiana University Press, 2015.

Klorman, Edward. *Mozart's Music of Friends: Social Interplay in the Chamber Works.* Cambridge: Cambridge University Press, 2016.

Knapp, Raymond. " '*Selbst dann bin ich die Welt*': On the Subjective-Musical Basis of Wagner's *Gesamtkunstwelt.*" *19CM* 29 (2005): 142–160.

Kneller, Jane. *Kant and the Power of Imagination.* Cambridge: Cambridge University Press, 2007.

Koch, Heinrich Christoph. *Kurzgefasstes Handwörterbuch der Musik.* Leipzig: Johann Friedrich Hartknoch, 1807.

Koch, Heinrich Christoph. *Musikalisches Lexikon.* Frankfurt am Main: Johann André, 1802.

Koch, Heinrich Christoph. *Versuch einer Anleitung zur Composition.* 3 vols. Rudolstadt: Löwesche Erben und Schirach; Leipzig: Böhme, 1782–93.

Kohl, Katrin. "No Escape? Goethe's Strategies of Self-Projection and Their Role in German Literary Historiography." *Goethe Yearbook* 16 (2009): 173–91.

Konrad, Ulrich. *Mozarts Schaffensweise: Studien zu den Werkautographen, Skizzen und Entwürfen.* Göttingen: Vandenhoeck & Ruprecht, 1992.

Kopitz, Klaus Martin, and Rainer Cadenbach, eds. *Beethoven aus der Sicht seiner Zeitgenossen in Tagebüchern, Briefen, Gedichten und Erinnerungen.* 2 vols. Munich: G. Henle, 2009.

Köpke, Rudolf. *Ludwig Tieck: Erinnerungen aus dem Leben des Dichters nach dessen mündlichen und schriftlichen Mittheilungen.* 2 vols. Leipzig: F. A. Brockhaus, 1855.

Kramer, Lawrence. *Franz Schubert: Sexuality, Subjectivity, Song.* Cambridge: Cambridge University Press, 1998.

Kramer, Lawrence. *Musical Meaning: Toward a Critical History.* Berkeley: University of California Press, 2002.

Kramer, Richard. "Diderot's *Paradoxe* and C. P. E. Bach's *Empfindungen.*" In *C. P. E. Bach Studies*, 6–24. Edited by Annette Richards. Cambridge: Cambridge University Press, 2006.

Kramer, Richard. "Improvisatori. Improvisiren. Improviser . . . " *AfMw* 73 (2016): 2–8.

Kraus, Beate Angelika. "Beethoven and the Revolution: The View of the French Musical Press." In *Music and the French Revolution*, 302–14. Edited by Malcolm Boyd. Cambridge: Cambridge University Press, 1992.

Kraus, Joseph Martin. "Ausdruck." In his *Wahrheiten die Musik betreffend*, 96–117. Frankfurt am Main: Eichenbergsche Erben, 1779.

Kretzschmar, Hermann. "Anregungen zur Förderung musikalischer Hermeneutik." *Jahrbuch der Musikbibliothek Peters* 9 (1902): 47–66.

Kretzschmar, Hermann. *Führer durch den Konzertsaal.* 3 vols. Leipzig: Liebeskind, 1887–90.

Kreuzer, Gundula. "*Heilige Trias, Stildualismus,* Beethoven: On the Limits of Nineteenth-Century Germanic Music Historiography." In *The Invention of Beethoven and Rossini: Historiography, Analysis, Criticism*, 66–95. Edited by Nicholas Mathew and Benjamin Walton. Cambridge: Cambridge University Press, 2013.

Kuhn, Thomas. *The Structure of Scientific Revolutions.* 3rd ed. Chicago: University of Chicago Press, 1996.

Kunze, Stefan, ed. *Ludwig van Beethoven: Die Werke im Spiegel seiner Zeit.* Laaber: Laaber-Verlag, 1987.

Kurz, Gerhard. "Alte, neue, altneue Hermeneutik: Überlegungen zu den Normen romantischer Hermeneutik." In *Krisen des Verstehens um 1800*, 31–54. Edited by Sandra Heinen and Harald Nehr. Würzburg: Königshausen & Neumann, 2004.

Lachenmann, Helmut. "Musik als Abbild vom Menschen." In his *Musik als existentielle Erfahrung: Schriften 1966–1995*, 111–15. Edited by Josef Häusler. 2nd ed. Wiesbaden: Breitkopf & Härtel, 2004.

Lam, Basil. *Beethoven String Quartets 2*. London: British Broadcasting Corporation, 1975.

La Mara [Lipsius, Ida Marie]. *Musikalische Studienköpfe*. Leipzig: Hermann Weißbach, 1868.

Lamartine, Alphonse de. *Harmonies poétiques et religieuses*. Paris: Charles Gosselin, 1830.

Le Huray, Peter, and James Day, eds. *Music and Aesthetics in the Eighteenth and Early Nineteenth Centuries*. Cambridge: Cambridge University Press, 1981.

Leistra-Jones, Karen. "Staging Authenticity: Joachim, Brahms, and the Politics of *Werktreue* Performance." *JAMS* 66 (2013): 397–436.

Lenneberg, Hans. "Revising the History of the Miniature Score." *Notes* 45 (1988): 258–61.

Lenz, Wihelm von. *Beethoven: Eine Kunststudie*. 4 vols. Kassel: Ernst Balde; Hamburg: Hoffmann & Campe, 1855–60.

Lenz, Wihelm von. *Die grossen Pianoforte-Virtuosen unserer Zeit aus persönlicher Bekanntschaft*. Berlin: B. Behr, 1872.

Lesser, Wendy. *Music for Silenced Voices: Shostakovich and His Fifteen Quartets*. New Haven, CT: Yale University Press, 2011.

Lessing, Gotthold Ephraim. *Werke*. Edited by Jost Perfahl. 3 vols. Munich: Winkler, 1969.

Leventhal, Robert S. *The Disciplines of Interpretation: Lessing, Herder, Schlegel and Hermeneutics in Germany, 1750–1800*. Berlin and New York: Walter de Gruyter, 1994.

Levy, David B. "Early Performances of Beethoven's Ninth Symphony: A Study of Five Cities." Ph.D. diss., University of Rochester, Eastman School of Music, 1980.

Liebert, Andreas. *Die Bedeutung des Wertesystems der Rhetorik für das deutsche Musikdenken im 18. und 19. Jahrhundert*. Frankfurt am Main: Peter Lang, 1993.

Lilti, Antoine. *The Invention of Celebrity, 1750–1850*. Translated by Lynn Jeffress. Cambridge: Polity, 2017.

Liszt, Franz. *F. Chopin*. Paris: M. Escudier, 1852.

Liszt, Franz. *The Life of Chopin*. Translated by Martha Walker Cook. 4th ed. Boston: O. Ditson, 1863.

Liszt, Franz. "Marx und die Musik des neunzehnten Jahrhunderts." *NZfM* 42 (1855): 213–21, 225–30.

Lobe, Johann Christian. *Aus dem Leben eines Musikers*. Leipzig: J. J. Weber, 1859.

Lochhead, Judy. "Refiguring the Modernist Program for Hearing: Steve Reich and George Rochberg." In *The Pleasure of Modernist Music*, 325–44. Edited by Arved Ashby." Rochester, NY: University of Rochester Press, 2004.

Lockwood, Lewis. *Beethoven: The Music and the Life*. New York: W. W. Norton, 2003.

Lockwood, Lewis. "Beethoven's Sketches: The State of our Knowledge." http://www.bu.edu/beethovencenter/beethovens-sketches-the-state-of-our-knowledge/

Lodes, Birgit. " 'Von Herzen—möge es wieder—zu Herzen gehn': Zur Widmung von Beethovens Missa solemnis." In *Altes im Neuen: Festschrift Theodor Göllner zum 65. Geburtstag*, 295–306. Edited by Bernd Edelmann and Manfred Hermann Schmid. Tutzing: Hans Schneider, 1995.

Loesch, Heinz von. "Tschaikowskys *Pathétique*: Lebenssymphonie oder schwules Bekenntniswerk? Ein kurzer kommentierter Literaturbericht." In *Musik und Biographie: Festschrift für Rainer Cadenbach*, 344–51. Edited by Cordula Heymann-Wentzel and Johannes Laas. Würzburg: Königshausen & Neumann, 2004.

Loh, Maria. *Still Lives: Death, Desire, and the Portrait of the Old Master*. Princeton, NJ: Princeton University Press, 2015.

Loos, Helmut. "Arnold Schmitz as Beethoven Scholar: A Reassessment." *Journal of Musicological Research* 32 (2013): 150–62.

Loughridge, Deirdre. "Magnified Vision, Mediated Listening and the 'Point of Audition' of Early Romanticism." *18th-Century Music* 10 (2013): 179–211.

Lühning, Helga. "'. . . an diesem geht die ganze Welt auf und nieder': Bettine Brentano zwischen Beethoven und Goethe." In *Goethe und die Musik*, 145–65. Edited by Walter Hettche and Rolf Selbmann. Würzburg: Königshausen und Neumann, 2012.

Lukes, Steven. *Individualism*. New York: Harper & Row, 1973.

Luserke-Jaqui, Matthias, ed. *Handbuch Sturm und Drang*. Boston: Walter de Gruyter, 2017.

Lütteken, Laurenz. *Das Monologische als Denkform in der Musik zwischen 1760 und 1785*. Tübingen: Niemeyer, 1998.

Maass, Johann Gebhard Ehrenreich. "Ueber die Instrumentalmusik." *Neue Bibliothek der schönen Wissenschaften* 48 (1792): 3–40.

Macaulay, Thomas Babington. Review of John Milton, *A Treatise on Christian Doctrine . . . translated from the original by Charles R. Sumner. Edinburgh Review* 42 (1825): 304–46.

McAuley, Tomas George. "The Impact of German Idealism on Musical Thought, 1781–1803." Ph.D. diss., King's College London, 2013.

MacAuslan, John. *Schumann's Music and E. T. A. Hoffmann's Fiction*. Cambridge: Cambridge University Press, 2016.

McCarthy, John A. *Crossing Boundaries: A Theory and History of Essay Writing in German, 1680–1815*. Philadelphia: University of Pennsylvania Press, 1989.

McClary, Susan. "Constructions of Subjectivity in Schubert's Music." In *Queering the Pitch: The New Gay and Lesbian Musicology*, 205–33. Edited by Philip Brett, Elizabeth Wood, and Gary C. Thomas. New York: Routledge, 1994.

McClary, Susan. *Modal Subjectivities: Self-Fashioning in the Italian Madrigal*. Berkeley and Los Angeles: University of California Press, 2004.

McColl, Sandra. *Music Criticism in Vienna, 1896–1897: Critically Moving Forms*. Oxford: Clarendon, 1996.

McGann, Jerome J. *The Romantic Ideology: A Critical Investigation*. Chicago: University of Chicago Press, 1983.

Magill, R. Jay, Jr. *Sincerity*. New York: W. W. Norton, 2012.

Mahler, Gustav. *Briefe*. Edited by Herta Blaukopf. 2nd ed. Vienna: P. Zsolnay, 1996.

Mainwaring, John. *Memoirs of the Life of the Late George Frideric Handel*. London: R. and J. Dodsley, 1760.

Makari, George. *Soul Machine: The Invention of the Modern Mind*. New York: W. W. Norton, 2015.

Mariner, Francis. "From Portraiture to Reverie: Rousseau's Autobiographical Framing." *South Atlantic Review* 57 (1992): 15–31.

Marpurg, Friedrich Wilhelm. "Anmerkungen über den Anhang etc. des Herrn Weitzler." *Historisch-kritische Beiträge zur Aufnahme der Musik* 3 (1757): 107–23.

Martin, Peter. *Edmond Malone, Shakespearean Scholar: A Literary Biography*. Cambridge: Cambridge University Press, 1995.

Martin, Raymond, and John Barresi. *The Rise and Fall of the Soul and Self: An Intellectual History of Personal Identity*. New York: Columbia University Press, 2006.

Marx, Adolph Bernhard. "Als Recension der Sonate Op. 111 von L. van Beethoven . . . Brief eines Recensenten an den Redakteur." *BAmZ* 1 (17 March 1824): 95–99.

Marx, Adolph Bernhard. *Die alte Musiklehre im Streit mit unserer Zeit*. Leipzig: Breitkopf & Härtel, 1841.

Marx, Adolph Bernhard. "Beurtheilungen. Quatuor pour 2 Violins, Alto et Violoncelle par L. van Beethoven. Oeuvr. 135." *BAmZ* 6 (30 May 1829): 169–70.

Marx, Adolph Bernhard. "Erstes grosses Konzert im Winterhalbenjahre 1825–26, in Berlin." *BAmZ* 2 (9 November 1825): 364–66.

Marx, Adolph Bernhard. "Louis van Beethoven: Esquisse biographique." *Gazette musicale de Paris* 1 (21 December 1834): 405–09.

Marx, Adolph Bernhard. *Ludwig van Beethoven: Leben und Schaffen*. 2 vols. Berlin: Otto Janke, 1859.

Marx, Adolph Bernhard. *Ludwig van Beethoven: Leben und Schaffen*. 2 vols. 2nd ed. Berlin: Otto Janke, 1863.

Marx, Adolph Bernhard. "Recensionen: Sonate für das Pianoforte von Ludwig van Beethoven. 110tes Werk." *BAmZ* 1 (10 March 1824): 87–90.

Marx, Adolph Bernhard. "Recensionen: Symphonie mit Schlusschor . . . von Ludwig van Beethoven, 125tes Werk." *BAmZ* 3 (22 November 1826): 373–78.

Marx, Adolph Bernhard. *Ueber Malerei in der Tonkunst: Ein Maigruß an die Kunstphilosophen*. Berlin: G. Fink, 1828.

Marx, Wolfgang. "Ligeti's Musical Style as Expression of Cultural Trauma." In *György Ligeti's Cultural Identities*, 74–91. Edited by Amy Bauer and Márton Kerékfy. New York: Routledge, 2018.

Massow, Albrecht von. *Musikalisches Subjekt: Idee und Erscheinung in der Moderne*. Freiburg: Rombach, 2001.

Mathew, Nicholas. *Political Beethoven*. Cambridge: Cambridge University Press, 2013.

Mattheson, Johann. *Der vollkommene Capellmeister*. Hamburg: Herold, 1739; repr., Kassel: Bärenreiter, 1954.

Maus, Fred. "Agency in Instrumental Music and Song." *College Music Symposium* 29 (1989), 31–43.

Maus, Fred. "Music as Drama." *Music Theory Spectrum* 10 (1988): 56–73.

Meisner, Sanford, and Dennis Longwell. *Sanford Meisner on Acting*. New York: Vintage, 1987.

Mersmann, Hans. *Beethoven: Die Synthese der Stile*. Berlin: Julius Bard, 1922.

Messiaen, Olivier. "Le rhythme chez Igor Strawinsky." *Revue musicale* 20 (May–June 1939): 91–92.

Messing, Scott. *Neoclassicism in Music: From the Genesis of the Concept through the Schoenberg/Stravinsky Polemic*. Rochester, NY: University of Rochester Press, 1996.

Michaelis, Christian Friedrich. "Ueber das Humoristische oder Launige in der musikalischen Komposition." *AmZ* 9 (12 August 1807): 725–29.

Milewski, Barbara. "Chopin's Mazurkas and the Myth of the Folk." *19CM* 23 (1999): 113–35.

Mill, John Stuart. *Essays on Poetry*. Edited by F. Parvin Sharless. Columbia: University of South Carolina Press, 1976.

Millán-Zaibert, Elizabeth. *Friedrich Schlegel and the Emergence of Romantic Philosophy*. Albany: State University of New York Press, 2007.

Millgram, Elijah. "Was Hume a Humean?" *Hume Studies* 21 (1995): 75–93.

Miltitz, Carl Borromäus von. "Ueber musikalische Begeisterung." *AmZ* 36 (2 April 1834): 213–18.

Mirka, Danuta, ed. *The Oxford Handbook of Topic Theory*. New York: Oxford University Press, 2016.

Mole, Tom, ed. *Romanticism and Celebrity Culture, 1750–1850*. Cambridge: Cambridge University Press, 2009.

Monahan, Seth. "Action and Agency Revisited." *Journal of Music Theory* 57 (2013): 321–71.

Monahan, Seth. " 'I Have Tried to Capture You . . . ': Rethinking the 'Alma' Theme from Mahler's Sixth Symphony." *JAMS* 64 (2011): 119–78.

Moritz, Karl Philipp. *Über die bildende Nachahmung des Schönen*. Braunschweig: Schul-Buchhandlung, 1788.

Morrow, Mary Sue. *German Music Criticism in the Late Eighteenth Century: Aesthetic Issues in Instrumental Music*. Cambridge: Cambridge University Press, 1997.

Mozart, Wolfgang Amadeus. *Briefe und Aufzeichnungen*. Rev. ed. Edited by Wilhelm A. Bauer, Otto Erich Deutsch, and Ulrich Konrad. 7 vols. Kassel: Bärenreiter, 2005.

Müller, Adam. "Die Lehre vom Gegensatze" (1804). In his *Kritische, ästhetische und philosophische Schriften*, 2:193–248. Edited by Walter Schroeder and Werner Siebert. 2 vols. Berlin: Luchterhand, 1967.

Murray, Penelope, ed. *Genius: The History of an Idea*. Oxford: Basil Blackwell, 1989.

Nägeli, Hans-Georg. *Vorlesungen über Musik, mit Berücksichtigung der Dilettanten*. Stuttgart and Tübingen: Cotta, 1826.

Neefe, Christian Gottlob. "Ueber die musikalische Wiederholung." *Deutsches Museum* 2 (1776): 745–51.

Newcomb, Anthony. "Once More 'Between Absolute and Program Music': Schumann's Second Symphony." *19CM* 7 (1984): 233–250.

Newcomb, Anthony. "Schumann and the Marketplace: From Butterflies to *Hausmusik*." In *Nineteenth-Century Piano Music*, 258–315. Edited by R. Larry Todd. 2nd ed. New York: Routledge, 2004.

Nicholls, Angus. *Goethe's Concept of the Daemonic: After the Ancients*. Rochester, NY: Camden House, 2006.

Nicholls, Angus, and Martin Liebscher, eds. *Thinking the Unconscious: Nineteenth-Century German Thought*. Cambridge: Cambridge University Press, 2010.

Niemetschek, Franz. *Leben des k.k. Kapellmeisters Wolfgang Gottlieb Mozart, nach Originalquellen beschrieben*. Prague: Herrlische Buchhandlung, 1798.

Nietzsche, Friedrich. *Zur Genealogie der Moral* (1887). In his *Sämtliche Werke*, 15 vols., 5:245–412. Edited by Giorgio Colli and Mazzino Montinari. Munich: Deutscher Taschenbuch Verlag, 1980.

Nissen, Georg von. *Biographie W. A. Mozarts*. Leipzig: Breitkopf und Härtel, 1828.

Nivelle, Armand. *Kunst- und Dichtungstheorien zwischen Aufklärung und Klassik*. 2nd ed. Berlin: Walter de Gruyter, 1971.

Noack, Friedrich. "Eine Briefsammlung aus der ersten Hälfte des 19. Jahrhunderts." *AfMw* 10 (1953): 323–37.

Nohl, Ludwig. *Die Beethoven-Feier und die Kunst der Gegenwart*. Vienna: Wilhelm Braumüller, 1871.

Nohl, Ludwig. *Beethovens Leben*. 4 vols. Vienna: Hermann Markgraf, 1864–77.

Nohl, Ludwig. *Mozart*. Stuttgart: Friedrich Bruckmann, 1863.

Nono, Luigi. Liner notes to his . . . *sofferte onde serene*. . . . DG 2531 004. Polydor, 1979.

Notley, Margaret. "Late Nineteenth-Century Chamber Music and the Cult of the Classical Adagio." *19CM* 23 (1999): 33–61.

Nottebohm, Gustav. *Ein Skizzenbuch von Beethoven*. Leipzig: Breitkopf & Härtel, 1865.

Novalis [Friedrich von Hardenberg]. *Schriften*. Edited by Paul Kluckhohn and Richard Samuel. 4 vols. 2nd ed. Stuttgart: W. Kohlhammer, 1977.

Novello, Vincent, and Mary Novello. *A Mozart Pilgrimage, Being the Travel Diaries of Vincent and Mary Novello in the Year 1829.* Edited by Rosemary Hughes. London: Novello, 1955.

Nüsslein, Franz Anton. *Lehrbuch der Kunstwissenschaft zum Gebrauche bei Vorlesungen.* Landshut: Philipp Krüll, 1819.

Orlova, Alexandra. *Tchaikovsky: A Self-Portrait.* Translated by R. M. Davison. Oxford: Oxford University Press, 1990.

Ortega y Gasset, José. *The Dehumanization of Art and Other Essays on Art, Culture, and Literature.* Translated by Helen Weyl. 2nd ed. Princeton, NJ: Princeton University Press, 1968,

Ortega y Gasset, José. *La deshumanización del arte* (1925). Edited by Valeriano Bozal. Madrid: Espasa-Calpe, 1987.

Ortlepp, Ernst. *Beethoven: Eine phantastische Charakteristik.* Leipzig: Johann Friedrich Hartknoch, 1836.

d'Ortigue, Joseph. "Du mouvement et de la résistance en musique" (1841). In his *Écrits sur la musique 1827-1846*, 231–38. Edited by Sylvia L'Écuyer. Paris: Société française de musicologie, 2003.

d'Ortigue, Joseph. "Grand concert dramatique de M. Berlioz." *Gazette musicale de Paris* 2 (10 May 1833): 159–61.

Oulibicheff, Alexandre. *Beethoven: Ses critiques et ses glossateurs.* Leipzig: Brockhaus, 1857.

Oulibicheff, Alexandre. *Nouvelle biographie de Mozart.* 3 vols. Moscow: Auguste Semen, 1843.

Paddison, Max. "Mimesis and the Aesthetics of Musical Expression." *Music Analysis* 29 (2010): 126–48.

Painter, Karen. "W. A. Mozart's Beethovenian Afterlife: Biography and Musical Interpretation in the Twilight of Idealism." In *Late Thoughts: Reflections on Artists and Composers at Work*, 116–43. Edited by Karen Painter and Thomas Crow. Los Angeles: Getty Research Institute, 2006.

Panofka, Heinrich. "Aus Paris: Ueber Berlioz und seine Kompositionen." *NZfM* 2 (17 February and 3 March 1835): 67–69, 71–72.

Panofka, Heinrich. "Correspondence particulière." *Revue et gazette musicale de Paris* 4 (27 August 1837): 390–91.

Pärt, Arvo. "Acceptance Speech for the International Bridge Prize of the European City of Görlitz." In *The Cambridge Companion to Arvo Pärt*, 200–201. Edited by Andrew Shenton. Cambridge: Cambridge University Press, 2012.

Pasler, Jann. "The Ironies of Gender, or Virility and Politics in the Music of Augusta Holmès." *Women & Music* 2 (1998): 1–25.

Paulin, Roger. *The Critical Reception of Shakespeare in Germany 1682-1914: Native Literature and Foreign Genius.* Hildesheim: Georg Olms, 2003.

Pederson, Sanna. "Beethoven and Masculinity." In *Beethoven and his World*, 313–31. Edited by Scott Burnham and Michael P. Steinberg. Princeton, NJ: Princeton University Press, 2000.

Pekacz, Jolanta T. "Deconstructing a 'National Composer': Chopin and Polish Exiles in Paris, 1831-49." *19CM* 24 (2000): 161–72.

Pekacz, Jolanta T., ed. *Musical Biography: Towards New Paradigms.* Aldershot: Ashgate, 2006.

Peraino, Judith A. *Giving Voice to Love: Song and Self-Expression from the Troubadours to Guillaume de Machaut.* New York: Oxford University Press, 2011.

Perkins, David. *Wordsworth and the Poetry of Sincerity*. Cambridge, MA: Harvard University Press, 1964.

Perle, George. *Style and Idea in the "Lyric Suite" of Alban Berg*. Rev. ed. Hillsdale, NY: Pendragon Press, 2001.

Perry, Seamus. "New Impressions VII: *The Mirror and the Lamp*." *Essays in Criticism* 54 (2004): 260–82.

Peyre, Henri. *Literature and Sincerity*. New Haven, CT: Yale University Press, 1963.

Pinkard, Terry. *German Philosophy, 1760–1860: The Legacy of Idealism*. Cambridge: Cambridge University Press, 2002.

Plato. *Republic*. Translated by G. M. A. Grube. Revised by C. D. C. Reeve. In Plato, *Complete Works*, 971–1223. Edited by John M. Cooper. Indianapolis: Hackett, 1997.

Plebuch, Tobias. "Dark Fantasies of the Dawn of the Self: Gerstenberg's Monologues for C. P. E. Bach's C minor Fantasia." In *C. P. E. Bach Studies*, 25–66. Edited by Annette Richards. Cambridge: Cambridge University Press, 2006.

Podewski, Madleen. "Konzeptionen des Unverständlichen um und nach 1800: Friedrich Schlegel und Heinrich Heine." In *Krisen des Verstehens um 1800*, 55–73. Edited by Sandra Heinen and Harald Nehr. Würzburg: Königshausen & Neumann, 2004.

Poe, Edgar Allan. "The Philosophy of Composition." *Graham's Magazine* 28 (April 1846): 163–67.

Pryer, Anthony. "Hanslick, Legal Processes, and Scientific Methodologies: How Not to Construct an Ontology of Music." In *Rethinking Hanslick: Music, Formalism, and Expression*, 52–69. Edited by Nicole Grimes, Siobhán Donovan, and Wolfgang Marx. Rochester, NY: University of Rochester Press, 2013.

Quantz, Johann Joachim. *Versuch einer Anweisung die Flöte traversiere zu spielen*. Berlin: J. F. Voss, 1752.

Quillin, Jessica K. *Shelley and the Musico-Poetics of Romanticism*. Farnham, Surrey: Ashgate, 2012.

Quintilian. *Institutio oratoria*. Translated by H. E. Butler. , 4 vols. Cambridge, MA: Harvard University Press, 1946.

Rameau, Jean-Philippe. *Traité de l'harmonie*. Paris: Ballard, 1722.

Rebs, Christian Gottlob. "Ueber mehrere Musikaufführungen in Leipzig." *BAmZ* 3 (1826): 203–4, 213–17, 225–28, 248–49.

Reckwitz, Andreas. *Das hybride Subjekt: Eine Theorie der Subjektkulturen von der bürgerlichen Moderne zur Postmoderne*. Weilerswist: Velbrück, 2006.

Reed, Edward S. *From Soul to Mind: The Emergence of Psychology, from Erasmus Darwin to William James*. New Haven, CT: Yale University Press, 1997.

Reichardt, Johann Friedrich. *Briefe eines aufmerksamen Reisenden die Musik betreffend*. 2 vols. Frankfurt am Main and Leipzig: n. p., 1774–76.

Reichardt, Johann Friedrich. *Vertraute Briefe, geschrieben auf einer Reise nach Wien und den oesterreichischen Staaten zu Ende des Jahres 1808 und zu Anfang 1809*. 2 vols. Amsterdam: Kunst- und Industrie-Comptoir, 1810.

Reichardt, Sarah. *Composing the Modern Subject: Four String Quartets by Dmitri Shostakovich*. Aldershot: Ashgate, 2008.

Reid, Charles. *The Music Monster: A Biography of James William Davison, Music Critic of "The Times" of London, 1846–78*. London: Quartet Books, 1984.

Rellstab, Ludwig. "Ueber Beethovens neuestes Quartett." *BAmZ* 2 (25 May 1825): 165–66.

Reynolds, Christopher. *Motives for Allusion: Context and Content in Nineteenth-Century Music*. Cambridge, MA: Harvard University Press, 2003.

Richards, Annette. *The Free Fantasia and the Musical Picturesque*. Cambridge: Cambridge University Press, 2001.

Richter, Jean Paul Friedrich. *Vorschule der Ästhetik*, 2 vols. Hamburg: Friedrich Perthes, 1804.

Richter, Jean Paul Friedrich. *Vorschule der Ästhetik*. 2 vols. 2nd ed. Stuttgart: J. G. Cotta, 1813.

Riezler, Walter. *Beethoven*. Berlin and Zurich: Atlantis, 1936.

Rihm, Wolfgang. "'Im Innersten,' Drittes Streichquartett (1976)." In his *Ausgesprochen: Schriften und Gespräche*, 2:303–6. Edited by Ulrich Mosch. 2 vols. Winterthur: Amadeus, 1997.

Riley, Matthew. *Musical Listening in the German Enlightenment: Attention, Wonder and Astonishment*. Aldershot: Ashgate, 2004.

Roach, Joseph. *The Player's Passion: Studies in the Science of Acting*. Newark: University of Delaware Press, 1985.

Rochberg, George. *The Aesthetics of Survival: A Composer's View of Twentieth-Century Music*. Revised and expanded ed. Ann Arbor: University of Michigan Press, 2004.

Rochberg, George. "Notes by the Composer." In Joan DeVee Dixon, *George Rochberg: A Bio-Bibliographic Guide to His Life and Works*, 103–5. Stuyvesant, NY: Pendragon Press, 1992.

Rochberg, George, and Istvan Anhalt. *Eagle Minds: Selected Correspondence of Istvan Anhalt and George Rochberg (1961–2005)*. Edited by Alan M. Gillmor. Waterloo, Ontario: Wilfrid Laurier University Press, 2007.

Rochlitz, Friedrich. "Der Besuch im Irrenhaus." *AmZ* 6 (1804): 645–54, 661–72, 677–85, 693–706.

Rochlitz, Friedrich. "Den Freunden Beethovens." *AmZ* 29 (17 October 1827): 705–10.

Rochlitz, Friedrich. "Noch einige Kleinigkeiten aus Mozarts Leben, von seiner Witwe mitgeteilt." *AmZ* 1 (11 September 1799): 854–56.

Rochlitz, Friedrich. "Über den zweckmässigen Gebrauch der Mittel der Tonkunst." *AmZ* 8 (1805): 3–10, 49–59, 193–201, 241–49.

Romain, Louis de. *Essais de critique musicale*. Paris: Alphonse Lemarre, 1890.

Ronge, Julia. *Beethovens Lehrzeit: Kompositionsstudien bei Joseph Haydn, Johann Georg Albrechtsberger und Antonio Salieri*. Bonn: Beethoven-Haus, 2011.

Rosen, Charles, and Henri Zerner. *Romanticism and Realism: The Mythology of Nineteenth-Century Art*. New York: Viking, 1984.

Rosenbaum, Susan B. *Professing Sincerity: Modern Lyric Poetry, Commercial Culture, and the Crisis in Reading*. Charlottesville: University of Press of Virginia, 2007.

Roulston, Christine. *Virtue, Gender, and the Authentic Self in Eighteenth-Century Fiction: Richardson, Rousseau, and Laclos*. Gainesville: University of Florida Press, 1998.

Rousseau, Jean-Jacques. *Les confessions* (1782). Edited by Jacques Voisine. Paris: Classiques Garnier, 2011.

Rousseau, Jean-Jacques. *The Confessions*. Translated by J. M. Cohen. Harmondsworth: Penguin, 1953.

Rousseau, Jean-Jacques. *Dictionnaire de musique*. Paris: Veuve Duschesne, 1768.

Rousseau, Jean-Jacques. *Julie, or the New Heloise*. Translated and edited by Philip Stewart and Jean Vaché. Hanover, NH: University Press of New England, 1997.

Rousseau, Jean-Jacques. *Julie ou La nouvelle Héloïse*. Ed. René Pomeau. Paris: Classiques Garnier, 2012.

Ruffner, J. A. "Newton's Propositions on Comets: Steps in Transition, 1681–84." *Archive for History of Exact Sciences* 54 (2000): 259–77.

Rushton, Julian. *Mozart*. Oxford: Oxford University Press, 2006.

Ruskin, John. *The Queen of the Air*. London: Smith, Elder, 1869.

S. "Tonstücke für 2 Violinen, Alto und Violoncello." *Allgemeine Musikzeitung zur Beförderung der theoretischen und praktischen Tonkunst* 1 (10 November 1827): 303–4.

Sacks, Ethan. "Taylor Swift Blasts Ex-Boyfriend in New Song, 'Never Ever Getting Back Together,' from Upcoming Album 'Red'." *New York Daily News*, 14 August 2012. http://www.nydailynews.com/entertainment/music-arts/taylor-swift-releases-new-song-back-upcoming-album-red-article-1.1135999#ixzz23d1E6O8k

Sadie, Stanley, ed. *The New Grove Dictionary of Music and Musicians*. 29 vols. 2nd ed. New York: Oxford University Press, 2001.

Sallis, Friedemann. *Music Sketches*. Cambridge: Cambridge University Press, 2015.

Saloman, Ora Frishberg. *Listening Well: On Beethoven, Berlioz, and Other Music Criticism in Paris, Boston, and New York, 1764–1890*. New York: Peter Lang, 2009.

Samson, Jim. "The Great Composer." In *The Cambridge History of Nineteenth-Century Music*, 259–84. Edited by Jim Samson. Cambridge: Cambridge University Press, 2002.

Samuel, Claude, and Péter Várnai, eds. *György Ligeti in Conversation with Péter Várnai, Josef Häusler, Claude Samuel, and Himself*. London: Eulenburg, 1983.

Scheer, Monique. "Topographies of Emotion." In *Emotional Lexicons: Continuity and Change in the Vocabulary of Feeling 1700–2000*, 32–61. Edited by Ute Frevert et al. New York: Oxford University Press, 2014.

Scheding, Florian. "Where Is the Holocaust in All This? György Ligeti and the Dialectics of Life and Work." In *Dislocated Memories: Jews, Music, and Postwar German Culture*, 205–21. Edited by Tina Frühauf and Lily Hirsch. New York: Oxford University Press, 2014.

Schelling, Friedrich Wilhelm Joseph. *System des transzendentalen Idealismus*. Tübingen: Cotta, 1800.

Schenk, Erich. *Wolfgang Amadeus Mozart: Sein Leben, seine Welt*. 2nd ed. Vienna: Amalthea Verlag, 1975.

Schiller, Friedrich. "Sprache." In *Musenalmanach für das Jahr 1797*, 177. Tübingen: Cotta, 1797.

Schiller, Friedrich. *Über die ästhetische Erziehung des Menschen in einer Reihe von Briefen* (1794–95). Edited by Wolfgang Düsing. Munich: Hanser, 1981.

Schilling, Gustav. *Franz Liszt: Sein Leben und Wirkung, aus nächster Beschauung dargestellt*. Stuttgart: A. Stoppani, 1844.

Schindler, Anton. "Das ähnlichste Bildnis Beethovens: Schreiben an den Redacteur." *AmZ* 37 (14 January 1835): 17–25.

Schindler, Anton. *Biographie von Ludwig van Beethoven*. Münster: Aschendorff, 1840.

Schlegel, August Wilhelm. "Etwas über William Shakespeare bey Gelegenheit Wilhelm Meisters." *Die Horen*, 4. Stück (1796): 57–112.

Schlegel, August Wilhelm. *Sämmtliche Werke*. 16 vols. Edited by Eduard Böcking. Leipzig: Weidmann, 1846–48.

Schlegel, August Wilhelm. "Über das Verhältnis der schönen Kunst zur Natur." *Prometheus* 5/6 (1808): 1–28.

Schlegel, August Wilhelm. *Vorlesungen über schöne Litteratur und Kunst, erster Teil: Die Kunstlehre* (1801–02). Edited by Jacob Minor. Heilbronn: Gebrüder Henninger, 1884.

Schlegel, Friedrich. *Friedrich Schlegel's "Lucinde" and the Fragments.* Translated by Peter Firchow. Minneapolis: University of Minnesota Press, 1971.

Schlegel, Friedrich. Kritische Friedrich-Schlegel-Ausgabe. Edited by Ernst Behler et al. Munich: F. Schöningh, 1958–.

Schlegel, Friedrich. "Über die Unverständlichkeit." *Athenäum* 3 (1800): 335–52.

Schlegel, Johann Elias. "Abhandlung, daß die Nachahmung der Sache, der man nachahmet, zuweilen unähnlich werden müsse" (1745). In his *Aesthetische und dramaturgische Schriften*, 96–105. Edited by Johann von Antoniewicz. Heilbronn: Gebrüder Henninger, 1887.

Schleiermacher, Friedrich Daniel Ernst. *Hermeneutik und Kritik* (1838). Edited by Manfred Frank. Frankfurt am Main: Suhrkamp, 1977.

Schleuning, Peter. *Die freie Fantasie: Ein Beitrag zur Erforschung der klassischen Klaviermusik.* Göppingen: A. Kümmerle, 1973.

Schlosser, Johann Aloys. *Beethoven: The First Biography.* Translated by Reinhard G. Pauly. Edited by Barry Cooper. Portland, OR: Amadeus Press, 1996.

Schlosser, Johann Aloys. *Ludwig van Beethoven: Leben und Schaffen.* Prague: Buchler, Stephani und Schlosser, 1828.

Schlutz, Alexander M. *Mind's World: Imagination and Subjectivity from Descartes to Romanticism.* Seattle: University of Washington Press, 2009.

Schmidt, Jochen. *Die Geschichte des Genie-Gedankens in der deutschen Literatur, Philosophie und Politik, 1750–1945.* 2 vols. 3rd ed. Heidelberg: Winter, 2004.

Schmidt, Julian. *Geschichte der deutschen Nationalliteratur im neunzehnten Jahrhundert.* 2 vols. Leipzig: Herbig, 1853.

Schmitz, Arnold. *Das romantische Beethovenbild: Darstellung und Kritik.* Berlin and Bonn, 1927; rpt., Darmstadt: Wissenschaftliche Buchgesellschaft, 1978.

Schoenberg, Arnold. *"Stile herrschen, Gedanken siegen": Ausgewählte Schriften.* Edited by Anna Maria Morazzoni. Mainz: Schott, 2007.

Schoenberg, Arnold. *Style and Idea: Selected Writings of Arnold Schoenberg.* Edited by Leonard Stein. Berkeley and Los Angeles: University of California Press, 1975.

Schoenberg, Arnold, and Wassily Kandinsky. *Arnold Schönberg, Wassily Kandinsky: Briefe, Bilder und Dokumente einer aussergewöhnlichen Begegnung.* Edited by Jelena Hahl-Koch. Salzburg: Residenz-Verlag, 1980.

Schoenberg, Arnold, and Wassily Kandinsky. *Arnold Schoenberg, Wassily Kandinsky: Letters, Pictures, and Documents.* Edited by Jelena Hahl-Koch. Translated by John C. Crawford. London: Faber & Faber, 1984.

Schöning, Matthias. *Ironieverzicht: Friedrich Schlegels theoretische Konzepte zwischen "Athenäum" und "Philosophie des Lebens."* Paderborn: Ferdinand Schöningh, 2002.

Schopenhauer, Arthur. *Parerga und Paralipomena.* Edited by Gerd Haffman. 2 vols. Zurich: Haffmans, 1988.

Schopenhauer, Arthur. *Die Welt als Wille und Vorstellung.* Edited by Gerd Haffman. Zurich: Haffmans, 1988.

Schubart, Christian Friedrich Daniel. *Ideen zu einer Aesthetik der Tonkunst.* Vienna: J. V. Degen, 1806.

Schuhmacher, Eckhard. *Die Ironie der Unverständlichkeit: Johann Georg Hamann, Friedrich Schlegel, Jacques Derrida, Paul de Man.* Frankfurt am Main: Surhkamp, 2000.

Schumann, Robert. "'Aus dem Leben eines Künstlers': Phantastische Symphonie in 5 Abtheilungen von Hector Berlioz." *NZfM* 3 (1835): 1–2, 33–35, 37–38, 41–44, 45–48, 49–51.

Schumann, Robert. "Etuden für das Pianoforte." *NZfM* 11 (1839): 97–98, 113–14, 121–22.

Schumann, Robert. *Robert Schumanns Briefe: Neue Folge*. Edited by F. Gustav Jansen. 2nd ed. Leipzig: Breitkopf und Hartel, 1904.

Schweikert, Uwe. "Das literarische Werk: Lektüre, Poesie, Kritik und poetische Musik." In *Schumann Handbuch*, 107–26. Edited by Ulrich Tadday. Stuttgart: J. B. Metzler, 2006.

Seigel, Jerrold. *The Idea of the Self: Thought and Experience in Western Europe since the Seventeenth Century*. Cambridge: Cambridge University Press, 2005.

Senner, Wayne M., Robin Wallace, and William Meredith, eds. *The Critical Reception of Beethoven's Compositions by His German Contemporaries*. 2 vols. Lincoln: University of Nebraska Press, 1999–2001.

Seyfried, Ignaz Ritter von. *Ludwig van Beethoven's Studien im Generalbasse, Contrapuncte und in der Compositions-Lehre*. Vienna: Haslinger, 1832. Translated by François-Joseph Fétis as *Études de Beethoven: Traité d'harmonie et de composition*, 2 vols. Paris: Maurice Schlesinger, 1833.

Shapiro, James. "Unravelling Shakespeare's Life." In *On Life-Writing*, 7–24. Edited by Zachary Leader. New York: Oxford University Press, 2015.

Shelley, Percy Bysshe. "A Defence of Poetry." In his *Essays, Letters from Abroad, Translations and Fragments*, 1:1–57. Edited by Mary Wollstonecraft Shelley. 2 vols. London: Edward Moxon, 1840.

Sisman, Elaine. "After the Heroic Style: *Fantasia* and the 'Characteristic' Sonatas of 1809." *Beethoven Forum* 6 (1998): 67–96.

Sisman, Elaine. "Haydn, Shakespeare, and the Rules of Originality." In *Haydn and His World*, 3–56. Edited by Elaine Sisman. Princeton, NJ: Princeton University Press, 1997.

Sisman, Elaine. "Haydn's Career and the Idea of the Multiple Audience." In *The Cambridge Companion to Haydn*, 3–16. Edited by Caryl Clark. Cambridge: Cambridge University Press, 2005.

Sisman, Elaine. "Music and the Labyrinth of Melancholy: Traditions and Paradoxes in C. P. E. Bach and Beethoven." In *The Oxford Handbook of Music and Disability Studies*, 590–617. Edited by Blake Howe, Stephanie Jensen-Moulton, Neil Lerner, and Joseph Straus. New York: Oxford University Press, 2016.

Smith, Amand Wilhelm. *Philosophische Fragmente über die praktische Musik*. Vienna: Taubstummeninstitutsbuchdruckerey, 1787.

Solomon, Maynard. *Beethoven*. 2nd ed. New York: Schirmer Books, 1998.

Solomon, Maynard. *Beethoven Essays*. Cambridge, MA: Harvard University Press, 1988.

Solomon, Maynard. "Franz Schubert and the Peacocks of Benvenuto Cellini." *19CM* 12 (1989): 193–206.

Solomon, Maynard. *Late Beethoven: Music, Thought, Imagination*. Berkeley: University of California Press, 2003.

Solomon, Robert C. *Continental Philosophy since 1750: The Rise and Fall of the Self*. Oxford: Oxford University Press, 1988.

Solvik, Morten, and Stephen Hefling. "Natalie Bauer-Lechner on Mahler and Women: A Newly Discovered Document." *MQ* 97 (2014): 12–65.

Sponheuer, Bernd. *Musik als Kunst und Nicht-Kunst: Untersuchungen zur Dichotomie von "hoher" und "niederer" Musik im musikästhetischen Denken zwischen Kant und Hanslick*. Kassel: Bärenreiter, 1987.

Staël-Holstein, Anne Louise Germaine de. *De l'Allemagne*. 3 vols. Paris: H. Nicolle, 1813.

Steinberg, Michael P. *Listening to Reason: Culture, Subjectivity, and Nineteenth-Century Music*. Princeton, NJ: Princeton University Press, 2004.

Stenzel, Jürgen. " 'Si vis me flere . . .' —'Musa iocosa mea': Zwei poetologische Argumente in der deutschen Diskussion des 17. und 18. Jahrhunderts." *Deutsche Vierteljahrsschrift für Literaturwissenschaft und Geistesgeschichte* 48 (1974): 650–71.

Stenzl, Jürg. "Igor Strawinskys Manifest von 1924." In his *Auf der Suche nach Geschichte(n) der musikalischen Interpretation,* 71–91. Würzburg: Köngishausen & Neumann, 2012.

Stoepel, Franz. "P. S. des Uebersetzers." In Anonymous, "Ueber den gegenwärtigen Zustand der Musik in London," *Münchener allgemeine Musik-Zeitung* 1 (3 November 1827): 73–80.

Stone, George Winchester, Jr., and George M. Kahrl. *David Garrick: A Critical Biography.* Carbondale: Southern Illinois University Press, 1979.

Straus, Joseph N. *Extraordinary Measures: Disability in Music.* New York: Oxford University Press, 2011.

Straus, Joseph N. "Stravinsky the Serialist." In *The Cambridge Companion to Stravinsky,* 149–74. Edited by Jonathan Cross. Cambridge: Cambridge University Press, 2003.

Stravinsky, Igor. *An Autobiography.* New York: Simon & Schuster, 1936.

Stravinsky, Igor. *Chroniques de ma vie.* 2 vols. Paris: Denoël et Steele, 1935.

Stravinsky, Igor. Liner notes to *Stravinsky Conducts.* Columbia MS6548. New York: Columbia, 1963.

Stravinsky, Igor. "Some Ideas about My Octuor." *Arts* 6/1 (1924): 4–6.

Stravinsky, Igor, and Robert Craft. *Expositions and Developments.* Garden City, NY: Doubleday, 1962.

Stravinsky, Igor, and Robert Craft. *Themes and Episodes.* New York: Knopf, 1966.

Strecker, Ivo, and Stephen Tyler, eds. *Culture and Rhetoric.* New York: Berghahn Books, 2009.

Sullivan, Elizabeth Way. "Conversing in Public: Chamber Music in Vienna, 1890–1910." Ph.D. diss., University of Pittsburgh, 2001.

Sullivan, J. W. N. *Beethoven: His Spiritual Development.* New York: Knopf, 1927

Sulzer, Johann Georg. *Allgemeine Theorie der schönen Künste.* 2 vols. Leipzig: M. G. Weidemanns Erben und Reich, 1771–74.

Swafford, Jan. *Beethoven: Anguish and Triumph.* New York: Houghton Mifflin Harcourt, 2014.

Talbot, Michael. "The Work-Concept and Composer-Centredness." In *The Musical Work: Reality or Invention?,* 168–86. Edited by Michael Talbot. Liverpool: Liverpool University Press, 2000.

Taruskin, Richard. "Resisting the Ninth." *19CM* 12 (1989): 241–56.

Taylor, Charles. *The Ethics of Authenticity.* Cambridge, MA: Harvard University Press, 1992.

Taylor, Charles. *Sources of the Self: The Making of Modern Identity.* Cambridge: Cambridge University Press, 1989.

Taylor-Jay, Claire. "The Composer's Voice? Compositional Style and Criteria of Value in Weill, Krenek and Stravinsky." *Journal of the Royal Musical Association,* 134 (2009): 85–111.

Tchaikovsky, Piotr Ilich. *"To My Best Friend": Correspondence between Tchaikovsky and Nadezhda von Meck, 1876–1878.* Translated by Galina von Meck. Edited by Edward Garden and Nigel Gotteri. Oxford: Clarendon Press, 1993.

Thayer, Alexander Wheelock. *Ludwig van Beethoven's Leben.* 5 vols. Edited by Hermann Deiters and Hugo Riemann. Leipzig: Breitkopf & Härtel, 1901–08.

Theodore Presser Company. *George Rochberg: Composer Scrapbook.* King of Prussia, PA: Theodore Presser, 2013. https://issuu.com/theodorepresser/docs/scrapbook_rochberg

Thiel, Udo. *The Early Modern Subject: Self-Consciousness and Personal Identity from Descartes to Hume*. Oxford: Oxford University Press, 2011.

Thomas, Downing A. *Music and the Origins of Language: Theories from the French Enlightenment*. Cambridge: Cambridge University Press, 1995.

Thorau, Christian. *Semantisierte Sinnlichkeit: Studien zu Rezeption und Zeichenstruktur der Leitmotivtechnik Richard Wagners*. Stuttgart: Steiner, 2003.

Thorau, Christian. "'What Ought to Be Heard': Touristic Listening and the Guided Ear." In *The Oxford Handbook of Music Listening in the 19th and 20th Centuries*, 207–28. Edited by Christian Thorau and Hansjakob Ziemer. New York: Oxford University Press, 2019.

Thorau, Christian, and Hansjakob Ziemer, eds. *The Oxford Handbook of Music Listening in the 19th and 20th Centuries*. New York: Oxford University Press, 2019.

Thumpston, Rebecca. "The Embodiment of Yearning: Towards a Tripartite Theory of Musical Agency." In *Music, Analysis, Experience*, 331–48. Edited by Costantino Maeder and Mark Reybrouck. Leuven: Leuven University Press, 2015.

Tieck, Ludwig. *Franz Sternbalds Wanderungen*. 2 vols. Berlin: Johann Friedrich Unger, 1798.

Tiessen, Heinz. *Zur Geschichte der jüngsten Musik (1913–1928): Probleme und Entwicklungen*. Mainz: Melosverlag, 1928.

Tolstoy, Leo. *What Is Art?* Translated by Aylmer Maude. New York: Thomas Crowell, 1899.

Tomas, Vincent. "Kandinsky's Theory of Painting." *British Journal of Aesthetics* 9 (1969): 19–38.

Tottmann, Albert. *Kurzgefaßter Abriß der Musikgeschichte von der ältesten Zeit bis auf die Gegenwart*. 2 vols. Leipzig: Otto Lenz, 1883.

Treitler, Leo. "Speaking of the I-Word." *AfMw* 72 (2015): 1–18.

Triest, Johann Karl Friedrich. "Bemerkungen über die Ausbildung der Tonkunst in Deutschland im achtzehnten Jahrhundert." *AmZ* 3 (1801): 225–35, 241–49, 257–64, 273–86, 297–308, 321–32, 369–79, 389–401, 405–10, 421–32, 437–45.

Trilling, Lionel. *Sincerity and Authenticity*. Cambridge, MA: Harvard University Press, 1972.

Tucker, Brian. *Reading Riddles: Rhetorics of Obscurity from Romanticism to Freud*. Lewisburg, PA: Bucknell University Press, 2011.

Tucker, Herbert F. "Dramatic Monologue and the Overhearing of Lyric." In *Lyric Poetry: Beyond the New Criticism*, 226–43. Edited by Chaviva Hošek and Patricia Parker. Ithaca, NY: Cornell University Press, 1985.

Twining, Thomas. *Aristotle's Treatise on Poetry*. London: Payne and Son, 1789.

Unseld, Melanie. *Biographie und Musikgeschichte: Wandlungen biographischer Konzepte in Musikkultur und Musikhistoriographie*. Cologne: Böhlau, 2014.

Varèse, Louise. *Varèse: A Looking-Glass Diary*. New York: W. W. Norton, 1972.

Varga-Behrer, Angelika. *"Hut ab, ihr Herren, ein Genie": Studien zur Chopin-Rezeption in der zeitgenössischen Musikpresse Deutschlands und Frankreichs*. Mainz: Schott, 2010.

Vaszonyi, Nicholas. *Richard Wagner: Self-Promotion and the Making of a Brand*. Cambridge: Cambridge University Press, 2010.

Vogel, Oliver. "Berlioz als Harold: Ein romantisches Selbstporträt im Zeichen des Liberalismus." *Mf* 68 (2015): 136–64.

Völmicke, Elke. *Das Unbewusste im Deutschen Idealismus*. Würzburg: Königshausen & Neumann, 2005.

Voss, Egon. "Das Beethoven-Bild der Beethoven-Belletrisik: Zu einigen Beethoven-Erzählungen des 19. Jahrhunderts." In *Beethoven und die Nachwelt*, 81–94. Edited by Helmut Loos. Bonn: Beethoven-Haus, 1986.

Wagner, Richard. *Beethoven.* Leipzig: E. W. Fritzsch, 1870.

Wagner, Richard. "Ein Brief von Richard Wagner über Franz Liszt." *NZfM* 46 (10 April 1857): 157–63.

Wagner, Richard. *Drei Operndichtungen nebst einer Mittheilung an seine Freunde als Vorwort.* Leipzig: Breitkopf und Härtel, 1852.

Wagner, Richard. *Das Kunstwerk der Zukunft.* Leipzig: Otto Wigand, 1850.

Wagner, Richard. *Oper und Drama.* 3 vols. Leipzig: J. J. Weber, 1852.

Wagner, Richard. *Sämtliche Briefe.* Edited by Werner Breig. Wiesbaden: Breitkopf & Härtel, 1967–.

Wald, Elijah. *Dylan Goes Electric! Newport, Seeger, Dylan, and the Night that Split the Sixties.* New York: Dey Street, 2015.

Wald, Elijah. *Escaping the Delta: Robert Johnson and the Invention of the Blues.* New York: Amistad, 2004.

Wallace, Robin R. *Beethoven's Critics: Aesthetic Dilemmas and Resolutions during the Composer's Lifetime.* Cambridge: Cambridge University Press, 1986.

Wasielewski, Joseph von. *Robert Schumann: Eine Biographie.* 2 vols. Dresden: Rudolph Kunze, 1858.

Wasserman, Earl R. "The Sympathetic Imagination in Eighteenth-Century Theories of Acting." *Journal of English and Germanic Philology* 46 (1947): 264–72.

Watkins, Holly. *Metaphors of Depth in German Musical Thought: From E. T. A. Hoffmann to Arnold Schoenberg.* Cambridge: Cambridge University Press, 2011.

Weber, Gottfried. "Über die Echtheit des Mozartschen Requiem." *Cäcilia* 3 (1825): 205–29.

Weber, William. *The Rise of Musical Classics in Eighteenth-century England: A Study in Canon, Ritual, and Ideology.* Oxford: Clarendon Press, 1992.

Webster, James. *Haydn's "Farewell" Symphony and the Idea of Classical Style: Through-Composition and Cyclic Integration in His Instrumental Music.* Cambridge: Cambridge University Press, 1991.

Webster, James. "Music, Pathology, Sexuality, Beethoven, Schubert." *19CM* 17 (1993): 88–93.

Webster, James. "The Rhetoric of Improvisation in Haydn's Keyboard Music." In *Haydn and the Performance of Rhetoric,* 172–212. Edited by Tom Beghin and Sander M. Goldberg. Chicago: University of Chicago Press, 2007.

Wegeler, Franz, and Ferdinand Ries. *Biographische Notizen über Ludwig van Beethoven.* Koblenz: K. Bädeker, 1838.

Weiler, Georg von. "Ueber den Geist und das Auffassen der Beethoven'schen Musik." *Cäcilia* 9 (1828): 45–50.

Weintraub, Karl Joachim. *The Value of the Individual: Self and Circumstance in Autobiography.* Chicago: University of Chicago Press, 1978.

Wellbery, David E. *Lessing's "Laocoon": Semiotics in the Age of Reason.* Cambridge: Cambridge University Press, 1984.

Wellbery, David E. "The Transformation of Rhetoric." In *The Cambridge History of Literary Criticism,* vol. 5, *Romanticism,* 185–202. Edited by Marshall Brown. Cambridge: Cambridge University Press, 2000.

Wendt, Amadeus. "Ausdruck in der Musik." *Cäcilia* 4 (1826): 173–86.

Wendt, Amadeus. "Gedanken über die neuere Tonkunst, und van Beethovens Musik, namentlich dessen Fidelio." *AmZ* 17 (1815): 345–53, 365–72, 381–89, 397–404, 413–20, 429–36.

Wendt, Amadeus. *Über die Hauptperioden der schönen Kunst, oder die Kunst im Laufe der Weltgeschichte.* Leipzig: J. A. Barth, 1831.

Wendt, Amadeus. "Ueber Beethovens neueste Symphonie." *Leipziger Kunstblatt für gebildete Kunstfreunde, insbesondere für Theater und Musik* 1 (14 February 1818): 280–81.

Wheelock, Gretchen. "Mozart's Fantasy, Haydn's Caprice: What's in a Name?" In *The Century of Bach and Mozart: Perspectives on Historiography, Composition, Theory and Performance*, 317–41. Edited by Sean Gallagher and Thomas Forrest Kelly. Cambridge, MA: Harvard University Department of Music, 2008.

White, Eric Walter. *Stravinsky: The Composer and His Works.* 2nd ed. Berkeley and Los Angeles: University of California Press, 1979.

Whyman, Rose. *The Stanislavsky System of Acting: Legacy and Influence in Modern Performance.* Cambridge: Cambridge University Press, 2008.

Whyte, Lancelot L. *The Unconscious before Freud.* New York: Basic Books, 1960.

Wiedeburg, Michael Johann Friedrich. *Der sich selbst informirende Clavierspieler.* 3 vols. Leipzig: Waisenhaus, 1765–75.

Wieland, Christoph Martin. "Einige Nachrichten von den Lebens-Umständen des Herrn Willhelm [*sic*] Shakespear." In William Shakespeare, *Theatralische Werke, aus dem Englischen übersetzt von Herrn Wieland*, 8:1–30. Zurich: Orell, Gebner, 1766.

Wiemer, Wolfgang. "Carl Philipp Emanuel Bach Fantasie in c-Moll—ein Lamento auf den Tod des Vaters?" *Bach-Jahrbuch* 74 (1988): 163–77.

Wilde, Oscar. "The True Function and Value of Criticism." *The Nineteenth Century* 28 (1890): 435–59.

Wiley, Christopher. "Re-Writing Composers' Lives: Critical Historiography and Musical Biography." Ph.D. diss., Royal Holloway, University of London, 2008.

Wilson, John David. "Beethoven's Popular Style: *Der glorreiche Augenblick* and the Art of Writing for the Galleries." In *Beethoven und der Wiener Kongress (1814/15): Bericht über die vierte New Beethoven Research Conference, Bonn, 10. bis 12. September 2014*, 219–88. Edited by Bernhard R. Appel et al. Bonn: Beethoven-Haus, 2016.

Wittkower, Rudolf, and Margot Wittkower. *Born under Saturn: The Character and Conduct of Artists.* London: Weidenfeld and Nicolson, 1963.

Wordsworth, William. *Lyrical Ballads.* 2 vols. 2nd ed. London: T. N. Longman and O. Rees, 1800.

Wordsworth, William. *Lyrical Ballads.* 2 vols. 3rd ed. London: T. N. Longman and O. Rees, 1802.

Wordsworth, William. *Poems . . . With Additional Poems, a New Preface, and a Supplementary Essay.* 2 vols. London: Longman, Hurst, Rees, Orme, and Brown, 1815.

Wordsworth, William. *The Poetical Works of Wordsworth.* Edited by Paul Sheats. Boston: Houghton Mifflin, 1982.

Wyn Jones, David. "Beethoven and the Viennese Legacy." In *The Cambridge Companion to the String Quartet*, 210–27. Edited by Robin Stowell. Cambridge: Cambridge University Press, 2003.

Wyzewa, Théodore de. "À propos du centenaire de la mort de Joseph Haydn." *Revue des deux mondes* 79 (1909): 935–46.

Young, Edward. *Conjectures on Original Composition.* London: A. Millar and R. and J. Dodsley, 1759.

Young, James O., and Carl Matheson. "The Metaphysics of Jazz." *Journal of Aesthetics and Art Criticism* 58 (2000): 125–33.

Yudkin, Jeremy. "The Naming of Names: 'Flamenco Sketches' or 'All Blues'? Identifying the Last Two Tracks on Miles Davis's Classic Album *Kind of Blue.*" *MQ* 95 (2012): 15–35.

Zaminer, Frieder. "Über die Herkunft des Ausdrucks 'Musik verstehen.'" In *Musik und Verstehen: Aufsätze zur semiotischen Theorie, Ästhetik und Soziologie der musikalischen Rezeption*, 314–19. Edited by Peter Faltin and Hans-Peter Reinecke. Cologne: Arno Volk, 1973.

Zaslaw, Neal, and William Cowdery, eds. *The Compleat Mozart.* New York: W. W. Norton, 1990.

Ziolkowski, Theodore. "Language and Mimetic Action in Lessing's *Miss Sara Sampson.*" *Germanic Review* 40 (1965): 262–76.

Zöllner, Frank. " 'Ogni pittore dipinge sé': Leonardo da Vinci and 'Automimesis.'" In *Der Künstler über sich in seinem Werk*, 137–60. Edited by Matthias Winner. Weinheim: VCH, 1992.

Index